Chicago to Appo

Chicago to Appomattox

The 39th Illinois Infantry in the Civil War

Jason B. Baker

McFarland & Company, Inc., Publishers
Jefferson, North Carolina

ISBN (print) 978-1-4766-8620-2
ISBN (ebook) 978-1-4766-4551-3

Library of Congress and British Library
cataloguing data are available

Library of Congress Control Number 2021059321

On the cover: "Fall of Petersburg" Kurz & Allison,
Published, Chicago 1893 (Library of Congress)

Printed in the United States of America

McFarland & Company, Inc., Publishers
Box 611, Jefferson, North Carolina 28640
www.mcfarlandpub.com

To the citizens of Illinois who have answered the call, in all its forms, to preserve and protect our Union that we may strive to make it more perfect,

and

*in memory of my Grandpa "Tools" for teaching me our history,
in honor of my dad who taught me to appreciate history,
and to my son, who I hope makes his own history.*

Contents

Preface

THE 39TH ILLINOIS VOLUNTEER INFANTRY REGIMENT was made up of young men from Chicago and the modern-day suburbs, and areas stretching from Boone County in the north to DeWitt County in the central portion of the state. Towns like Wilmington, Marseilles, LeRoy, Santa Anna, and Bloomington dot the roster. They answered the call in their hometowns, formed under a lawyer in Chicago, and were among the few Illinois regiments to fight in the eastern theater. Seeing only sporadic, small scale action in the early parts of the war, they fought at places like Kernstown against "Stonewall" Jackson and Charleston Harbor alongside the 54th Massachusetts of *Glory* fame. After most of the unit decided to re-enlist together, they spent the last year of the war in Virginia fighting near Petersburg and Richmond in the campaign to end the war. The regiment took part in the sustained and brutal warfare of the Siege of Petersburg and saw two of their members awarded the Congressional Medal of Honor. The 39th would travel over 6,000 miles by rail, waterway, and foot, and take part in the final combat before witnessing the Confederate surrender at Appomattox Courthouse on April 9, 1865.[1]

I had long known that my great-great-great-grandfather, John Barber, served in the Civil War. My grandfather had told me about it, and my uncle had some letters and even the saber he carried in his cavalry service. The story I was always told was that he was General Grant's bodyguard. As a younger kid, nothing seemed more impressive to me. As I got older and joined the military myself, I realized that it was probably founded in some truth but embellished like most good military stories. However, when motivated to research further, I discovered that while not Grant's *personal* bodyguard, Private Barber was a 15th Illinois Cavalry Regiment member. Among other services in the western theater, his specific company was at one time known as "Grant's Guard," providing him security and reconnaissance. Grandpa had not been embellishing—in fact, he had probably been selling him short.

Thanks to websites like Ancestry.com, and the fantastic online records of the Illinois Gen Web Project, I soon found out that John Barber had two brothers, my great-great-great-grand uncles Alden and Cicero Barber, who likewise fought in the war. While my earliest days of research were intended to simply learn about my ancestors, and share their story with my family, my fascination with the 39th Illinois continued to grow. They were one of the few Illinois regiments to fight in the east and made up of small-town young men from where I grew up. The regiment didn't just have two relatives, it was made up of young men from towns my friends and family are from, towns I played school sports in, areas my father farms in, and the suburban area my wife spent her childhood in.

The 1889 regimental history of surgeon Charles M. Clark and the published letters and diaries of regiment members Homer Plimpton, Joseph Ward, Anthony Taylor, and Valentine Randolph made putting the 39th Regiment's story into one modern book a possibility I began to consider. I told a friend I had the basics of their history, with some engaging first-hand accounts, and I wished there was a work that put it all together with the scholarship and background of the broader war. Wouldn't it be interesting to learn more details of the war by following the experience of a unit from home? I didn't need to break some new fascinating ground—I just wanted to bring all the information together to tell the totality of their story. My friend's reply: "Write the book you'd want to read."

After I tracked down a physical copy of the 1889 regimental history, my motivation to turn the research and knowledge I was gathering into an actual book was jump-started partly by the new amount of free time I had on my hands during the pandemic of 2020. Much more so, however, the dialogue and discussion stemming from the civil unrest in the country left me longing to know my ancestors' involvement with the war. I needed something to occupy my mind productively and grappled with my understanding of our Civil War as much of the country was doing the same. Strangely, I found refuge in immersing myself in that period and having debates with myself. As a military officer, I gravitated towards the discussion of leadership and battle. However, I was also compelled to understand better the non-military forces that shaped the struggle and moved it through its four years.

This book became a story about the path—the journey—that a group of young men from Illinois took from the beginning to the end of the war. Like a journey on any route, much of your travel is under your control. Some of it, however, is not. Wrong turns are taken, there's traffic, roads are blocked, or perhaps someone forces you to go a different route in some form or fashion. Many regimental histories are vivid accounts of soldiers' day-to-day life, what they wore, what they ate, and how hard an existence it was. While these themes very much come up in the book, I believe those are topics most people are already well acquainted with. This book discusses how a group of young Illinois men came to form a regiment, why they moved from place to place, and the political and military factors that dictated such things.

Space is not spent so much on camp stories, descriptions of gear, and images of violence beyond what is required to tell the story. This also means that I do not get too far into the weeds on minute details of military tactics save for when it tells a specific account of the 39th. For troop movements and battles, I stay very much at the strategic and operational levels—those that explain why a battle was fought and what its objectives were. This means I limit my discussion of generals and high-ranking officers, of each side, to the top brass or most well-known names. I did this both to not saturate the book with people to keep track of and prevent myself from spending entire chapters describing only a day or two of movement or a couple of specific individuals.

This does also mean that many individual stories of members of the 39th do not neatly fit into the book's narrative. To include as many as possible, however, and build the background of some of the more notable members, I begin each chapter with a short "mini-biography" that not only tells stories but creates a sense of the regiment. I recreate the regiment's roster in an appendix that provides many personal details.

In the way of research, my outline for this book is based on Doctor Charles Clark's *The History of the Thirty-Ninth Regiment, Illinois Volunteer Veteran Infantry, In the War of the Rebellion, 1861–1865* from 1889. Filling in details, dates, names, and experiences with the previously mentioned published journals, I then consulted the most recommended and informational works on the various campaigns, locations, and battles in which the regiment took part. Doctor Clark's book was *their* story, and I wanted to find out how that story was written. Living in Virginia during the bulk of my research and writing, I also visited many of the sites the regiment took part in battle. Capturing images and seeing the land for myself allowed me to not just better describe it but feel a sense of what happened. My young son and I traveled to Petersburg to see the well-preserved ground of Fort Gregg in the summer of 2020 and later writing of the regiment's bloody struggle there moved me to tears as I remembered seeing it with my own eyes.

The resulting book, I hope, is one that uses my family story and "hometown" regiment as a vehicle for exploring three distinct portions of the war of which I previously knew so little myself: the importance of the 1862 Shenandoah Valley Campaign, the often-overlooked 1863 struggle for Fort Sumter in Charleston Harbor, and the long, bloody, and complex Siege of Petersburg, combined with the impact of the 1864 election. Hovering over all of it was slavery in America, and the politics not just of America's leaders, but the men fighting the war. A note on politics: I reference Republicans and Democrats throughout the book to identify or illustrate why arguments existed. Just as today, and especially over slavery and secession, all members of a party did not see eye to eye. The nature of the two parties has been fluid since the war, and commentary offered in the book presents the issues of the time and is meant as nothing more. The same is true for the discussion of the Confederacy and any of their stated causes. I do not shy away from some of that discussion; however, it is not the focus of this book, and I sought to limit it to what was required for my narrative.

All that said, at its core, this is a regimental history of a Civil War fighting unit, and the bulk of the book deals with the 39th Illinois' experience of war. It is the story of an Illinois regiment in a war rarely associated with the state besides President Lincoln's prominent contribution. Just shy of 260,000 individuals from Illinois fought bravely in service of the United States, but the 39th Illinois Infantry Regiment now holds a special place in my heart.[2] They were my family. They came from where I came from, where my family came from, where my loved ones still live, and where I will return when my own service is over. While not *the* Civil War story, it is *a* Civil War story that shows how volunteers from Illinois shaped, and were shaped by, four years of war.

However, there is no delight to take in the horrors of the war, and I do not seek to romanticize it. Close to 35,000 Illinois service members died in the war.[3] Eighty-three members of the 39th were killed in battle. Sixty-one died of battle wounds, 25 died in prisons, and 90 more from disease. Four hundred eleven were wounded, and 118 were subjected to places like Andersonville, an unimaginably horrific Confederate prisoner of war camp.[4]

We must, however, find comfort in remembering the sacrifices made for our Union. We know now and are forever grateful because these sacrifices were not conducted in vain. However, the Civil War is not over if we don't remember it, and we must strive not to let its sacrifices be undone. I hope that this book teaches us not to take our history for granted and be forever vigilant in protecting the country that was saved and the freedoms it's supposed to offer—to every American. Doctor Clark said it best in opening his history:

> It will remind you of old comrades who fell at your side, and who now lie far away from their homes in the hurried graves you made for them. Your children, I hope, will appreciate this record of your achievements at a time when the very foundations of this government were being undermined and threatened with destruction, and human liberty was poised in the balance; and may it teach them a greater love for their country.[5]

I would like to acknowledge the assistance of a few individuals and organizations in making this book happen. Were it not for my uncle, I would have never gotten interested in my ancestral tie to the Civil War, and my gratitude for that extends far beyond just being able to write a book. Clark's 1889 history of the regiment provided the outline, but I could never piece the information together without the Illinois Gen Web Project's *Illinois in the Civil War* resource online. Hal Jespersen's maps not only look terrific in the book, but his diligent work in preparing them allowed me to visualize places the 39th fought. A huge thank you to organizations and individuals like the National Park Service, the American Battlefield Trust and the authors of books on the Civil War that allowed me to see this history with my eyes and imagine it with my mind. I am merely telling a story, and that would not have been possible without the work of experts and historians. Most of all, thank you to my loving wife, who patiently endured my Civil War stories, daily progress updates, and waking up early and coming to bed late to fit in writing when I could.

Finally, a heartfelt thank you to McFarland for giving a first-time author the opportunity to share a story he was passionate about, and all their support throughout. I alone bear responsibility for any errors or omissions.

❖   ❖   ❖

The views and opinions expressed in this book are my own, in my personal capacity, and do not reflect the official policy or position of the U.S. Department of Defense, the U.S. government or any other organization.

Introduction:
"Here My Children Have Been Born"

IN 1858, THE CITIZENS OF ILLINOIS had a front-row seat to the arguments and ideas that were watering the seeds of the looming rebellion. Illinois residents were reading about, and maybe even attending, a series of senate election debates throughout the state where Stephen A. Douglas jousted with his challenger, Abraham Lincoln, in seven Illinois towns. Lincoln was the nominee for the recently formed Republican party, a party formed largely in response to the dissolving of the Whigs and in response to issues such as the Douglas sponsored Kansas-Nebraska act that had brought the issue of slavery racing to the fore.[1] Lincoln's "House Divided" nomination acceptance speech had caused Douglas to brand him as a threat to the stability of the Union, and thus Lincoln challenged him to debates and Douglas suggested seven districts throughout the state.[2]

Across the state, people formed great crowds to watch the three-hour events where the great orators held forth for 30–90 minutes at a time, arguing, counter-arguing, and rebuking each other. The overwhelming focus of the debates was on slavery and the question of its extension into the new territories and its fate in the future of the nation. While the two men may have been campaigning for votes to become a U.S. Senator from the state of Illinois, they were passionately debating the very core issue that was tearing the nation apart and threatening to split it in two.

Alden and Cicero Barber may very well have traveled, with their brother, the short distance up the road to Ottawa for the first of these debates.[3] Over 50 eventual members of the 39th Illinois Infantry Regiment lived within 20 miles of Ottawa and may have heard from their future commander-in-chief. With the 39th Illinois companies being formed primarily from counties in the north and east-central portions of the state, a good number of the young men would have been within a day's travel of four of the seven debates. Regardless of whether they or their families attended any of them, there is no doubt they would have heard and read reports and realized the crisis in the country and Illinois' growing role.

Despite a loss to Douglas in Illinois where Douglas' popular sovereignty was better received by the western, diverse, and slave-state bordering populace, Lincoln's view that the *Dred Scott* decision would nullify popular sovereignty, and his opposition to disunion, ingratiated him to a broad section of Republican—and northern in general—voters.[4] It would soon become clear that the state of Illinois would continue to be at the center of forces leading up to the Civil War. Not only would Lincoln become the 1860 Republican nominee for President, but the nominating convention itself was held in Chicago.[5]

❖   ❖   ❖

By the fall of 1860, it was clear to the citizens of Illinois that the coming election of Abraham Lincoln threatened to split the country. On Illinois ballots with Lincoln that November was 45-year-old Richard Yates running for Governor. Born in Kentucky, Yates moved to Jacksonville, Illinois, at 16 and graduated from Illinois College in 1835. After studying law in Kentucky, Yates returned to Jacksonville and opened his own practice in 1837. He was elected to the Illinois State House of Representatives and served in two separate instances from 1842 to 1845 and from 1848 to 1849. Yates was then elected as a Whig to the United States House of Representatives, where he served from 1851 to 1855.

Yates had followed a political path like Lincoln's as a former Whig who climbed the ranks of the new Republican party with his oratory skills and strong desire to preserve the country as an anti-slavery union. As if those similarities weren't enough, Yates too was born in a log cabin in Kentucky, the men had each represented the same district in the Illinois legislature, and Lincoln was the one who encouraged him to run for Governor after some political setbacks.[6] Motivated by the same ideas and events in the period between him leaving the House and running for governor of Illinois, Yates would have been particularly pleased to see his friend and fellow Whig turned Republican nominated for the Presidency in his home state. The two men supported each other's 1860 campaigns. They emerged victorious together, with the consensus at the time being they were vital to each other's success.[7] Adding to the Illinois involvement in Lincoln's victory was that Stephen Douglas was one of the Democrats' candidates in the election. One of, because the party had been

Photograph of Richard Yates taken between 1855 and 1865 (Library of Congress: LC-DIG-cwpbh-00717).

unable to come to any agreement and split their votes between a northern and southern democrat.

❖   ❖   ❖

On February 11, 1861, a crowd gathered at the Springfield rail station to see Lincoln off to Washington, D.C. The pride of the crowd that one of their own was headed off to be President would have been muted by the situation the country found itself navigating. John Brown's 1859 raid on Harpers Ferry had primed the charge on the growing powder keg of slavery and its place in the Union, and the election of Abraham Lincoln had ignited it.[8] "The south will never submit to such humiliation and degradation as the inauguration of Abraham Lincoln," wrote a Georgia newspaper.[9] In fact, Lincoln wasn't even on an overwhelming majority of southern ballots. Seven southern states had seceded since Lincoln's election, and those wishing to forestall violence might have been ignoring that it had already arrived. In the first issue of his newspaper *The Liberator* in 1831, noted abolitionist William Lloyd Garrison "had prophesied that slavery would eventually result in a bloody scourge on American soil."[10] Two months after Lincoln's departure from Illinois, the four-year bloody scourge, and a battle for unity and the soul of a nation, would begin.

With a divided country and looming war weighing on his heart, Lincoln delivered an impromptu speech from his train car. An address to the people and place he called home:

> My friends, no one, not in my situation, can appreciate my feeling of sadness at this parting. To this place and the kindness of these people, I owe everything. Here I have lived a quarter of a century, and have passed from a young to an old man. Here my children have been born, and one is buried. I now leave, not knowing when, or whether ever, I may return, with a task before me greater than that which rested upon Washington. Without the assistance of that Divine Being who ever attended him, I cannot succeed. With that assistance I cannot fail. Trusting in Him who can go with me, and remain with you, and be everywhere for good, let us confidently hope that all will yet be well. To His care commending you, as I hope in your prayers you will commend me, I bid you an affectionate farewell.[11]

In town, that day would have been a handful of other Springfield residents who would also soon leave Illinois, head east, and wonder when, or whether ever, they may return.

PART I

"A Good Ways from Home"

October 1861–December 1862

As President Lincoln rode down our lines at a gallop … his eye caught sight of our flag, which had our name and number emblazoned upon it, and partly turned and stopped and called out, "What regiment is that?" "Thirty-Ninth Illinois!" was answered. "Well! You boys are a good-ways from home, a'int you?"[1]

1

From Chicago

Charles Clark was born in 1834 in upstate New York. After moving to New York City, in 1840 then moved to Albion in the western part of the state. Clark received an excellent education at Albion Academy and then took up the study of medicine before beginning work as a clerk in a drugstore in New York City. In 1855, Clark enrolled in medical school at the University of the City of New York and graduated in March 1857. Shortly thereafter, Clark moved to Portage City, Wisconsin where he joined a medical practice, then removing to Chicago in the winter of 1858.

In 1860, Doctor Clark went west to seek fortune in the Rocky Mountain gold rush, but was unsuccessful. Trying his hand at writing, a skill that would later come in handy, he published a book in 1860 regarding his experiences near Pike's Peak.

In April 1861, Clark was one of the men who gathered with Thomas Osborn to raise a company—then regiment—for service to the United States. In August, after passing an examination with the state board, Clark was commissioned as assistant surgeon of the regiment.[1]

WHEN THE NEW ILLINOIS LEGISLATURE assembled in January 1861, Governor Yates used his inaugural address to make it crystal clear how he felt about the United States, the Constitution, and his state's role in the struggle he feared lay ahead:

> Referring to national affairs, whatever may have been the divisions of parties hitherto, the people of Illinois will, with one accord, give their assent and firm support to two propositions: First. The obedience of the Constitution and the laws must be insisted upon and enforced, as necessary to the existence of the Government. Second. That an election of Chief Magistrate of the nation, in strict conformity with the Constitution, is no sufficient cause for the release of any State from any of its obligation to the Union.[2]

Governor Yates left little doubt how he felt about not just the secession of southern states, but whether they even have a right to do so. He clarified that, in his mind, "the whole material of the government—moral, political, and physical, if need be—must be employed to preserve, protect, and defend the Constitution of the United States."[3] Had anyone in the Illinois Assembly wondered what kind of Governor Richard Yates would be with war looming, they were left to wonder no more. "Yates was Illinois, and Illinois was Yates. He was earnest, decisive, courageous, and persistent in his efforts to put down the rebellion,"[4] said L.U. Reavis, an Illinois lecturer and public speaker, in 1881. President Abraham Lincoln had a friend in the Illinois governor seat as dedicated as he was to the preservation of the Union.

It is no surprise then, that Governor Yates acted quickly and decisively at the onset of war. On April 13, 1861, the day after rebels fired on Fort Sumter, Yates convened the Legislature amid worries about loyalty in southern portions of the state bordering Missouri and Kentucky. Yates wanted troops sent to Cairo, a city of great importance to the U.S. cause because of secessionist sentiments, its location on the Ohio and Mississippi Rivers, and proximity to the border of two potential Confederate states. Compounding all of this was a Federal arsenal just up-river in St. Louis that could fall into southern hands just as Fort Sumter had. Yates sent urgent word to Lincoln explaining the situation and stated that Cairo and the arsenal required securing and that Illinois could provide the men to do so. Lincoln agreed, and as early as April 19, Yates sent troops to southwest Illinois to ensure southern sympathizers could not gain the upper hand. With Cairo secured, and additional forces sent to the arsenal, on April 25, Federal troops brought considerable arms and ammunition across the Mississippi and into Illinois, where Governor Yates and President Lincoln undoubtedly agreed it would serve them better used by United States troops as opposed to rebel ones. Beyond the strategic success of military necessity, the actions taken by Lincoln and Yates had the additional benefit of nailing down the support of citizens in the southern part of the state. As one southern farmer stated: "I tell you what it is, them brass missionaries has converted a heap of folks was on the anxious seat."[5]

Yates was no less instrumental to Illinois' contribution to the war effort when Lincoln called for the states to supply volunteers on April 15. Yates "translated it into an appeal for a gathering of regiments"[6] and soon became known as the "soldier's friend," while

Shenandoah Valley with 39th Illinois points of interest (map by Hal Jespersen).

initially sending more troops to aid the Union than any other state.[7] So confident were Illinois bankers of Yates' abilities, that they made $1,000,000 available to equip Illinois volunteers, although the Legislature would need to approve the appropriations for the money to fund.[8] Had each group known that Illinois would furnish over 50 generals during the war they might have given him more, and appropriated it for anything he liked. This would have been especially true if they knew the future of the Galena leather goods store clerk that Yates appointed as a state mustering officer: A West Point graduate and distinguished Mexican War veteran named Ulysses S. Grant.

❖   ❖   ❖

While Yates was busy shaping Illinois' contributions to the war effort, 28-year-old Chicago lawyer Thomas Osborn was busy considering what shape his contribution to the Union would take. Osborn was born in Ohio in 1832 and graduated at the head of his class from the University of Ohio. Following his graduation, he studied law in Crawfordsville, Indiana, under Lewis Wallace. While not just learning the law, Osborn may have picked up his sense of duty to the nation from his mentor. Wallace had served in the Mexican-American War, became a Major General in the Civil War, and served in various governmental and political roles to include governor of the New Mexico Territory, and United States Minister to the Ottoman Empire. As if all that would not be enough for a lifetime of accomplishment, Wallace was the author of the classic novel *Ben-Hur: A Tale of the Christ.* After being admitted to the bar, Osborn moved to Chicago in 1858 and took up his practice.[9]

During what Doctor Charles Clark described as a period of "great excitement and intense feeling of indignation" following the events at Fort Sumter, Osborn consulted a group of men about what they could, or would, do.[10] Gathering in the law office of Moore and Osborn on Dearborn Street in Chicago, Osborn's group expressed their anger, sadness, and longing to help. The all-volunteer, professional military of modern America makes such a thing hard to imagine, but men from all corners of the state were clamoring to sign up even before Lincoln called for troops. Governor Yates called for 6,000 volunteers just two days after Fort Sumter, and companies were formed all over the state. Osborn and his group (which included Dr. Clark) took actions to create a company, and scour the area for other companies of men that were looking to be organized into an organized regiment.

The method and manner by which they formed Civil War volunteer companies and regiments would be something wholly unfamiliar to the modern professional military. In a rush to service and to answer their state and country's call, men would travel throughout their communities and surrounding counties, forming groups to present to the army for service. While these groups often voted to elect their commanders, being able to pull together a company of men might make you a Captain and organizing an entire regiment might make you a Lieutenant Colonel—maybe even a Colonel if you had the means and resources to put your regiment in uniform and supply weapons. While the desire to serve was commendable, this led to some early growing pains. Having such a small regular force before the war, the U.S. army needed bodies badly, and officers to lead them. While a few had veteran experience, many did not, and would require just as much training as the enlisted men. In fairness to this point, however, many served admirably and become decorated Federal officers—Thomas Osborn included.

In less than six weeks, the group recruited 1300 men ready to muster into the United States' service. The War Department had initially asked for six regiments, or roughly 6,000 men, from Illinois but in a "characteristic excess of patriotism" the General

Undated wartime photograph of Colonel Thomas Osborn. Images of him during the war are almost non-existent, even in the 1889 regimental history (**National Archives: Identifier 528153**).

Assembly had authorized ten.[11] The state was facing the admirable problem of having far more volunteers than the state could handle, and Osborn's regiment-to-be was out of luck. This led to the loss of some recruits as time passed, awaiting a second call, with some men even traveling to neighboring states to fill their ranks. Learning that the state of Missouri was behind in its recruiting, Osborn also tried making the group's services available to their bordering governor to no avail.

Amidst all of this, the regiment named itself in honor of Governor Yates and came to call itself the "Yates Phalanx."[12] Whether Osborn or other recruiting officers had a connection to Yates, or wanted to flatter him into accepting their services, is unclear. Governor Yates had an abundance of volunteers ready to serve and after early losses, the country needed more troops. Yates sent "Phalanx" recruiting officer Orrin Mann to Washington with letters to President Lincoln and Secretary of War Cameron urging the acceptance of the regiment.[13] While Lincoln acknowledged his good friend's commitment to the war, and desire for his home state to do all it could, it was not until Congress allowed the President to call for 500,000 more troops, and three-year enlistments, after the Federal defeat at Bull Run that the Yates Phalanx was accepted into service.[14]

The regiment prepared to be mustered into service, and members soon gathered in Chicago in a temporary building, The Wigwam, that had been erected

Doctor Charles Clark in 1889, inset from 1863 (reproduced from Clark, *History*).

for the Republican convention the previous year. Young men like 23-year-old Valentine Randolph, from Lincoln, wrote in his journal the day he was recruited, "We have but few days to live; one had as well die fighting for his country as not."[15] A 22-year-old immigrant farmer from Bremen named Joseph Ward, who answered the call of a nation he had only known for 11 years.[16] Or men like 23-year-old Northwestern graduate Homer Plimpton, a schoolteacher who planned to enroll at Garrett Biblical Institute in Evanston, but "heard the clarion call of God to enter the armed forces" after Bull Run and a recruitment pitch from a minister to the "Preacher's Company."[17] Then there was the case of a man like Emile Guntz from Chicago. At the very outset of the war, Guntz enlisted in the 19th Illinois Infantry for a three-month stint and was sent to Cairo to help stop ships running the Federal blockade. His regiment had no uniforms, inadequate—and often no—weapons, and Guntz was so disillusioned that he took his discharge and went home. "I soon got tired of staying at home after seeing so many of my friends leave for the war," wrote Guntz, "so I made up my mind to enlist again."[18]

Imagine the scene as farmers and laborers came together with lawyers and entrepreneurs from around the state, bound by the counties they called home, their desire to preserve the Union, and a complete lack of soldiering skills. Young men in their late teens and early twenties, and a 52 year old, and a 67-year-old cook, brothers and cousins, democrats and republicans—all ready to serve but needing guidance and organization.[19] In the early part of August, the regiment received an experienced army veteran named Austin Light, who would help organize the regiment and eventually become the Colonel.[20] The regiment received tents and equipment for making camp and traveled to Camp Mather outside the city to begin daily drills and learn the basics of military life.[21]

The men began drilling in morning and afternoon sessions in "awkward squads" as Clark put it.[22] Early in September, the State Commissioners of

Agriculture sponsored a competition to award a flag to the best drilled company in the Chicago camp. Spending ten days drilling hard, a group of men led by Adjutant Frank Marshall, of Chicago, won the competition and were awarded the flag.[23] Finally, late in September, elections were held for officers. While Light and Osborn's positions were already awarded, a heated race for Major arose. Orrin Mann and William Ranstead were the candidates, and their camps became evenly split. Doctor Clark was selected as judge of the election—and ultimately cast the deciding vote for Mann, breaking a tie after the men of the regiment had cast their ballots.[24]

❖   ❖   ❖

On the morning of October 11, 1861, 806 officers and men formed up in the camp to be officially "mustered in" to service and formally received their orders to report to the Camp of Instruction at Benton Barracks in St Louis.[25] The regiment set out in front of thousands who had gathered to see regiments off to war that day, marching down Michigan Avenue towards Madison street and waiting for train cars to the tune of "The Girl I Left Behind Me." It was the first of over 1425 miles the Yates Phalanx would march between then and April 1865.[26]

2

Trains, Steamboats and Twists of Fate

Valentine Randolph was born 1838, the seventh of fourteen children. His parents had moved from Virginia to Illinois in 1831 and settled in Logan County in the central portion of the state. Randolph was raised on a farm, and his family was hard working and religiously devout. At 19, Randolph enrolled at Illinois College, and three years later in 1860 began at Dickinson College in Pennsylvania. When the war broke out, however, Randolph returned home and enlisted in what became Company I of the 39th Illinois.

Company I was a "magnificent body of men—the majority of them were large in form, robust in muscle, young and spirited," wrote Doctor Clark in his 1889 history. While Randolph was an educated man, young, and spirited in the sense of wishing to serve his country, he did not fit the large and robust description coming in just shy of five and a half feet tall. Nevertheless, Randolph's daily diary is well written, well organized, and while often contains critique and judgement of the men and situations around him, portrays a man who believed in, and was loyal to, the cause of preserving the Union.[1]

AFTER A TRAIN RIDE down to Alton, Illinois, and a steamboat trip to St Louis, the 39th found itself at the Camp of Instruction at Benton Barracks. The regiment was now in the company of other infantry units receiving last-minute training and under the command of regular army officers. Benton Barracks was on 300 acres made up partially of old fairgrounds, and the men soon adjusted to army life. With arms now in hand, and bellies full of pork, beans, and hardtack, the 39th drilled and further learned how an infantry unit moves in battle. The overwhelming majority of Illinois units mustered into service would be headed to serve in the western theater, but random occurrence intervened to change that.[2]

Colonel Ward H. Lamon, a Marshal of the District of Columbia, arrived late in October, making efforts to round out a brigade that would head east. Lamon, a native Virginian, was attempting to form regiments for a brigade made up of loyalist men from Virginia. Lamon was one regiment short of a full brigade and traveled to other states to recruit men. Speaking to Governor Yates in Illinois, the governor told Lamon he would not permit Illinois men to be recruited to out-of-state regiments but would allow units already credited to the state to be taken. For this reason, and perhaps thinking a regiment in the east would have a chance at Richmond, the Governor offered the Yates Phalanx. The decision was made that the 39th Illinois Infantry Regiment would head to Hagerstown,

"Off to the Front." Illustration of the 39th Illinois leaving Chicago (reproduced from Clark, *History*).

Maryland, assigned to General Nathanial Banks' V Corps. This did not come without some controversy however, as Lamon's credentials were later questioned, and Congress made an inquiry into the cost of moving the 39th east. Regardless, it was a twist of fate that sent the 39th east, when most Illinois units were sent to the western theater.[3]

❖   ❖   ❖

On October 31, the 39th boarded trains and began their trip to Hagerstown via Alton, Illinois, then Indianapolis. The regiment was greeted at stops by cheering crowds offering food (not to mention drinks, cigars, and the attention of adoring women) and comfortable sleeping accommodations for overnight stops. From Indianapolis, they moved towards Pennsylvania and finally south reaching Hagerstown, Maryland, as November 2 turned to November 3. The regiment's reward for reaching their destination was a six-mile march, with their knapsacks, in the pouring rain. The unit took up shelter in an old warehouse where they remained for three days before a train arrived to transfer their gear and head to Williamsport.

Only five days later, on November 10, the 39th was settling into their tents for the night when the "long roll" sounded throughout the camp. The long roll of the drum starts with a slow, methodical drumbeat that would get a regiment's attention while quickly accelerating its pace into a long consistent drum roll that would drive the urgency of the situation. This was the first time The Phalanx would have heard this sound outside of training, and you can imagine the adrenaline, emotion, and commotion that would have erupted. Out of their tents, the roll became faster and men grabbed rifles and followed the sound of the drums. Non-commissioned officers form their platoons, captains form their companies, and the senior officers form the regiment in line of battle. Colonel Light came galloping through the camp, "Fall into ranks, boys, quickly."[4] Drums, shouting voices, and clattering rifles would have been simultaneously drowning each other out yet equally distinctive as each man's heart raced faster and faster to head into battle with the rebels for the very first time. The regiment moved to a new drum cadence now, and they maneuvered towards the river.

The official history of the 39th Illinois does not record a battle this day, however, because one did not happen. "Drill is dismissed," yelled Colonel Light.[5] The regiment had gotten its first good scare out of the way and proved it knew the sense of urgency that would one day be required.

Unfortunately, just a couple of weeks later, the regiment had a more severe scare in an event that put the unit's esprit de corps at risk. Towards the end of November, it became known that the War Department had seen fit to remove Colonel Austin Light from command of the regiment. Dr. Clark's account states that "it would serve no good purpose" to repeat the reasons for his dismissal and insinuates that he did not believe them to be true.[6] In his diary, G Company Private Homer Plimpton of Sterling, goes further and details a story from Colonel Light's previous army service. The story went that while a Corporal, Light had received a furlough yet did not return to service at the ordered date, or at all. According to Plimpton, he was court-martialed and removed from the service.[7]

Both Clark and Plimpton's accounts allude to some regimental politics coming into play and that a small group of Light's detractors had it out for him. Records also show most of the men were dismayed by this, and his goodbye to the regiment was exceedingly sorrowful. There is no sign any of the officers, including Lieutenant Colonel Osborn, were in on this, as they had been grateful for his experience and counted on him for success. Osborn was now in one of the toughest imaginable leadership positions: Being the new Colonel and commander of a unit that had just lost the leader they loved because of some mysterious dynamic. With only a few weeks of experience under Light, Osborn would have to continue learning his job on the fly while earning the respect of the men he would lead into battle.[8]

The orders received in early December brought that battle closer to hand as the regiment received orders to reinforce Brigadier General Benjamin Kelley near Romney, Virginia. He was engaging rebels to re-open the Baltimore and Ohio Railroad. On December 15, the 39th departed for Hancock, Maryland, where they crossed the Potomac into Alpine Station, Virginia.

The Phalanx was about to encounter one of the Confederacy's top generals on his home turf.

3

Trial by Fire

Ezra Cook was born in Connecticut and was the son of a Methodist minister. Never spending more than a two-year term in any place, Cook spent his boyhood in various small villages of New England.

Aging, and unable to keep up with the schedule of ministering to many small churches, his father engaged in a manufacturing business for some time, before selling it in 1853 when Cook was 12, and moving to a farm near Wheaton, Illinois, 30 miles west of Chicago. Cook was attending Wheaton College—a school with a strong abolition streak that played a role in the Underground Railroad—and Cook was called to action. "I did not doubt that it was the death-knell of slavery," he wrote, "and my heart was in the battle for freedom."

Acknowledging his father, however, the 19-year-old Cook would not go without his consent. While reluctant at first, Cook's father was eventually swayed by the appeal of Methodist minister William Slaughter's appeal for young Christian men to join his "Preacher's Company."[1]

UNDERSTANDING LIFE FOR THE 39TH over the next few weeks requires an understanding of the geography of the land they now found themselves in. The regiment marched 25 miles west to Hancock from Williamsport, following the Potomac the whole way. The area was of growing importance because of the routes of travel it provided into the Shenandoah Valley to the southeast. Nestled between the Blue Ridge Mountains to the east and Appalachians to the west, and capped by the Potomac and James Rivers, the Shenandoah Valley was an area of immense importance at this stage in the war. The valley was an invaluable source of fertile farmland tasked with feeding the Confederate Army, but more importantly, its control was vital to the defense and assault of each side's capital. To gain, or maintain, access to the Valley, each side also needed access to the railroads and bridges in the region the 39th now found itself.

On the macroscale, the regiment was now 95 miles northwest of Washington, D.C., and 200 miles northwest of Richmond, where the Potomac serves as a border between Maryland and modern-day West Virginia. The town of Winchester was 40 miles to the south, with Harpers Ferry 50 miles southeast. In the immediate vicinity was Alpine Valley just on the other side of the Potomac from Hancock, St. John's Run four miles to the east, and the small town of Bath (modern day Berkeley Springs, West Virginia) four miles to the southeast on the other side of Great Cacapon Mountain. Romney, and General Kelley with 5,000 men, was 55 miles southwest. The companies of the 39th were spread amongst these

View from Cacapon Mountain looking towards Bath (modern-day Berkeley Springs, West Virginia) on the left (author's photograph).

locations, providing security for railroad repair crews and protecting bridges over river crossings and mountain passes. The garrison of Bath was being commanded by now Lieutenant Colonel Mann, along with Companies D, K, and I, and two cannons from the 4th U.S. Artillery.[2] Company E was at Sir John's Run, and Company G was at Great Cacapon Bridge. Meanwhile, Colonel Osborn established himself in Alpine at the abandoned home of a Confederate legislator, and the remaining Companies A, B, C, and F.[3] The men assigned to duties guarding the bridges and rail stations fared well for accommodations, finding comfortable lodging in the vacated homes of the area, many of which were well appointed summer homes of well-to-do southerners. Christmas and New Year passed without incident, and the regiment was now established, and part of Major General Nathanial Banks' roughly 23,000-man V Corps in and around the Valley.[4]

Private Plimpton started a diary with the new year, and on January 2 wrote that "I think that judging from the preparations the Government is now making a 'big strike' will soon occur which will tell with tremendous effect upon secession."[5] While the Federal government was in fact planning efforts for an assault on Richmond in the coming weeks, the 39th would have work to take care of beforehand. Confederate Army Valley District commander, General Thomas "Stonewall" Jackson, was headquartered 40 miles to the south in Winchester with 9,000

View from Prospect Peak, near Bath (modern-day Berkeley Springs, West Virginia) looking south at the Potomac River and Cacapon Mountain (author's photograph).

men and had designs on destroying Federal access to rails, roads, and canals, and causing headaches for the U.S. army attempting to operate in the valley.[6]

❖   ❖   ❖

Fortification was made of the Colonel's headquarters, now called "Fort Osborn," but through Christmas and the New Year was never needed. Although rumors of troop movements and nightly alarms became somewhat frequent, the situation had remained calm, and work on the railroads continued uninterrupted. The men at the various outposts formed scouting parties and liberated the various "sesh" homes of contraband that might be useful to the regiment: food, horses—and applejack whiskey.[7]

Early on January 3, a Black man came to the 39th's headquarters, stating that a large force of Jackson's army was on the move and five miles from Bath. This was a common occurrence, where free Blacks or those who had recently escaped enslavement attempted to help Federal forces. Unlike the litany of rumors and alarms the 39th were previously made aware of, this one would prove true, and the warning would be immeasurably helpful.[8] Lieutenant Colonel Mann took Captain Samuel Linton, of Willow Creek, and 60 men from Linton's D Company, and set off on a scouting expedition with six cavalry couriers.[9] Yet unknown to Mann, Captain Slaughter, of Blue Island, and a portion of G Company, to include

Private Plimpton, were on Prospect Rock atop Cacapon Mountain taking observations from various prominent points. Captain Slaughter's men observed about 3,000 men and two large camps.[10]

Lieutenant Colonel Mann and his scouting party proceeded south out of Alpine on the Winchester Road. Four to five miles outside of town they encountered a small group of rebel cavalry troops. Not knowing the numbers and disposition of Jackson's forces Mann engaged and pursued the cavalry, and the Phalanx found itself engaged with the enemy for the first time.[11]

❖   ❖   ❖

Laying in wait were 150 infantrymen from Jackson's 21st Virginia who sprang an ambush after the cavalry drew Mann into them. Attempting to cut off Mann and Linton's retreat, a "lively skirmish" ensued, as the two tried to drive off the enemy force.[12] Mann likely assessed the object of Jackson's current movement was to move the 39th Illinois off their locations and take Alpine and Hancock. This would give Jackson access to Maryland and Pennsylvania, cut off communications and lines of retreat for Federal forces, and give him unfettered access to General Kelley's troops at Romney. Given Romney's access to the south branch of the Potomac, points on the Baltimore and Ohio Railroad, and its direct road to Winchester, control of the town was currently vital to both sides.

Between the current location on the Winchester Road, and Hancock, was a range of high hills extending many miles in either direction. Bath itself was the only real location a force could cross the Potomac in that area and reach Alpine and Hancock. Keeping all of this in mind, Mann sought to maintain his option to make a fighting retreat to Bath and not let the ambush cut him off. Captain Linton spaced out his men in multiple locations along the skirmish line and gave the impression that their strength was more than it was. Keeping up their fire while maneuvering to a position to retreat, Linton's men successfully held off the significantly larger force even as it received reinforcements. As daylight ran out, Linton and his infantry began their retreat to Bath, while the cavalry and Lieutenant Colonel Mann (who was also mounted) continued to skirmish with the rebel force to slow down any pursuit.[13] Staying in the vicinity longer than he should have, Mann's horse navigated thick timber and jumped three fence lines, narrowly avoiding capture through the "good running qualities of his young stallion."[14]

Linton and his men made their way into Bath after dark, and Jackson's men decided not to follow without daylight or a firm idea of the force stationed there; and because heavy snow had begun to fall.[15] Mann and Linton had commanded well, and the group had killed five rebels, including one Lieutenant, and wounded several. Linton's D Company had only suffered three members with minor wounds but lost eight men taken prisoner—although one of those prisoners would later prove to be a silver lining.[16]

Knowing Jackson would follow up his attack in the morning, Colonel Osborn put the entire regiment on alert and sent word to General Kelly that he needed support. The 84th Pennsylvania had just arrived outside Hancock, and even though they had just received their arms after travel, the unit crossed the

Potomac at 10:00 at night with 550 men to strengthen the position at Bath. His regiment only four days out of training, Colonel William Murray assumed command from Osborn based on date of rank. The two men had only 1,500 troops combined.[17] Wrote Valentine Randolph, a Company I private from Lincoln, "The night was cold, dark and the snow continued to fall. Till midnight we stood in readiness to fire at a minute's warning; there being then no appearance of an attack a heavy guard was stationed along the road and the rest were permitted to go to quarters. I volunteered to guard the road. In the morning we expected to be attacked."[18]

On Cacapon Mountain, Captain Slaughter was gaining an appreciation for what might soon transpire. The 39th Illinois had seen its first day of combat and would not wait long to see the second. Wrote Homer Plimpton that night, "The Captain extended the pickets on the mountain during the night and ordered us to sleep on our arms."[19]

❖   ❖   ❖

Before sunup on the morning of a frigid January 4, Colonel Osborn set his regiment to work to prepare for an assault on Bath, Hancock, and the railroads and bridges under their control. The 84th Pennsylvania was stationed with the Fourth U.S. Artillery on Warm Springs Ridge overlooking Bath and companies of the 39th Illinois were spread atop Mount Alpine and the hills overlooking Winchester Road. The valley narrows significantly at Bath, and the Federal forces were using the heavily wooded hills to their advantage. On Great Cacapon was Captain Slaughter and his element of Company G, who had spent a frosty night on the mountain sleeping with their rifles for pillows. Slaughter now sent 32-year-old Lieutenant Oscar Rudd, of Blue Island, and twenty-one men near the top of the 2,600-foot mountain (Bath's elevation is 600 feet) to observe enemy movement towards Bath and "embarrass the approach" of any force that might be sent against the position.[20]

Between 9:00 and 10:00 a.m., a company of Confederate cavalry advanced on a road moving northwest towards Alpine and engaged the 39th's pickets. Sixty men from Company B moved to check the rebel advance. Not long after, a regiment of Jackson's men appeared in the woods flanking the position at Bath where fire was exchanged. The Fourth U.S. Artillery rained down on the rebel position for an hour, keeping their advance in check and preventing Confederate rifles from getting in range of the infantry at Bath.[21]

As the skirmishing near Bath and Alpine subsided with some small Confederate losses, the situation escalated at Great Cacapon. At 11:00 a.m., spotters atop the mountain sighted a column of three regiments moving north up the Bath Road. As Captain Slaughter ensured that word made it back to Bath and Hancock, Company G now also spotted enemy movements from two directions directly towards them at Cacapon. Slaughter took his men of Company G, and an element of Company E under Lieutenant Lewis Whipple of Rockville and forded the Great Cacapon Creek to establish a defense of the bridge there. After fortifying defenses at each end of the bridge, Lieutenant Whipple and his men posted at the bridge.

The rest of Company G took a position in the bluffs overlooking the creek. Still atop the mountain was Lieutenant Rudd and his group of 21 men.[22]

Late in the afternoon, Jackson's army of roughly 8–9,000 men presented themselves near Bath with 22 pieces of artillery. The men of the 39th, and their 84th Pennsylvania reinforcements, had courageously defended Bath all morning and maintained a sufficient presence throughout the day. Still, they now risked being surrounded by an overwhelming force. Colonel Murray feared he could not hold the position until reinforcements could arrive and ordered a retreat to Alpine via Sir John's Run. Men forded the icy water as companies I, K, and D of the 39th engaged the enemy to cover the retreat.[23]

A true testament to their willingness to stay and fight, and allow men and artillery to get to safety, is that several Phalanx members were captured in the skirmish surrounding the retreat. The last two men to cross were Company K men, Sergeant Elbanis Myers of Bloomington and Captain Joseph Woodruff of Marseilles. As the two were ensuring all the men got across, Myers discovered a dozen loaded rifles that had been left behind by men more concerned about crossing the frigid water. The two knew the enemy was closing in and decided they could use all 12 rifles in short order to give the appearance of a bigger force and buy one last bit of time for their men. The two did not have to put their plan into place, however, as they witnessed a man pull a boat ashore then run into the woods "at a lively pace, as though he had some important business."[24] Assuming none of their own were heading in the wrong direction, the two men took possession of the boat and crossed the river.

Several things were now happening at once, as the sands of winter daylight ran short. Jackson divided up his command sending two brigades toward Sir John's Run, Alpine, and Hancock, and one was sent towards Big Cacapon to burn the railroad bridge.[25] Meanwhile, Dr. Clark arrived near Bath, hoping to deliver medical supplies for the wounded but realized the 39th had abandoned their position. Fearing the rebel cavalry on the road from Bath to Alpine, and needing to get word to Colonel Osborn, the surgeon quickly made his way back to headquarters to report his findings. Wrote Dr. Clark, "at Alpine Station on January 4th all was excitement. We knew that our boys were engaged with the enemy at Bath, but as to what extent and how progressing nothing was known."[26]

While Osborn had spent the day requesting reinforcements and receiving orders from Generals Kelley and Brigadier General Frederick Lander (one of Banks' Division commanders in Williamsport), Clark's intelligence was the first he had received all day. Stonewall Jackson was advancing towards Alpine, and Osborn still had men on Cacapon Mountain, down below guarding the bridge, and forces at Alpine that needed time to retreat to Hancock. While the 39th would soon abandon Alpine, they used its strategic location one last time to their advantage. Osborn ordered Company A Commander, Major Sylvester Munn of Wilmington, along with members of Company F, to set up an ambush in the pass.[27]

As twilight set in, those in Alpine were busy loading wagons with equipment and supplies as quickly as possible to move across the icy cold Potomac. Soon the "rebel yell" was heard as Jackson's cavalry made their way towards Alpine, and

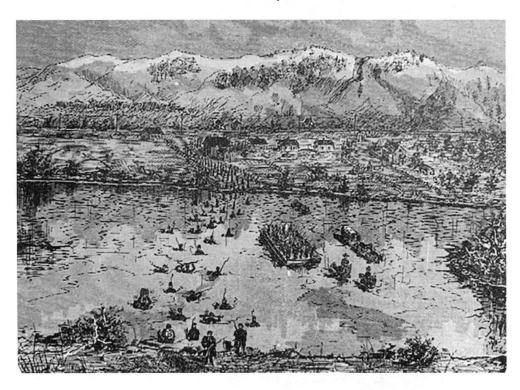

The Retreat from Alpine Station, a sketch by Dr. Clark (reproduced from Clark, *History*).

Major Munn's detachment sprang their ambush. Musket fire peppered the cavalry charge from all directions, and unable to see their opposing force, the Jackson men fell back after Munn's forces "emptied ten saddles."[28] Munn lost three men, but the ambush curtailed the immediate danger of enemy advance and allowed forces at Alpine to cross the river.[29]

Given the availability of resources for moving equipment and no time to spare, three-fourths of the command had to wade shoulder-deep, freezing, water. "Into it boys, wade it," ordered Lieutenant Colonel Mann.[30] Wrote Clark afterward, "The passage of the river at a temperature considerably below the freezing point was a most trying ordeal and resulted afterwards in much sickness. As the men emerged from the water, the frosty air gave their clothing a most uncomfortable stiffness."[31] Clark's notes in the regimental roster are dotted with accounts of men who forever suffered from rheumatism after the icy plunge. "I became so chilled through that I could hardly stand," wrote Company F Private Martin Van Buren Peters of Elgin. "With my clothes dripping and stiffening on me, I made a rush for a house where some of the other boys had gathered around a red-hot stove."[32] Their warming did not last long however, as shells fell in the city and the men had to head for better cover.

◆ ◆ ◆

Lieutenant Rudd continued to witness the day's events from the mountain top, and in the last bit of light spotted an infantry regiment and artillery headed for Great Cacapon. Rudd and his men now took cover at a bend in the narrow road and waited for the enemy advance. Rebel infantry was less than 200 feet from Rudd's position when he ordered his men to fire. The sound of 21 simultaneous rifles firing filled the air, and several rebels fell to the ground. The shock of the moment threw the column into disarray, and Rudd used the moment to move further down the mountain taking fire the whole way, but not losing any men.[33]

Further down the mountain at the railroad bridge was Private Plimpton and the elements of E and G Companies led by Lieutenant Whipple and Captain Slaughter. One of the Company E Men was Private William Jewett of Wesley. "Jackson was coming upon us," Jewett recalled, "and we were awaiting events."[34] Now in the darkness of night, they received rebel artillery and musket fire from 300 feet beyond the bridge and by cavalry attempting to ford the water near the bridge. Hearing a shot pass just over his head, Lieutenant Whipple caught his foot and fell, fearing he had been shot. "Bury me where I lay, boys!" he yelled.[35] Recovering quickly from his embarrassment, Whipple ordered the men to return fire. Much the same as Rudd on the mountain, the men of companies E and G used the darkness and fire from multiple locations to their advantage and made themselves seem a much larger force. "We poured our minnie balls from our rifle muskets into them as fast as we knew how," wrote Plimpton, "and with effect, for we drove them back to the foot of the mountain."[36]

No longer in immediate danger but fearing that their retreat may soon be cut off, Captain Slaughter rallied his men and made for the train cars that had been moving troops into the area. He couldn't return to Alpine or Hancock, but he couldn't keep his men here. They would head towards Cumberland and attempt to rally back up with the 39th. Twenty-five men were missing, and the men would later learn five were killed and ten wounded and taken prisoner.[37] Astonishingly, the other ten missing men eventually made their way to the U.S. army camp at Cumberland in the coming days.

One of the wounded men that was located and accessible, however, was Company G Private Frank Sherwood of Shabbona. Private Ezra Cook, of Wheaton, petitioned Captain Slaughter to take some men and carry Sherwood to the train. According to Cook, Slaughter was adamant the detachment needed to move, and that Sherwood would need to be left behind. Lieutenant Rudd approached Private Cook and risking the consequences of an enlisted man speaking ill of one officer to another, Cook plead his case to the Lieutenant. Rudd was appalled at the notion of knowingly leaving a wounded man behind, and in defiance of Slaughter, took some men and secured Sherwood. Knowing they would not make it to the train in time slowed down by a wounded man, the group found an old couple loyal to the Union and left him at the home. While it was a risky call to make, it was the only chance they had to make it out of the area before sunup. True to their promise; Cook, Sergeant W.W. Spencer of Bainbridge, and Private Henry Parkhurst of Le Roy returned a few days later for Sherwood.[38]

While the men of Companies E and G had left the bridge undefended for the rebels to destroy come morning, their courageous stand prevented the destruction of the retreating forces. The soaking wet and freezing cold men who had crossed the Potomac into Hancock could not start fires. Irate that his men had allowed the Federal troops to escape across the water, Jackson had planted multiple cannons on the bluffs opposite Hancock and began targeting the town.[39] The Fourth U.S. Artillery moved their two guns to Hancock, and as Colonel Osborn later wrote "the ball opened at last" as the Federal cannon returned fire for an hour and forced Jackson's guns out of range.[40] With enemy forces now observed in Alpine, a brigade of reinforcements arrived, as did General Lander, who assumed command. They spent the next 12 hours wondering what the morning would bring, as the temperature approached zero overnight.[41]

❖   ❖   ❖

At 10:00 a.m. on January 5, the force at Hancock saw a white flag advancing towards the Potomac from the Alpine side. Lieutenant Colonel Mann assembled a few men and met the enemy envoy at the river. Mann returned with Jackson's top cavalry commander, Colonel Turner Ashby, who wished to speak to General Lander on behalf of General Jackson.[42] Lieutenant Colonel Mann took great satisfaction of now dealing in this fashion with the blindfolded man he and his men had thwarted many times over the last couple of days. During the trip over the river, Ashby asked Mann, "what unit do you belong to?"

"The Thirty-Ninth Illinois!"

"My God!" responded Ashby. "Where in hell is not the Thirty-Ninth! They seem to be ubiquitous."[43]

Needing to keep up the appearance of a much larger force a little while longer, Lieutenant Colonel Mann undoubtedly smiled and said little else for the rest of the trip. The deception was continued even at General Lander's headquarters. When fearing that Ashby may understand the telegraph machine, the meeting was moved to a location away from it. Jackson's letter demanded the surrender of United States forces in Hancock and stated he would cross the river with 15,000 men and bombard the town if opposed. Two hours were given for non-combatants to leave the place, and presumably for Lander's force to surrender, before Jackson would open fire.[44]

General Lander turned to Colonel Ashby and said, "give my regards to General Jackson," before raising his voice and adding, "and tell him to bombard and be damned!" Lander continued that it was a "secesh" town anyway, and Colonel Murray added that Jackson would be the one responsible for the damage. As a stunned Ashby readied himself to leave, Lander calmed himself and set someone to writing. The general told Ashby he would deliver a "polite and soldierly" reply just as Jackson did. He added, however, "General Jackson and yourself, Colonel Ashby, are gentlemen and brave men, without a question, but you have started out in a God dammed bad cause!" Ashby was then sent safely on his way.[45]

Two hours later, the 39th Illinois raised their flag to the top of the flagpole in Hancock's town center, showing they had no intent to surrender to Jackson, and soldiers stood ready with buckets of water to extinguish any flames. Men took up positions with their rifles, the 4th U.S. Artillery put two guns in place on high ground behind the town, and then waited. Late on his own deadline, Jackson's artillery eventually sent two shells over, before The Federal battery, with a more extended reach than Jackson's, pummeled Alpine for the next hour. Neither side reported much injury, and no troops assembled to cross the river, only setting fire to the town before retreating. Stonewall's bluff was called, and the gamble paid off.[46]

Because of the constant movement of forces, and the use of concentrated ambushes, Jackson believed he had been facing a much larger force. One of the Company D men captured on the 3rd had been questioned by Jackson himself as to the number of Federal troops in the vicinity. The "most accomplished liar" told Jackson with a straight face that "we have on the Virginia side of the river between six and seven thousand men, and this morning it was reported that General Banks' army had reached Hancock to reinforce Lander."[47] This bit of "statecraft" by the captured soldier caused Jackson to halt his assault and regroup and allowed Colonel Murray and the 84th Pennsylvania time to reinforce Bath. Jackson had left Winchester intent on capturing up a small force, controlling the northwest access to the Shenandoah Valley, and gathering food and supplies for his men. Instead, wrote Dr. Clark, "his force of 10,000 men was held at bay for a day at Bath, and for hours at different points by mere detachments from an Illinois regiment. This affair might have had a more sorrowful and tragic ending had Jackson fully understood the number of our troops and their disposition."[48]

❖   ❖   ❖

The 39th Illinois was about to be on the move again in the frigid January cold. While he had failed to achieve his ultimate objectives, Jackson had still burned the Cacapon bridge, and destroyed Federal communications between the Allegheny Mountains and the Potomac. As Peter Cozzens states in *Shenandoah 1862: Stonewall Jackson's Valley Campaign*, Jackson's "rear was now secure for the march on Romney." Stonewall's efforts in the Shenandoah were far from over.

The Phalanx was about to head into the Valley for the biggest chess match in the first half of the war.

4

Into the Valley

Homer Plimpton was born in 1838 near Erie, Pennsylvania, and his family moved to Illinois in 1840. His father, a doctor, suffered from poor health and the family moved to a more populated area in Ohio in 1847. In 1854, however, the family again moved to Illinois and two years later Plimpton enrolled at Northwestern University; graduating with honors in 1860.

Following graduation, Plimpton began work as a teacher, but when the war broke out, was called to serve. His devout religious nature led him to Captain Slaughter and the "Preacher's Company" where he began a fascinating wartime journey as a member of the 39th Illinois.[1]

WHILE THE SUCCESS AGAINST Jackson in his Bath-Romney expedition was not a pitched or set-piece battle and is merely a minor footnote in Jackson's Valley campaign, it was a taste of fighting for the 39th Illinois and a successful one at that. Colonel Osborn had passed his first test as a leader, and Lieutenant Colonel Mann had proved himself extremely capable in the field. The actions of the various companies had proven their training effective, and their successes staved off what could have snowballed into a considerable problem for Federal efforts in the Valley.[2]

Making Osborn's success that much more impressive was that the 39th had been "pursuing a sort of independent existence" in Lander's division.[3] "Lamon's Brigade," intended to be formed when the 39th Illinois was poached from Benton Barracks to head east, had never materialized. In fact, nothing more was ever heard of it by the men. What would have been done with Osborn's regiment had that brigade formed is unknown, but its absence had left them at Alpine and Hancock for their skirmish, and now sent them to Cumberland, Maryland. The U.S. army in the Valley knew Jackson intended to move on Romney, and the 39th Illinois and 84th Pennsylvania, as well as the recently arrived 110th Pennsylvania, were requested as reinforcements.[4]

The 39th left Hancock on January 11, 1862, for a 40-mile march to Cumberland in snowy, mountainous terrain and arrived on the 12th. Besides the Pennsylvania regiments, they were now camped with a cavalry unit and the Fourth U.S. artillery that had been in Hancock. After receiving some new clothing and supplies, a necessity brought on by the hasty exit from Alpine, the 39th boarded trains for New Creek, where two additional regiments from Ohio joined the growing organization.[5]

❖　❖　❖

Roughly 20 miles southwest of Cumberland, New Creek was a station on the Baltimore and Ohio Railroad, 60 miles west of Winchester, with Romney in between. The area was so unfit for living because of a cycle of weather, including snow, freezing, thawing, then more snow, the regiment elected to live out of the train cars. The days became consistently rainy, and Dr. Clark wrote that "sickness came as a flood-tide among us." He continued, "The experiences of both officers and men at New Creek, VA., will be remembered as among the saddest and most sorrowful of any that were encountered in their history as soldiers."[6] Homer Plimpton's February journal entries were filled with reports of lousy weather, and sick men, as he had been detailed to work in the hospital at Cumberland. On February 5, he wrote, "I learned today that there are some fourteen hundred sick in the hospitals here. Three funerals have taken place today. There are eight of Company G here who are considered dangerously sick."[7]

In early February, Colonel Osborn received orders to have the 39th move to Patterson's Creek, which found the regiment retracing much of its travel of the last couple of months. The regiment reached Patterson's Creek on February 5. It was now part of the First Brigade of Lander's First Division, part of Major General Nathanial Banks' V Corps of the Army of the Potomac.[8]

On February 22, Washington's Birthday, the regiment had an inspection and parade review and received news of General Ulysses S. Grant's "great victory at Fort Donelson and the bravery of our Western boys."[9] Many Illinois regiments were serving in the western theater, specifically under Grant, and the 39th undoubtedly felt great pride in their Illinois brothers—literally in the case of Company I Private George Riddle, of LeRoy, whose brother was killed at Fort Donelson.[10] At this point in the war, the United States found itself in an excellent position. Federal forces had made tremendous advances in Missouri, Kentucky, and Tennessee, and the Army of the Potomac had over 150,000 men nearing Richmond—three times the number of Confederates facing them. While there was no Federal presence in the Shenandoah Valley there were roughly 30,000 men in the vicinity to Stonewall Jackson's 6,000.[11]

However, President Lincoln was concerned that General George McClellan's upcoming Peninsula Campaign would leave Washington vulnerable since it included forces of General Irvin McDowell being used simultaneously for capital defense and an attack on Richmond and counted Nathaniel Banks' 23,000 men near the Valley as part of Washington's defense. In the President's mind, this would open the door for the Valley to be used for a rear assault on Washington, while leaving no force between Richmond and the capital. McClellan, commanding not just the Army of the Potomac but all United States armies, needed to position his pieces on the board to assuage the President's fears while giving him the conditions he desired for his assault on Richmond. Not knowing how greatly he outnumbered Confederate General Joseph Johnston, the ever-cautious McClellan ordered General Banks' V Corps into the Valley on February 27. This set in motion the series of events he believed would soon end the war: Secure the Valley, leave a minimal force to hold it while shifting men east to defend Washington, and perform a pincer movement on Richmond with McDowell.[12]

❖   ❖   ❖

As politicians and generals devised a grand strategy, the 39th continued to provide security of railroad repairs near Patterson's Creek until receiving orders on March 1 as part of the V Corps' movement into the Valley. Lieutenant Colonel Mann traveled to Lander's headquarters to retrieve the letter and witnessed Lander's imposing nature in person. After detailing the instructions to Mann and handing him the letter, Mann replied, "General, I will try and see your orders obeyed."

"TRY! God damn your soul to hell! Try!!" exclaimed Lander. "What in the hell do you mean, Sir, by such talk? Is that any language for a soldier to use, damn you!"

Mann overcame the shock of the moment and mustered a confident "General Lander, your orders shall be obeyed to the letter!"

The General immediately extended his hand to Mann. "That is right, Colonel; that is soldierly! I bid you goodbye, and hope we shall soon meet again."[13]

General Lander's orders for Colonel Osborn stated, "I have [intrusted] you with a highly important service—that of opening the railroad to Martinsburg." After giving further logistical information, he closed with "If the rebels come on you in force, *fight* under any circumstances, and if you are taken prisoner, I will release you [to-morrow] morning. I start on a forced march across the country to cut them off from Winchester."[14]

General Lander called on the 39th to have the courage and fight that it did at Bath and Alpine and take the lead in opening-up the Baltimore and Ohio Railroad towards dislodging Jackson from Winchester. The 39th would retrace its route back through Cumberland, Hancock, and Alpine, then move south with the railroad crews towards Martinsburg—25 miles north of Winchester. Meanwhile, Lander would march his forces 50 miles east from his headquarters in Paw Paw to get between Jackson and the rail repairs. Between movements such as this of troops already in Virginia, and the rest of Banks' forces moving west from Harpers Ferry; the entire 38,000 strong V Corps would be in the Valley.[15]

The General, however, would never meet Lieutenant Colonel Mann again, and Lander's letter to Osborn was "perhaps one of the last he ever penned."[16] While traveling from Patterson's Creek, the 39th stopped at Alpine Station when they received news of General Lander's death. The general was battling pneumonia and passed away in his sleep during the night of March 2 into the 3rd. Assuming command of the First Division was Brigadier General James Shields. The 39th now had an Illinois man as their division commander. Shields had been an Illinois House of Representatives member, sat on the Illinois Supreme Court, and, after serving in the Mexican American War, was then a U.S. Senator from Illinois.[17]

The 39th remained near Alpine for a time, re-supplying and guarding continued railroad repair and bridge construction. On the night of March 7, they moved to Cherry Run, where a bridge needed constructing and remained for two days before being ordered to abandon their train cars and march towards Martinsburg, arriving on the 10th. They gathered, with the entire division, and were greeted by their new division commander. "General Shields has arrived!" wrote Private Randolph. "We're glad to be commanded by a man, once a citizen of Illinois. Said he (Shields to the 39th) I will give you plenty of fighting to do and if you disgrace Illinois, you had a damn sight better never return home."[18] While Shields, having great respect for the Illinois boys, would have honored Lander's promise to "free you tomorrow," the effort would not be required as the movement towards Winchester continued the next day. The division moved within two miles of Winchester, unopposed by the enemy. Aware of the massive moment of Federal troops into the Valley advancing on Winchester, Jackson had withdrawn up the Valley.[19]

❖　❖　❖

General McClellan was now satisfied that his army controlled the Valley, and Jackson's retreating force was not a threat. Lincoln conditioned his approval of the Peninsula Campaign on McClellan leaving enough troops at Manassas Junction to "leave Washington entirely secure." To that end, McClellan ordered Shields' First Division to hold Winchester while the rest of Banks' V Corps began preparations to move east.[20]

Early on March 18, the 39th packed three days rations and formed a column with all three brigades of infantry, four artillery batteries, and a cavalry regiment; to march up the Valley towards Winchester and beyond to Strasburg. While Jackson's Division was not assessed as a threat, they were serving as a covering force for V Corps' movement east. Shields' reconnaissance in force was ordered by General Banks to find out Jackson's strength and clear the path for V Corps to move to Centerville and Manassas.[21]

As Confederate scouts realized the movement of Banks' army out of the Valley, Jackson's mission in the Shenandoah took on a new twist. Whereas before, Stonewall Jackson was charged with attempting to evict Federal forces from the Valley; he was now ordered by Richmond and Johnston to keep the U.S. army *in* the Valley. With events transpiring as they had and a need for troops elsewhere, Jackson's Division was down to three Virginia brigades, a handful of artillery batteries, and Colonel Turner Ashby's cavalry regiment. Jackson could not be expected to take on and defeat much larger forces, but it was hoped that constant harassment might force the Federals to divert troops back to the Shenandoah and away from Richmond.[22]

The column passed through Winchester, once the Jackson stronghold, finding only Federal troops there now. General Shields took a position at the front of his division, and it must have been a sight to see for the residents of Winchester who hadn't fled. Nearly 10,000 U.S. soldiers marching in step, rifles in hands, packs on their backs, moving freely and unopposed through Winchester. The column passed through more small towns, void of Confederate troops with only sullen-looking women to watch them march. "The only delighted and happy expressions," wrote Dr. Clark, "were seen in the shining faces of the many [negroes] who had gathered together in little groups at various points."[23]

During the mid-afternoon, and five miles north of Strasburg, the troops saw smoke rising from a bridge into Strasburg that Jackson's men had torched. Shortly after, the boom of cannons was heard, and it appeared the column's advance guard was being engaged. The cannon fire continued, and the crack of rifle fire began as the column picked up a quick time march. The column soon had to open ranks and step off the road to allow artillery to pass forward quickly.[24] "In a gallop four batteries rushed, the drivers putting whip at every jump. The earth trembled beneath the tread of the horses," wrote Valentine Randolph in his journal that night.[25] Homer Plimpton added that they stopped moving only once after the shooting began "to allow our artillery, twenty-four pieces, to pass from the rear to the front, which it did on the keen run; and a more exciting scene I never saw."[26]

The shooting ended before the main column reached Cedar Creek as the sun set. The advance guard of cavalry had encountered a forward presence of Turner Ashby's cavalry, with some infantry, and a skirmish had ensued. Smoke the division had seen was the rebel force burning the bridge on their retreat. Men in the column saw one casualty move past them in Winchester's direction, but otherwise, the division was unscathed in the attack. The column had covered 17 miles during the day and now placed their cannons, set out their pickets, and slept on their rifles under the stars.[27]

❖   ❖   ❖

After finishing their breakfasts of pork fat and coffee on the fire, General Shields' column reformed early the morning of the 19th and continued its movement to Strasburg. A temporary bridge was laid down over the shallow creek, and movement was cautious as the occasional rebel shell was sent toward the advancing column. Jackson was fully implementing his plan to keep Federal troops occupied somewhere that didn't involve reinforcing McDowell or McClellan further east. Should the northerners continue to move south, Jackson would have gladly used the high ground of Mt Jackson to tie them up even longer. The column halted a mile outside of Strasburg and deployed artillery and snipers that again engaged with Turner Ashby's cavalry for an hour. With Jackson's forces falling back once more, Shields and his division marched through Strasburg, stopping on the other side. Federal artillery was put in place and began firing in the enemy's direction as the division formed into lines of battle. Ashby was seen organizing his cavalry, and the artillery firing ceased to ensure Federal troops could retreat under the cavalry charge, but no charge ever came. Night fell, a steady rain began, and Shields' division, and the men of the 39th, set up camp for the evening. When morning broke, nothing was seen of the enemy and Shields turned his division around back toward Winchester.[28]

After 40 round trip miles of marching, often in rain and snow, the division arrived back at camp late on the 20th, with leadership satisfied that all was well. Shields spoke to his commanders confidently about the situation, and Banks was so sure Jackson was no longer a threat that all plans would move forward. The men, however, were exhausted.[29]

Little did they know how much they would need to recover, and how little time they would have to do it.

The Battle of Kernstown
and a Pursuit of Stonewall

Simon Brucker was one of the 39th's recent American immigrants, having been born in 1838 in Alzey, Germany. Brucker received a public school education in that place, graduating at 14, and moving to America with his brother that same year. Brucker remained in New Jersey for one year while learning English, before setting off for Ohio and eventually Illinois—settling in Pontiac.

Brucker began work in the mercantile business in Pontiac until the beginning of the war. Eager to support the cause of preserving his new home, Brucker enlisted in the 20th Illinois in April 1861 for 30 days' service. Quickly realizing the war would last so much longer, Brucker returned to Pontiac and re-enlisted in August in what became Company C of the 39th, before actively recruiting additional members of the company.[1]

ON MARCH 21, 1862, Stonewall Jackson received reports from Ashby's cavalry and civilian sources that Banks was splitting his force and moving out of the region. Fearing that Banks was doing precisely what he was tasked to prevent, Jackson turned his men around and began a grueling 40-mile march back to Winchester in terrible weather through worse terrain.[2] As part of Banks' movement out of the valley, Lieutenant Simon Brucker, of Pontiac, was ordered by General Shields to take 50 men of Company C and 50 men from the Thirteenth Indiana to relieve picket outposts belonging to men leaving with Banks. Brucker could not track down the soldiers they were replacing and thus established his picket lines where he had been instructed to.[3]

Saturday, March 22, was a quiet day in camp, for the men of the 39th and the First Division. Still resting up from the three-day excursion to Strasburg, the men were made aware of U.S. victories in Newbern, North Carolina, and at Pea Ridge, Arkansas. Spirits were high, and the division was preparing to move again on the following Monday. South of Winchester, on a picket line between Strasburg and Front Royal, things were about to get more exciting, however. Lieutenant Brucker wrote that just as the sun was coming up, a corporal thought he spotted Banks' pickets coming in. As the men soon found out, however, it was fifteen of Colonel Ashby's cavalrymen who closed within 50 yards and opened fire. Brucker and his men returned fire, but the enemy had already turned their horses and ran off.[4]

Thirty minutes later, the cavalrymen returned and "quite a lively skirmish took place for an hour's time," remembered Brucker.[5] Brucker's detachment took cover behind a stone fence that allowed them to fire without being exposed, while maintaining access to the road between Strasburg and Front Royal, and the main pike to Winchester. Soon the enemy brought artillery to bear while the Confederate cavalry continued attempting to flank Brucker's picket line.[6] Brucker's men bravely held the advance at bay, even as he continually looked back towards Winchester for reinforcements after sending a messenger. Around 11:00 a.m., Brucker finally heard a bugle and horsemen coming towards them. "They still found us masters of the situation," wrote Brucker. "We had been attacked and had successfully repulsed the enemy's pickets and skirmishers at least a dozen times."[7] One man from the 13th Indiana was killed, and the 39th suffered two wounded and had five taken prisoner. The Confederate loss, however, was three killed and fifteen wounded.[8] The action of Brucker and his men had slowed down an unexpected attack and served as notice to be ready.

◆   ◆   ◆

Back in camp, the quiet day had been interrupted by the long roll and the men formed lines of battle. The 39th was put into position with the 5th Ohio on the Romney turnpike as the picket skirmishing unfolded. Hearing that fighting had erupted, General Shields' rode out to the location of his artillery to get a sense of the skirmish.[9] No sooner had he arrived than a rebel shell exploded near him, knocking him from his horse and shattering his left arm above the elbow. Ashby retired from the field, never having entered Winchester. The entire division spent the night on duty, and the 39th was placed on picket duty five miles west of Winchester until midnight before returning to camp for a restless night of sleep.[10]

The encounter didn't dissuade Ashby of his assumptions, but he was convinced more than ever of the enemy disposition in and around Winchester. His spies in the area had witnessed movement by Banks, and Ashby had only spotted some cavalry, a single company of infantry, and some artillery. In reality, after his injury, Shields had sent a large part of the division in various directions outside of Winchester to wait in reserve, then put First Brigade Commander Colonel Nathan Kimball in charge. Late on the 22nd, Ashby reported to Jackson, now only 15 miles from Winchester, that he had encountered only a rear guard. Not realizing Ashby had encountered the picket line of a 9,000-man force, Jackson now saw an opportunity. He would heed his directive to force Federal reinforcements back into the Valley, but potentially recapture Winchester and threaten Washington. Even after his grueling 25-mile march had whittled his numbers down to 3,087 men, Jackson decided to attack the next day.[11]

◆   ◆   ◆

It was around noon on March 23, 1862, when the division heard cannon fire south of Winchester. Jackson had thrown Ashby down the main Valley Turnpike earlier in the morning where heavy skirmishing had ensued. Dismayed Ashby had

GEN! SHIELDS AT THE BATTLE OF WINCHESTER, V.ª 1862.

Currier and Ives depiction of General Shields the day before the Battle of Kernstown (Library of Congress: LC-DIG-pga-08945).

not taken Winchester and had ceded the high ground in front of him, Stonewall chose to attack—still believing he only faced a rear guard. Arriving on the scene, Stonewall sent Ashby forward towards Kernstown. Meanwhile, Jackson intended to take the rest of his force and move west, then north, to flank the Federal forces and drive into Winchester. Ignorant of the numbers he was facing; however, Jackson did not understand that Colonel Kimball was creating a two-mile front with his 9,000 men comprised of three infantry brigades, a cavalry brigade, and five artillery batteries on the high ground of Pritchard Hill in the center of the line. Members of the 39th hurried to the left end of the line with the rest of Second Brigade under Colonel Jeremiah Sullivan as a tremendous artillery exchange ensued.[12]

"The missiles of death began to fall everywhere. How the dirt flies!" wrote Valentine Randolph.[13] The 39th and rest of the Second Brigade were formed in line of battle and quickly lay in the dirt face down to avoid the enemy shells flying overhead. Shells were falling and exploding all around the 39th's position as Jackson sought to pin down the Federal flanks while attacking the guns at the center.

Jackson's initial launch at Pritchard's Hill, and the center of the line, was turned back, and thus he now moved more troops to the west, again not fully grasping the size of the force that opposed him. Recognizing this, and aware of his numerical advantage, Kimball shifted Colonel Erastus Tyler's Third Brigade further to the west, while also dispatching three companies of his First Brigade off Pritchard's Hill in support. Also included in this movement was the 5th Ohio, which the 39th was reinforcing.[14]

The situation now required an advance from the 39th and a distraction that allowed all this orchestration to occur. "We soon discovered the batteries and regiments on the right falling back, taking up new positions. In the meantime, the shot and shell of the enemy were being directed at us, some of the time coming a little closer than desirable," wrote Plimpton.[15] Sullivan ordered two artillery pieces to the left flank considering all this, and the 39th's old friends from the 4th U.S. Artillery rained shot down on the rebel batteries while the 39th provided for the defense of the position. Both sides kept up their firing, as shells sent debris from the earth and parts of trees flying around the men. As the artillery silenced the rebel guns on their right flank, Captain Linton and Company D deployed to run off some of Ashby's cavalry, which had remained in the area and was attempting to move with the cessation of artillery fire. The scene on the left near Kernstown became quiet, the 39th having played an essential part in the Second Brigade's ability to stop Ashby's cavalry, cover Kimball's movement of forces, and hold the left flank of the Division's line.[16]

Late in the afternoon, however, Jackson's forces had mounted a somewhat sustained show of force against the Federal right, when Colonel Tyler launched 50 companies of his Third Brigade in a merged offensive against Jackson.[17] "Soon the firing became incessant," wrote Valentine Randolph watching the scene unfold. "There was one continual sound not unlike a very heavy hailstorm."[18] Added Homer Plimpton, "The engagement now became very severe; one continual roar of musketry."[19] Jackson's brigade on his left side could initially hold off Tyler's attack taking cover behind a stone wall, but Jackson soon received word of the actual numbers he was facing. Speaking to the aide who delivered the news, Jackson replied, "Say nothing about it, we are in for it."[20]

With batteries still in place and an overwhelming number of men, Tyler's offensive eventually broke through after brutal fighting and many Federal advances. The 84th Pennsylvania advanced three times, their commander Colonel Murray being killed in the last.[21] Kimball's men were undeterred though, and as more reserves were brought forward, more and more rebel regiments withdrew, emboldening the Federal advances. "Just at dark, we saw the rebel line give way and heard the triumphant shouts of our men, we knew that they were victorious, at least for this day," wrote Plimpton.[22]

Out-numbered, out-flanked, and out of ammunition, the rebels were in full retreat before Jackson's final reinforcements could arrive on the field. The day had been disastrous for Jackson, with 740 killed, wounded, or captured, roughly 20 percent of his engaged force. First Division suffered 575 combined casualties and captured, with the 39th Illinois suffering no losses and only one man injured in their action.[23] Possibly unsure of what General Shields would want to do, and aware his men were exhausted and hungry, Colonel Kimball did not mount a pursuit of the retreating Jackson, no doubt just relieved to have won the day after Shields' injury the day before.[24] Having not eaten since early morning, the men of the 39th camped in place for the night, laying on their rifles expecting to fight again at a moment's notice. The 39th's first taste of major combat would always stick with them, and Valentine Randolph, and everyone else most likely, did not sleep: "The groans of the wounded loaded the air. The cattle bellowed, said to be occasioned by the smell of blood. The horrors are indescribable."[25]

❖   ❖   ❖

General Banks arrived early in the morning, and the men of the 39th were up before dawn and in the lead of pursuit towards Strasburg of the retreating Jackson. Banks and his staff were concerned about Jackson's aggressiveness and potential for reinforcements, but McClellan wanted a serious pursuit, to bring about the conditions for his campaign.[26] The force spent days moving forward and firing artillery, to probe for Jackson's rearguard. So it went, day after day, the brigades in pursuit would deploy cavalry and infantry ahead and send some artillery shells in Jackson's direction. Jackson's rearguard would give token defensive fire and lob some shells themselves. The pursuit kept up, day after day, with the men encountering rebel dead and wounded along the road. As General Shields' men advanced, Jackson's men continued to retreat, destroying railroads and bridges along the way.[27] By April 1, Jackson's retreat had reached Mt. Jackson, where he set fire to rail cars and a bridge before retreating further, still flanked on all sides. By this time, General Banks, who had been commanding in person, was receiving word that Jackson might link up with reinforcements and ended the pursuit. "On the evening of April 4th, the sutler reached our camp, bringing several casks of ale, and it is hardly necessary to add that it was soon transferred from the barrels to the thirsty throats of its admirers," wrote Doctor Clark.[28]

6

Final Days In (and Out of)
the Valley

Joseph Ward was born in 1838 near Norfolkshire, England, another of the regiment's recent immigrants, Ward immigrated to America with his family in 1850, and made their way to New Bremen—a modern day Cook County township near Tinley Park.

In his introduction to *An Enlisted Soldier's View of the Civil War, The Wartime Papers of Joseph R. Ward Jr.*, D Duane Cummins writes that Ward was "descended from a sturdy lineage of farm folk" and that the family took up farming in their new American home. That Ward would have been a useful farm worker and soldier is evident from his "sturdy" appearance. In photos in the book, Ward is tall and broad shouldered, with large features.

When enlistments were called for after it appeared the war would go on longer than expected, Ward answered the call of his home of only a decade. A religious man, Ward—just like Plimpton—was drawn by Captain Slaughter's "Preacher's Company" and made his way into Company G and the 39th, enlisting on August 29th. His frequent letters, and occasional diary entries—while filled with spelling and grammatical errors—tell the story of a humble man who sought to serve his country, wished to see the end of slavery, and did his duty without fuss or fail.[1]

By April 12, 1862, General Shields had recovered well enough to review his command now in camp at Strasburg. Shields told the First Division that he was "ready to give the rebels another chance at him."[2] Whether the General was rallying his troops or was not aware of the national strategy dilemma about to unfold is unclear. Homer Plimpton noted that "the men greeted him everywhere with cheers." Demonstrating that it was most likely not known that Jackson's tactical defeat had been a strategic victory, Plimpton added, "The general feeling now is that the war will soon be over. Bets are being made in regard to the time of our discharge; some putting it within thirty days."[3] Adding to the 39th's excitement, the regiment had most likely heard by now of General Grant's success at Shiloh, on April 6–7, where nearly forty Illinois regiments and batteries fought bravely.

All the generals up through the 39th Illinois' chain of command, to include General McClellan, had offered high praise to the division for their efforts at Kernstown. For the 39th individually, while not involved in the central portion of the battle, it was their first involvement in a pitched battle, and the regiment performed well. Valentine Randolph reported that "Colonel Osborn and Lieutenant

Colonel Mann acted as cooly as if they had been on battalion drill."[4] The Yates Phalanx had seen its most aggressive action to date and performed well. President Lincoln and his cabinet were so elated at a significant victory that they visited the battleground themselves.

However, Lincoln had also become very disturbed by Jackson's bold attack on Winchester and grew even more concerned about Washington's defense. This set a series of things in motion: Lincoln ordered Banks back into the Valley, creating a new Department of the Shenandoah, which meant McDowell's Corps (now the Army of the Rappahannock) would hold in place instead of joining the assault on Richmond. Instead of using Banks to guard Washington, and having McDowell join the assault on Richmond from the north, McClellan's Army of the Potomac alone would move from the southeast. More yet, Lincoln also transferred a division of McClellan's army to General John Fremont's Mountain Division in western Virginia, intending to strike into Tennessee.[5] McClellan was now only in charge of the Army of the Potomac, and Lincoln was essentially acting as commanding general of the armies.

Three separate U.S. armies now existed between the Alleghenies and the peninsula, and "unity of command was lost," notes Valley Campaign historian Peter Cozzens.[6] General Shields had complimented his men for "opening the campaign on the Potomac," but it was Jackson who had opened his Shenandoah Valley campaign. While Kernstown had been a tactical defeat for Jackson, it was "suddenly turned into an important strategic victory."[7]

❖   ❖   ❖

Poor weather prevented General Banks from making major troop movements until April 17 when the 39th received orders to move. In a letter home to his parents, Joseph Ward wrote "this division was on the move after her old antagonist Jackson."[8] Banks intended to move his Department of the Shenandoah south up the Valley beyond Mt Jackson to expel Stonewall Jackson from the region and deny him reinforcements. Equally important to this effort would be denying Jackson the ability to reinforce Confederate General Joseph Johnston, who had positioned 55,000 men on the Peninsula to counter McClellan. The first two days of movement were slowed by awful roads, the need to cross the winding Shenandoah in multiple locations, and the occasional brush with Turner Ashby's cavalry harassments.[9]

The First Division reached New Market on April 19, and the 39th was ordered east across the Massanutten mountain to guard bridges over the Shenandoah's south fork at White House Landing. While the regiment likely crossed at the New Market Gap, this would have still been a ten-mile march over rough terrain reaching as high as 1,800 feet. Half of the regiment was assigned to the Columbia bridge, with the other half at White House bridge, sharing the duty with two companies of the 1st Vermont Cavalry.[10]

Major Munn was in command of the group assigned to the Columbia Bridge, and to his surprise, learned they would need to take control of the bridge from some of Ashby's cavalry before he could follow his orders to guard it. Taking the rebels by surprise, the Vermont cavalrymen stormed the bridge, backed up by the men of the 39th, and quickly took possession of the bridge and 17 prisoners. Major Munn then posted his men to defend the long, covered bridge. Sometime later, a Confederate officer who had been away returned to the bridge, not understanding that the 39th had taken possession and unable to see inside the covered structure. As he casually approached on his horse, Munn told his men to allow his closer advance. When he was very close, Munn ordered "halt!"

"Halt!?" replied the officer. "What the devil are you halting me for? I'm no dammed Yankee!"

"Well, we are," replied Munn as his armed men stepped forward, "halt!"[11]

Aside from the capture of an unsuspecting Confederate officer, the 39th's time near White House Landing lasted the month and "passed smoothly away" until the beginning of May.[12] As all of this was occurring, portions of Banks' army had advanced as far south as Harrisonburg on the opposite side of the Massanutten range, a full 70 miles south of Winchester. During the Banks advance, Jackson had maneuvered his force to Swift Run Gap, 25 miles east of Harrisonburg, and kept his distance from Banks' main body. This placed him in a position to outflank Banks should he push beyond Harrisonburg, move east to join Johnston in defense of Richmond, or link up with General Richard Ewell who had arrived in Port Republic, to the south, with 8,000 men. On April 29, Jackson left Swift Run Gap moving far to the south, but then west. Banks believed Jackson was leaving the Valley, and President Lincoln ordered Banks to withdraw to Strasburg.[13]

On May 6–7, Banks' forces on the east side of the Massanutten range saw signs of Confederate troop movements, and various units found themselves in heavy skirmishing. To the east, along the Blue Ridge Mountains, was seen miles of enemy campfires at night, which seemed to confirm Jackson had marched east to link up with Johnston's army.[14] "Jackson, it is said, is making his way toward Richmond as fast as [possible]," wrote Joseph Ward.[15] No longer needed to expel Jackson from the Valley, Banks continued to Strasburg, and General Shields' Division, and the 39th, received orders to reinforce General McDowell near Fredericksburg.[16] Jackson linking up with Johnston meant Banks could offer men for McDowell's use in once again proceeding from the north as part of General McClellan's assault on Richmond. "This war is now to be pushed to the end." wrote Joseph Ward to his parents. "We are going to reinforce McDowell and push on toward Richmond."[17] On May 12, the 39th joined General Shields and 1st Division in crossing the Blue Ridge Mountains.

❖   ❖   ❖

Out of the valley for what they assumed was the last time, the 39th joined General McDowell's 35,000-man force, which was actively preparing to move when Shields and his Division arrived on the 22nd. Morale was extremely high for the troops. New Orleans had just fallen to Federal control to go along with the other western theater successes. McClellan and his 100,000 men were within "hearing of Richmond's church bells," and the men were about to join him from the north and crush Johnston's army that was just half their size.[18] To add to the excitement of the situation, President Lincoln and Secretary of War Stanton arrived to perform a grand review of the army. On the afternoon of May 23, the entire command assembled in formation, and the President rode along the lines with General McDowell. "What regiment is that?' asked Lincoln when he spotted the 39th Illinois' flag.

"Thirty-Ninth Illinois!"

"Well! You boys are a good ways from home, a'int you?"

Afterward, the President made a tour of quarters, and "seemed delighted to find a regiment from his own state in the Army of the Potomac."[19] All this, however, would be the highlight of the regiment's brief trip out of the Shenandoah Valley: General Jackson had not given up his campaign to keep U.S. armies tied up and away from Richmond, and much had happened during the 39th's travels.

❖   ❖   ❖

Jackson had indeed marched his men out of the Valley as the Federals believed, and he also crossed the Blue Ridge Mountains as the fires had evidenced. However, what Stonewall Jackson did next threw a wrench into the Peninsula Campaign for a second time. He took his men as far east as Charlottesville, then put them on trains to head back over the mountains to Staunton, where he previously had a supply depot.[20] A small brigade of only 6,500 men from Fremont's Mountain Division moved towards Staunton, and on May 8 Jackson sprang an offensive. His force, now 11,000 strong, defeated the Federal brigade near the small town of McDowell—an ironic name given the events it would set in motion—then turned back to the east intent to move on Banks.[21]

With word of the May 8 battle, and the knowledge that Jackson was now moving down the Valley, Banks' army dug in at Strasburg to make a stand. The return to Strasburg that had been ordered back at the start of May, however, meant that Jackson's road north was wide open, and Stonewall could dictate his movement and attack on his terms.[22] With Jackson's army moving down the central Valley pike, Banks' dug in using Strasburg's fortifications with, 4,476 infantry, 1,600 cavalry and 16 guns; and on May 21 deployed a small force of roughly 900 to guard his left flank at Front Royal.[23]

Jackson used his freedom of maneuver to cross Massanutten Mountain and link up with Ewell's force, continuing his advance on Banks with 17,000 men. Turner Ashby and his cavalry kept along the central pike, causing Banks to believe his defensive positioning was appropriate. In reality, however, Jackson and Ewell had stuck to a smaller valley east of the mountain, and on May 23, Federal forces were entirely overwhelmed at the Battle of Front Royal. Jackson was now 15 miles southeast of Banks with twice as many men, and a race for Winchester was on.[24]

Jackson's army caught portions of Banks' supply train on May 24, but the Federal main body made it to Winchester and prepared to fight the best they could. Banks had very little hope against Jackson's numbers but elected to fight to give his remaining supply wagons a chance to make it to Williamsport 35 miles north. Early on May 25, Jackson's 15,000 attacked Banks' 6,000 and sent the remnants of the Department of the Shenandoah retreating to the safety of the Potomac.[25]

◈   ◈   ◈

The day after their grand review by President Lincoln, the 39th learned that General Banks had been driven back to the Potomac. *Again* Stonewall Jackson threatened roads and rails through the valley, *again* he was a threat to attack Washington, and *again* the Phalanx would return to the Shenandoah. Jackson had moved his force toward Harpers Ferry to give the impression of threatening the capital. On May 24, Lincoln ordered General Fremont into the valley at Harrisonburg and suspended General McDowell's movement from Fredericksburg towards Richmond.[26]

The 39th thought it had left the valley for good and would embark on a journey to end the war, but the next day, the regiment set out on a forced march with the rest of Shields' division, back in the direction they had come from just days ago. Once again, General McClellan's pincer movement on Richmond reverted to a southern assault by his army alone. Wrote General McDowell to Lincoln, "I shall gain nothing for you there, and shall lose much for you here."[27]

President Lincoln gave orders to Banks, Fremont, and McDowell creating an elaborate orchestration of the three armies that would trap and destroy Jackson once and for all, "but a strange lethargy seemed to paralyze the northern commanders," wrote famed Civil War historian James McPherson in *Battle Cry of Freedom*.[28] Tired troops, multiple chains of command, and weather and road conditions had three different U.S. armies chasing Stonewall Jackson through the Valley. Between June 6–9, Jackson won three more battles in Harrisonburg, Cross Keys, and Port Republic before heading east—his only loss being the death of Turner Ashby.[29] Now in command of Confederate forces, and considering Jackson's work in the Valley done, General Robert E. Lee summoned Jackson to support Richmond's defense. The 39th had spent three weeks continually moving from place to place, with only the occasional skirmishes for their part. They arrived at Port Republic only in time to aid the wounded after Jackson's last victory. His work to distract Federal forces from the Peninsula Campaign a success, Jackson left the Valley, and so did the 39th.[30]

The march to and from Fredericksburg and back took three weeks and covered 360 miles. Tired, and distressed at the outcome and its implications, the 39th was headed to join General McClellan and a second chance to march on Richmond.[31]

7

McClellan, Waiting Games
and Emancipation

Amos Savage was born in 1836 on his family's farm near Homer, in recently organized Will County, Illinois. Savage had opportunities available rare to many other "farm grown" members of the 39th in that the new county offered a good district school. At 19, Savage became a teacher; working the fields in the spring and fall and teaching in the winter. In 1860, he was a delegate to the state convention that nominated Richard Yates for Governor and elected national delegates to nominate Lincoln for President. Savage then took in active role in campaigning for Lincoln, and was even elected supervisor of Homer in April 1861; but never took the position.

Savage resigned the position after the firing on Fort Sumter and attempted to join a regiment that wasn't accepted for service. Undeterred, he traveled to Chicago and enlisted in Company G of the 39th Illinois, chosen by the men to be their Second Lieutenant. Savage was the powerful mix of a bright and educated man with a physical stature that commanded attention. He was promoted to First Lieutenant during the summer of 1862 and would eventually become a Captain by necessity in 1864—but wholly deserving of the duty.[1]

THE ARMY OF NORTHERN VIRGINIA had used General McClellan's delays to act, and Stonewall Jackson's exploits in the Shenandoah, to buy time to strengthen their position defending Richmond. McClellan had moved his army to Fortress Monroe on the Chesapeake and began moving up the James and York rivers, arriving on the outskirts of Richmond by mid–May 1862—a movement that would become familiar to the 39th two years later.[2] During the last weeks of May, Jackson's expedition in the Valley had been crucial to keeping Federal reinforcements away from Richmond, however, and stalling out McClellan's Peninsula Campaign. Still, after taking command from the wounded Joseph Johnston on June 1, General Lee decided he would need to take action to avoid a Federal siege of Richmond.[3]

During the 39th's journey east towards Alexandria near the nation's capital, Lee struck McClellan's railroad supply line with the newly arrived Stonewall Jackson and began pushing the Army of the Potomac back to the James River. Wrote Dr. Clark of the situation upon reaching Alexandria on June 28, "a rest was given us to recuperate from so long a march; but it was not to be a protracted or even a sufficient one, for McClellan's army was engaged with Lee's in what has been recorded in history as the Seven Days fight, in front of Richmond."[4]

The Seven Days' Battles took place between June 25–July 1, 1862. The theme of United States tactical success, but strategic failure, continued as the Federals inflicted heavy Confederate losses at the Battle of Mechanicsville on July 26. Much as in the Shenandoah Campaign, Stonewall Jackson had a role in a Confederate tactical loss that became a strategic success. Jackson's men were late to the fight at Mechanicsville, most likely because of battle fatigue and their long and rough journey east. However, despite a resounding tactical success at Mechanicsville, Jackson's arrival near his right flank forced McClellan to realize he couldn't protect his supply line.[5]

Lee launched a full pursuit, now with Jackson's forces fully integrated, and looked to prevent the Army of the Potomac from making an orderly retreat, while forcing McClellan to reassess his plans for Richmond. The coming days saw extremely bloody fighting with Federal troops falling back to defensive positions and turning to face the Confederates. On June 27 at the Battle of Gaines' Mill, Lee scored his first significant victory of the war. In a savage battle with over 80,000 men engaged, the Federal line briefly collapsed. McClellan was now firmly committed to abandoning his designs on Richmond and retreating to the James.[6]

Federal rear guards held their own, however, and on June 30, managed a counterattack when Confederate troops broke the Federal line again. This allowed the Army of the Potomac to reach the high ground of Malvern Hill with support of naval guns from the James. General Lee was frustrated; however, as even though he had saved Richmond and turned the tide, he knew an opportunity to destroy McClellan's army had been missed.[7]

Attacking a 150-feet-high hill over open ground, the Confederate force on July 1 was shredded by four Federal divisions and 100 guns.[8] Lee had lost a quarter of his army during the 7 Days Campaign. McClellan had "won" all but one battle yet retreated to his starting point feeling the Malvern Hill victory a suitable cover for "successfully changing his base of operations."[9] In total, 30,000 men were killed and wounded during the week, with each side feeling like it had squandered opportunities. McClellan knew he should have captured Richmond, and Lee thought he should have destroyed the Army of the Potomac. The only thing known for sure was the war was again nowhere near over, and that, in the words of James McPherson, a "pattern for harder fighting and greater casualties" between the two armies had been established.[10]

❖ ❖ ❖

Following their brief respite in Alexandria, where the men enjoyed decent food and drink and the chance to stock up on personal items, the First and Second Brigades of Shields' division boarded steamers on June 29 and began the journey south. Traveling down the Potomac, then the Chesapeake, the soldiers anchored outside Fort Monroe near Hampton, Virginia, and the mouth of the James River the following evening. The 39th Illinois men realized just how far from home they were as they passed George Washington's Mount Vernon earlier in the day, then slept amidst the "forest of masts" containing U.S. ships and gunboats of all shapes and sizes.[11] Traversing the James River and passing large Federal guns, the

Congress and *Cumberland* wrecks, and seeing the U.S.S. *Monitor* ironclad might have seemed like the stuff of stories, but was the new reality for the Yates Phalanx. On July 2, the traveling soldiers reached Harrison's Point and General McClellan's Army of the Potomac encampment.

The 39th Illinois was now assigned to the Third Brigade, part of the Second Division of the Army of the Potomac's IV Corps. Brigadier General Erasmus Keyes was the corps commander. Brigadier General John James Peck was in command of the Second Division, soon to be made Major General for his leadership at Malvern Hill. The Army of the Potomac's camp at Harrison's Landing, named for the birthplace of President William Henry Harrison, was a massive one with troops and the material of war everywhere one looked. It was "indeed a warlike scene," wrote Homer Plimpton.[12] Private Plimpton had been assigned as a temporary aide to Doctor Clark and would have been a busy man. Journals and diaries of the men all pointed to heat, bad water, and crowding. The temperature often reached "102 in the shade," wrote Doctor Clark. The water was "scarce and totally unfit" and "mosquitos disturbed sleep at night." Clark continued, "sickness in many forms was widespread, and Death was busy reaping a rich harvest in the Army of the Potomac."[13] On top of all this was the army's exhaustion that came from a week of bloody fighting and the uncertainty over what would happen next.

The regiment settled into a life that saw a week at a time being spent on outpost and picket duty, then returning to the camp for garrison duties and training. In camp, the 39th was back to days that included drill, inspections, instruction, and more drill.[14] Between the conditions in the swampy camp and the garrison schedule's rigors, the week on outpost duty became the desirable assignment. The 39th did finally have the company of fellow Illinois men, however. The 8th Illinois Cavalry was in camp, and Joseph Ward wrote of them being the "only Illinois boys I have seen since we left St. Louis."[15] Homer Plimpton even found a schoolmate from his time at Northwestern and had friends from the 8th visit him during his hospital duties.[16]

The present position of the Army of the Potomac was a strong one, and defensible enough that Lee had no appetite for an attack. McClellan, as always, felt he needed more reinforcements to resume an offensive against Richmond. As he had in the past, McClellan believed Lee had far more men than he did and was reticent to leave his stronghold without more men. President Lincoln made a trip to Harrison's Landing on July 8 to speak with McClellan and review the troops. McClellan reaffirmed his commitment to Lincoln to resume his campaign against Richmond as soon as he received more reinforcements. This commitment and request; however, came in a letter to Lincoln where he lectured the President on how to run a war while absolving himself of any blame in the failures thus far. While Lincoln said nothing of it at the time, it accelerated his souring feelings of the General.[17]

Washington sent what they could throughout July: This included Company H finally joining the 39th Illinois, led by Captain Chauncy Williams. Along with a smattering of recruits for the other companies, Company H had been guarding prisoners at Illinois' Camp Butler and was sent east to link up with their regiment for the renewed drive on Richmond.[18]

While the regiment was gaining some men during this time, they were also losing some. Captain Slaughter of Company G resigned his commission, with Lieutenant Rudd, and Lieutenant Amos Savage, of Homer, receiving promotions. The resignation of Captain Slaughter appears to have been an issue long in the brewing, ever since the January skirmish with Stonewall Jackson, and Company G's actions on and around Cacapon Mountain. The men were rightly impressed with Lieutenant Rudd's leadership in holding off superior rebel numbers on the mountain, while various accounts implied the men were cold to Slaughter. On February 4, Ward had written to his parents that "Rudd is all the officer we have."[19] He also spoke of the respect the men had for Lieutenant Savage, and that Slaughter often spoke of resigning. Ezra Cook was more direct, writing that Slaughter had sent home an account of the actions on Great Cacapon of his "great services" and seemingly took all the credit. Cook, in contrast, had written to his father of Lieutenant Rudd's actions, bemoaning Slaughter, and the letter was published in the *Northern Illinoisan.* According to Cook, Slaughter noticed the account, but took no action against him.[20]

Additional officers had resigned commissions as well. Captains Gray, Hooker, and Wilmarth of Companies C, E, and B had also resigned their commissions. Major Munn was also soon forced to resign his commission because of poor health. All this was in addition to a handful of Lieutenants, and the Adjutant Frank Marshall.[21] Whether it was the fighting, the rough conditions, the weather, and hardships, or the prospects of a long war—it does not appear that leadership at the top was the issue. Colonel Osborn had been tapped by superiors to lead the brigade on multiple occasions temporarily and, according to Valentine Randolph, he was "more popular with the regiment than he was a few months ago."[22]

❖   ❖   ❖

Whether through battle, disease, or resigning officers, losing men was not unique to the 39th, nor was the difficulty in recruiting replacements. It was becoming more apparent that the fighting was going to be bloody; it would not be over soon, and that only a policy of total war would bring success. Even though 700,000 men from northern states had volunteered to serve in the last year, Lincoln understood that calling for more troops—or instituting a draft—would bring panic and further depress northern sentiments for the prospect of success. McClellan continued to ask for more troops, but Lincoln and the War Department wanted him to fight.[23]

Like other states, Illinois had stopped actively recruiting in December 1861 but now realized more men would need to be called forth. Governor Yates also realized the war's conduct and recruiting efforts would need to change to bring the war to an end. In mid–July, he sent President Lincoln a letter stating that "the time has come for the adoption of more decisive measures."[24] Put succinctly; Governor Yates wanted to attack the heart of the Confederacy—the source of their economic power and reason for fighting—and make available all able-bodied men who wished to fight for the Union. Of course, Yates was advocating for emancipation if for no other reason than as a measure to win the war.

While he had reservations about whether he even could, and what impact it would have, Lincoln informed his cabinet on July 22 that he planned on a proclamation of freedom and sought feedback. Being mostly positive, the President decided that he would wait for a victory to implement it and keep it from looking like desperation.[25] In the meantime, the President called for 300,000 new volunteers in a call to "follow up recent successes of the Federal arms and speedily crush the rebellion."[26] In Illinois, the call for troops to end the war, but more likely the looming threat of conscription, brought about a new wave of volunteers. Yates' efforts in Illinois brought in a fresh stream of recruits throughout the rest of the summer, and an even more significant influx in October and November from rural areas after the harvest. To his credit, Illinois citizens saw Yates as the "soldier's friend," as he had shown up to bring supplies and offer support following the battles of Fort Donelson and Shiloh.[27]

In one striking example of how up close and personal Yates got with the war, he rode to the front with General Grant during the battle of Port Gibson in May. When the two came under fire, Yates got jumpy in the saddle, causing Grant to remark, "Governor, it's too late to dodge after the ball has passed."[28] Ultimately, Illinois ended 1862 with 20,000 men over the state's quota, a testament not just to their belief in the Union, but their Governor's call to service.[29]

Between July and the end of 1862, a combination of veteran recruiting, threats of a draft, bonuses, officer commissions, and crafty messaging brought the recruiting numbers desired. Throughout his time at Harrison's Landing, however, it was apparent that no amount of reinforcements to the Army of the Potomac would appease McClellan to re-start his advance on Richmond. Further, in both the letter he gave the President when he visited and in discussions since, he made clear his distaste for total war and emancipation as a war tactic. Out of patience for McClellan's constant call for troops and aversion to the war's developing nature, Lincoln would soon order the Army of the Potomac north.[30]

❖　❖　❖

The men of the 39th were becoming just as frustrated as Lincoln, but not for the same reasons. Aside from the occasional cannon fire along the James, the only action was the never-ending drill and being told by officers to be ready. Back and forth from picket duty, the men were in the dark about the future of the Army of the Potomac. "We depend on the New York and Philadelphia papers for the latest and most reliable news from the Army of the Potomac," wrote Valentine Randolph on August 4.[31] The journals and letters of Randolph, Plimpton, and Ward, along with Doctor Clark's history, all paint the same picture of life for the 39th at Harrison's Landing: Heat, sickness, inactivity, and a mounting frustration by the men.

Interestingly enough, Valentine Randolph correctly predicted what was next for the Army of the Potomac, but not for the same reasons as Lincoln and Stanton.

Writing in his diary on August 13, Randolph assessed that the army was not ready to move on Richmond and would most likely abandon the peninsula. This was the correct assumption, but Randolph attributed it to the fact that McClellan had not received enough reinforcements after the Seven Days Campaign.[32] Having heard of the call for 300,000 more recruits, Homer Plimpton wrote that the soldiers "have the utmost confidence in General McClellan."[33] Joseph Ward would soon write letters to his parents saying "I think McClellan is a good Gen."[34] Whether the chain of command was covering for their commander, didn't know the back and forth he was having with Lincoln or some combination thereof; at this point in the war, the men appeared to be blaming inactivity on the government.

Perhaps both arguments had merit. It was indeed true that McClellan never ceased asking for more troops the Union didn't have, and that frequently he could have seized the initiative with his superior numbers. That said, the army had taken a beating in the Seven Days Campaign, and sickness was ravaging it at Harrison's Landing. The man in the field could envision success with some fresh bodies and a renewed operation. However, the government wanted to fight a new and more total war with the army it had. For the majority of enlisted men, and even many younger officers, the war was the first time they had ever thought about strategy, or politics, or war aims. To men not accustomed to such thoughts and aware only of their immediate surroundings and not the complete picture, they most likely trusted and supported the views of their immediate superiors.[35]

In his book *A Republic in the Ranks: Loyalty and Dissent in the Army of the Potomac*, Zachery Fry discusses that while much of the institutional Army leadership had a Democratic background that sought to avoid political influence, many fresh volunteers were of a Republican and pro-administration slant.[36] This dynamic shifted throughout the war, as men became more politically aware, developed an understanding of strategy, and debated the politics driving the war—mainly slavery. The men of the 39th would have witnessed the clash of officer political views in their chain of command: Their Corps Commander, General Keyes, was a well-known Republican that many in Washington used as their "eyes and ears" inside McClellan's Army, and who McClellan did not care for.[37]

The waiting soon ended, and the Army of the Potomac began evacuating the peninsula on August 14. On August 16 General Keyes' IV Corps was the last to leave—more or less cast off by McClellan. Wrote Doctor Clark, "we were the tail end and rearguard of that magnificent army that a month or two before had been mobilized for the purpose of taking Richmond; and now it was ingloriously retreating to Yorktown, its rear protected by a western brigade."[38] The men marched east, crossing the Chickahominy River the next day on a 2000-foot pontoon bridge the Army of the Potomac had been crossing since the 14th. The men marched for five days to Yorktown on dusty roads packed with wagon trains and men in stifling heat with scarce water.[39]

❖   ❖   ❖

The regiment reached Yorktown on August 21, and the men collected oysters and crabs and enjoyed a more pleasant camp location. Ever mindful of history throughout his diary, Valentine Randolph wrote of the Revolutionary War and visited historical spots. On the 24th the regiment was on the move again, moving southeast to Fort Monroe near Hampton, Virginia. Finally, on the 30th, the men knew their fate. Most of McClellan's Army traveled north to link up with General John Pope's Union Army of Virginia. The General was brought from the west to lead the newly formed army made up of divisions that had been fighting in the Shenandoah. Pope himself was a proponent of the need for the United States to fight a total war, advocating, among other things, the seizure of rebel property. The move wasn't just another signal towards a changing Federal strategy, but a further rift between Lincoln and McClellan.[40]

General Peck's division, however, was split between Yorktown, Fort Monroe, and Suffolk. "Vale, Peninsula!" wrote Valentine Randolph, as the 39th and their brigade headed for Suffolk.[41] It wasn't just farewell to the peninsula and campaign, but to the old way of war. As James McPherson wrote in *Battle Cry of Freedom*: "From now on the North would fight not to preserve the old Union but to destroy it and build a new one on the ashes."[42]

❖ ❖ ❖

By September 3, the 39th and the Third Brigade were encamped at Suffolk with 5,000–6,000 men. The 39th settled into garrison life once again, clearing trees, putting up defenses, and serving their time on picket duty and reconnaissance excursions. The regiment received daily New York papers while at Suffolk and kept a keen eye on the news of the war, as unfavorable as it currently was. In the first two weeks of the month, Valentine Randolph wrote that the news was "discouraging" and lamented how just two months ago, Richmond was threatened.[43] Doctor Clark added that the "news is most discouraging from all points."[44]

Receiving regular news from the papers, the men of the 39th could hardly be blamed for their discouragement. Less than two weeks after the 39th left Harrison's Landing, Stonewall Jackson captured a Federal supply depot at Manassas Station. This sent General Pope's Army of Virginia on the retreat, and they were routed at the Second Battle of Bull Run, August 28–30. Lee, along with Stonewall Jackson and James Longstreet, had turned the tide. While the Army of the Potomac had been 20 miles from Richmond a month ago, the Army of Northern Virginia was now fighting a Federal rear guard only 20 miles from Washington.[45]

The change that had occurred in less than two months had leadership concerned, and northern citizens panicked. There was concern McClellan had wanted Pope to fail, and Lincoln was inclined to agree, but McClellan was the only General that had done any real winning. With the fear Lee would now attempt an invasion of the North, Pope's Army of Virginia was absorbed by the Army of the Potomac, and McClellan was put in charge of defending the capital. Furthering the notion that the rank and file enlisted men loved and supported McClellan are accounts of Pope's retreating army sending up cheers and celebrating when they heard General McClellan was returning to lead them.[46]

"Maryland is invaded!" wrote Valentine Randolph on September 10. "The people of the North are just beginning to realize the fact that the war has actually begun."[47] Doctor Clark also expressed his frustrations and an understanding of what Robert E. Lee was now doing. Echoing Randolph, he wrote that the rebels were looking to dictate "their own terms of settlement," while the Federal Government's policy seemed to be "wait while the rebels win."[48]

Pressing his recently won momentum, Lee was trying to dictate politics just as much as a military strategy with his crossing into Maryland. While he had been successful in repelling the Federals, a victory on northern soil could invite European governments to recognize the Confederacy. Success in the north could also affect the upcoming mid-term elections, recruiting, and overall support by northern citizens.[49] Perhaps sensing that Lee's foray into the North would awaken citizens to the reality of the war, Joseph Ward wrote to his parents in mid–September that "[w]e all think the [rebles] have done the best thing for us they could by crossing into Maryland." Although he added, "[t]he government seems to send us the [fartherst] from danger."[50]

The "danger" was now developing near Sharpsburg, Maryland. As the 39th continued to pull guard duty, clear timber, and follow the news of the war that left them behind; their former comrades of the Army of the Potomac met the Army of Northern Virginia at Antietam on September 17. History has well recorded the fierce and bloody fighting that took place on that day—the deadliest day in U.S. history—with entire books dedicated to the battle alone. Antietam's carnage was horrific, with 6,000 dead and 17,000 wounded—four times the American casualties of D-Day.[51] Whether the 39th was disappointed they had missed out on such a decisive battle or glad to have avoided Antietam's horror, the results of General McClellan's army once again affected their future. The Confederacy still didn't have a victory in the north to gain European recognition or turn the Union against the administration and they were in no position to sue for peace. While McClellan neglected to press the retreating Lee, he had turned away a threat to the capital. Abraham Lincoln now had the victory he needed to change the entire narrative of the war.[52]

❖   ❖   ❖

On September 22, 1862, President Lincoln signed Proclamation 95—The Emancipation Proclamation. The men of the 39th, and the entire U.S. army, no doubt knew the effect it would have on the war. The issue made European recognition of the Confederacy almost impossible and practically assured both sides would now fight for a total victory. There would be no return to the status quo: The Confederacy would either achieve its full independence, or the United States would re-emerge, whole, and with slavery eradicated for all time. Joseph Ward seemed to have a full grasp of the war in front of him when writing to his parents on October 10: "As long as it [seemes] to look ahead I have no wish to return to stay until this once happy land shall be what it never was before free and there shall be no more slaves, no never."[53]

One is hard-pressed to avoid intense feelings when reading such words from a soldier in the field. Ward had volunteered a year earlier, feeling that he owed it to his adopted home as an immigrant. Valentine Randolph wrote of despising war but wanting to see peace and unity in his country. Homer Plimpton wanted to be a minister, but after the failure at First Bull Run felt called by his country. All three joined for similar reasons but referenced emancipation in their own ways. While Ward's emotions were clear, Randolph and Plimpton were less direct in what impact they felt emancipation would have. Randolph wrote on October 19, of "upwards of 100 negroes" coming into the camp that morning, adding "[t]his is, perhaps, the first fruits of Lincoln's Emancipation Proclamation, if so it has ripened prematurely."[54] Plimpton does not reference the proclamation directly, but wrote fondly and approvingly of attending a Black church on October 5, and mentions his faith and eradicating slavery to preserve the Union throughout his journal. Clark's *History* makes no mention of Lincoln's proclamation.

The myriad of views, however, is most likely representative of the regiment as a whole—they themselves being a cross-section of the state. Back home in Illinois, feelings about the Emancipation Proclamation varied throughout the state. Geographic location played a role, as did one's profession, family background, or even religion. Douglas type Democrats did not always *endorse* slavery, they simply thought such matters should be left to the citizens of a state. Others just saw themselves as pragmatic about it. They were democrats, and slavery was not an issue in Illinois, but the enslavers were democrats and gave the party power. In his book *Illinois in the Civil War*, Victor Hicken discusses the "strangely contradictory" attitudes western and southern Illinois had regarding the enslavement of Blacks. "They disliked the former, and yet were conservative in respect to the concepts of equality." He wrote about those who volunteered from those parts of the state, "it would be infinitely safer to write that most did so simply to save the Union."[55]

Another increasingly prevalent school of thought on emancipation were those in favor of emancipation not for moral reasons, but as a military necessity. Like Richard Yates, abolitionist Union governors had been firmly pressing Lincoln for emancipation but knew many of their citizens didn't see it as a reason for war. Yates presented the proclamation as such and went further in encouraging Illinois representatives to allow Black immigrants into the state to fill the ranks.[56]

For many, emancipation was a moral imperative, but for others, it took away the primary thing the South was fighting for and could ease Federal recruitment demands. The benefits of emancipation as a military necessity became increasingly accepted inside the army as the war went on and even changed many reluctant soldiers' hearts. Men realized that if their commander-in-chief saw it as a necessity to end the war and preserve the Union, then maybe it was a good idea. Federal soldiers slowly developed a loyalty to Lincoln's vision of a free and whole America, and Republicans convinced the men that Democrats were the ones preventing unity.[57] Spending time in southern states likely also helped as they realized the essential nature of slavery to the Confederate cause, spent time with Blacks who escaped to Federal lines, and realized, in the words of Hicken, "that their only true friends in the South were the Negroes themselves."[58] The 39th experienced plenty of this interaction while at Suffolk. By early October, hundreds of enslaved Blacks had made their way to the Federal lines at Suffolk after hearing of Lincoln's proclamation, and more came every day.[59]

❖   ❖   ❖

While much news was being made by politicians in Washington and the Army of the Potomac in other parts of the state, the 39th continued life of garrison duty, drill, fortifying camp, and going on patrol. There was a sizable confederate force roughly 20 miles from the camp the entire time the regiment was at Suffolk. However, the most action the regiment saw during their time were some modest skirmishes near the Blackwater River, where they captured two pieces of artillery and did not suffer any casualties. While the enemy's presence led to the constant need for patrols and building fortifications, the skirmishes never amounted to much. In fact, the 39th Illinois only lost two men during their entire stay at Suffolk, neither to combat. One man was killed by a falling tree while reinforcing entrenchments, and the other succumbed to typhoid fever.[60]

The 39th had realized that their current role in the war was to await developments elsewhere that would dictate their future. The men were kept busy with a considerable amount of work and little downtime. That being said, the men were not at places like Antietam, and realized, "We are certainly having very easy times," wrote Homer Plimpton. "[M]uch easier than at this time last year, or most of the time since."[61] However, given the downtime, Plimpton was dismayed at repeated denials for a furlough to visit his sick father. While Colonel Osborn approved his request frequently, it was disapproved by the Generals above him. Plimpton was very dismayed at the loss of "all feelings of humanity as to refuse one a request of the nature such as his."[62] Later on, Plimpton found out that an officer got a leave of absence and lamented that he failed to get his own "because I lack shoulder straps."[63] Plimpton often wrote with such critiques of officers who only cared for themselves, as he saw it, and was perhaps formulating thoughts about how he would lead should he ever have the opportunity.

As the year wound down, the men learned that once again; news was being made elsewhere that would affect them and the war. After failing to pursue Lee following the strategic Victory at Antietam, Lincoln lost his patience with McClellan for the last time. "I am glad he has been removed," wrote Homer Plimpton. "He was as good as 150,000 men to the rebels."[64] While many men in the Army of the Potomac were crestfallen at the loss of their General, a shift in thinking was occurring, as evidenced by Plimpton's writing.

❖   ❖   ❖

Christmas came, with the only other notable eastern battle having taken place at Fredericksburg in mid–December. Major General Ambrose Burnside, now in command of the Army of the Potomac, had intended to cross the Rappahannock River at Fredericksburg in November while Lee was out of place—a move that would have put him 60 miles north of Richmond. Burnside experienced delays in acquiring pontoon bridges and assembling his entire army to cross, however, and the attack was delayed until December. By this time, Lee's army had completely dug in at Fredericksburg, and Burnside's attack resulted in a slaughter. Another attempt to reach Richmond had been thwarted. "If there is a worse place than Hell," said President Lincoln, "I am in it."[65]

The mood of the 39th was no cheerier. "Dull Christmas," wrote Valentine Randolph, who had waxed poetically in his Christmas entry a year earlier.[66] "Christmas again has returned," wrote Homer Plimpton, "and it finds me still in the service." Plimpton recalled that the previous Christmas saw him believing he'd be home by this time, but that now they were "no nearer the end than on Christmas of 1861."[67]

The 39th had traveled east in June 1862, seemingly to get their second chance at a drive on Richmond to end the war. Instead, they arrived at a retreat at the end of the Seven Days Campaign and suffered brutal summer heat and diseases while political and strategic fighting took place. In all this, they had nothing to show for it other than some built up fortifications, some minor skirmishing, men lost to activities other than war, and following news that seemed to happen everywhere but where they were. The New Year, however, brought a new mission. On January 5, Brigadier General Peck's 2nd Division struck camp at Suffolk and headed for the Chowan River, roughly 50 miles southwest in North Carolina. In 1863, the 39th Illinois was headed to the heart of secession.[68]

PART II

"Until Hell Freezes Over"

January 1863–February 1864

"If you Yanks expect to stay on Folly Island to combat the sandflies and fleas until you drive us into the Union, you will have to stay there until hell freezes over!"
—Note received from Confederate soldiers in a Charleston newspaper mocking the Federal losses at Chancellorsville, May 13, 1863[1]

8

Sailing to the Heart of Secession

Orrin Mann was born in an area just east of Cleveland, Ohio in 1833. Mann came from a family tree of service to the nation; his grandfathers on both sides having fought in the Revolutionary War, and some of his uncles fighting in the War of 1812. At age five, Mann's family moved to Michigan, where his father died shortly after. With many mouths to feed, Mann worked hard on the family's farm from a young age, with just the occasional schooling in the old one-room log cabin schoolhouse.

At age 20, he went to work as a blacksmith in Ann Arbor, Michigan, before giving it up to spend time better educating himself. Mann moved to Chicago, arriving to the city the very night the news of Fort Sumter made its way to Illinois. It is unknown what business Mann planned to engage in, or how he came to know Osborn, but he soon became actively involved in recruiting for the 39th Illinois. His efforts both in Chicago, and Washington D.C., to bring men to the regiment were rewarded with being elected Major. This then led to becoming the Lieutenant Colonel when Osborn took command and stepping into temporary command himself during Osborn's various stints of brigade command.[1]

IN JANUARY 1863, the Civil War was just under two years old and had just over two years remaining. In the east, the first half of 1862 saw the Federals arrive on Richmond's doorstep only to be turned away. The Confederates then briefly put Washington, D.C., in danger, only to have their first offensive onto northern soil turned back but rallying with a significant victory to end the year. In the west, the U.S. army drove the rebels out of Kentucky, and most of Tennessee, with Ulysses S. Grant making a name for himself with victories at Fort Donelson, Fort Henry, and Shiloh. The Federals had been victorious in a month-long siege of Corinth, Mississippi, and controlled New Orleans.

Eighteen sixty-three would see the war not just reach its halfway point in terms of time but serve as a turning point that would dictate how the second half was fought. The year produced three of the war's five bloodiest battles, the most famous one, and arguably the most important strategic one.[2] While Federal victories at Gettysburg and Vicksburg around America's 87th birthday get 1863's historic attention, a third campaign took place during a good portion of the year. Important both for strategic reasons and the development of new military doctrines, the Federal campaign against Charleston, South Carolina, was a campaign against the rebellion's birthplace.[3]

❖   ❖   ❖

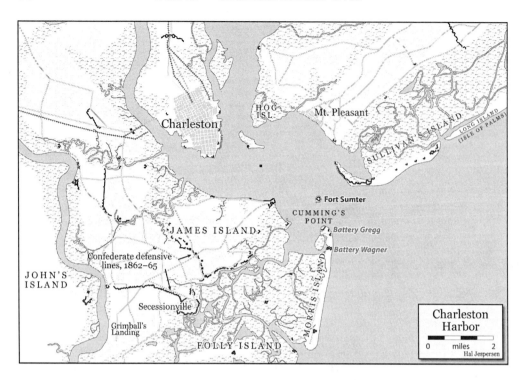

Charleston Harbor with 39th Illinois points of interest (map by Hal Jespersen).

Following a long march where the men foraged and acquired tobacco from various plantations along the way, the 39th took transports down the Chowan River, arriving at Newbern, North Carolina, on January 9, 1863. The 39th was now in the Second Brigade, Third Division, part of the Department of North Carolina, and XVIII Army Corps under Major General John G. Foster. Brigadier General Orris Ferry moved up to become the division commander for the time being, and the 39th's very own Colonel Osborn was commanding the brigade. The Second Brigade consisted of the 39th, the 62nd and 67th Ohio, and the 176th Pennsylvania. While the position was temporary, Colonel Osborn was thought of well enough by General Ferry and other superiors to be given brigade command. Lieutenant Colonel Mann commanded the 39th Illinois during Osborn's time at the brigade level.[4]

The regiment left Chicago 15 months prior with 806 men and had received 147 recruits while they were at Harrison's Landing for a total on the rolls of 953 men. Nineteen officers had resigned, two dismissed, and one had died. One hundred one men had been left behind on marches, sent to a hospital, or discharged for medical reasons, while 39 had deserted, and 18 had died. While the 767 officers and men fit for service had gotten no news of the outside world since leaving Suffolk and knew nothing of their immediate future, they gathered that a large expedition was in the works.[5]

Ever since the Union surrendered Fort Sumter in April 1861, northerners had seen Charleston as the origin of the rebellion and personified it as the beating heart of secession and the Confederacy. The government had long desired to take

Charleston and hold Fort Sumter—not just for symbolic reasons but for important strategic ones. The city provided many goods to Confederate troops, was the South's main blockade-running port, and could serve as a base for operations throughout the southeast. Naval leadership saw a successful assault of Charleston as a way to boost the prestige of the ironclad program, and President Lincoln knew taking the city would be a trifecta of strategic, political, and moral victories. The Army's X Corps, Department of the South, was commanded by Major General David Hunter, who was being timid regarding supporting a Charleston assault. Major General Foster was being sent, with 10,000 men, to the Department of the South to motivate Hunter to provide army support to the cause.[6]

On Sunday, January 18, the 39th had a dress parade, after which Colonel Osborn presented the regiment with a flag sent by Governor Yates. Made of blue silk with golden trim, the flag had a picture of the Governor and "Yates Phalanx, 39th Regiment Illinois Infantry" on one side, and the Illinois coat of arms on the other. "It is decidedly the handsomest banner that I ever saw," wrote Homer Plimpton, "and we are glad for the evidence that our noble Governor has not forgotten us."[7] Cheers went up, and a speech was given by Colonel Osborn telling the regiment to "[n]ever submit to its dishonor or permit its capture by the enemy!"[8] Little did Osborn know how much his mandate to the color-bearers would be tested before the war's end.

While the flag was sent as a gesture to support esprit de corps in his namesake unit, Yates undoubtedly had ulterior motives in ensuring the Illinois regiment viewed him favorably. Fiery political discourse was alive and well both at home and within the U.S. army, especially after conservative democrats made gains in mid-term elections. However, as Zachery Fry argues in his book *A Republic in the Ranks: Loyalty and Dissent in the Army of the Potomac*, "the period from late January to April 1863 was the critical refining moment in the army's political education."[9] Yates was dealing with anti-war democrats, pejoratively referred to as copperheads, who were fighting him hard on issues like emancipation, Black enlistments, national conscription, and the entire nature of the war.[10]

In the face of the divisiveness, Yates knew that the continued bonds formed by troops through bloody battle and witnessing the reality of slavery in the south could be used to his advantage. The men had grown to see emancipation as a military necessity, and political division as a military impairment. An ever-increasing number of Federal volunteers viewed politicians not supporting the war or men from home, not volunteering, as an affront to their service to the republic. For all of Yates' sincere views on saving the Union and abolishing slavery, he was also a skilled politician. Regiments were increasingly writing letters home to newspapers, or even sending resolutions to support the administration, and being sent on furloughs to recruit. Encouraging the men of the 39th to honor their native state and reminding them how much their Republican governor—the "soldier's friend"—supported them would serve the war effort both in the field and back home.[11]

Presumably, during the same review and flag presentation, the 39th learned on the 18th that they would head to South Carolina. One week later, the regiment struck camp and boarded train cars for a 35-mile trip to Morehead City on the North Carolina coast. The rail line ran out on a pier to a harbor busy with the loading of men and supplies, and the regiment embarked on two transport ships of their own. The transport ships were designed for nothing more than moving men and material from point A to B and did not contain sleeping berths or any such comforts. The men were forced to sleep on deck or crammed down below for their ocean voyage. Troops, baggage, and equipment were ferried from land to awaiting ships for four days. Finally, on the evening of January 29, as pleasant weather was being replaced by wind and rain, General Foster ordered the ships out to sea for the voyage south.[12]

❖　❖　❖

"The storm that had been brewing since early morning now broke in all its fury, and we got more than a taste of old Ocean in one of its tragic moods," wrote Dr. Clark.[13] Men spent the night getting sick as the wind increased, and the ocean grew rougher. The men spent the first 24 hours of their voyage on a rolling sea, trying in vain to find a spot in the ship that wasn't taking on water, or didn't contain the contents of a fellow soldier's stomach. "At inspection in the morning," remembered Dr. Clark, "the hold of the vessel was found to be in a most foul and filthy condition."[14] By the morning of the 31st, the storm ceased, and the water calmed, and men were at last able to eat, enjoy the fresh sea air, and even see some dolphins—a novelty for a young man from Illinois in 1863. Off in the distance during the day, the men heard firing in what they assumed was Charleston's direction. In fact, it was a Confederate blockade runner being fired upon by Federal vessels. A reminder that the war had been near constant in the area ever since Fort Sumter.[15]

On the 1st of February, the ships carrying the 39th arrived off Port Royal near Hilton Head, South Carolina. However, the men were forced to stay aboard the boats in the harbor for a few days. One reason was that many of the ships sailed from Morehead City were quite delayed because of the weather. Still, there were also the usual military issues to be sorted out, such as who was going where, with what material, and by what methods. According to Homer Plimpton, a sizable fleet of transport and warships was growing in the harbor, but the men had little to do but wait on the ships and debate politics. "[T]he discussions become too heated at times for the preservation of an even temper."[16] Such debates were undoubtedly fueled by the news reaching the men that General Burnside was removed from command of the Army of the Potomac, and General Joseph Hooker now led. Hooker's leadership would lead to the continued growth of pro-administration and pro "hard-war" sentiment in the U.S. army.[17]

On February 8, the men moved up the bay to St. Helena Island and could finally disembark their squalid accommodations and get back on dry land. The troops still did not understand what the expedition would do, although being less than 50 miles southwest of Charleston Harbor most rightly assumed there would be an assault there. The men were given free time to establish their camp, and they began exploring and collecting fruit and oysters. Perhaps thinking they were just being given some time to recover from the awful journey, the real reason for delays in further movement resulted from leadership conflicts.[18]

General Foster began studying Charleston Harbor to help design a joint assault with the navy. Foster soon consulted with Brigadier General Truman Seymour, who he had been garrisoned with at Fort Sumter when it fell in 1861. Seymour was a regular army officer who had served well during the Peninsula Campaign and at Antietam. Along with Foster, he was the type of aggressive officer with a personal tie to Fort Sumter that the government hoped would spur action in General Hunter and naval commander Rear Admiral Samuel Francis Du Pont. Seymour and Foster both advocated a joint assault where the army captured Morris Island, and associated Confederate batteries, then focused guns on Fort Sumter. Once Fort Sumter was neutralized, the ironclads could move into the harbor and lay siege to Charleston.[19]

The Confederate defenders did not have any leadership disputes and very much knew what their plan was: Hold Charleston. General Pierre G.T. (commonly P.G.T.) Beauregard, a military engineer, had been the commanding officer of the Confederate forces who fired on Fort Sumter in April 1861. Like many in the Confederate higher ranks, Beauregard had been a United States military officer before the war and had served as an engineer helping defend American coastline forts. After overseeing the rebuilding and fortification of Sumter following its surrender, Beauregard led troops at First Bull Run, and commanded armies at Shiloh and the Siege of Corinth, before returning to Charleston to put his leadership and engineering expertise to use. Beauregard developed a formidable defense of Charleston, fortifying guns, blocking approaches with obstructions and underwater explosives, and developing a plan to blunt a Federal assault while nearby reinforcements arrived by rail. "What the general feared most," wrote Stephen Wise in *Gate of Hell*, "was a dual sea and land attack that would force him to spread thin his men and artillery."[20]

While Du Pont was iffy on the expedition's ability to take out Charleston's improving defenses, Hunter was absolutely opposed to the idea. Seymour had originally approached Hunter with the plan before Foster and his men even arrived. Hunter disliked it so much he made Seymour his chief of staff putting his thumb on Seymour and preventing him from leading any operations. The idea fared no better when Foster joined the cause, and a leadership controversy arose. Hunter had apparently been unaware Foster was coming, and when Foster didn't report to him but began making plans, tempers flared.[21]

Foster left for Washington to take the matter up with senior leadership, which led to Valentine Randolph's diary entry of February 15 that noted the "forces of Foster's Expedition are turned over to Gen. Hunter, Commander of this department" (X Corps, Department of the South). Randolph added that passes were revoked, and a grand review was scheduled to occur soon.[22]

On George Washington's birthday, February 22, all the ships in the harbor were decorated with flags and bunting. This would have been quite the sight given the armada of ironclads, gunboats, and vessels carrying heavy siege guns assembled. "It is evident," wrote Homer Plimpton, "that there will be a heavy bombardment at some point soon."[23] Yet for the time being, the 39th's time was taken up by inspections, grand reviews, drill, and exploration of St. Helena Island and nearby Beaufort. However, the drilling was not for nothing as the Inspector General of the U.S. Army visited in early March to inspect the troops. Men, equipment, and quarters were examined, and each regiment was observed in various drill exercises. The 39th was apparently making good use of their downtime and was reported as the "best drilled and disciplined regiment in the Department of the South."[24]

Even though currently leading the brigade, this is continued evidence that Colonel Osborn was doing a standout job of training his men. His leadership team was keeping the men properly focused, without burning them out, during their downtime. This most notably included Lieutenant Colonel Mann acting as the regimental commander and Captain Linton serving in Mann's old position.

❖   ❖   ❖

The men did not spend all their downtime exploring the surrounding area, however, and continued to keep up with the news—especially that from Illinois. They received mail from Illinois in the first few days of March that included distressing sentiments from the Prairie State. Valentine Randolph wrote that "[t]he North is divided! It tolerates traitors in Illinois!"[25] "[W]e not only have an enemy in the field to fight," wrote Homer Plimpton, "but enemies at home to contend with."[26] The men were no doubt referring to the ongoing battles Governor Yates was having with anti-war Democrats in the state legislature. While several Illinois Democrats were of the pro-war, pro-union slant, many realized that the source of their power as a party lie with the Democratic stronghold of the south. The Illinois Democratic majority had adjourned their session just a couple weeks prior and were postponing their return until summer to buy time to lobby Washington for a peace deal.[27] Seeing the reality of slavery up close, and forging bonds in the hardships of war in service to their country, caused many men to take great offense at the anti-war sentiment. "The emergence of the Democratic Party's vocal anti-war wing," wrote Zachery Fry in *A Republic in the Ranks*, "made partisanship unavoidable for even the most apolitical enlisted men."[28]

On March 3, Colonel Osborn addressed the regiment with the confidence and uncompromising words that only a commander with his men's respect and trust could make. "No sacrifice, he thought, was too great to make for the preservation of the Union," recalled Randolph. "He was willing to fight Northern traitors as well as Southern rebels."[29] As was becoming the trend among frustrated regiments in the field, especially those with strong pro-administration feelings, the 39th adopted a series of resolutions detailing their "indignation in regard to this state of affairs" to be sent to publications in Illinois.[30] The resolutions were adopted via a voice vote, and "[n]o disloyal sentiment can find lodgement in the 39th Illinois," wrote Randolph.[31]

While much of the anti-war sentiment coming from the North continued to stem from those merely wishing to end the war and return to the status quo, a great deal of it came from an aversion to Lincoln's methods of fighting the war and disbelief that Blacks could be equal in America. However, the 39th was one of the many regiments in the U.S. army, getting a first-hand look at former plantations, the Confederate way of life, and the plight of Blacks in the south. A great deal of work was being done in the Port Royal and Beaufort areas by northern missionary groups providing aid and education to recently freed Blacks in the region. The writings of Clark, Plimpton, and Randolph all mention the men talking with Blacks in town and enlisting their services as guides or boatmen to explore the area or go fishing. Beaufort itself had been the site of the first Black regiment mustered into service when the Emancipation Proclamation took effect.[32]

At first, "regiments met with opposition and racism from the white troops in the Department of the South," wrote Stephen Wise in his book *Gate of Hell.* Wise notes, however, that the "attitudes softened" as the "white regiments worked closely with their black counterparts."[33] Writing in his journal on March 8, Homer Plimpton noted that the talk of Black regiments was growing, and attitudes were changing. He noted that many men were considering applying for commissions to lead Black soldiers, "[s]ome too, who heretofore have been down upon the negroes are among them."[34] Positive interactions in both personal and professional settings were doing something that couldn't occur when these Blacks were enslaved: It humanized them. Views were rapidly evolving, and more and more Federal soldiers saw the war not just as a battle to save the Union but to bring freedom to their fellow man.

❖ ❖ ❖

On March 9, three more Monitor ships arrived, and General Hunter also gave orders detailing the need to train disembarking boats with enemy troops nearby. On March 14, the regiment performed "surf boat drills," wearing their knapsacks and carrying their weapons while jumping out of boats and wading into battle lines.[35] The men knew action was drawing close, as drilling continued, and more warships arrived in the harbor. On March 26, General Hunter had a grand review, and many changes were made to division and brigade structures as it became apparent General Foster would not be returning. The 85th Pennsylvania was now part of the 39th's brigade, and as their commander was senior, Colonel Osborn returned to his duty with the regiment. The men rightly guessed that the drills, inspections, and organizational changes signaled action would soon take place. Admiral Du Pont had put off his attack for many months, fearing Charleston's improving defenses, but he also feared the impact on his reputation if he continued to wait.[36] Before the sun on April 2, the men of the 39th were up and preparing for movement. Wagons began moving their things towards the docks, a sure sign that this was a permanent move. The day was spent loading men and equipment, and late in the evening, they put out to sea in rough storms, once again suffering from a lack of sea legs.[37]

❖ ❖ ❖

Almost a year had come and gone since an original plan for seizing Charleston had been formulated, but on April 3, 1863—Good Friday—Admiral Du Pont ordered his squadron out of Port Royal Sound. Sailing with his flagship frigate *New Ironsides* was the newest ironclad *Keokuk¸* and seven original Monitor class ironclads.[38] Du Pont's armada rallied near Edisto Island that evening, just south of Kiawah Island, where the 39th was also lying in wait. "There are eight monitors lying here at anchor," wrote Homer Plimpton, "also a large number of vessels, nearly all loaded with ammunition and stores."[39] Du Pont's objective was for the ironclads to bombard Fort Sumter, then focus on Morris Island. Quieting Fort Sumter, then firing on Morris Island would hopefully allow the army to land and seize the island. Control of the island, and the ability to place heavy siege guns on it, would allow for a continuous bombardment of Sumter and the surrounding Charleston defenses.[40]

After a few days of slow, northward movement, the 39th disembarked on Folly Island—less than five miles from Morris Island, and six to seven miles from Fort Sumter itself; "plainly to be seen and the flag on it," wrote Valentine Randolph.[41] As if the site of the fort itself wouldn't have driven the point home, "the enemy is within a short distance on nearly every side," wrote Homer Plimpton. "We can see the smoke rising on nearly every side."[42] The men could also see the fleet or ironclads in the water between them, and the symbolic fort and "[m]atters began to look like business again, and we were all glad to have the dull and monotonous routine of camp-life dissolved," wrote Dr. Clark.[43] The men spent the 6th, slowly probing the island for Confederate troops, and finding none, spent the night camping on the Atlantic coast's wet sand.

On the morning of the 7th, more probing was done, leadership finally convinced there was no enemy presence on the Island, although they could see armed rebels on the nearby islands. Transports had moved 10,000 of General Hunter's men to the surrounding area with siege guns in tow. As Stephen Wise wrote in *Gate of Hell*, "the general did not expect to take any major role in the action but wanted to be in a position to occupy Charleston should the attack prove successful."[44] Further proof that Hunter did not feel he could be successful but was more than willing to accept the appearance of such should the opportunity present itself.

❖   ❖   ❖

Around 2:00 p.m. on the afternoon of April 7, the men of the 39th watched the warships move towards the harbor. At 3:00, Fort Moultrie kicked off the festivities, firing on the Federal ships from Sullivan's Island on the harbor's northeast side.[45] Fort Wagner on Morris Island, south of the harbor, soon joined in, and the symbolic Fort Sumter—guarding the center of the port—rained shot down towards the ironclads. "We could see the water fly where the cannon balls struck," wrote Valentine Randolph. "Fort Sumpter [*sic*] was enveloped in a cloud of smoke."[46] Reflecting on the symbolism of the ongoing attack, Homer Plimpton noted that just like two years ago, "men are looking with eager eyes towards Fort Sumter.... It was the fall of that flag on that fort that stirred every true American's heart to arise in its defense."[47]

Many accounts of the fight point to ship commander's being excessively cautious because of underwater mines and obstructions, and difficulty navigating their ships in the channel. This is not to mention that the Confederates had the Federal force out-gunned three to one and could fire faster. Stephen Wise's research states that the ironclads sent 154 shots or 16,000 pounds in the Charleston defenses direction, and the rebels replied with 2,209 shots—roughly 162,000 pounds. He also points out that the defenders had the advantage of range markers that allowed twenty percent of their shots to be effective.[48] "A heavy cannonade was kept up for two hours," wrote Valentine Randolph, "[w]e could feel the air vibrate when some of the heaviest guns were discharged."[49]

After two hours, with three of his vessels unable to continue fighting, Du Pont called off the attack. One was sinking, and others were heavily damaged. While Du Pont had intended to continue the assault on the 8th, he changed his mind and had the surviving ships sail for Port Royal to be inspected. Surprisingly, the ironclads proved tough and would soon be fit for battle again after repairs.[50]

Despite this proven resilience, Du Pont made no plans for a renewed assault and was further convinced Charleston could not be taken. Joining Du Pont in pessimism was General Hunter. During the fight, and days immediately following, General Seymour had positioned two guns and a regiment of men to the north of Folly Island, and observing Morris Island, believed he could successfully attack. Hunter denied the request. Seymour had a portion of the men establish a picket line and hid a two-gun battery.[51] On April 8, portions of the 39th helped to conceal the guns with earthworks, and on the 11th and 12th, Confederate forces fired toward the guns. The Federal troops were ordered not to return fire, to keep themselves and the guns concealed. The 39th spent the day of April 11 deployed across the entire island, crawling through thick brush to ensure no enemy presence.[52]

Writing off General Hunter, General Seymour petitioned Admiral Du Pont to join an assault on Morris Island, but the Admiral was unmoved. Hunter pulled most of his men back to Port Royal, but Seymour somehow managed to keep a brigade, that included the 39th, under Brigadier General Israel Vogdes on Folly Island. General Seymour, however, was not the only one who was writing off Hunter and Du Pont. Army, Navy, and national political leadership—to include Stanton and Lincoln, believed in Seymour's plan and were done tolerating inaction.[53]

The 39th's brigade, sleeping without tents, in makeshift beds on Folly Island, was the only Federal force currently in front of Charleston. "The attack has, for the present at least, been abandoned," wrote Valentine Randolph.[54] The brief excitement would soon return to boredom and inactivity on an inhospitable island. New leadership, and an alternative plan, would quickly be on its way, however; and the 39th's location on Folly Island would be critical to its success.

9

Laying Siege

Captain Joseph Woodruff was a native of central New York who moved to Ottawa, Illinois, 80 miles southwest of Chicago on the Illinois River. In 1846, at 17, he enlisted in a battalion raised to reinforce Illinois volunteers fighting in the Mexican American War. Traveling from Ottawa to Fort Leavenworth, Kansas via the Illinois, Mississippi and Missouri Rivers, the battalion then marched across the plains to Santa Fe, New Mexico where they took part in the United States victory at Cerro Gordo. Leading the army was Winfield Scott, the commanding general of the U.S. Army at the very beginning of the Civil War, with such notable officers at Ulysses S. Grant, P.G.T. Beauregard, and Robert E. Lee.

Upon returning to Illinois, Woodruff became a resident of Marseilles, Illinois, a small river town eight miles east of Ottawa with a population under 700. Woodruff ran a mercantile business with his brother-in-law, and served as a leader in a local company of "Wide Awakes," an organization of young free-state men who wanted to see a Republican candidate in the 1860 election. When the war broke out, Woodruff was a respected local leader that had no difficulty raising a company with a core of members from the Marseilles area.[1]

WHILE THE FIRST BATTLE of Charleston Harbor was symbolically significant, it had resulted in fewer than 40 total casualties. The Emancipation taking effect at the beginning of the year, and the attack on Fort Sumter, were both significant for what they did to the attitudes about the war and its conduct, but May 1863 would usher in the bloody, all-out, total war that the conflict would become. The first week of May saw the Army of the Potomac and the Army of Northern Virginia clash at Chancellorsville with nearly 30,000 total casualties, and a Confederate victory that caused Lincoln to exclaim, "[my] God! My God! What will the country say?"[2] Lee's victory would compel another attempt at invading the North, ultimately leading to the armies meeting again at Gettysburg in July. Meanwhile, in the west, Grant was beginning his siege of Vicksburg that May, with him being the aggressor who would drive towards decisive action the first week in July.

May 1863 for the 39th Illinois, however, was a quiet time. The only real action was the occasional firing by the Federal ships on Confederate vessels trying to run the Charleston blockade, and the occasional fire on men—of either side—trying to do work on fortifications. The men were kept busy with placing batteries and constant picket duty. On May 13, the Confederate soldiers floated a Charleston newspaper across to the men on Folly Island with details of the Chancellorsville battle. While it alerted the men that the half-mast flag on Fort Sumter was for the death of Stonewall Jackson, it also told the story of a Federal defeat with a significant number of casualties and men taken prisoner. Written on the margin of the paper was "If you Yanks expect to stay on Folly Island to combat the sandflies and fleas until you drive us into the Union, you will have to stay there until hell freezes over!"[3]

If the Confederate soldiers were attempting a psychological operations campaign on the Union men, it would have been effective. The rebel flag still flew above Fort Sumter, the Federals had suffered another defeat at the hands of Robert E. Lee, and the men were suffering in the heat and elements on a beach constantly battered by storms, digging entrenchments, standing guard, and fighting off sickness.

Federal leadership, however, did not intend to wait until hell froze over and was still determined to find the leaders and plan to take Charleston Harbor. For the task, the government now turned to Brigadier General Quincy Gillmore. A distinguished West Point graduate, Gillmore was a skilled artillery and engineering officer who had helped seize Port Royal and build defenses at Hilton Head Island, earning him a reputation as "the foremost artillery and engineer officer in the army."[4] Gillmore was called to Washington and arrived to find General Seymour already there, making his case to get rid of Hunter and Du Pont and enact his plan for a joint expedition. To Seymour's relief, his pleas were finally being accepted, and he found Gillmore's intentions—a landing on Morris Island combined with a naval assault—to be quite agreeable.[5]

While the Federal high command was busy choosing its leaders and building the alternative plan, the men of the 39th continued their life on Folly Island. When they weren't busy building fortifications or standing guard duty, they passed the time, as so many soldiers do, griping about the leaders they didn't like and looking for ways to keep up morale. Fortunately for the men on Folly Island, and unfortunately for Brigadier General Israel Vogdes, these two diversions converged on one man. While considered an officer quite skilled in artillery and defensive positions, and a kind man who cared for his troops, Vogdes was also a demanding officer called "old regulations" who hammered men for violations.[6]

However, the General had a habit of moving about the island without his full uniform, yet fully expected everyone to recognize him and render the proper customs and courtesies. On one occasion, Vogdes was out after dark, and encountering one of his picket lines, was caught without the appropriate reply or countersign to his troops' challenge. While the men knew it was their commanding officer, the General was delayed for quite some time while they properly sorted out the matter.[7]

Despite the trading of sporadic fire and threatening notes scribbled on newspapers, there was quite the market for goods across the lines, and an agreement between the warring soldiers on carrying it out. The men had a system of holes dug along the inlet, or floats to carry items back and forth, and traded coffee for tobacco, and northern papers for southern papers. The pickets were very keen to be on the lookout, keep the system fair and square, and ultimately look out more for their own officers than the enemy. When an officer approached, hasty picket firing was carried out to ensure the guard duty was being taken seriously.[8] As is the case in war, however, the "good" or "easy" times end for one reason or another. One reason is usually getting caught doing something unwise, and the other is typically new leadership taking charge. The 39th supplied the former, immediately preceding the latter.

On the night of June 10, a rebel vessel trying to run the blockade ran aground on Folly Island's northern end. The ship's crew abandoned their boat and set fire to it with little success. Confederate troops fired artillery in the vessel's direction to destroy it and keep Federal forces away. Federal forces fired artillery to prevent any attempts to rescue it. Following up on his effective leadership at Bath and Kernstown, Major Linton assembled a boat crew and made out for the abandoned vessel under cover of darkness. Onboard the ship, the men found pineapples, cigars, and scotch, and loaded themselves up as best as possible and returned to shore. Not wanting to waste the opportunity, the men returned the next night, but their small float drifted off during their looting. Attempting to make it back, regimental surgeon William Woodward was so weighed down with his loot that he struggled in the water. Doctor Clark recalled that within thirty feet of the shore, Woodward began yelling that he was drowning. He was recovered by his mates, where a comical scene of his haul ensued.[9]

General Vogdes was rightfully upset with the situation, and a few of the men found themselves in the bad graces of the general. Not only had they put themselves at risk, but the episode had led to more back and forth shelling by each side that threatened damage and injury at no real benefit. "I hear that the men at the head of the island are going out to that blockade runner and get lots of fruit, cigars, and liquor," remarked Vogdes to his staff one day, "[i]t's a little strange that none of it has found the way to these headquarters."[10] The "raids" continued quietly, and more carefully until there was no more treasure to loot. On June 14, General Gillmore arrived to inspect the situation on Folly Island. It would seem that no amount of contraband arriving at headquarters could have kept the situation from changing. "The amicable relations between our pickets and those of the enemy have ceased," wrote Valentine Randolph.[11] Between the recent increase of artillery fire, and Gillmore's desire to begin attack preparations, the relaxed island life was over, and the men knew fighting would soon begin.

❖   ❖   ❖

The overall plan for taking Charleston was to take the south end of Morris Island, bombard the forts, then use Morris Island as a staging point for destroying Fort Sumter, before using the navy to bring about the surrender of the city itself. General Gillmore was impressed with the work that General Vogdes and the men had been doing. Knowing Folly Island would be where the Morris Island attack was launched from, he assigned Vogdes the job of constructing batteries on the island's northeast tip.[12]

The work was hot and exhausting, even while it was being carried out in silence at night to avoid the enemy's detection. Much of the work was being done within a few hundred yards of the enemy, and great care was taken to be as silent as possible with only officers and engineers speaking. Thus began a series of rotations for the 39th whereby companies put in time on Folly Island performing picket duty and constructing the batteries, while other companies rotated south to Cole's Island for rest and recovery. The work was hard, consisting of digging, building, and unloading the never-ending arrival of guns and supplies. The heat was oppressive, and injuries and death occasionally occurred because of accidents, sickness, or rebel shells. Despite such conditions, the men knew an attack on Morris Island, and the heart of secession was close, and morale remained high.[13]

As the work came together, General Hunter was organizing his forces for the attack. Brigadier General Alfred Terry led one of his new divisions. The Second Division, of which the 39th now found itself assigned to, would be led by Truman Seymour, who had felt the plan was the right one all along. General Gillmore had roughly 20,000 men in the Department of the South, "all well drilled and disciplined," wrote Doctor Clark.[14] Troops were arriving daily, and Gillmore would continue to grow his numbers. Notably, these numbers included the 2nd South Carolina and 54th Massachusetts, two all-Black volunteer regiments. The attack on Charleston planned to use 11,000 infantry, 250 artillerymen, and 400 engineers.[15]

❖   ❖   ❖

On July 4th, the harbor ships, now including vessels specifically designed to clear obstructions, were adorned with flags and fired salutes to America at noon—not yet aware they were also saluting Lee's retreat at Gettysburg and Grant accepting the surrender of Vicksburg on that very day. Rear Admiral John Dahlgren also arrived on the 4th and took command of the naval forces. After weeks of hard work, over forty guns had been mounted and fortified on Folly Island, and General Hunter was eager to add Charleston to the same breath as Gettysburg and Vicksburg.[16]

Refining his plan with Dahlgren, Hunter intended two diversions: He sent a regiment to cut the Charleston and Savannah Railroad and prevent reinforcements, and ordered General Terry's First Division to James Island, adjacent to Morris Island and closer to Charleston itself. Terry was to give the impression of an attack there to split Confederate forces and fire. The main attack on Morris Island would be led by the man whose original idea a joint expedition had been. The Second Brigade of Seymour's First Division, led by Brigadier General George Strong, would assault Morris Island with the cover of the ironclads and recently built guns.[17]

Beauregard was aware an attack was coming and used the time to prepare as much as he could. However, his efforts had been hindered over the past month by a constant need to send men to Vicksburg in an urgent attempt to hold that city. Late in June, six Confederate deserters had shown themselves in Federal camps and stated the force inside Charleston was shrinking as men were sent to Vicksburg.[18] Beauregard had 2,600 infantry, 3,800 artillerymen, and 550 cavalrymen available for Charleston's defenses. While these numbers were down, he had the advantage of every unit being native South Carolinians, many from Charleston itself. What Beauregard had lost in manpower, he hoped to make up for in native sons being willing to defend their home, and such a symbolic city, to the last man. Waiting for the Second Division on Morris Island was a force of 665 infantrymen, 330 artillerymen, and 26 cavalrymen.[19]

After the weeks of bringing in supplies, building batteries and entrenchments, and readying men for battle, the final, and most grim, battle preparation took place: Sick and wounded members of the 39th, and all other regiments, were sent to Hilton Head, and medical tents and tables for surgery and amputations were moved forward.[20] On the evening of July 9, Valentine Randolph observed warships moving into position, followed by nine transports loaded with troops. "All things are now about ready to make an attack on Morris Island."[21] The men struck their tents, packed their knapsacks, and awaited the attack.

❖   ❖   ❖

Very early on the morning of the 10th, 2,500 men of Strong's brigade were in boats, 1,350 men operated the batteries and stood ready to bring artillery ashore, and 1,450 men—to include the 39th—were held as reinforcements.[22] Just after 5:00 a.m., General Seymour gave the order, and "[t]he batteries on Folly Island opened, in good earnest."[23] Thirty-two guns and fifteen mortars interrupted the early morning routine of the rebels on the southern end of Morris Island. Four of Dahlgren's ironclads soon joined the performance to the loud cheering of U.S. troops who no longer felt the need to conceal themselves. As Confederate batteries joined the fight, the engagement's noise became so loud that Federal forces at Port Royal heard the booming over fifty miles away.[24]

After almost two hours of bombardment, with Strong's men moving closer and closer, Confederate artillery could soon not aim low enough and shot passed over the top of the assault force. The Confederate long roll sounded as General Strong led his men onto the shore and drove the defending force out of their rifle pits and continued to advance up Morris Island. Confederate troops were abandoning their positions and retreating to Fort Wagner on the northern end of the island, and many were taken prisoner along with artillery pieces.[25]

An officer from a New Hampshire regiment ran among the Federal soldiers waving his hat and holding a newspaper he found in the captured works, "Vicksburg captured. Great victory at Gettysburg!"[26] The men cheered wildly, celebrating their own victory and those of their comrades in other locations, but the mood quickly returned to the realities of war. Now free of Confederate soldiers, Fort Sumter began unloading shot on the southern end of Morris Island, and as the men pushed north, Fort Wagner fired on them as well. Taking some losses, and no longer able to press forward, the assault ended. Doctor Clark's account of the attack states that 14 men were killed and 39 wounded, with 204 Confederate casualties, and 127 taken prisoner. Twelve guns were also soon to be repurposed for the Union cause.[27]

A pontoon bridge was constructed across the inlet. That afternoon, the entire 39th was moved to Folly Island's head to help load artillery and material for transport across the strait and prepare for future operations. Seymour ordered the offensive resumed in the morning with an attack on Fort Wagner, but the Federal forces were repelled with ugly losses. Strong's attacking brigade lost over 300 men to only a handful of Confederate losses. In *Gate of Hell*, Stephen Wise writes that the assault "never had a chance." Wise discusses that the force was too "overconfident" from the previous day's work and that there was no detailed planning or preceding artillery fire "thinking a quick bayonet assault would easily overrun Wagner."[28]

Developing a sense of strategy after almost two years in the service, Valentine Randolph wrote that "the fort could not be taken by a charge without too great a loss of life; so it must be taken by approaches."[29] Thus began the dangerous work of constructing breaching batteries, digging rifle pits and entrenchments, and preparing for the siege life that would soon dominate the next two months—all of this being done under artillery and sniper fire, while working long shifts in the oppressive heat. Admiral Dahlgren had his warships positioned to provide cover fire on Wagner to protect the work.[30]

❖   ❖   ❖

On July 16, General Gillmore issued a memo congratulating the men for their work and especially thanked General Vogdes' men, which specifically included the 39th, for their work building the batteries and preparing Folly Island for offensive operations. While the regiment was no doubt grateful to be recognized for their efforts and know that they contributed, they were likely disappointed they had not taken part in the assault. The decision to have the 39th held in reserve was no doubt a result of having spent weeks doing hard labor and requiring rest, but that does not make watching your comrades fight and die any easier.[31]

Throughout the day on July 17, Dahlgren's fleet kept a steady barrage on Fort Wagner in a continued effort to weaken the structure, take out its defenses, and, if nothing else, prevent its occupants from getting rest. During the day, and into the 18th, Gillmore was moving men from the other islands to Morris Island for another offensive on Wagner. One of these regiments was the all-Black 54th Massachusetts volunteers depicted in the movie *Glory*. Their commander, Colonel Robert Gould Shaw, had been adamant that for Black regiments to be taken seriously, and not just seen as army labor, they must be given the opportunity to fight. Shaw's men had been engaged in smaller skirmishes with success, and he now volunteered his men to be the lead element of such a critical attack. Their selection to lead the assault was not purely a symbolic or ideological one, however. Because of the number of sick or wounded in other regiments, the 54th—650 men strong—was the strongest regiment on the island and made the most sense to put in front.[32]

The events Homer Plimpton witnessed on July 18, he wrote, were the "grandest sights I ever had the good fortune to behold."[33] Federal cannon fire began slowly early in the day, and by noon, all the guns from the land and the sea were firing on Wagner at the rate of one projectile every two seconds.[34] Just after dark, the 54th, followed by five other regiments, took off on the double-quick up the beach towards Fort Wagner. When within 100 yards, the column began their charge, and soon the scene was a "sheet of fire" in the words of Valentine Randolph.[35] Fort Wagner and Fort Sumter dropped shot onto the Federal ranks, while the Confederate garrison and attacking U.S. troops exchanged musket fire. Many men of the 54th never even made it off the beach, but a good portion made it to the ditch in front of Wagner and took cover. Colonel Shaw regrouped his men, and some made it up the slope and into parts of the battery where they continued firing and engaging in brutal hand to hand combat. Making it to the top of one wall, Colonel Shaw began waving his sword in the air, encouraging his men and was torn to pieces by musket fire. Still, the 54th "fought like tigers," in the words of Valentine Randolph, "like devils," in the words of Homer Plimpton.[36]

It would be inappropriate not to take stock of the courage and bravery displayed by the 54th Massachusetts, fighting against an enemy seeking to preserve enslavement and part of an army where many still did not see them as equals. However, the 54th begged their commander for the opportunity, and when granted one, they fought with pride for the Union cause. The 54th lost forty-two percent of their men, in what Valentine Randolph described as "desperate fighting ... on this horrible night."[37] The brave men of the 54th Massachusetts joined the U.S. army, by choice, fought bravely for its cause, and died with honor alongside their fellow countrymen—taking their emancipation into their own hands.

As the 18th turned to the 19th, the 39th Illinois crossed over to Morris Island expecting to reinforce and continue the attack but found nothing but the dead and dying. According to Wise, 5,000 men took part in assaulting Wagner, with 246 killed, 890 wounded, and 391 captured.[38] As noted, the loss of officers was exceptionally heavy, and as Valentine Randolph put it, "no advantage was gained." General Gillmore's men had bravely charged Fort Wagner, but the Federal bombardment had not done as much damage to the defenses of Fort Wagner as thought. Advancing up a narrow beach for a frontal assault under heavy fire was a tall order. The men of the 39th lay on the beach overnight, the only noise now being crashing waves and the desperate cries of the wounded.[39]

❖　❖　❖

Organizational changes were again made to account for losing leadership, loss of men, and the allocation of siege duties. Brigadier General Alfred Terry was now in charge of the division on Morris Island, which was comprised of three infantry brigades, twelve artillery batteries, a cavalry company—and most importantly—the 1st New York engineers. The 39th was part of Second Brigade, commanded by Colonel Joshua Howell.[40]

The engineers, not the infantrymen, were now most important to the war effort. Work began constructing siege lines, or trenches, to advance slowly on Wagner while engineers built fortifications to defend the men and placed guns. Soldiers spent their days digging with the spade or on picket duty. The work was hot and challenging, not to mention dangerous. Men would advance to the ditches often under fire, and begin digging as fast as possible, pressing themselves into the earth when they heard cannon fire headed their way. Cannon, artillery,

Regimental staff on Morris Island. Colonel Osborn seated on left, a rare wartime photograph of the regimental commander. Lieutenant Colonel Mann seated on right. Of note: The Black man on the far right is likely one of the former enslaved in the area that regiments hired for help navigating the area or working in camp (reproduced from Clark, *History*).

and sniper fire were common occurrences as each side sought to prevent the other from working. Confederate cannons were placed on James Island to the west, and Sullivan's Island to the north to disrupt Federal work and U.S. warships returned the favor from the ocean. Simple tasks such as digging a trench, or loading a cannon, became dangerous ones when performed in the open.[41]

So it went as days turned into weeks. Men dug trenches, built fortifications, and placed guns under the engineers' direction in unbearable heat. The sappers, from a French word meaning to undermine, would then detonate charges to open new parallels to advance towards Wagner. On July 23, a new parallel was opened 750 yards from the fort.[42] Early in August, reinforcements arrived on Folly Island, many who were Gettysburg veterans and more than happy to follow up their success with a chance at the heart of secession. The new men allowed for a rotation of three days in front of Wagner, one day in camp, and another day doing picket duty away from Wagner.[43]

On August 9, the distance was closed to 450 yards.[44] All accomplished under

Line officers on Morris Island, consisting of the captains and lieutenants from the companies (reproduced from Clark, *History***).**

constant sniper and artillery fire. Amazingly, even while actively taking part in the work duties and picketing close to Wagner, the 39th didn't suffer their first casualties until a picket duty rotation on August 15. One man lost a portion of his leg to fragments of a shell explosion, and one sustained a head injury at the hands of a sharpshooter. "These are the first men the 39th has had wounded since we left the valleys of Virginia," wrote Homer Plimpton. "It is a common saying that none of the 39th can be harmed."[45] Unfortunately, the luck of the 39th had run out.

❖   ❖   ❖

Early on August 17th, the recently constructed batteries opened-up on Sumter and Wagner. Soon after, seven of Admiral Dahlgren's warships joined the affair firing their big guns from the ocean. At one point, the Confederate flag on Sumter came down, to the great cheering of the Union men, but apparently had just been cut down by the fire and was soon raised once again. The industrial advantage of the northern cause was showing itself in the form of 12 batteries of 38 heavy guns—"the war's largest concentration of heavy ordnance."[46] For days, the Federal guns pounded the fortifications of Charleston Harbor and its surrounding islands. Beauregard and his force had been expecting a vast Federal artillery barrage but did not understand the power and accuracy of the new guns being used.

The Confederate response was muted, mostly coming from James Island, and only a sporadic shot from Sumter and Wagner. The response was enough to keep the Union men honest, however. On one occasion, Confederate infantry attempted to push Federal engineers back away from the line and had to be run off by pickets and guards protecting the work. Despite the weakening response, Gillmore's men still suffered death and wounds most every day, with not even the officers being safe. Colonel Howell sustained a terrible head injury when a bomb shelter collapsed on him. Temporarily put in command of the brigade, Colonel Osborn suffered a concussion from cannon fire that put him in hospital for a few days.[47]

Part of all the building and fortifying on Morris Island had been erecting a site for a parrot gun that fired 200-pound shells.[48] The gun was nicknamed the "Swamp Angel," apparently because of a comment made by Corporal John Kipp, from Marseilles, of Company K. Upon returning from building a pathway across marshland to the gun, Corporal Kipp remarked that "[w]e have been out in the great marsh, and as nearly as I can guess we have been constructing a pulpit of sand for some swamp angel to preach from."[49]

On August 21, Gillmore sent a message under a flag of truce, informing Beauregard of his intent to fire on the city as it had an arsenal and was a legitimate military target. Only if Fort Wagner and Battery Gregg were surrendered would Gillmore hold off. Receiving no reply, the Swamp Angel targeted the spire of St. Michael's Church inside the city with over 30 rounds before the rear end of the gun was blown out. Beauregard now sent his own message under a white flag stating that there were elderly and injured people inside the city, and that it was not a legitimate military target. Perhaps hoping that the threat would change Beauregard's calculus, perhaps not wanting to be associated with targeting civilians, or perhaps because the gun was no longer functioning, Gillmore refrained from further targeting of Charleston proper.[50]

On August 24, General Gillmore sent word to Washington of the "practical demolition" of Fort Sumter, noting that the symbolic fort was a "shapeless mass of ruins."[51] With almost all attention now on Fort Wagner, by August 26, the Federal force was 250 yards from the fort. Now at such a close distance that the parallels became sharp zigzags, the close-in work was a nasty affair for all involved. Wagner's defenders had a rifle pit only 100 yards in front of the Federal engineers that was making work difficult at best, and deadly at worst. Fire on the 25th was focused on the rifle pits, and that evening the 39th's brigade went to the front on picket duty, with Colonel Osborn at the helm.[52]

Early in the evening of the 26th, General Gillmore was ready to move and ordered General Terry to take the rifle pits. Over 250 men from the 24th Massachusetts prepared themselves on the left with bayonets fixed for a charge, and many with spades that would immediately begin rebuilding fortifications when the pits were taken. Other members of the brigade were stationed to the right, providing cover with sharpshooters. When given the command, the men who had crept as close as possible charged up and into the rifle pits engaging in hand-to-hand combat with the rebel defenders. Fort Wagner briefly opened-up

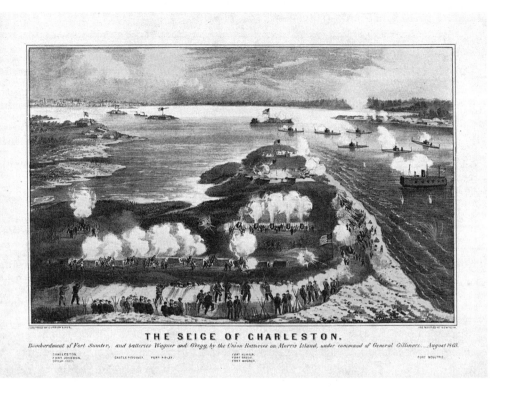

THE SEIGE OF CHARLESTON.

Bombardment of Fort Sumter, and batteries Wagner and Gregg, by the Union Batteries on Morris Island, under command of General Gillmore. August 1863.

Currier and Ives depiction of the Siege of Charleston in August 1863 (Library of Congress: LC-DIG-pga-09796).

on the attackers, with little effect because of the proximity. The men in the rifle pits were so overwhelmed that many did not even get shots off before being captured. Federal losses in the assault were minimal, with accounts varying, but all counting less than five dead and ten wounded. As many as 75 Confederate soldiers were taken prisoner, and the Federal force now controlled the beach to within 200 yards of Fort Wagner.[53] Remembered Doctor Clark, "[f]rom that time until the fall of Wagner no Confederates ventured outside the fort in our direction."[54]

The day was a successful one for the division, but a day that saw the Phalanx's luck run out. Earlier in the day, a man had been severely wounded by a sharpshooter while on picket duty, and three men were wounded by artillery fire during the assault on the rifle pits. Killed by artillery fire during the assault was a corporal from Company K. Corporal James Welcome, of Bloomington, became the first man killed by enemy fire since leaving Virginia.[55]

❖　　❖　　❖

While Fort Sumter had been reduced to rubble, and Fort Wagner's days were numbered, Beauregard was still not ready to give it, or the city, up. The stand at Wagner had done its job in buying time to fortify Charleston's defenses, allowing the movement of men and resources to hold the city. Beauregard even stationed infantry troops at Fort Sumter to defend what was now purely a symbolic location of no military value.

On the evening of September 1, U.S. warships opened-up a barrage on Fort Sumter that lasted through the night and into the next morning that brought no response from Sumter, and an ineffective one from Sullivan's Island. By September 4, General Gillmore was ready to end the siege of Fort Wagner. Early on the 5th, a heavy bombardment of Wagner began intending to drive the Confederate garrison into their bombproofs and allow Federal engineers to move their lines up to the fort. The fire was kept up over forty hours, and on the evening of the 6th, the 39th moved to the front as "grand guards" of the trenches and the engineers under the command of Lieutenant Colonel Mann. General Terry readied his division to take the fort, and by the early hours of the 7th, General Gillmore's guns had put 1,247 artillery rounds onto Wagner. By 3:00 that morning, however, it seemed the assault wouldn't be required.[56]

A Confederate deserter from Fort Wagner showed himself to Lieutenant Colonel Mann in the trenches, just after midnight, and reported that Wagner was being evacuated and a fuse will blow the powder magazines intending to destroy the fort and kill as many Federal soldiers as possible. While Lieutenant Colonel Mann had his men take control of the prisoner and send word to headquarters, the soldiers now sitting on a literal time bomb were eager for their orders. Mann received word back to direct the guns firing on Battery Gregg on the northern end of the island, to focus on Wagner for fifteen minutes before sending five men to assess the situation. Private Camillus Cox, of Chicago, was one who volunteered for the assignment. Cox and four others climbed on top of the parapet, circled the fort, and met at the center, finding the fuse. While the fuse was cut, one man returned with the news that all was quiet inside Wagner.[57]

Captain James Wightman, of Odell, took twenty men from Company C and entered Fort Wanger, capturing a handful of the last men who had been setting the fuse and ensuring the powder would not blow. At 3:30 a.m. on September 7, Lieutenant Colonel Mann telegraphed General Terry: "Captain James Wightman and twenty men have gone in and the colors of the Thirty-Ninth Illinois are planted on the ramparts."[58] After months of hot, exhausting, dangerous work full of sickness and recent injury and death, the Yates Phalanx flag flew above Fort Wagner. Cox and his four comrades were awarded thirty-day furloughs for bravely volunteering to inspect the unknown.

❖   ❖   ❖

Battery Gregg fell quickly after Wagner was silenced, and following the bombardment, it too had endured. Gillmore's army now controlled all of Morris Island, and the guns of the two batteries were turned on the remaining Confederate guns in the harbor. The scene was a grisly one. Men worked around bodies from inside Wagner and those from the last assault that had emerged from their shallow graves because of tides, explosions, and the struggle of men in the sand. The Wagner garrison had buried torpedoes meant to protect the harbor in the sand around Wagner and Gregg, and injuries in the division mounted in the ensuing days.[59]

Even with the "battle" over, death and destruction did not wholly cease. The

39th had two men badly injured by Federal shells falling short, and a man of the 85th Pennsylvania lost his leg stepping on one of the torpedo mines. The 39th now garrisoned Morris Island, taking part in refortifying the island and going on picket duty as the island served as a staging ground for Charleston's continued assault. Confederate artillery fire continued, and the work was becoming no less dangerous. On the night of the 10th, Private George Burke of Bloomington was killed by a shell that cost another man's leg.[60]

As the month wore on, it became apparent that no amount of destruction done to Fort Sumter, or risk the city was held in, would cause Beauregard to surrender symbolic Charleston. Even as Sumter lay entirely in ruins, with no military capability, a rebel flag continued to fly. Death continued to find the 39th as well. On the evening of the 23rd, while on picket, three men of Company K were wounded, two badly. Captain Joseph Woodruff succumbed to his wounds. Woodruff was the man who waited on the bank of Sir John's Run in January, ready to fight a last stand and ensure the men of the regiment would get across. Homer Plimpton remembered him as "one of our best officers."[61] Woodruff had left behind a lucrative business in Marseilles to volunteer to serve his country and had done it well—often called upon to command the regiment in the absence of other officers. "A sad record for today," wrote Valentine Randolph.[62]

The 39th had gone from a regiment of tiny successes, relative safety, and missing out on significant battles, to veterans of a dangerous major offensive. With this, however, had come the reality of the horror that war inflicts.

10

Furlough

George Snowden was born in Pittsburgh, Pennsylvania, on the last day of 1835. He received a fair amount of schooling growing up, and at a young age worked in a printing office. In 1855, he moved west to Illinois, settling in Oregon and working as a clerk. In 1858, he tried his hand at the steam-boating business in the south but returned to Oregon in 1860 as a clerk in his father's drugstore.

It was back in Oregon that Snowden encountered Samuel Linton recruiting for what would become Company D of the 39th. Linton convinced Snowden to travel to Chicago with him to gain a better understanding of the regiment, and Snowden enlisted on August 12, 1861.

Snowden apparently impressed his superiors early on and was made First Sergeant while the regiment was in St. Louis. After being in temporary command of his company at the Battle of Kernstown, Colonel Osborn commissioned Snowden as a Lieutenant in June 1862, and Snowden was made a Captain just before the veterans went on furlough.[1]

LIFE HAD NOT GOTTEN more comfortable for the 39th Illinois since the fall of Fort Wagner, but it seemed to get worse and worse. Even though Fort Sumter was in ruins and of no value to the Confederacy, and the Union now controlled all access to the city of Charleston, death and injury still found the Phalanx. During twelve days from October 6–18, the regiment had eight more men wounded by Confederate shells and one killed.[2] Considering this, and with it becoming apparent that no further action would be taken against Charleston, the 39th Illinois was likely quite happy to be sent back to Folly Island on October 28.[3]

The roughly six months, on and off, Charleston offensive by Gillmore's X Corps was one with a mixed legacy. Fort Sumter, the symbolic beginning of the Civil War, had been demolished, and the rebels could no longer make use of it militarily. However, the Confederate flag did still fly above it. The city of Charleston itself had been cut off from the ocean, and Federal forces controlled all access to Charleston Harbor. Yet, Beauregard had not surrendered the city, and the heart of secession beat on, if only symbolically. Both sides would settle for small strategic and moral victories as further Federal efforts proved not worth the loss of life and use of men and supplies. The city and the fort would remain formally in the Confederacy's hands until General William Tecumseh Sherman's arrival in 1865.[4]

The campaign served one very notable political and strategic end on the

Union home front, that of the demonstrated use of Black regiments in combat. Much of the Northern news covered the bravery of units like the 54th Massachusetts, and Lincoln and the Republicans capitalized on this. Military commanders were commenting on Black troops' effectiveness not just for their actual fighting, but the psychological impact on southerners. As James McPherson put it, "[o]pposition to emancipation became opposition to northern victory."[5] However, much of this sentiment was quickly put to the back of Northern minds as shortly after ceasing major operations on Morris Island, the deadly Battle of Chickamauga took place in north Georgia. One of the deadliest battles of the war, the Federals suffered over 16,000 casualties at Chickamauga.[6] After a summer of splitting the Confederacy in two at Vicksburg, repelling a second Lee invasion of the North at Gettysburg, and all but ending the prospect of European backing of the Confederacy; northern eyes would have only stopped briefly on Morris Island before turning in concern back to the western theater at Chickamauga in late September, and Lincoln's Gettysburg Address in November.[7]

❖   ❖   ❖

After months of hot, tiring, dangerous work on the front, with twenty-five killed and wounded, the 39th Illinois was happy for the change of pace.[8] The firing was continuing in and around the harbor but was no longer the regiment's immediate concern. Life now consisted of rest and recovery; sick and wounded men were cared for, and aside from the occasional drilling, the rest of the men enjoyed free time. On December 5, the men boarded a ship for Hilton Head, arriving there to make camp on the 7th. Drilling continued here in the winter camp, as the Department of the South awaited its orders for the upcoming year. The 39th's chain of command remained familiar, as they were assigned to a brigade led by Colonel Howell in General Seymour's Division.

A quiet Christmas passed, the regiment's third in the service, and it was around this time the issue of veteran reenlistment came up. Regiments throughout the U.S. Army who had enlisted for three-year terms in 1861 were asked whether they would reenlist for another three years. A myriad of factors to include political leanings, a call to duty, a desire to stick with war-forged comrades, and worry for family at home were competing against each other. Secretary Stanton offered several incentives to maintain as many veterans as possible: Regiments where 75 percent or more of the men reenlisted would maintain their flags and designations, men who reenlisted would receive a $400 bonus, and those who reenlisted would receive a 30-day furlough.[9] Lieutenant Cyrus Knapp, from Chicago, was appointed the regiment's recruiting officer, and Colonel Osborn and other officers made patriotic speeches to generate excitement for reenlisting.[10]

Pride in the unit, and not wanting to let others down, played a large role in men deciding to reenlist. Much of the scholarship surrounding reenlistment has long pointed to political motivations. While true that many Republicans and Democrats reenlisted, and did not, for their respective political reasons, the opposite was also true. As Zachery Fry points out in *A Republic in the Ranks*, "a unit's ideological commitment could not predict its desire to reenlist."[11] Many men who had advocated for hard and total war against the south were glad to see it finally arrive, while many who believed it the proper course thought they had done their share, and it was someone else's turn. One can understand a soldier's desire to stick with his brothers in arms and fight for the cause, as much as one can appreciate feeling that three years of honorable service and hardship was enough. Every service member has their own unique reason they volunteer, and after serving honorably, continue or pass the flag to a replacement. This was as true as it is today.

Scholarly assessments of Federal reenlistment numbers are challenging to ascertain and vary wildly, but 15 percent throughout the war is an often-cited figure. Factors such as a soldier's initial enlistment, the length of the enlistment, what theater they were in, and when exactly it was up all had an impact alongside the usual partisan or patriotic factors. In his book *For Cause and Comrades: Why Men Fought in the Civil War,* James McPherson assesses that "more than half" of the U.S. soldiers who enlisted in 1861 reenlisted in 1864, a group that most closely represents the 39th Illinois.[12] This was the group of men who answered the call immediately following the events of Fort Sumter and Bull Run and were, in theory, the most ideologically driven to serve the Union cause.

Whatever their reasons for joining, and whatever their feelings of the war currently were, every man now had to make their choice as 1863 drew to a close. The 39th had been in the service of the United States for just over two years. Twice it was thought they were making ready to march on Richmond, only to see such plans dissolve. Now seeing the total war and bloody battles of Vicksburg, Gettysburg, and Chickamauga—and their own experience at Charleston—the men knew that whatever lie ahead would be hard. Would the men who so eagerly volunteered at the start of the war stick with the effort and brave the unknown, or would they consider their duty done and hope to survive a final ten months of service with no furlough?

Decisions were required to be made by January 5, and Colonel Osborn's initial report cited 408 men—enough to return home as a regiment and keep the 39th's designation. Osborn then learned, however, that Company H could not be counted as part of the 408. Having not yet been in the service two years after joining the regiment late at Harrison's landing, they were not eligible, and the 39th was in danger of losing their regiment.[13]

Congress, however, extended the deadline to March. With numbers varying wildly across the U.S. Army, the War Department wanted to maximize the time it gave men to decide. After a challenging year of war, the middle of winter would have been a tough time to make such a decision. However, the administration and the army realized that more time being persuaded by their officers and brothers in arms may bring them their numbers. While the hard battles of 1863 brought significant losses of men, they had also mostly brought positive momentum to the Union cause. More importantly, the 1863 state elections had brought further pro-administration attitudes to the military.[14]

Former General of the U.S. Army George McClellan endorsed Democrat

George Woodward for Governor of Pennsylvania. Along with this endorsement was an endorsement of a view that the war should be fought without injury to property rights and be only about reuniting North and South.[15] The continually growing sentiment that many politicians and citizens were undermining the war effort was now one being endorsed by their former general, and the opinion soon became that the Lincoln administration's actions all along had been ones of support for the United States, its soldiers, and their ability to win the war. Thus, hearing reports of these growing sentiments, the deadline to reenlist was extended.[16]

While the political factors may not have been what put the 39th over the 75 percent threshold—only a few extra men reenlisted during the extended time—the extension allowed time for the 39th to keep their unit designation. Upon examination of sick, wounded, or injured men, noted Homer Plimpton, "[t]he difference has been met in another direction." Forty-two men were designated for the Invalid Corps by Doctor Clark, and the 39th Illinois once again had 75 percent of its active men reenlisting in the service of the United States.[17] For his part, Plimpton urged his brother who had been serving with him to return home at the end of his enlistment. He spoke very little of his brother, Olin, in his journal, but advised him it would make it "satisfactory to the people at home by having one of us with them." While Plimpton himself seemed a little unsure about whether to return home and pick up his profession, something—thankfully—seemed to pull him to stay with the regiment.[18]

On January 27, the men of the 39th not heading home on furlough were attached to the 62nd Ohio, while the now roughly 450 men heading home prepared to head for their transport. On the 28th, they began a march to the harbor to the men of the division's applause. Regimental bands played music. The Phalanx marched between lines of troops, passing by their two generals' headquarters, with Colonel Osborn no doubt rendering a salute to the two men whose letter he was carrying home to Illinois:

> *HEADQUARTERS, HILTON HEAD*
> *January 25, 1864*
>
> *To His Excellency, the Governor of Illinois:*
>
> *Sir:—The Thirty-Ninth Regiment Illinois Volunteers, Colonel T.O. Osborn, having reenlisted as a "veteran regiment," has been furloughed and will soon proceed homeward. I cannot permit it to leave my command without expressing, so far as I am able, my entire satisfaction with its conduct under all circumstances.*
>
> *It will display to you, possibly, a state of discipline and excellence of instruction that will not be diminished by contrast with the very best of our volunteer regiments, and you may justly be proud of its past and present efficiency, for which Colonel Osborn, a most excellent officer, deserves great praise.*
>
> *Your Excellency will, I am sure, afford Colonel Osborn every reasonable facility for filling his command, and you can entrust the interests of your citizen-soldiers to no better hands. And I am*
>
> > *Your Excellency's Obedient Servant,*
> > *T. Seymour, Brig. Gen'l Commanding.*

(reverse)

HEADQUARTERS, DEPARTMENT OF THE SOUTH
HILTON HEAD, January 25, 1864

I heartily endorse everything Brigadier-General Seymour says of the Thirty-Ninth Regiment Illinois Volunteers, and their commanders, and hope the Governor of Illinois will use his influence to have the regiment returned to my command when recruited, unless Colonel Osborn prefers some other.

Q.A. GILLMORE, Maj. Gen'l Commanding.[19]

❖　❖　❖

The regiment was afforded travel on two modest, but comfortable, ships for their four-day journey north to New York City. While there was a brief incident of running aground on a shoal, a loose horse, and some spilled water caskets that caused a few injuries—the trip was decidedly more enjoyable than their previous ocean voyage. The men were set up at a Federal encampment at Park Barracks, with many splurging for hotel rooms with a proper bath and bed. The men explored the city, bought clothes, went to the theater, and enjoyed the foods that do not present themselves amidst Civil War campaigning.[20]

On February 3, the men boarded rail cars and enjoyed the scenery in the relaxed nature of an elegant passenger train ride. The train arrived in Chicago close to midnight on the 6th, and the men had resigned themselves to thinking they would find little fanfare or food and head to camp. The regiment marched through the city to Bryan Hall, where to their surprise, the women of the Chicago Soldiers' Rest organization had a substantial meal awaiting them. They were met by Lieutenant Colonel Mann, who had returned to Chicago in mid–November for recruiting purposes. He and Colonel Osborn gave speeches praising the men and thanking the "pretty waiters" whose company the men enjoyed.[21] The men camped for the night at North Market Hall and were treated to an equally lovely breakfast by the ladies of the Chicago Soldiers' Rest the following morning as well.

The men were given ten days to travel to see family, at which point they were to return to Chicago to take part in the regiment's recruiting efforts. Camp Fry, near the corner of modern-day Clark & Diversey, was the 39th's home with the men being less than enamored with continued camp life while a major city was so near. Colonel Osborn offered passes to visit the city, however, and men took advantage of his good nature and turned twenty-four-hour passes into forty-eight-hour ones regularly. The regiment took its recruiting duties seriously amidst the diversions of city life and building on Lieutenant Colonel Mann's efforts brought in around two hundred fifty men. Combined with the 80–100 men still in Hilton Head, this pushed the regiment close to 800 men.[22]

One very notable diversion of city life was a performance at McVicker's Theater near the end of the regiment's time in Chicago. All around the city, the men saw posted a sign:

BENEFIT
OF THE TREASURER OF THE THEATER
HENRY WARREN!
WHO HAS THE PLEASURE OF ANNOUNCING TO HIS FRIENDS,
THAT THE DISTINGUISHED
DOCTOR WM. WOODWARD
ASSISTANT SURGEON,
THIRTY-NINTH ILLINOIS INFANTRY,
HAS KINDLY VOLUNTEERED TO APPEAR AS
—HAMLET—
IN THE THIRD ACT OF SHAKESPEARE'S TRAGEDY OF THAT NAME[23]

Fresh off his performance as the nearly drowning pirate on Folly Island, Doctor Woodward was volunteered for the role by some of his friends after becoming known for reciting Shakespeare in camp. The theater was full that evening, and the regimental band performed before the show. Doctor Clark and Colonel Osborn joined Governor Yates, and his wife, in a box while the men of the regiment were scattered throughout the house. While the regiment, and the audience, enjoyed the spectacle if, for no other reason than the novelty of the situation, the *Chicago Times* offered its own tongue-in-cheek review: "If the Doctor of the Thirty-Ninth Illinois murders the men of his regiment in the same manner he did Hamlet last night, he had better leave the service."[24]

❖   ❖   ❖

The tone became more serious when the regiment learned it would leave Chicago for Washington, D.C., on the last day of February. Before leaving, the men of the 39th Illinois assembled in Bryan Hall, which was packed with men and women, many unable to find a spot inside. Governor Yates appeared to a flurry of applause from both the regiment and the audience. He spoke at length about the struggle for preserving the Union and the contributions of the state and his namesake Phalanx. Yates spoke with pride about how quickly and earnestly the state had raised recruits, to include members of the 39th, who now brought even more honor to themselves by reenlisting. The men unfurled their flags as Yates boldly declared, "[y]ou see them there, tattered and torn, riddled by shot and shell, and stained by blood of brave men, but you will find no blot upon their escutcheon."[25]

Wild applause erupted, but the masterful political speaker was not done with his performance. The regiment had brought fragments of shot fired from Morris Island and placed them on the stage in front of Yates. Yates offered to the crowd that perhaps representatives *should*, in fact, be sent to meet with Confederate leaders to discuss peace as the Copperheads so wished. Before the crowd could give an adverse reaction, he placed his foot on one shell and pointed to the other stating, "I would name this for one of them, and I would name that for the other."[26] The crowd erupted in patriotic applause as Governor Yates finished his two-hour speech declaring that the 39th Illinois would do its part in crushing the rebellion.

Early on the morning of February 29, the men of the 39th Illinois Infantry found themselves once again marching through the streets of Chicago, cheered by a crowd, just as they had in October 1861—but this time as veterans. Once again, they marched towards a train that would carry them east. The U.S. Army had a new commander, one of Illinois' own, and for a third time, the Yates Phalanx eyed a chance to strike towards the capital of the Confederacy. They would not be denied this time, but there was a year of bloodletting to get through before that time would come.

PART III

"All This Bloodletting"

March 1864–April 1865

"There was, with all of this bloodletting, little pleasure to serving with the Army of the Potomac or the Army of the James. As Private Ransom Bedell, a Cook County soldier of the 39th Illinois, noted, it was not uncommon for a general officer of those commands to call upon his few western regiments to lead the various assaults. There was sufficient reason for this, Bedell added, for when the 39th charged, it moved like an 'avalanche.'"[1]

11

Bermuda Hundred

Leroy Baker was born in 1835 in Cortland County, a rural portion of upstate New York. At 20, he moved west to Illinois and settled near Wilmington. It was here, in the very first days after Fort Sumter, that Baker assisted Sylvester Munn, and Joseph Richardson—also of Wilmington—in the formation of a company. So many local men enlisted that the company became too large, which became a blessing in disguise. The company attempted to become a part of the 20th Illinois, but another company received its place. When some men left to join the 20th, the company fell to a more proper size. Made up almost entirely of men from Wilmington, with some from adjacent towns, men from Chicago and Cook County rounded out the roster when the regiment arrived in Chicago to join the 39th.

Baker was voted the company's Second Lieutenant for his efforts and quickly became First Lieutenant when Joseph Richardson died of typhoid. Not long after, Baker became Captain of the company during the shuffle resulting from Colonel Light's dismissal. During the regiment's earliest days at Hancock, Maryland, Baker came down with a serious case of typhoid that prevented him from joining in the fight against Stonewall. Baker soon recovered, however, and proved himself worthy during service in the valley, and performed excellent service as a frequent "officer of the day" during the Morris Island siege.

Baker's leadership would be put to the test often during the Bermuda Hundred campaign, as his seniority of rank, and the misfortune of others, would require him to command the regiment on multiple occasions.[1]

MARCH 1864 FOUND THE United States Civil War just short of three years old, and it had taken Abraham Lincoln that long, but he finally had his man to lead all U.S. armies. Ulysses S. Grant's successes in the west had earned the President's trust for taking action in a war where too many Federal generals had been guilty of inaction. Grant was now called on to coordinate the overall war effort. The West Point graduate had left the service amidst accusations of drinking too much, struggled to make a living as a farmer and in other occupations, and worked at his father's leather good shop in Galena, Illinois, when the war broke out. Pressed back into service, Grant led successfully at Fort Henry, Fort Donelson, and Shiloh in 1862. In 1863 he commanded the Federal capture of Vicksburg after a months-long siege and split the Confederacy in two. Later in the year, by then commanding all forces in the western theater, Grant rescued Federal forces during the Chattanooga Campaign, turning the momentum of Gettysburg and Vicksburg back in the Union's favor after the defeat at Chickamauga.[2]

Now called on to defeat the Confederacy, end the war, and restore the Union; Lieutenant General Grant devised a plan of simultaneous advances that would put pressure on the Confederacy—everywhere they were—and strain their growing supply and personnel problems. The spring of 1864 would see two major Federal offensives, complimented by three supporting efforts, all aimed at the principal objective: Capture Richmond, defeat Lee's army, and end the war. In the west, Major General William Tecumseh Sherman would drive from Tennessee and through Georgia as part of his eventual "March to the Sea." In the east, Major General George Meade, who had successfully led at Gettysburg, would advance the Army of the Potomac towards Richmond and General Lee while defending Washington.[3]

One of the supporting efforts involved a Federal force moving up the James River from the south towards Richmond, cutting Lee's supply lines, and eventually squeezing the Confederate capital with the Army of the Potomac. This newly formed Army of the James, commanded by Major General Benjamin Butler, would be created with men that needed to be put to better use than garrison duty to press the war to a conclusion. Butler, who had been commanding the Department of Virginia and North Carolina, would form the Army of the James with men from his command and other organizations in the southeast. One of these groups of men was Major General Quincy Adams Gillmore's X Corps from South Carolina.[4]

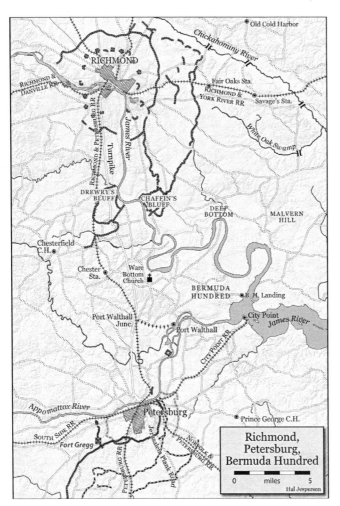

Richmond, Petersburg, Bermuda Hundred with 39th Illinois points of interest (map by Hal Jespersen).

❖   ❖   ❖

While the members of the 39th who had not reenlisted were still in South Carolina, the veterans returning from Chicago arrived in Washington, D.C., and crossed the Potomac into Virginia on March 4. The regiment established a camp at Fort Barnard, one of the defensive artillery positions protecting the capital. While the commander of the artillery unit garrisoning the fort made every accommodation for the men of the 39th, the stay at Fort Barnard was a miserable return to army life. There was snowy weather, followed by rain, and the location of the 39th's camp at the bottom of a hill was a flooded, muddy mess. At the end of March, Colonel Osborn came down with a severe case of pneumonia, and Doctor Clark credited the artillery commander giving up his dry and comfortable quarters with Osborn's recovery.[5]

Tasked to sit with the feverish Colonel overnight was Company A Private Anthony Taylor of Wilmington. Taylor had received a diary to write in just before the furlough and began using it shortly after the regiment arrived outside Washington, D.C. Taylor wrote of little more than collecting regimental mail and the occasional inspection between early March and late April, which would have still been preferable to the many men who suffered from pneumonia and typhoid. The men had reenlisted to fight the Confederacy, not languish in a sickly camp, and were undoubtedly ready to move.[6]

Throughout the first two weeks of April, regiments serving under Butler were making their way to Yorktown. The men were unaware of their task, destination, or anything other than the drilling and inspections they were undergoing. By mid–April, the XVIII Corps, from North Carolina, was set up at Yorktown, but Gillmore's X Corps experienced some delays. The Corps was more dispersed, and there were delays in orders arriving, but some blame rested solely with the corps' commander. Gillmore was spending more time concerning himself with his upcoming Senate confirmation to Major General than preparing for the campaign. While it is unknown if Butler believed Gillmore was fully deserving of the promotion, he would have been growing concerned about meeting Grant's timeline to begin the campaign. Butler, always noted as more of a political rather than tactically minded general, wrote to a Senate friend and asked that the matter be handled.[7]

After weeks of rumors, on April 26, the 39th Illinois broke camp and marched from Arlington to Alexandria, to board transports and head for Gloucester Point on the York River. The regiment arrived late in the day to an overwhelming scene of military activity with camps laid out across Gloucester Point and across the river near Yorktown. The regiment also encountered the men of the 39th who hadn't reenlisted and had arrived in camp ahead of them from South Carolina. The 39th Illinois Infantry was back as one, in the X Corps' First Division commanded by Brigadier General Alfred Terry, and in First Brigade with many familiar faces. The 39th had been in a brigade with the 62nd Ohio since Kernstown, the 85th Pennsylvania since Harrison's Landing, and the 67th Ohio since Charleston. Colonel Joshua Howell of the 85th was once again their brigade commander.[8]

The time at Gloucester Point and Yorktown was spent preparing for campaign life, as regiments rid themselves of extra baggage and prepared themselves to be an army on the move. Instead of carrying knapsacks with a few days' supplies, the men would now move with all the essentials they would need to include shelter tents in the absence of larger walled camp tents. Any time not spent being outfitted with necessities and requirements was spent doing more and more drilling in bayonet charges and skirmishing. The joke among the men was soon to call the newly formed Army of the James the "Army of the Games."[9]

On April 28, General Butler received word from General Grant that the campaign would begin the night of May 4. The Army of the James would begin their movements simultaneously with the Army of the Potomac. Butler was tasked with cutting Confederate rail and supply lines and advancing on Richmond. Cutting off Richmond from Petersburg's rail connections would cut them off from the rest of the south. Forcing Lee to send reinforcements in Butler's direction, or preventing reinforcements from coming to Lee, would be an additional success. If, and when, Lee's Army of Northern Virginia fell back towards Richmond, Grant wanted Butler ready to link up with Meade and end the war. On April 30, still not knowing the plan or their destination, the men of the X and XVIII Corps were formed up for General Butler's grand review of the Army of the James. Afterward, men were issued two good pairs of shoes and 100 rounds of ammunition and told to be ready to break camp and march with three days of food.[10]

❖   ❖   ❖

On May 4, the 39th, and the rest of the Army of the James, awoke early in the morning to strike their camp and march to the river to board transports. The scene was a grand one, as ships of all shapes and sizes made ready to begin the expedition. Navy gunboats would lead the way, with ironclads following the force up the James. Loading men and equipment took all day and come night; the transports moved out into the water to anchor overnight. Doctor Clark described the "vast fleet" as seeming "like a fairy scene—the brilliant lights of varied colors swinging from the masts; bands of music here and there discoursing lively tunes, and the glorious Stars and Stripes above all, floating and flaunting in a delicious breeze."[11]

The flotilla got underway early on the 5th, heading southeast to the Chesapeake and Fort Monroe—giving the appearance of threatening Petersburg from the rear—before entering the James and proceeding up-river. Major General William "Baldy" Smith's XVIII Corps was in the lead with its 16,978 infantrymen and 1,012 artillerymen. Following closely behind was General Gillmore's X Corps and his 16,812 infantrymen and 1,114 artillerymen.[12] Much as they had in 1862, the 39th undoubtedly enjoyed the scenery of the river travel and would have had occasion to spot their former camp at Harrison's Landing. Landing at Bermuda Hundred in the early hours of May 6, the regiment was a little over five miles from their previous summer home of two years ago. The weather was just as hot, but the situation could not be more different. There would be no languishing in camp while leaders and politicians squabbled. The Army of the Potomac was beginning the Overland Campaign and would soon engage General Lee in the Wilderness north of Richmond. South of Richmond, the Army of the James, had begun the Bermuda Hundred Campaign.

❖   ❖   ❖

Upon debarkation, the X Corps formed up and began a march to the west with the 39th in the lead and deployed as skirmishers. Bermuda Hundred is near a bend in the James, near where it converges with the Appomattox River, roughly 12 miles northeast of Petersburg and 20 miles southeast of Richmond. The movement was slow going, as firing was heard nearby, and scouts and skirmishers were frequently deployed forward to check the way. The march's path was filled with blankets, heavy coats and pants, and all manner of extra gear that men discarded throughout the day. Not only was the excess weight cumbersome on their backs, but the weather was so warm that such gear was not thought necessary. After being in the lead the entire day the 39th, and the rest of X Corps, stopped in the early evening and deployed pickets while setting up to bivouac for the night. The landing had achieved surprise, with only sporadic firing being heard as Federal gunboats and some small detachments of infantry had taken control of a few lightly or un-garrisoned defensive positions along the two rivers. Most importantly, the expedition took control of City Point, securing Federal access to the James and Appomattox Rivers.[13]

Shortly after this, Lieutenant Colonel Mann heard a great cheering building from the back of the line of troops, building as it neared the bivouac site. General Butler had come riding among the men. Upon reaching his picket line, Mann asked the General to stop for his safety. Butler asked if they had "seen any rebs," to which Mann replied that some cavalry had appeared a quarter mile ahead.[14] However, General Butler had a great interest in scouting forward with his staff to a creek and small church before heading back. While Mann offered to advance his line forward for the General's safety, Butler would have nothing of it and went ahead. Mann watched as Butler rode to a high point near Ware Bottom Church with his staff and inspected the surrounding area.

To Mann's horror, a Confederate cavalry squad appeared out of a thicket, yelling to halt and firing their weapons. With no armed escort, Butler's two orderlies soon had their horses shot out from under them and were taken prisoner. Butler and his staff turned and willed their horses back through the trees and towards the X Corps lines. General Butler no longer advanced beyond the lines, and Confederate forces were now well aware of the Federal presence. As he had recently done in Charleston, tasked to defend Petersburg from the X Corps was Confederate General P.G.T. Beauregard.[15]

Beauregard was frantically working to position forces in light of the Federal landing at Bermuda Hundred. Trains of men were being rushed towards Petersburg from North Carolina. The vast buildup up Federal troops at Gloucester Point and Yorktown had not gone unnoticed, but where precisely the U.S. forces would attempt to land wasn't known. The Confederate best guess had been an assault on Petersburg from the south via Fort Monroe. Now witnessing men land at Bermuda Hundred and move towards Petersburg and Richmond, Beauregard did the best he could with what he had. Similar to Stonewall Jackson's orders in the Shenandoah Valley, Beauregard was asked not to win any decisive victories, but to protect a vital interest and buy time for reinforcements. Working with his sub-ordinate generals Braxton Bragg and George Pickett, Beauregard had arriving forces concentrated at Port Walthall Junction, where the Richmond and Peters-burg Railroad connected with another line. In the estimation of the Confederate leadership, this is where Butler would attack.[16]

The men spent the 7th establishing a fortified camp roughly halfway between Petersburg and Richmond. Entrenchments were thrown up, while men cut down trees and spades "once more turned up as the trump card."[17] The firing they heard the day prior, and as they now established camp, was that of the XVIII Corps engaged with the enemy. After setting their end of Butler's line roughly three miles southeast of X Corps at a high point near a bend in the Appomattox River, Butler ordered units from XVIII Corps to the Richmond and Petersburg Railroad with support from X Corps. With this order, a series of continued arguments and disagreements continued between Gillmore and Butler. Perhaps because not all of X Corps had arrived from the march yet, Gillmore refused to offer X Corps men for the effort.[18]

Advancing only with XVIII Corps units, the Federal forces probed toward Port Walthall Junction late on the 6th. Some minor skirmishing, with very few casualties, had convinced Smith that the movement should be stopped for the day. Even though Smith's men outnumbered the Confederates by 4 to 1 and had artillery support, a well-placed rifle pit and return of fire had given him pause. Southern trains had been running in and out of the area, often empty, to give the appearance of a larger number of reinforcements.[19]

On the 7th, Gillmore gave in and provided men for an assault on the rail-road. With a brigade from the XVIII Corps, 8,000 men moved once again for Port Walthall Junction, where "quite a little fight" ensued.[20] The Federal force success-fully moved Confederate troops away from the junction and was able to cut 100 feet of track and burn a bridge. Army of the James casualties in the fighting were 24 dead, 268 wounded, and 53 missing. Confederate losses totaled just under 200 casualties.[21] Butler, however, decided not to pursue the retreating Confederate forces.

❖   ❖   ❖

Much of the Bermuda Hundred campaign's academic study is dedicated to understanding why Butler's Army of the James went on the defensive so soon instead of pressing the surprise of their landing and following up the victory at Port Walthall Junction. Grant himself would later write in his memoirs that "[But-ler] made no great effort to establish himself on that road and neglected to attack Petersburg, which was almost defenseless."[22] There are many potential reasons for the delay. Butler did not fully know the Confederate forces' total size and dispo-sition in the area and wanted to fortify a defensive line. Butler wanted to ensure he would not lose ground if reinforcements arrived from the south, or if Lee had success in the north and could turn towards Petersburg. The Army of the James was also still landing late movements of men and supplies at Bermuda Hundred, and then there was his relationship with the X Corps commander, which likely created trust issues. Grant had written to Halleck that he wished to link up with Butler as soon as possible, and knowing Grant was tied up with Lee in the Wilderness, Butler would delay a push to Richmond until Grant and Meade were closer. Thus, May 8 was a day for the Army of the James to rest and continue building reinforcements. The 39th spent an uneventful day on picket duty, returning to their camp that evening to await their next moves.[23]

Even though the Army of the James would now fortify their position at Bermuda Hundred and wait for the Army of the Potomac, there was still work to be done to damage Confederate supply lines. The 39th was up before the sun on May 9 and prepared to move with the entirety of both corps minus the three brigades that had actively fought at Port Walthall Junction. The XVIII Corps would return to the vicinity of Port Walthall Junction to complete destruction of the railroad there, while X Corps would head west to cut the rail near Chester Station. General Butler's goal was only to present a force that gave the appearance of threatening Petersburg long enough to tear up railroads and remain close enough to fall back if required and maintain the line at Bermuda Hundred.[24]

May 9 saw both Corps tearing up the railroad and one encountering the enemy. The XVIII Corps tore up more railroad at Port Walthall Junction, and X Corps destroyed the railroad, a telegraph line, and the depot at Chester Station. The work of the early day was unopposed by the enemy, but oppressive triple-digit heat made the physical labor of destroying the railroads all the worse. Upon leaving Port Walthall Junction, XVII Corps encountered a Confederate force after coming out of the woods into a clearing near their next objective—the road and rail bridges over Swift Creek. The Second Division's First Brigade fought off a small, disorganized Confederate attack in the sweltering heat, inflicting 137 casualties. However, First Brigade suffered 13 killed and 100 wounded, with Second Brigade suffering 26 losses in support. X Corps elements had filled in as reinforcements but given Confederate artillery in front of them and the exhaustion of the day, no follow up attack was made. The men buried the dead, ate what food they had, and set up in line of battle as best they could.[25]

❖   ❖   ❖

Late on May 9, Butler considered his plans for the following day. At his headquarters, he read a series of messages from the war department discussing Grant and Meade's Battle of the Wilderness. In the fighting that developed into nearly blind combat in dry woods set ablaze by the battle, the total casualties neared 30,000 men. While Secretary Stanton's letters to Butler talked of a significant victory in the Wilderness, most historians consider the struggle to have been tactically inconclusive. What was true, and what Stanton was relaying to Butler, was that Grant had disengaged and was heading southeast in a series of movements intended to put the Army of the Potomac between Richmond and General Lee's Army of Northern Virginia. Given that Butler's long-standing order from Grant was to stand ready to link up and drive on Richmond, he decided the Army of the James could no longer wait where they were.[26]

On May 10, the Army of the James began moving in Richmond's direction, tearing up more railroad as it went. The 39th, for the second day in a row, was near Ware Bottom Church. The day prior, they acted as a picket line, ensuring no movement came south from Richmond or Drewry's Bluff. On the 10th, they and the rest of the Brigade served as a rearguard covering the Federal advance. Around midday, a Confederate probe attempting to ascertain Butler's intentions ran into the Army of the James along the Richmond turnpike between Chester Station and the James.[27]

Portions of General Terry's X Corps First Division fought a Confederate force of roughly 2,000 men for approximately 90 minutes in heat approaching triple digits. While wooded area prevented the 39th from seeing the action, Valentine Randolph wrote that they could hear constant fire and yelling, and that "three or four of the musket balls came whistling past where we were stationed."[28] The 67th Ohio turned back multiple Confederate advances, and as Federal reinforcements arrived to the field, Confederate forces retired toward Drewry's Bluff. General Terry's division suffered 280 casualties, inflicting 249 on the Confederate force.[29] Nothing was gained by either side in the engagement, other than some additional railroad torn up by the Army of the James, and the Confederates taking solace in stopping the Federal advance.

❖ ❖ ❖

For the second day in a row, and as the story had gone throughout the entire war, the 39th Illinois was often near major fighting—often their own division or even brigade being engaged—but remained just off to the side. The situation would soon change that, however. Beauregard's field commanders, Generals Braxton Bragg and George Pickett had protected Petersburg from a larger force's landing at the expense of only some railroad and a few casualties. However, Major General Philip Sheridan's cavalry, detached from the Army of the Potomac, was moving towards Richmond from the north, and it was apparent Butler intended to move towards Richmond from the south.

Finally, receiving his full complement of reinforcements, Beauregard decided that his forces must take the offensive. General Lee was engaged in heavy fighting with Grant at Spotsylvania Courthouse and could not detach reinforcements. If the Army of the Potomac got past or outflanked Lee and headed for Richmond, Beauregard's force would have nowhere to go. Beauregard would rally his current and arriving forces near Drewry's Bluff and look to attack south to push the Army of the James off of Richmond and Petersburg's doorsteps.[30]

The next ten days would see fighting that spared no element of the Army of the James, most especially not the 39th Illinois.

12

The Battle of Drewry's Bluff

Hiram Phillips was born in Piketon, Ohio, in 1822, and at seven his family moved to Indiana. Phillips received an excellent education, and became a teacher himself. In 1846, at age 24, Phillips enlisted for one year in the 1st Regiment of Illinois Volunteers to fight in the Mexican-American War. During this service, he fought in the battle of Buena Vista under General, and future President, Zachary Taylor.

Phillips was living in LeRoy, Illinois, when the Civil War began, and given his previous experience was determined to serve. Garnering the respect of a 39-year-old war veteran, Phillips had little trouble recruiting men, filling it in good part with LeRoy men and those from adjacent counties, and took them to Chicago where they became Company I of the 39th Illinois.

Given the age, and experience, of Captain Phillips, Company I became one of the most efficient and disciplined companies in the regiment—mettle that would be put to the test at the Battle of Drewry's Bluff.[1]

LATE ON MAY 11, 1864, a terrible rain and lightning storm erupted on the 30,000 men encamped with the Army of the James, and 18,000 Confederate troops near Drewry's Bluff and Proctor's Creek. The men assumed the morning would bring movement after a day of rest and fortifying the camp and assumed it would be the beginning of a drive on Richmond. However, Butler planned to demonstrate forces in such a way that would prevent Beauregard from moving reinforcements to Lee while he continued to disrupt Confederate lines of communication.[2]

General Smith's XVIII Corps would move in Richmond's direction on the main turnpike, while General Gillmore's X Corps would form a rearguard against attack from Petersburg. The demonstration of forces would serve as a cover for Brigadier General August Kautz's cavalry division to perform a raid in the Confederate rear and tear up the Richmond and Danville Railroad. An additional aim would include the movement of XVIII Corps' Third Division. Under the command of Brigadier General Edward Hincks, The Third Division was made up of an artillery company and two brigades of all-Black infantry regiments. These regiments would seek to create a second fortified position for Butler's Army, opposite the current one, on the Appomattox River. While all of this alone would be a success, accomplishing it would also allow Butler to retain the possibility of fully pressing an attack and advancing on Richmond.[3]

As a mile-long column of the Army of the James set off on the morning of May 12, the 39th was part of the X Corps element forming the rear guard to deter an attack from Petersburg. Likely dejected at feeling left out once again, the regiment spent the day improving trenches and fortifications with their weapons nearby, ready to move at a moment's notice. In a heavy downpour, the Army of the James was creeping forward, driving off some Confederate pickets, and occasionally receiving musket and artillery fire. The main body of XVIII Corps reached Proctor's Creek but took up a defensive position. The rain made visibility difficult and moving slow. General Smith knew he would need reinforcements to cross the creek because of the Confederate disposition on the other side and decided against further movement until they arrived. Portions of X Corps arrived in the late afternoon, and the front line of the Army of the James spent the night trying to stay dry, unable to start fires for warmth or cooking.[4]

While the men at the front lay miserably on the wet ground, the night and following morning were so quiet that the 39th could sleep in and enjoy a day of rest—rest they soon would be glad to have gotten.[5] During the day on the 13th, General Butler sent Gillmore and his X Corps element west to outflank the Confederate position facing Smith at Proctor's Creek. Still moving in a downpour of rain, the men overtook a small Confederate cavalry unit, and otherwise operated without harassment as they moved toward the Confederate rear.[6]

To Gillmore's right, XVIII Corps continued their advance of the previous day. Gillmore had ordered elements to the top of a hill overlooking Proctor's Creek and sent others across but found no opposition as the rebels had dropped back to the fortifications of Drewry's Bluff overnight. General Smith's force continued into thick woodland and spent midday into the early afternoon encountering growing opposition from Confederate pickets as they approached a line of enemy earthworks. Not knowing the disposition of the Confederate defenders, more reinforcements were called forward.[7]

As XVIII Corps was skirmishing along their line in front of the Confederate left, X Corps had called up artillery and was preparing to lay into the Confederate line's right flank. In very heavy skirmishing that saw both Confederate and Federal lines falling back and reforming, Gillmore's men eventually took positions vacated by Confederate soldiers who had retreated to the east and the fortifications of Drewry's Bluff. The advance and skirmishing of the last two days had caused a fair number of casualties, but Butler now had the Army of the James in what he felt was an excellent position. X Corps had turned the Confederate right flank, and the Federal line stretched from west of the Richmond and Petersburg Railroad, over the Richmond Turnpike, and in front of the Confederate left. Kautz's cavalry was behind enemy lines tearing up railroads and telegraph lines, and the Confederates could not send any reinforcements north to Richmond or Lee's aid. With strong fortifications to his rear to guard against attack from Petersburg, Butler's plan was unfolding as desired.[8]

◈   ◈   ◈

Shortly after 2:00 a.m. on May 14, the 39th was called out from camp to move up. At 4:00 a.m., the regiment was marching up the Richmond Turnpike, headed for the Richmond and Petersburg Railroad to guard an ammunition train preparing to head to the front. The regiment arrived at Chester Station, roughly two miles from the emerging front, where they waited for two hours for some coal cars to arrive to transport wounded men. G and I Companies were dispatched to push the coal cars to the front while Company F was sent to do reconnaissance left of the fighting. The balance of the regiment stayed at Chester Station to guard the ammunition train. Near the front, the men from G and I would load wounded men from the roadside into the coal cars, then push them to Chester Station, returning to find more men ready to be loaded. "There were some horrible sights to be seen," wrote Valentine Randolph recalling his duties with Company I, "but this was only a foretaste of what we were soon to witness."[9]

The Army of the James had continued their advance at roughly the same time the 39th had left camp that morning. XVIII Corps sent skirmishers forward towards the Confederate fortifications but found only rebel skirmishers. Smith's corps moved forward slowly, and by 8:00 a.m. had driven the Confederate guards back. Widening the probe, by 9:00 a.m., the XVIII Corps had overtaken the entire line that had faced them and now saw a second and more formidable looking line in the distance. The new Confederate line was made up of well-dug fortifications that extended west, just over the Richmond and Petersburg Railroad, then turned north towards Drewry's Bluff.[10]

On the left, or X Corps, side of the advance, General Gillmore ordered Alfred Terry's First Division to cross Proctor's Creek. The Division linked up with John Turner's Second Division to its east and began its advance forward. Terry's division was the left flank of the almost two-mile-wide Army of the James line. Just to the west of the railroad was the First Brigade of XVIII Corps First Division, detached as reinforcement and commanded by Gilman Marston. Brigadier General Marston and his four New York regiments were the Federal line's far left, with only some cavalry to the west. Just as their XVIII Corps counterparts had done, the X Corps slowly advanced on the left, driving off Confederate skirmishers, and came to a halt in front of the imposing second line of Confederate defenses.[11]

Late in the morning, skirmishers in the center of the Federal line began probing forward once again, while regiments began occupying and refortifying the abandoned Confederate works. To the right of the Richmond Turnpike, Federal skirmishers cleared a wooded area and came into view of Confederate fortifications. As the rain returned, the sound of muskets and artillery joined the thunder across the entire two-mile line. Beauregard's artillery accurately targeted Butler's line, and Federal artillery attempted to answer as sharpshooters from both corps did their best to neutralize the Confederate gunners.[12]

On the left end of the line, General Terry's First Division took the worst of the day's punishment with eventual casualties reaching 117.[13] Terry called for First Division reinforcements, likely from First Brigade, which was manning the fortifications at Bermuda Hundred. Since the 39th had been detached to guard the ammunition train at Chester Station, they were the closest, and the call to the front was for the Phalanx. At 1:30 p.m., the regiment, minus Company H, who remained with the ammunition train, was marching towards the sound of rifles and artillery, headed for the Federal left. As the regiment reached the rear of the

line, Osborn and his company commanders had the men hug the ground as musket balls whizzed by, and the occasional shell crashed in. During this time, a handful of men were wounded by artillery rounds and sharpshooters. After what must
have seemed an eternity, Terry sent the regiment to the far-left end of the line and
attached them to Marston's Brigade.[14]

The regiment was tasked to support an artillery battery and waited in the
woods just left of the railroad while the battery was positioned on a small ridge.
The battery in position and beginning its work, the regiment moved to the base
of the rise once again amidst artillery and musket fire. Leading his men out of the
woods, Osborn rode into a clearing now in full view of the Confederate fortifications. A shell crashed in amongst the men, sending grapeshot into Osborn's arm
and fracturing his elbow. In great pain and losing blood, the 39th commander
remained on the field as he hurried his men to the ridge's base. Reaching a relatively safe position, the 39th laid flat as the battery did its work with its own heavy
losses.[15]

As darkness approached, Osborn realized his regiment's position was as
secure as possible and finally gave in to the pain and blood loss. As Lieutenant
Colonel Mann was in camp on the sick list, Osborn passed command to Major
Linton and turned his horse towards a field hospital. Being told the offending shot
could not be located in his arm, the Colonel was bandaged up and told to return
to the fortifications at Bermuda Hundred. Arriving back in camp, Osborn was
met by Lieutenant Colonel Mann, who saw his commander's condition. "The rebels are going to give us hell!" Osborn told him. "The regiment is fully officered,
Major Linton will handle it well; and bear in mind you will soon have a chance to
command it in battle." The next morning, Osborn took the hospital boat full of
wounded men to Fort Monroe.[16]

❖   ❖   ❖

Back at the Federal left flank, Major Samuel Linton was grateful for the
opportunity to "handle it well" after a ball had ripped through his coat earlier
in the day. The firing waned after dark, the artillery battery retired to the rear,
and the 39th moved forward, their right side now on the Richmond and Petersburg Railroad. All along General Butler's line, reinforcements moved forward
where required, fortifying their positions the best they could in the dark. Along
the turnpike, some center regiments ran telegraph wire amongst tree stumps in
front of the defenses for an extra layer of protection. The men of the 39th took
turns sleeping with their weapons in hand. A third of the regiment slept while the
others kept watch. Foretelling how difficult rest would be on the cold, wet ground;
around midnight, there was firing across the line, and the regiment was on its
feet. Two men were shot, and the episode was over as quickly as it had begun.[17]

Aside from some moderate casualties on his line's far left side, the day had
been a good enough one for Benjamin Butler. The probes and push forward
had forced the Confederates back from their outer works, and Butler's two-day
advance had troops straddling both the Richmond and Petersburg Railroad and
the Richmond Turnpike. While the James River was too shallow for gunboats to

be brought in to pound the position, the Army of the James had established a line roughly ten miles from Richmond while the cavalry cut more railroad. With an entire X Corps Third Division at Port Walthall Junction still to pull from, Butler could launch an offensive that broke open a hole to Richmond.[18] The 39th's contributions to the day's efforts had come at the cost of 14 wounded and two killed.[19]

❖　❖　❖

Sunday, May 15 would not be a day of rest for those who might have wished it to be. At first light, the 39th moved off the top of the ridge they had spent the night on and went to work, establishing a line of rifle pits and earthworks. With the hill protecting the left of the regiment and piled up earthen material on the right, the 39th had the occasional Confederate shell sail safely overhead. The 39th's position with Marston's Brigade on the X Corps left was roughly 600 yards from the Confederate rifle pits and slightly uphill. Another 400 yards beyond the Confederate entrenchments were the forts of Drewry's Bluff that were on ground level with where the 39th was. Between the two armies was a bare field of tree stumps framed to the Confederate north by a creek and the wooded area of the bluff, and the Federal south by woods and Proctor's Creek. The Federal left sat against the Richmond and Petersburg Railroad and a wooded area, while the right sat against a wooded area that opened up before the James River another mile to the east. Through the approximate center of it all ran the Richmond Turnpike.[20]

In the very early hours of the day, Baldy Smith planned an attack on the Confederate line at Butler's behest. Smith would use a brigade from the right and one from Third Division at Port Walthall Junction, and send a column toward the fortifications in front of them. Needing a force to guard the assault's flank, Smith requested Marston's Brigade be returned from the X Corps left. Unaware of the left flank's casualties the day prior and owing to the time it would take to move the brigade, the attack planning was called off until reinforcements could be better placed. Smith also had reservations about the fact that the Federal line did not stretch to the James. The decision to abort plans for an offensive was a de facto decision to move the Army of the James to defensive operations.[21]

A defensive posture likely did not bother Butler and perhaps was his preferred course of action. Major General Philip Sheridan had arrived nearby the day prior, and on the 15th he gave Butler the details of the Army of the Potomac's Battle of the Wilderness. Upon telling Butler his cavalry would need a week to return to fighting condition, Butler reportedly told Sheridan that Grant would reach Richmond by then. His army had control of the railroad and turnpike between Petersburg and Richmond, had tied up Beauregard's forces, and prevented them from moving to Lee's aid. He had established a fortified base of operations and forward defensive line. In Butler's mind, Grant would arrive at a location prepared for the two armies to join and drive on Richmond.[22]

If the state of affairs made General Butler satisfied to take a defensive stance, they were forcing P.G.T. Beauregard to plan for an offensive. With Grant attempting to push Lee towards Richmond, and the situation such that it was with the Army of the James, Beauregard needed to act. The Confederate general contacted

General William Whiting, stationed near Petersburg, to notify him that the situation required his support. While Confederate leadership considered having Whiting's Division march far to the left of the Federal flank to join up with the men at Drewry's Bluff, it was not believed they could afford the time that would require. Beauregard ordered Whiting to advance north towards Port Walthall Junction and wait for the sound of battle to begin. At such a time, Whiting was to determine where the bulk of the fight was occurring and smash his division into the Federal flank or rear.[23]

The rest of the morning was mostly quiet along the Federal line with an occasional exchange of fire between sharpshooters and men on picket. Confederate artillery did some firing, and the 39th was again called on to support a battery brought forward to answer it. Within range of Confederate guns, the men were ordered to keep their heads down, but the regiment still suffered two more dead and two severely wounded. The Army of the James spent an afternoon of alternating rain and scorching sun dodging the sporadic fire, reinforcing their entrenchments, and ensuring their flanks were secured as re-supply wagons were brought forward. On the left, General Terry's brigade commanders had a bad feeling, however. The men along the railroad could see Confederate trains arriving regularly to the north, and their position along the ridge afforded a view of large numbers of Confederate troops repositioning along their lines.[24]

The 39th used the cover of darkness to make final improvements and strengthen their works. Near the Richmond Turnpike, Doctor Clark and other surgeons put the finishing touches on a field hospital in a clearing inside a wooded area near Butler's headquarters. Retiring early, the doctors feared what may come in the morning. Back on the Federal line, sharing the surgeon's fears, many men held makeshift religious services.[25]

A fog drifted in from the river late in the night and filled the dark, soon to be, battlefield. A Confederate cavalry unit rushed a Federal picket line and was run off by XVIII Corps men firing blindly into the fog. Reinforcements were requested by Brigadier General Charles Heckerman, whose First Brigade of Second Division was the right flank of the Federal line. The request never made it to General Smith; however, an ominous sign for the right flank come morning. More Confederate cavalry drove back Federal pickets on the right flank shortly after midnight as Beauregard probed the line, and parts of XVIII Corps lost contact. The right flank of the Army of the James was soon to be in danger, but in the confusion, darkness, and fog of the evening, that message did not make it to Baldy Smith.[26]

❖   ❖   ❖

At 3:00 a.m., on May 16, 1864, a 39th Illinois member who wasn't even on the line was one of the first to learn a battle would soon occur. Doctor Clark and his fellow surgeons were jarred awake by a Confederate shell that came crashing through the top of their occupied house. The men hurried outside, unable to even see the debris in the blinding fog.[27]

XVIII Corps pickets began sounding the general alarm around the same time as their outposts encountered Confederate skirmishers on the Federal right flank. At 4:45 a.m., Confederate General Robert Ransom ordered his Division on the Confederate left forward through the fog. The Federal pickets on the right flank headed back towards the XVIII Corps line, as regiments anxiously awaited their entry into the rifle pits so they could start firing. The pickets safely inside the lines, Heckerman's brigades sent the first round of musket fire blindly through the fog towards the advancing rebels. After the first Federal volley, Ransom's men picked up their pace toward the Federal line, as more brigades followed them, and Confederate artillery began firing over the top of the advancing infantry.[28]

The scene was soon one of disarray, as XVIII Corps men were firing blindly into the advance, and Confederate infantry fell to the ground. The second wave of advance also fell to the ground, just as many from tripping over bodies and tree stumps in the fog as from being shot. On the right flank the Army of the James continued to fire and reload as the rebels struggled to maintain their lines but continued forward. The two lead Confederate brigades were stalling and becoming separated from each other in the fog, with a couple of regiments becoming tangled in the telegraph wire that had been strung out.[29]

While the Confederate attacks were stalling further down the line, however, the Confederate left was soon close enough to see through the fog that the Federal right could be turned. Two Confederate regiments swung wide, then crossed over Old Stage Road and into the far-right regiment of Heckerman's Brigade, the 9th New Jersey. Companies bent back their lines to form a new flank, but the effort only worked for a short time. Heckerman was soon forced to order the 9th to retreat and fall back with Confederate attackers close behind. The retreat now left the road that XVIII Corps—or worse, Confederate forces—could use to reach the Bermuda Hundred camp undefended.[30]

Heckerman's Brigade's remaining regiments continued to do their job, however, and were stalling the other Confederate attacks and inflicting heavy losses further down the line. To the right, however, another Confederate regiment had discovered Old Stage Road had no opposition, and the Federal right flank was about to be peeled back. In the fog, General Heckerman lost his way in the woods and was taken prisoner. Following the 9th's retreat, the flank was now held by the 23rd Massachusetts. However, their commander had been killed early in the battle, and now without a brigade commander, the 23rd's senior Captain retreated. Their casualties were significant, as they hurried to join the 9th New Jersey remnants in a fallback position.[31]

The chain of events was now fully set in motion. The retreat of the 23rd left the next regiment, the 27th Massachusetts, now fully exposed on their flank. Even though they had fought off three separate Confederate advances in their original position, they could now do nothing more than fire one last volley from their muskets before many of them were captured. The 25th Massachusetts was now the exposed regiment, and something needed to be done to secure the Federal line. Losing various commanders, and the confusion of being surrounded by the fog, led to lower-ranking officers needing to make immediate decisions. The Lieutenant Colonel of the 25th ordered his men to fix bayonets and charge to the Confederate attackers' rear. All organization was lost in the foggy rearward attack, and they lost 140 men, but the action allowed the 98th New York to align themselves to the right and establish a new flank.[32]

The time was now roughly 5:45 a.m., and the first bits of light were trying to break through the still thick fog. The temporary stabilizing of the XVIII Corps right allowed the Army of the James to plug holes and attempt to push back. Meanwhile, the quick success of only parts of the Confederate advance had become an issue in the fog, as regiments became disoriented when losing contact with each other. Realizing his successful regiments were now disoriented, others were getting cut up at the line, and nearly all were out of ammunition, Ransom paused his assault to regroup, re-arm, and call for reinforcements.

Twenty minutes prior, Baldy Smith had apprised General Butler of the situation and ordered Albert Ames to send a regiment from his reserves towards the right side of the line to re-secure Old Stage Road and the Federal right flank. With the new flank currently holding and awaiting the reinforcements, Smith had his artillery pieces, and supply wagons moved to the rear. Batteries could not find, and range targets in the fog, and the XVIII Corps commander didn't want to see his equipment captured by a surrounding force. As the hour approached 6:00 a.m., Butler wrote to his X Corps commander that an urgent movement from his force, into the Confederate advance's flank, was desperately needed.[33]

❖　　❖　　❖

On the X Corps side of the fight, men had been awake since the firing began, wondering when the battle would reach their position. Butler's message reached Gillmore at 6:20 a.m., and he ordered General Terry's First Division and General John Turner's Second Division to prepare for the attack. Thirty minutes prior, however, Confederate troops had engaged the center of the Federal line on either side of the turnpike. As regiments had made successive moves to the right in their efforts to preserve the flank, X Corps Brigades had thinned themselves out, moving right to stay in touch with their counterparts. Now, just as Terry received the order to prepare to move, he reported that a significant force of Confederate skirmishers had probed his brigades, but that it had been easily repelled. Gillmore, however, reported this to Butler as an assault on the left flank.[34]

The figurative, and quite literal, fog of war was wreaking havoc on Federal command and control. As Turner was preparing to join forces with Terry and advance to the right, the XVIII Corps brigade just to his right was shifting in continued reinforcement of the turned flank and protecting the Army of the James' access to the turnpike. As had been the case all morning, the Army of the James had been pulling from the left to plug on the right. While the tactic had been working, and was stalling, the assault, something would eventually have to give. Soon Terry was sending a regiment to the aid of XVIII Corps, as Turner continued to struggle to stay in contact with them. The actual fog of the battlefield prevented him from seeing. The metaphorical fog of deciphering his commanders' messages caused Gillmore to believe his forces' rearward movement were retreats and not reinforcements to the right. Even though an hour had passed since ordered by Butler, Gillmore continued to hold back the attack fearing for his own position on the left.[35]

On the left, the 39th, and the rest of Marston's brigade, noticed regiments around them moving to the rear and the right. Moving from double to single rank, the 39th filled in the space left by departing regiments. The 39th was now spaced rather thinly and had no forces behind them either. Receiving occasional skirmishing fire in front of them, the noise to the right of the 39th continued to grow. The gap between the two corps continued to grow, and Turner was continually moving Second Division elements to the right. By 8:30, five X Corps regiments had been moved to the right to support XVIII corps in some form or fashion. The X Corps' right side was in a fight for their lives to save the right flank, while the left side was rapidly thinning.[36]

Shortly after 8:30, Gillmore finally made his movement—over two-and-a-half hours after initially ordered. Finally, seeing more clearly the situation on the right, Gillmore realized that a thrust to the right by X Corps could smash into the Confederate attack's left side and turn the tide of the battle. Terry moved his own three brigades to the right, along with Turner, while Marston's troops stayed in place on the left to disguise the movement. Both divisions struggled because of a delay in receiving the orders and the fact that Confederate infantry had finally exposed the gap between the two corps. By terrible coincidence, Confederate infantry had also begun advancing on the Federal left as all this was happening. The 39th was firing on a steady advance of Virginia infantry. The Yates Phalanx turned back two simultaneous attacks on their right and left, only to realize Marston's Brigade was the only one remaining.[37]

Unable to fully disengage X Corps and move to the aid of XVIII Corps, it became clear to Butler that the Army of the James needed to conduct a fighting withdrawal to their fortified entrenchments. There were reports that, combined with the initial forces that turned the Federal flank, Beauregard now had men crossing the James River. The delay in the X Corps movement had prevented Smith's men from doing anything other than attempting to preserve the right flank, and that effort was now failing. Butler ordered Gillmore to fall back to the rear of Smith's forces in movement designed to clear, and hold, the path back to the entrenchments. However, Gillmore was equally concerned about his own path of retreat and his own flank as he began this movement. At roughly 9:30 a.m., Gillmore ordered General Marston to bring two regiments, and whatever remnants of brigades were left on the right, to the rear of the X Corps line to ensure the Richmond Turnpike was held. This left one regiment, 550 men, west of the railroad, to protect the Army of the James' left flank.[38]

❖　❖　❖

The lone Illinois regiment in the Army of the James, the regiment from the westernmost state of the two corps, was now the lone and most western regiment on the line. The 39th's skirmishers along a fence near the railroad were driven back into the rifle pits, and the entire line of the regiment opened fire on the enemy. Confederate infantry fell to the ground directly in front of the 39th, and a great cheer went up as the attacking Virginians fell back. However, to the 39th's right, the Confederate column closed ranks around their fallen comrades and continued forward. Amidst the fighting directly in front of them, the regiment had not noticed, or been informed, of the X Corps full withdrawal. Spreading itself thinner and further right, the Phalanx realized it had not been confronting one or two enemy regiments, but five. The men watched as Virginia regiments' colors fell to the ground multiple times, only to be picked up and continued forward.[39]

Near the center of the former Federal line, Turner's Second Division had been flanked in the gap between X and XVIII Corps and fought its way out to follow their orders to retire and secure the roads back to camp. Regiment by regiment covering each other's retreat, the men passed the stations where surgeons were furiously trying to help men amidst the ongoing fighting. The division moved south of Proctor's Creek and took up a position on the east side of the Richmond Turnpike. While parts of Terry's Division made it quickly south of the creek, many continued in heavy fighting that delayed their movement. Finally, the Second Division made their way down the Turnpike.[40]

While the 39th had initially been ordered to guard the Federal left flank and hold their position at the railroad, they were now, very much unknown to them, serving as a desperate speed bump protecting the X Corps retreat. The 39th did not receive an order to withdraw with the rest of X Corps, and in fact, received no order at all. With Marston gone and General Terry directing First Division's movements, Samuel Linton was on his own to decipher his superiors' intentions and protect his regiment.

Acting on the last order he had received—to fill the trenches and hold them—Linton ordered the men of Companies C, G, and I to fall back to the woods behind the rest of the regiment to reform his thin line into two ranks. Linton planned that the 39th could then continue to fight and would also be in a position for the two lines to cover each other's withdrawal, which he knew would soon be required. The order was misunderstood by some, however, and many of these men took it as an order to retreat altogether. Frustrated, Linton ran into the woods himself, shouting for the men to return and re-form behind the original line. Fearing his efforts were in vain, Linton headed toward the left flank of the regiment. The 39th's right had been turned by a Confederate column advancing in the railroad cut's safety, and the rebels stormed up and over the railroad, firing into and occupying the rifle pits. Intending to have his left side fall back and to the right, to cover the regiment's full retreat, Linton shouted to his men.[41]

Crossing the open space between the woods and the 39th's line, Linton was struck by an enemy bullet. However, as he was hit, he saw Captain Leroy Baker, of Wilmington, rallying the men back to the line. Companies C, G, and I charged into the enemy fire coming from their recently occupied rifle pits and engaged in vicious close combat. Realizing that the regiment must drive back the enemy on the right before they could retreat, Linton struggled to his feet and headed that way when he was shot again in the lung. Regaining the rifle pits, and now attempting to run off the Confederate attackers, Company C Commander, James Wightman of Odell waved his sword atop the works to rally his men and was shot down. His men rallied to his side and ran off the Confederate attack. In the words of Doctor Clark, "the last feeling that he probably was ever conscious of in this life was one of pride and exultation at the success of his comrades." Momentarily, the 39th Illinois, now led by the 29-year-old Captain Baker, had stabilized the situation.[42]

However, the victory was short-lived as the men realized they were still flanked from the right, and an enemy force was moving north up the railroad cut from their rear. The men of G Company pointed their rifles at the Confederate troops calling for them to surrender. Ever present in the 39th's most trying moments, Captain Rudd ordered his men not to fire while giving the enemy a chance to surrender.

"Surrender!" yelled a Confederate officer.

"Surrender yourself!" answered Rudd.[43]

However, whether by accident or intent, somebody fired a shot, and the entire Confederate force joined the volley. Fire poured into the 39th's line as men looked for rifle pits or any cover they could find while returning the fire themselves, but the regiment was surrounded. Doing their best to cover their comrades, every man was now retreating for himself under heavy fire to the cover of the timber, and what they hoped was the new X Corps line.[44]

Roughly twenty minutes since Major Linton's second wounding, the regiment was now entirely in retreat. The 39th cut its way out of the engagement, no easy feat as they continued to face fire from all directions. They had to cross the open space from their pits to the timber while taking fire from the line, then move into the woods and take fire there. Men moved south, paralleling the railroad, towards Chester Station from where they had preceded to the front some 48 hours ago. Sergeant Spencer and Private Cook, of G Company, traversed down the railroad together when they saw Confederate troops on the other side. No sooner had the two men fired into the Confederate squad when others who had been hiding in the brush appeared and ordered them to surrender. Ignoring the request, Spencer and Cook ran, with Cook taking a bullet through the hand. Seeing how much blood Cook was losing, Spencer ran with Cook all the way to Chester Station and put him in one of the coal cars for the wounded.[45]

As Spencer and Cook neared Chester Station, they found the 39th and regiments from X Corps assisting the wounded while able-bodied men attempted to form up with their regiments. In command of the ambulance train evacuating the wounded was Company B Lieutenant Lesmore Kidder of Bloomington. He was badly wounded when a Confederate cavalry regiment swooped in and escaped only by virtue of having a horse.[46] The rebel cavalry detachment came storming through the throng of beleaguered men trying to round up prisoners. Company I Private George Riddle, of Le Roy, had been carrying Sergeant Samuel Gillmore, also of Le Roy, away from the line when he saw the cavalry coming. Riddle told Gillmore he couldn't carry him anymore as he looked for help.

"Oh, God! George, don't leave me!" cried Gillmore. However, Riddle promised to save him and found a member of the First New York Mounted Rifles who had been on picket duty and was now attempting to run off the enemy cavalry.

Riddle threw Gillmore on the New Yorker's saddle as the enemy closed within shooting distance.

"What, in the name of God, are you going to do?" asked the horseman.

"You take care of him and I'll take care of myself," answered Riddle. Riddle then grabbed hold of the stirrup as the horse took off and let himself be drug along the ground until he could hang on no longer and rolled off and under a log for cover. There he encountered company-mates John Berry of Santa Anna and Jeff Everts of Le Roy. The three men hid in some brush as the cavalry passed. All four, including Sergeant Gilmore who had better days to come, made it back to camp.[47]

Less fortunate were men like Company K sergeant Emile Guntz, of Chicago, Company E private Hugh Snee of Rockville, and the senior most enlisted man, Sergeant Major Reese Bishop of Le Roy. Marched off with guns to their heads in Guntz's case, or so badly wounded they were carried off in Bishop's case, they were put on a train to Macon, Georgia, and ultimately found themselves prisoners in "that hell-hole, Andersonville, the most God-forsaken place that men were ever put in—not fit for cattle." Snee found a way to escape and return to the regiment in September, and the German-born Guntz would be fortunate enough to return to the regiment after a prisoner exchange six month later. Bishop, however, was not as fortunate, and died at Andersonville in November. Homer Plimpton would soon begin acting in Bishop's stead.[48]

❖　❖　❖

At one point surrounded and in hand-to-hand combat with the enemy, the 39th Illinois Infantry had maintained the left flank while the Army of the James retreated and somehow extricated itself back to the entrenchments of Bermuda Hundred. After two days on the line, under constant fire, then nearly 13 hours of ongoing battle, the regiment took stock of what had happened. Colonel Osborn was in a hospital at Fort Monroe, Adjutant Joseph Walker, of Lockport, was mortally wounded, and Captain Wightman was dead. Company E privates Willy Ely, from Concord, and William Brown, of Chicago, had carried Linton away from the field under heavy pursuit—ultimately having to hide him and evade capture. Linton lay alone for some time before Captain Baker came upon him, making it back to camp but seriously wounded. Captains Andrew Wheeler and Hiram Phillips, and Lieutenants Lesmore Kidder and Elisha Kingsbury were all wounded as well. Phillips was taken prisoner and would languish in Libby Prison, in Richmond, for three months before being paroled and discharged. Kingsbury's arm wound was severe enough to require amputation. The 39th Illinois suffered approximately 120 killed, wounded, or missing in the time between leaving for Chester Station and returning to Bermuda Hundred—one fifth of the men who saw fighting.[49] Being told his wounds were mortal, Adjutant Walker told Doctor Clark, "it is well," and died shortly after.[50]

In the words of General Butler, the Thirty-Ninth had "fought most gallantly, and have suffered most severely" in their first experience of significant fighting during a major battle.[51] "It" was not "all well," however. What had started ten days

Army of the James entrenchments at Bermuda Hundred (Library of Congress: LC-DIG-ppmsca-35182).

ago as a promising opportunity to end the war now had the men on their heels. The Army of the Potomac was engaged in brutal fighting to the north, and the Army of the James was back behind the entrenchments of their Bermuda Hundred camp.

While back in camp on May 19, Oscar Rudd sat down to write a letter to the mother of Corporal Neriah Kendall in Joliet. As Kendall's company commander, Rudd was forced to relay the news of the battle, and that men had reported seeing Kendall shot in the head and crying out on the ground. No doubt painting a picture of the hasty withdrawal, Rudd informed Kendall's mother that his body could not be brought off. "It is my painful duty to announce to you that your noble son, Neriah, is probably dead," Rudd wrote, "though there is a bare possibility that he yet lives."[52]

What had been the first involvement by the Yates Phalanx in major fighting would most definitely not be their last.

13

Ware Bottom Church
and the End of a Campaign

Al C. Sweester was born in Maine in 1839, moving around the country
at a very young age to Mississippi, back to Maine, and then to Wisconsin before ending up in Bloomington, Illinois. In 1858, the excitement
of the Pike's Peak gold rush took Sweester west, but he soon realized
that his wealth would not be made there and returned to Bloomington.

Sweester was working in the milling business when the war broke out
and he enlisted in the 8th Illinois Infantry for the three months' service.
After mustering out and returning home, Sweester took an active role
in forming a company that eventually became Company B of the 39th
Illinois. Sweester was popular and well-liked among the men up until
he was wounded so badly on June 2 that one of his legs required amputation. He would come close to losing his life, but survive and return
home. His post-war days included being elected to the office of city collector and then an appointment to Deputy U.S. Collector of Internal
Revenue. He was also quite active in leadership positions of the states
Grand Army of the Republic organization.[1]

HAD THE BATTLE OF DREWRY'S BLUFF been a boxing title fight, it likely would
have been judged a split-decision in favor of Beauregard. Even though the Army
of the James re-formed a new line as the 39th was battling on the left flank, Butler
believed he was outnumbered and ordered a full withdrawal to the Bermuda Hundred entrenchments. Butler thought he had been accomplishing his mission to
disrupt lines of communication and prevent Beauregard from dispatching troops
to help Lee against Grant. Conversely, he now worried that part of Lee's army
could combine with Beauregard's to drive out the Army of the James. Falling back
to and continuing work on the Bermuda Hundred fortifications would ensure the
Army of the Potomac had a base to arrive at—and an army with which to link up.[2]

Butler attempted to paint a positive picture to his men and superiors in
stating that objectives had been accomplished. The smart decision was now to
improve the fortifications while waiting for Grant. However, this was a hard pill to
swallow for many of the men as they had seemingly lost the engagement, given up
positions on the railroad and turnpike, and suffered over 3,000 casualties—1,388
of which were now Confederate prisoners. Moreover, and equally damaging,
many of Butler's officers were questioning his abilities, and he was in open disagreement with his Corps commanders—and they with him. To this end, General Sheridan brought word back to Grant that he believed Butler unfit to lead.

Thinking he was outnumbered and under-served, Butler pleaded with Secretary of War Stanton for more men, claiming he had kept supply lines open and needed to prepare for Grant's arrival.[3]

For Grant's part, he was becoming distraught. Lee had blocked him from reaching Richmond once again in terrible fighting at Spotsylvania Court House, and Federal efforts in the Shenandoah were not going well. Grant thought Butler's efforts to destroy the railroad and supply lines had been a moderate success at best and was frustrated Butler had not struck at an almost defenseless Petersburg. Grant now needed to decide how to coordinate best the actions of the Army of the Potomac and the Army of the James. He knew Butler's position was geographically excellent, and that he could use the surrounding terrain to hold a large area with a single line of fortification. The good news was that Butler may send some troops to Grant's aid while still holding his position; the bad news was that the same geography that made it so defensible made it challenging to launch another offensive. The expression came that Butler was in a "bottle tightly corked." Beauregard had capped the Army of the James from spilling out through the neck of its location, but the contents were perfectly safe inside the bottle.[4]

While Butler and the U.S. high command sought to put a positive spin on a tactical setback, Beauregard and the Confederates were unsatisfied with their less than complete victory. Beauregard had his army occupy the abandoned Federal positions during the retreat on the 16th and claimed a great deal of left-behind equipment and supplies. Still, he had hesitated to continue his pursuit. For one, his men had fought themselves ragged all morning, and while mostly successful, the Confederates suffered close to 3,000 casualties themselves. However, what now incensed Beauregard was that he had held up his pursuit to wait for General Whiting. Afraid that a hurried pursuit would push Butler's troops back to their fortifications before Whiting could attack, Beauregard had given his general time to arrive—but it was to no avail. General Ames' force at Port Walthall Junction had demonstrated in such a way to give Whiting pause during his advance toward the fight. While the Army of the James generals were quarreling with each other over what had gone wrong, Beauregard felt that not enough had been done. The Confederates had given themselves some breathing room, but so much more could have been done. Smith and Gillmore were on thin ice, but Ransom and Whiting found themselves demoted.[5]

The weather and calmness of May 17 stood in stark contrast to the previous five days for the men in camp. After rainstorms and all the fighting, the 39th had an inspection and was left to enjoy the day. Regiments throughout the Army of the James had reviews, and leaders tried to assess not just the fighting state of the men, but what men they even still had. Soldiers did the best they could to eat, rest, recover, and take stock of their equipment. The feeling of loss would have been unable to shake, however. The man you had shared a tent with or made food with may not have been there anymore. Then there was the sight of wounded men being carried away for the hospital boats juxtaposed against clean looking reinforcements arriving into camp. Regardless of how one was managing their recovery from the battle, there was not much time to do it. The Army of the James needed to get back to work improving their defenses.[6]

As the Army of the James went to work preparing for a lengthy defense of the Bermuda Hundred position, the Confederates began a slow push from their positions at the end of the battle. May 17–19 saw Beauregard's forces pressing in on the Federal line, engaging pickets, and trying to fortify their line parallel to, and only a mile from, the Army of the James. A cycle developed where men took turns reinforcing the works, manning the trenches, performing picket duty, and resting. The firing came and went between skirmishers and artillery of both sides, and by Federal gunboats in the James River. While the smattering of engagements yielded relatively few casualties, occasionally, it was more severe. On May 18, the 97th Pennsylvania suffered fifty-seven losses defending its picket line.[7]

Beauregard was actively trying to reduce the length of his line with his movements and his building of fortifications and positions for artillery. While well aware he may not have the force required to drive the Army of the James out of Bermuda Hundred, he believed that a smaller force could keep the bottle corked and would allow him to send reinforcements to Lee's aid nearer Richmond. Beauregard informed Confederate President Jefferson Davis that he could slowly filter men towards Lee while improving his own lines, eventually providing him enough men to attack Grant's flank. Robert E. Lee was also petitioning Davis for Beauregard's men, but not for the same reason. Lee believed Grant was being reinforced and felt an influx of men was the only way to avoid retreat. Seizing on Beauregard's offer, Davis decided Beauregard could afford to immediately send 10,000 men in Lee's direction—ignoring Beauregard's plan. The move removed one-third of Beauregard's infantry in Bermuda Hundred and forced him to call General William Walker's Brigade from Petersburg. The move left Petersburg lightly defended, but Beauregard now felt he urgently needed to attack and consolidate his lines.[8]

❖   ❖   ❖

After another day of trading artillery fire and reinforcing entrenchments, Beauregard's forces made three charges on Federal pickets overnight from the 19th into the 20th. Yelling loudly and charging with great intensity, the attacks were met with artillery and short-lived. While the Army of the James picket lines held, and the Confederates took substantial losses, the men realized the next day would likely bring a full attack. On the morning of the 20th, Confederate infantry again charged the Federal right occupied by X Corps, specifically the areas handled by the First and Third Divisions. While initially under heavy artillery fire, the attackers were soon close enough to the X Corps line to render artillery unsafe. Under heavy picket fire by the Army of the James, the Confederate force successfully evicted X Corps men from the first line of rifle pits and occupied them. The worst of the attack was felt by Ames' Third Division. Ames' men made two attempts to charge and re-take his first line of rifle-pits to no avail but gained enough ground to establish a new fighting position. Terry's Division had fared much better in the attack and could now re-gain its line and assist Ames with his.[9]

At 2:00 p.m. on May 20, the 39th's brigade commander, Colonel Howell, was ordered by General Terry to head to the line. The 85th Pennsylvania was already on duty, and Howell was to bring with him the 39th Illinois and 67th Ohio, along with the 6th Connecticut from 2nd Brigade. Howell's orders were to assume command of the men who had been skirmishing there, re-take the ground lost, re-capture the rifle pits, and re-establish—and hold—the line. General Terry rode into camp and called together Howell, and his regimental commanders spread out a map and said he "expected the First Brigade to do the work with neatness and dispatch."[10]

Not an hour after receiving the initial order, the 39th, led by Lieutenant Colonel Mann, who had recovered from his illness, marched out from behind the fortifications and into the woods. Two miles from camp Howell's men arrived at a position near Ware Bottom Church to a symphony of artillery and musket fire. There would be no establishing a position or waiting for the battle to begin this time. The 39th's second major piece of fighting had already started. Finding the 85th Pennsylvania about to be overrun, Howell sent his men forward on the double-quick, forming into a line of battle on the move and firing as they reached the line. The brigade had soon developed a line with the now recovering 85th Pennsylvania and connected it with the 2nd Division elements.[11]

A line of battle now established, Howell's brigade fired and re-loaded as they were able, taking a hefty amount of fire themselves. The 39th found themselves on the far right of the line, enveloped in thick undergrowth, firing blindly towards the smoke and sound of their enemies' guns. Howell soon ordered his right flank to swing forward and towards the left to sweep across the Confederate front and re-take the rifle pits. Lieutenant Colonel Mann passed the word to his company commanders: The 39th would charge forward into the undergrowth, to what was assumed to be the Confederate left, and swing into the enemy line.[12]

With a great yell, the men of the 39th began forward with a hurried advance. Moving through the undergrowth and entanglement, the men fired toward the Confederate position, the enemy fire being returned. Lieutenant Colonel Mann was positioned at the regiment's front-right, urging his men forward and filling the lines where men fell when he was struck by a bullet and badly wounded in the left leg. As Mann put it, "[w] e had been under fire for about twenty minutes— had crowded our way over a broad space of contested ground, but excepting the dead and wounded over whom we passed I did not see a Confederate soldier in that battle."[13]

As he did at Drewry's Bluff when commanding officers fell, Captain Baker took command of the regiment and rallied his men on the flags of the Yates Phalanx. Stepping out of the undergrowth into an opening, the 39th spotted the retreating Confederate infantry they had been advancing on, and some who were digging in the rifle pits. Baker ordered the regiment to charge forward, streaming into the open space firing at the enemy and chasing them off into the woods. Knowing their orders were to re-gain and hold the rifle pits, men jumped into the entrenchments, stuck their rifles in the ground, and pulled spades out of their packs. To the 39th's left, the brigade's remainder had been equally successful, and the original X Corps position was re-established. "I never saw officers and men behave better," wrote Colonel Howell in his official report. "Their promptness, zeal, dashing and daring courage was beautiful—their fire steady and deadly to the enemy."[14]

While the 39th had regained some of General Terry's original rifle pits, the Federals lost the overall battle. The 39th suffered 70 of the brigade's roughly 300 casualties—the Army of the James suffering 702 as a whole.[15] Those in the regiment since October 1861 had gone two-and-a-half years without playing a significant role in pitched battle and had now done so twice in five days. Colonel Osborn, Lieutenant Colonel Mann, and Major Linton were all in the hospital with serious wounds. Twenty-two men of the 39th Illinois had been killed or mortally wounded in the two battles. With shelling, skirmishing, and sharpshooters active every day, the regiment's total casualty count would be 200 men before the month was out.[16]

◆　◆　◆

Modern remains of Ware Bottom Church rifle pit (author's photograph).

The standoff at Bermuda Hundred had now reached a full-on stalemate status. Beauregard had consolidated his line, named the Howlett Line for a nearby Doctor's home, and hemmed in Butler with a stretch of artillery batteries, trenches, and rifle pits between the Appomattox and James Rivers. However, the work had come at the cost of 800 casualties he could not afford. The Confederate War Department had completed the transfer of some of Beauregard's troops to Richmond, and Beauregard's new defensive line led Jefferson Davis to believe he could now spare more. Beauregard wanted to continue making offensive moves, but the Confederate calculus was now simple: If

Butler's troops left to reinforce Grant, the Confederate forces needed to arrive first. If the Army of the James remained where it was, Beauregard's new position could spare men while keeping Butler in place.[17]

For now, Butler believed his army was staying put. There were growing rumors that some of his men may be dispatched to the Army of the Potomac, or that Grant may soon arrive in the area as he continued engaging Lee, then advancing to the southeast. To Butler's mind, Grant's arrival required the total control of the Bermuda Hundred landing and City Point. To that point, Grant absolutely agreed. However, Butler also felt that required keeping his men and being reinforced. To that point, General Grant did not agree. Grant felt that the events of May 16 and 20 had limited "very materially the further usefulness of the Army of the James as a distinct factor in the campaign."[18] While Grant sent envoys to Butler's headquarters in the last week of May to assess the situation, he had already decided. On May 22, Grant wired Army Chief of Staff, Major General Henry Halleck, in Washington that he wanted General Smith and 10,000 men to join the Army of the Potomac, and that Butler was to keep enough men to hold City Point and Bermuda Hundred.[19]

◈　　◈　　◈

The rest of May saw each army manning the trenches, performing picket duty, and reinforcing their defenses. There was a constant din of fire and shelling, some of which occasionally brought injury, but most of the fighting was now taking place among leadership entities. Confederate leadership believed that Butler's position could not be taken except by a force they were unwilling to commit, but also did not fear him as an offensive threat. U.S. leadership knew their hold on Bermuda Hundred and City Point was strong, but Butler could not break Beauregard's line nor prevent him from sending troops to Lee. For this reason, as William Glenn Robertson wrote in *Back Door to Richmond,* "[b]oth Lee and Grant were more than willing to accept a stalemate below Richmond in order to reinforce their own commands."[20]

After the bloody, but neutral, result at Spotsylvania Courthouse, Grant had disengaged and again flanked the Army of the Potomac to the southeast. The goal of Grant's Overland Campaign had become finding open ground to engage Lee on, then flanking closer and closer to Richmond. The rationale being, that Grant could break through Lee's line and head to Richmond, or possibly even destroy the Army of Northern Virginia. Should neither of those occur, the continued movement to the southeast was designed to link up with the Army of the James and put Lee on totally defensive footing facing a numerically superior and better supplied U.S. Army. Between the 23rd and 26th of May, Grant and Lee faced off in three days of skirmishing near the North Anna River with roughly 5,500 casualties and another stalemate. Again, Grant had Meade's Army of the Potomac flank southeast and head for Cold Harbor—only 10 miles east of Richmond, and 10 miles north of Bermuda Hundred.[21]

On May 26, Baldy Smith received orders from General Halleck to begin preparations for taking men to join the Army of the Potomac. While Grant had requested 10,000 men initially, he had doubled the request after realizing Lee was not falling back to Richmond after the fighting at North Anna River. While disappointed at feeling he had missed opportunities, and concerned about Beauregard's numbers, Butler also wanted to show he was ready to work with Grant to strike at Richmond. He estimated that he could send Smith with 17,000 troops and take measures to replace their position on the line safely. Natural barriers and fortifications well protected the center and left of the Army of the James' line, so the right would require adjustments. As a result, General Terry's First Division of X Corps, to include the 39th Illinois, would be assigned the task.[22]

On May 29, the Federal movements were complete, and the stalemate at Bermuda Hundred became even quieter. The firing had slackened, men worked on the trenches, and there was even some exchanging of goods across picket lines. As before, the only real fighting was the continued bickering between Butler and Gillmore, who was now in command of the entire line of defense. By the 1st of June, however, Beauregard could hear the increasing thunder of artillery fire as Lee and Grant moved closer. Still unsure of how many of Butler's men had left, where they were headed, and where they currently were, Beauregard decided he needed a reconnaissance to find out Federal intentions and determine his next move.[23]

❖   ❖   ❖

The 39th Illinois was on picket late on the night of June 1, when they heard the lumbering wheeled movements of Confederate artillery through the woods. The artillery opened-up for forty-five minutes in what was likely an attempt to range their targets for the morning. In the early morning darkness on June 2, the Confederate batteries began pounding the Federal center and right for an hour as U.S. artillery answered. Then, briefly, there was silence.[24]

Shortly after 6:00 a.m., Confederate infantry climbed out of their rifle pits and charged towards the X Corps picket line. Terry's Division answered the charge with a volley of fire, but the line's right side was soon in trouble. The attackers were turning the right side of the 7th Connecticut, and the left of the 39th. The two regiments were forced to begin an urgent but measured withdrawal that forced the 11th Maine to fall back. However, the men involved were all able to resist enough to make an orderly movement to fallback rifle pits and entrenchments. This was enough to allow the 7th Connecticut to re-gain portions of the line that had been lost, but most of it could not. General Terry's Division was forced to establish a new line even closer to camp and suffered 172 casualties on the day.

The 39th suffered 35–40 casualties, including another officer killed and one severely wounded. Lieutenant Albert Fellows, of Santa Anna, was killed by a bullet to the head, and Lieutenant Al Sweester, of Bloomington, suffered a horrible leg wound.[25] Sweester arrived at the field hospital smoking a cigar, and when told the leg would require amputation, Sweester replied, "[w]ell Doc, just go to work and do the very best you can for me."[26]

One of the captured that day was Company G Private Richard Warren of Bremen. He would later recount to Homer Plimpton the six-day trip to Andersonville prison camp in Georgia. In five pages of writing, Warren describes Andersonville in words that are almost unbearable to read. A dirty stream through the center of a camp with tens of thousands of men as their only water, an arbitrary line that if crossed would get someone shot, no food, rampant disease, and terrible wounds ignored by Confederate medics. Daily, a cart pulled by mules would come by and stack bodies "like so much cord wood." Warren survived to be paroled and leave but died soon after the war from sickness he contracted there. Others were not so lucky. Of the 25 members of the 39th who died in rebel prisons, 11 of them were at Andersonville. In its 14 months of operation, approximately 45,000 U.S. troops were held in the camp; nearly 13,000 died.[27]

As if the regiment had not suffered enough in the last two weeks, the following day Captain George Snowden, of Oregon, was wounded by sharpshooter fire across the lines.[28] One heroic and notable moment arose as a result, however. Company D cook, Private Alexander Gaurley, of Dwight, ran to the position where Snowden had fallen and carried him to a place of safety before returning to his company in the small skirmish. Private Gaurley's age when he had enlisted three years prior: 67.[29]

❖   ❖   ❖

Beauregard's probe had been mildly successful, but he realized that he would not dislodge Butler from his position, and soon he would find himself vigorously defending the Confederate capital. The heaviest day of the fighting at Cold Harbor could be heard from Bermuda Hundred on June 3 and meant Grant would soon either break through to Richmond or join forces with Butler to assault Petersburg. As he had feared, this combination of factors led to Beauregard losing another brigade to the north.[30]

On June 2, Federal forces at Cold Harbor, including men of the XVIII Corps, had some moderate success. However, a June 3 frontal assault on the Confederate line was met with horrific losses. In his memoirs, Grant would later write that he "always regretted" the assault at Cold Harbor, which brought about no tactical advantage and cost 12,738 casualties to include 1,845 dead.[31] With Lee now so near Richmond, Grant decided he would take advantage of being so close to Butler and a secure base of operations. His next flank movement would again look to get around Lee's right, by crossing the Chickahominy and James Rivers and join forces with Butler. On June 6, a group of Grant's engineers delivered supplies for a pontoon bridge to Bermuda Hundred. On the 9th, Butler learned XVIII Corps would return to him—although with far fewer men after their service at Cold Harbor. Grant, along with General Meade and his Army of the Potomac, began their movement southeast on June 12, and Butler and Beauregard would soon see their forces joined with the respective incoming armies. For all intents and purposes, the Bermuda Hundred Campaign was over.[32]

❖   ❖   ❖

The 39th Illinois had arrived at Bermuda Hundred in early May after furlough. It soon saw significant combat for the first time in the campaign designed to pinch the Confederate capital between converging Federal forces. Instead, P.G.T. Beauregard had stalled a landing force of 30,000 men long enough to bring in reinforcements and spare Petersburg and Richmond for the time being. While Butler would receive harsh critique the rest of his life for his inability to strike fast and take Petersburg, he did do what he was asked. The Army of the James was tasked with securing a base as far north as possible on the James River, disrupt Confederate lines of communication, and keep the attention of Confederate troops that may otherwise have been sent to the Army of Northern Virginia. When considering that he only expected to do these things for ten days, Butler carried out his duties.[33]

Knowing that he himself contributed in part to the critiques levied against Butler, Grant would later write in his memoirs that Butler "certainly gave his very earnest support to the war."[34] A campaign of what-ifs, missed opportunities, and unpredictable and unavoidable factors was over—regardless of what might have been—and the final ten months of the war in the east would center on Petersburg.

❖　❖　❖

In Marseilles, Illinois, Huldah Barber had spent the last two-and-a-half years worrying about her oldest son John serving in the cavalry out west, her son Cicero who had been with the 39th Illinois since its inception, and her 17-year-old son Alden who joined when the regiment was home on furlough. She would soon receive word that Alden had been wounded and captured at the Battle of Drewry's Bluff. Cicero wrote a letter to his brother, Private John Barber, detailing the horror of watching Alden dragged away. Before the letter reached Arkansas, however, Cicero was killed at Ware Bottom Church. Alden, unfortunately, would not recover from his wounds and died in Libby Prison in Richmond on June 18. The story, and fate, of the Barber brothers—and the worry of a mother—was not unique to the army, or even the 39th. In February, the father and son team of John Denline and John Denline, Jr., of Fremont, had joined the regiment. No doubt leaving a Mrs. Denline at home in worry.[35]

A summer of sweltering heat and bloody battles was ahead, and the 39th would not be spared its horrors, but would not be denied its valor.

14

Grant's Arrival

Oscar Rudd was born in 1829 in Champion, New York, just east of Lake Ontario and close to the Canadian border. Regrettably, very little is known about Rudd's early life, or how his family came to find themselves in Illinois.

In August 1861, Rudd, joined with Amos Savage to help Reverend Slaughter recruit for his "Preacher's Company" that eventually joined the 39th Illinois. Clark laments in his Company G roster that "it has been impossible to learn anything concerning the antebellum history of Captain Rudd ... it is to be regretted that his record is incomplete."

What is not incomplete, however, is Rudd's contributions to the regiment, and the tremendous respect the men and officers of the regiment had for him. Rudd's actions on Cacapon Mountain in the skirmish with Stonewall Jackson may have very well saved the bulk of the regiment from being destroyed or captured. Clark further wrote in Rudd's roster entry that he was good and generous to those around him, and, as evidenced on Cacapon Mountain and the Battle of Drewry's Bluff, "asked none to follow where he would not lead."

The regiment suffering mightily from the casualties of battle, and things far from quieting down near Bermuda Hundred, Rudd's leadership would still be required.[1]

By THE FIRST WEEK OF JUNE 1864, over 50,000 men who crossed the Rapidan River with Grant in early May were casualties of brutal fighting in the Overland Campaign.[2] Over the same period, approximately 6,000 men who traveled up the James River with General Butler were casualties of the Bermuda Hundred Campaign. There was no doubt the rest of the war would be fought with such attrition rates.

The Army of the Potomac that triumphed at Gettysburg one year ago was now a battered one arriving in the oppressive summer heat around Petersburg. Stripped of some of its most loyal men and best officers, they would join with the Army of the James to begin the Richmond-Petersburg Campaign. General Butler's Army of the James that had arrived a month earlier with so much potential to strike the Confederacy was now essentially an extension of the Army of the Potomac. The two now "intimately associated," wrote Grant in his memoirs, and "substantially one body."[3] While the month had not gone as Grant and Butler had wished, they had at least prevented the Confederates from threatening Washington and had a force that could directly threaten Petersburg and Richmond.[4]

By mid–June, the temperature was occasionally reaching triple digits, and the 39th Illinois was doing their best to keep their heads down, stay cool, and wait for the inevitable movements of a new campaign. The Yates Phalanx had left Chicago in October 1861 and was now one of the remaining U.S. pieces on the board as the war entered its final stage. For almost three years, the regiment's path and fate had been decided by various circumstances of chance, political and military decision-making, and the enemy's actions. Now, their experience in the remaining ten months of war would be driven by men with names like Grant and Lee—carrying out the intent of men named Lincoln and Davis. The Richmond-Petersburg Campaign would last 292 days, with near-constant contact between two armies fighting over the soul of a nation on a thirty-five-mile-wide line.[5] Young men from nine counties in the central and north-eastern portions of Illinois would serve in one of just two regiments from the Land of Lincoln that would fight in the campaign. The 39th Illinois, now with their commanding general from Illinois on their side of the river, would serve from day 1 to day 292.

❖   ❖   ❖

Moving the Army of the Potomac from Cold Harbor to the area outside Bermuda Hundred and Petersburg was no simple task. Grant and Meade needed to move five army corps and a cavalry corps out of the elaborate Cold Harbor entrenchments, south for twenty miles, and then across a 2,000-foot-long pontoon bridge over the James River. A monumental task in logistics alone, Grant's plan also required the re-location to be protected from the enemy, and ideally, accomplished before Lee knew his intentions. The hope was that Lee would assume Richmond remained Grant's objective, and Federal forces would beat Confederate reinforcements to Petersburg. Grant sent Baldy Smith's XVIII Corps ahead of all the rest on June 13. Smith would link up with cavalry and other elements of Butler's force at Bermuda Hundred and secure Petersburg before the Confederates knew what was happening. Doing so would give Grant control of a city, and its rail junction, that connected the Confederate capital to all its sources of men and supplies.[6]

Throughout the day and night on June 14, Smith's XVIII Corps began arriving at Bermuda Hundred. The early movements and deceptive actions of the U.S. Army leaving Cold Harbor, had given Lee pause as he tried to anticipate Grant's next objective. Smith's arrival at Bermuda Hundred was causing Beauregard to fear for Petersburg's safety, but Lee was not yet convinced. While Lee was piecing together that Petersburg may be the new Federal aim, he could not shake the thought Grant would continue to drive towards Richmond. He knew that the strong fortifications McClellan had used at Harrison's Landing were still intact and that such a base of operations would give Grant access to Richmond or crossing the James towards Petersburg.[7]

The Federal movement had been achieving its intent. Petersburg had not yet been reinforced, and the XVIII Corps had arrived with 14,000 men opposing 4,000 rebels to man the city's defenses—half of which were hastily organized militia. At 1:00 a.m., on the 15th, Smith's men crossed the Appomattox River. Later in the morning, XVIII Corps began probing the outer defenses of the city while the

Army of the Potomac continued to arrive. Smith's approach soon brought him up against artillery fire from the formidable Dimmock Line. The line was ten miles wide, anchored at each end on the Appomattox River, and contained fifty-five artillery batteries. With massive fortifications, deep ditches to slow down attackers, and adequate cover for infantry protecting it, assaulting the line would be no simple task. However, effectively using the Dimmock Line required a number of men that the defenses currently did not have. While the Federal force perhaps no longer had total surprise on their side, speed and numbers could still carry the day.[8]

Baldy Smith, however, did not move with that kind of speed, and there were delays from Major General Winfield Scott Hancock's II Corps. An engineer by trade, Smith, was in awe of the Dimmock line upon seeing it firsthand and began a two-hour reconnaissance, followed by two hours of positioning his troops. Smith had lost nearly 1,000 men at Cold Harbor assaulting far less elaborate works and took his time to ensure that it did not happen again. Finding out Hancock's tired men had been delayed by not having rations and would not be ready to fight until after dark, Smith started his assault around 7:00 p.m. Opening up with artillery before deploying skirmishers and lines of battle, the XVIII Corps assault was initially successful. By 9:00 p.m., Smith's men had captured many of the guns and occupied over a mile of the entrenchments.[9]

Darkness and Smith's overabundance of caution halted the Federal momentum and prevented the successes from being followed up. Smith heard trains arriving in Petersburg all day and had also received reports that Beauregard had dispatched men from Bermuda Hundred, and Lee's army was inbound. Even though Hancock's II Corps was now on the field, Smith thought it better to maintain what he had gained rather than risk nighttime assaults against a growing enemy. Upon reinforcing the positions Smith's men took during the day, Hancock became quite anxious that more wasn't done before daylight, but Smith was satisfied with the day's work.[10]

However, Beauregard was not acting with caution; and took it upon himself to make an aggressive move. Without express permission from Davis or Lee, and behaving only under his orders to defend Petersburg, Beauregard ordered a division in front of Butler at Bermuda Hundred to move to the Petersburg line. The move paid off for the Confederates, as Lee had sent a division under George Pickett to back up the position at Drewry's Bluff. While Lee had done this thinking Richmond, via Harrison's Landing or Bermuda Hundred, may still be Grant's aim; it now served the purpose of backfilling the force Beauregard had shifted to Petersburg. Smith's hesitation to begin, then reluctance to follow up, his attack had limited the Federal gains. It allowed P.G.T. Beauregard to assemble a reputable defense of Petersburg by sun-up on June 16.[11]

❖   ❖   ❖

Throughout the night on June 15th into the 16th, the pickets in front of the Bermuda Hundred fortifications had heard a great deal of noise coming from the Confederate works. Early on the 16th, the men of the 39th were formed to march with the rest of the First Division of X Corps—a corps no longer commanded by General Gillmore. Following continued disagreements with Butler and a never-ending hesitation to carry out orders, Butler had Gillmore removed, and Brigadier General William Brooks would command X Corps. Brooks was very familiar with the Army of the James, having led a division of XVIII Corps at Cold Harbor.[12]

The Division marched towards the Confederate line and soon confirmed that Beauregard had pulled troops to Petersburg. Moving unopposed, Terry's division soon occupied the entire Confederate line that had been bottling up Butler at Bermuda Hundred. Receiving reports from Terry, Butler thought there was an excellent opportunity to cut off further reinforcements to reach Petersburg and wired Grant for instructions. Grant, in a rare cautious and defensive decision, however, ordered Butler not to jeopardize the Federal position at Bermuda Hundred by pressing deeper to attack and sent two divisions of VI Corps to reinforce Butler's men.[13]

Adhering to their orders, Terry's Division established themselves on the former Confederate line, and men went to work ripping up three miles of Richmond and Petersburg Railroad. The 39th was deployed forward as skirmishers to probe for any other Confederate positions in the area and warn against any efforts to retake their lines. In carrying out this duty, the regiment encountered roughly 40 confederate soldiers who gave themselves up under a white flag. Left behind as a token force on the Confederate line, these were the men who hadn't fled when witnessing the Division's approach. General Butler had his First Division of X Corps destroying more railroads, taking Confederate prisoners, and occupying the line that had kept him hemmed in for so long. While he wished to move more urgently, he would soon have reinforcements and would strike decisively to cut off Petersburg from further reinforcements.[14]

Lee was becoming more aware that Grant's aim was towards Petersburg. Maintaining the so-called Howlett Line in front of Bermuda Hundred wasn't necessary to protect Richmond but to preserve his ability to reinforce Petersburg. The 39th, still acting as skirmishers, continued their advance and soon found themselves near former battlefields between Chester Station and Ware Bottom Church. Here the regiment encountered a sizable Confederate force massed in the woods on the other side of a clearing. This was General George Pickett's Division, who now sent skirmishers charging against the 39th in action far less dramatic, but far more successful, than his ill-fated charge at Gettysburg. Captain Rudd, who had sprung the surprise attack on Cacapon Mountain and fought rebels face to face at Drewry's Bluff, was in command of the regiment's right flank and realized they were in danger of being turned. Rudd sent a runner with word to Division leadership while positioning his men to fight and preserve their flank.[15]

Shortly after noon, Pickett sent a strong skirmish line towards the First Division. To the right of the 39th was 2nd Brigade's 3rd New Hampshire, who was soon forced back. This brought Rudd's fears to reality as the 39th's right was now exposed. Adhering to the orders to not enter a full-on engagement, Captain Baker, in command of the regiment, ordered a fighting withdrawal to the Confederate works captured earlier in the day. While directing his men on the right flank, Captain Rudd was shot through the right shoulder, with the bullet passing through his vertebra and lodging into his left. Gravely wounded, his men completed the withdrawal and returned Rudd to the X Corps line, where he was immediately sent to the rear and on to Fort Monroe's hospital.[16]

First Division established themselves in the abandoned Confederate works, now postured opposite the direction intended when built, and used three artillery pieces to keep Pickett's Division in check. While injured men and supplies were safely removed to the rear, word came from Butler to fall back further. Without reinforcements, the Confederate line was too long to hold with one division against an unknown advance. The opportunity to block Lee from reaching Petersburg was fading. Terry's Division fell back further to the former Confederate picket line, and by 6:00 p.m., Confederate infantry retook most of their original main line. However, Grant had changed his mind and saw merit in an attack at Bermuda Hundred. Notifying Butler that reinforcements were headed his way, Butler ordered X Corps to occupy the Federal entrenchments closest to the Confederate line. The 39th returned to camp after dark, ate, and advanced beyond the line for a night on picket while gunboats on the James pounded the Confederate position. They had suffered seven casualties on the day.[17]

At Petersburg, June 16 had been a day of chess moves, reconnaissance, reinforcements, and sporadic fighting—fighting that did not begin in earnest until 6:00 p.m. Meade's advances lasted only three hours. Any Federal momentum was blunted by 9:00 p.m. Meade had a sizable advantage in men over Beauregard. Still, the Army of the Potomac was paying great respect to Petersburg's defenses and the Dimmock Line. The shuffle game of reinforcements and the use of earthworks and terrain had won the day for the Confederates once again.[18]

◆　◆　◆

Just before daylight on June 17, the Confederate force facing the 39th and X Corps near Bermuda Hundred made a large demonstration and advanced against the picket line. With the 24th Massachusetts, of Third Brigade on their right, the 39th fired into the Confederate infantry as they came with "their usual yell," wrote Valentine Randolph.[19] The attack was short-lived, however, and the 39th took 26 prisoners in the brief affair.[20]

As the day's fighting was getting underway at Bermuda Hundred, so too was the action at Petersburg. Just after daylight, the Army of the Potomac IX Corps attacked a battery and portion of the Confederate line that yielded 600 prisoners and took two Confederate guns. However, as was becoming the trend, the Federal force could not press its momentum when follow-up attacks were slowed by a ravine of slashed timber and Confederate fire. A second assault by IX Corps took place in the early afternoon, but one of the regiments guiding the assault lost its way, and Confederate artillery fire could put shells into an exposed Federal flank. Another offensive move had been stalled out, and Confederate infantry could shore up new lines where it had been broken. While Petersburg's defenders had avoided any catastrophic damage, Lee was further convinced that Grant's primary objective lie south of the Appomattox in Petersburg itself.[21]

As was this case with this, or any, war, the situation at Bermuda Hundred would now be directly affected by the situation elsewhere. Lee ordered the Confederate Third Corps, under A.P. Hill, to cross the Appomattox and head to Drewry's Bluff. The rationale was two-fold: If Federal attacks at Petersburg caused Beauregard to fall back, a line in front of Richmond would need to be established. Lee also had to guard against any breakthroughs from Bermuda Hundred, however, and ensure Federal forces could not wheel left and clamp down on Petersburg from the north. Adding the division of Charles Field to Pickett's, the Confederates considered an assault to retake the southern segment of the original Howlett Line Butler's army still held. Commanding the corps with Pickett and Field's divisions, Richard Anderson assessed the trenches at Bermuda Hundred and decided an attack was not worth it. The Confederate forces near Drewry's Bluff could form a line in front of Richmond and had the forces available to fight if Butler moved towards Petersburg.[22]

However, on the picket lines at Bermuda Hundred, the 39th, along with the 24th Massachusetts and 85th Pennsylvania, were exchanging an increasing amount of fire with Pickett's and Field's divisions. While Lee, and Anderson, had decided not to attack, portions of Pickett's Division did not get the word and were tired of taking constant fire. Late in the afternoon, the "rebel yell" joined the far-off sounds of battle at Petersburg, and Pickett's division charged the X Corps line. The 85th Pennsylvania was in front, and to the left, of the 39th and was quickly forced back, putting a break in the Federal line. Butler had been resting the VI Corps reinforcements Grant had sent him but was now forced to put them into action. While waiting for the reinforcements, however, the 39th also had to fall back to prevent the left flank from being turned by the advancing enemy.[23]

Under heavy fire, most of the 39th withdrew a quarter mile to the rifle pits behind them, while some men stayed in rifle pits to help protect the 24th Massachusetts. Captain Baker threw out a line of skirmishers that reached to the left of the 24th, stretching and staggering it in such a way to reach the Federal left while waiting for reinforcements. Baker's actions were successful, and XI Corps reinforcements arrived on the field as Pickett and Field leaned hard on the Federal left. The saga of Bermuda Hundred was maintaining its reputation as an action-packed stalemate. Confederates had re-established their original Howlett Line but failed to break through further. The Army of the James had prevented a Confederate breakthrough at Bermuda Hundred but given back the original Confederate defensive position. Amidst sporadic picket firing, the men went to work digging and reinforcing their new posts. The 39th Illinois had lost another nine men and spent another night on picket.[24]

As the Howlett line again changed hands at Bermuda Hundred, the Army of the Potomac was launching another offensive at Petersburg that made significant gains before a Confederate counter-attack near midnight forced the Federal infantry back. Beauregard had been fortunate to hold off the now four-to-one advantage Union forces had but was getting desperate. His engineers created a new line west, and to the rear of his current position. Besides battery placement, the new line took advantage of a ravine and slashed timber that would leave advancing Federal troops exposed to fire while navigating. As Beauregard moved his men, Lee received word from his cavalry that Grant had brought his entire army south of the James. Finally, fully convinced of Grant's strategy, Lee ordered most of the Army of Northern Virginia to Petersburg's defenses.[25]

❖　❖　❖

By the very early hours of June 18, only Pickett's division was holding the Howlett line, and there were almost no Confederate forces north of the James River. However, the movements took time to materialize, and the very first signs of light found the Army of the Potomac advancing on empty positions. Beauregard's withdrawal didn't just put his troops in a better position; however, it had a secondary effect of confusing the Federal chain of command. Word of the vacant positions funneled from brigade and division commanders, up through corps and to Meade, who then consulted with Grant. As time passed, and men on the field awaited orders, Lee's men moved into Petersburg, and Beauregard's were fortifying their positions.[26]

The Federal assault eventually resumed with the full break of day, led by the XVIII Corps still operating as a part of the Army of the Potomac, and II Corps. II Corps was now being led by one of its division commanders, Major General David Birney, as Winfield Scott Hancock had a wound from Gettysburg a year prior come open. II Corps made early progress because of Beauregard's forces' withdrawal but was soon engaged by heavy fire from the new Confederate position. Around midday, V and IX Corps attempted to join the push after traveling further but were soon ate up by fire from the Confederate line and crossfire from batteries still held on the Dimmock Line. Federal forces would make fantastic gains only to encounter thirty-five-foot-high earthworks. Advancing infantry would be forced to stop and cut steps into the mounds without accurately targeting artillery over the top. The slow-downs left Federal forces helplessly exposed to Confederate crossfire and further allowed Lee's reinforcements to trickle in.[27]

As the 39th listened to the distant fighting at Petersburg the entire day, they were busy keeping their heads down on picket duty as fire was traded across Bermuda Hundred lines. Late in the afternoon, Pickett's division opened-up with six pieces of artillery for almost an hour before quiet came, and the men knew what would come. The "rebel yell" was soon heard coming once again. Whereas their left had been forced to fall back the day before, now it was their right. The 11th Maine had relieved the 24th Massachusetts and was being pushed back. As it had been the day prior, this forced the 39th to fall back as well and pull in the picket line. The Confederate attack had done nothing to change the status quo other than adjust picket lines and bring about more death and injury. "I am heartily tired of this petty skirmishing," wrote Valentine Randolph the next day. "In it nothing of importance is to be gained."[28] Captain Leroy Baker led the 39th back to camp after three busy and tiring days of fighting that gained nothing more than a slight shift in the lines, at the cost of 35 casualties—to include five dead.[29]

Back at Petersburg, the Army of the Potomac was suffering through another hard day of starts, stops, and missed opportunities. Finding it hard to coordinate attacks across all his disparate forces, Meade ordered all his corps to make assaults as soon as possible wherever they were. This, however, had been the problem of the three days of attacks. The battle-weary Army of the Potomac had been fighting hard for over a month, made a lengthy move, and was now fighting an elaborate position on which they were not yet fully educated. There were issues of brigades not following orders, and officers questioning each other over the methods being used to assault such a defensive position. A frustrated Meade told Grant that his failure was due in part to "the moral condition of the army."[30] Grant agreed and knew he needed to fortify his line, rest his men, and devise an alternative plan.

Grant's crossing of the James, and linking up with Butler, had shifted the narrative of battle around Petersburg and Bermuda Hundred. Still, he could not capitalize on his numerical advantage. Conversely, Robert E. Lee and P.G.T. Beauregard had saved Petersburg but could not prevent Grant from beginning a siege. From June 15 to 18, U.S. forces lost 10,600 men to the Confederates, approximately 4,000. The end of the Federal offensives on June 18 was the de facto beginning of the Siege of Petersburg. U.S. and Confederate soldiers settled in for their new reality that would last the next ten months.[31]

❖　❖　❖

On June 22, President Lincoln rode along the lines with General Butler and received great cheers from the Yates Phalanx as he passed in front of their position. The men cheered enthusiastically, and Lincoln gave them his best encouragement, but there was little enthusiasm to be had. Since early May, the brutal and costly fighting and failure to take Petersburg was putting Lincoln's re-election bid in jeopardy. As June turned to July, the heat would be turned up both literally and figuratively on a Union cause becoming desperate to cool things off.

As the real and metaphorical heat built towards August, many would wither, but many in the 39th would rise nobly above it.[32]

15

Deep Despair and Deep Bottom

Lewis Whipple was born in Miamisburg, Ohio in 1840, the son of parents descended from New England Puritans. His parents had moved west to the Miami Valley of Ohio and lived a pioneer life.

In 1852, his family moved to Illinois and the Kankakee Valley, his youth spent working on the farm and occasionally attending the small district school. His mother, however, had received a decent level of education and provided him a more robust education than many Illinois pioneers received. Upon hearing the news of Fort Sumter falling, Whipple rushed to enlist and found his way into Company E of the 39th Illinois.

Whipple was voted First Lieutenant during the regiment's formation, and climbed to Captain when Company E Commander, James Hooker resigned in May 1862. Through this rank, and the seniority he now had in it, Whipple would soon find himself in command of the regiment.[1]

THE REST OF JUNE AND THROUGH JULY was a relatively quiet period for the 39th Illinois as General Grant re-organized his efforts. While the Army of the Potomac rested and solidified its positions, the Army of the James created a bridgehead at a place called Deep Bottom. Such a bridge was intended to keep the door open for operations north of the James. The 39th's work consisted mostly of marching from place to place in the heat, doing picket duty, and laboring in the sun to build fortifications. At Petersburg, Grant launched a brief offensive on June 22 with little effect and nearly 3,000 casualties. Looking to turn the stalled Federal efforts into Confederate momentum, Lee launched his own offensive on June 24. The XVIII Corps had not yet finished its defenses between the Appomattox River and City Point railroad, and Beauregard was tasked with exploiting that. The effort failed, with substantial Confederate casualties and fewer than 100 from XVIII Corps.[2]

"This failure demonstrated what the Federals had long since learned," writes Earl Hess in *In the Trenches at Petersburg*. "[A]ttacking even poorly made earthworks well-manned by veteran troops was unlikely to succeed."[3] For Beauregard, it was essentially the end of his time in the theater. While his efforts in May and June had saved Petersburg and Richmond, he grew frustrated at not having independent command following all his success and did not get along with Davis, Lee, and others. He was sent west and finished the war as General Joseph Johnston's number two.[4]

July 4 brought music from the regimental bands with the raising of flags and a celebratory volley of fire by Federal batteries. While the country's birthday brought a small bit of excitement, it mostly highlighted that the war was three years old and at a stalemate. For the 39th, it brought the close of two months of fighting that had led to 266 killed, wounded, or missing.[5]

During the lull, Doctor Clark proceeded to Fort Monroe and paid a visit to the men of the 39th who were there. Colonel Osborn and Lieutenant Colonel Mann were sharing a room together, and both were recovering well. Osborn was recovering enough to be soon sent to Chicago to recruit while regaining enough strength to return to the lines. Captain Rudd, however, would not be so fortunate. In a room near Osborn and Mann, and with his wife by his side, the beloved G Company Captain succumbed to his wounds on July 11. Less fortunate than Osborn or Mann, but at least avoiding Rudd's fate, Major Linton never recovered enough to serve again and would eventually be mustered out of service when his enlistment expired.[6]

A week after the nation's birthday, events just outside Washington, D.C., brought deep concern to U.S. leadership. Confederate general Jubal Early led forces out of the Shenandoah Valley and seriously threatened the capital after defeating Federal forces at Monocacy, less than 50 miles northwest of the Capital. The Federal forces—led by Osborn's pre-war mentor Lew Wallace—slowed Early down however, and reinforcements, and the Capitol's strong defenses, forced him to retire after two days of skirmishing outside the city. The U.S. high command was rattled, and the public was panicked. The second half of the month did nothing to make things better as General Sherman was stalling outside Atlanta. President Lincoln called for a draft of half a million men, and General Grant continued to suffer heavy losses while failing to take Petersburg. The price of gold and the value of the U.S. dollar reached wartime highs and lows, respectively.[7]

Robert E. Lee was counting on such distress both from U.S. leadership and their citizens. Dusting off the strategy from 1862, Lee had dispatched Early to the Shenandoah to clear out Federal troops and threaten Washington in a sequel to Stonewall Jackson's operations in the Valley. In Lee's mind, the strategy had many outcomes that would bring him positive results. Knowing how U.S. leadership reacted in 1862 to Washington's threat, he assumed reinforcements would be pulled from near Petersburg. Lee felt this would cause Grant to withdraw from the city altogether without the overwhelming numbers he preferred to employ. However, separate from the operational considerations, Lee's plan had a third objective: Add a severe threat to the capital to citizens' frustrations. With an election in less than four months, a Lincoln loss brought the prospects of peace negotiations and recognition of the Confederate States of America.[8]

As in 1862, troop shuffling began. Grant was forced to send a VI Corps division, followed by XIX Corps to ensure Washington's protection. Republican politicians were becoming concerned Lincoln could not win and questioned the war strategy and emancipation instead of just reunification. Capitalizing on all of this, Jefferson Davis sent peace commissioners to the north to further divide the Union. Backbiting even began among cabinet members, much of which was directed at U.S. generals in the field.[9]

Lincoln, however, had learned his lesson from 1862. While he would never be a President who would keep his hands off the war effort, he had learned to streamline his chain of command and empower someone he trusted to carry out his intentions. Grant and Lincoln knew what Lee's strategy was and knew the Confederacy's main chance of victory was a Lincoln electoral loss. Grant wished to maintain his plan that U.S. armies, wherever they were, needed to act as one. Withdrawal from the vicinity of the James River would allow Lee to send reinforcements to Georgia as Sherman's advance continued. Grant also believed in the unity of command. He convinced Lincoln that merging all the forces in the Shenandoah under one commander would allow better coordination both amongst themselves, and with Grant and Lincoln. To this end, Grant sent Major General Philip Sheridan and his cavalry operating north of Richmond into the Valley.[10]

The best intentions and efforts of Lincoln, Grant, and the men aside, the Confederate strategy continued to pay dividends, and the last days of July brought more bad news for the Union. While Sherman won a significant victory at Atlanta on the 22nd, he had still not captured the city. On the 24th, Federal forces not yet under Sheridan's unified command suffered a defeat where the 39th had previously fought at Kernstown and allowed Early to threaten Washington again. Late July U.S. action near Deep Bottom strengthened the position there and achieved moving Confederate troops off the Petersburg line. The minor victory, however, led to a costly defeat.

General Ambrose Burnside's IX Corps had been using men with mining experience to create a mine over 500 feet long to blow a hole under Confederate works. Grant was willing to attempt Burnside's gambit, having been talked out of further frontal assaults against fortified positions. With Lee having to move men to the Valley to counter Sheridan, and to Deep Bottom to counter the operations there; Grant thought the shock of the explosion and sudden ability to overrun a portion of the line would pay off. At 4:45 a.m. on July 30, 12,000 pounds of powder exploded, creating a crater that was 150 feet long, 60 feet wide, and 25 feet deep. The explosion's physical and mental shock delayed the initial assault, and things did not get better once it began. As Federal men advanced, Confederate fire from other portions of the line started a crossfire. Soon men were being funneled into the crater itself and could not escape. A Confederate counterattack became even more aggressive when they realized Black troops were taking part in the assault attempting to invade Petersburg. The Federals suffered almost 3,800 casualties, double the Confederates, and gained nothing in the attack. The end of July 1864 brought about one of—if not the—lowest points in the war for the Union.[11]

◈　　◈　　◈

The 39th had spent July continuing to work on fortifications, marching from place to place to protect troops movements and the Deep Bottom bridgehead, and generally attempting to survive the heat. Men suffering from the high temperatures and lack of water were now adding to the casualty counts that two months of battle had tallied up. Leroy Baker was doing his best to lead the regiment that had lost so many of its officers, but it was the emerging leadership of Sergeant Homer Plimpton making a difference. Plimpton had been organizing efforts among the men to write accounts for Illinois papers of the brave service of those killed in battle. When word of Captain Rudd's death reached the regiment, Plimpton had hoped the officers might do the same for him, but when they did not, Plimpton acted again. While the exercise required the men to re-live the battles that took their friends, it also allowed them to reflect on their duties, tell the story of what was happening, and encourage citizens at home to not let the struggle be made in vain.[12]

Plimpton was also working on another issue that would soon affect troop morale, the matter of expiring three-year terms. While leadership had been pushing for October 11, the date the regiment was mustered in, many men were making claims that they had signed up for three years of service at an earlier date. While ending the enlistments would take men from the regiment, Plimpton knew that unhappy men ready to go home would have a negative impact on the veterans and new recruits. In Plimpton's eyes, doing right by these men would garner positive service out of them until their last day. Like a good sergeant always does, Plimpton was looking out for the enlisted man's welfare, with benefit to the entire regiment. His efforts were not going unnoticed, and Plimpton was awaiting a commission to First Lieutenant.[13]

◆ ◆ ◆

The 39th, and X Corps, began the month of August with yet another leadership change. General Brooks was forced to resign because of poor health, and Major General David Birney took command. Birney was an experienced general, having led a brigade during the Seven Days Campaign, and divisions at Fredericksburg, Gettysburg, and during Grant's Overland Campaign. Wanting X Corps to be prepared for anything and ready to fight when called upon, Birney instituted a schedule whereby men not on picket duty were out in line at 3:00 a.m., then had multiple periods of drill or inspection throughout the day. The routine found little favor with the men only looking to beat the continuing heat, but Birney knew from his experience with Grant that X Corps would not be idle for long.[14]

In the second week of August, Grant's staff received word that Lee had, in fact, sent reinforcements from Petersburg to the Valley to counter Sheridan and to Atlanta to counter Sherman. Grant believed the removal of troops would allow him to man the lines at Petersburg and Bermuda Hundred with fewer men while affording him numbers to go on the offensive once again. Hancock's II Corps would board steamers and feint as if heading off to defend Washington before turning back up the James to debark just downriver from Deep Bottom. Simultaneously, Birney would take two divisions of X Corps and Brigadier General David Gregg's cavalry division and cross the James over the Deep Bottom pontoon bridge. While the operation's principal aim was to divert forces from Petersburg that would allow for further offensives on the railroad, additional goals could be achieved through the Deep Bottom offensive. Lee might be forced to recall his

Pontoon bridge across the James River at Deep Bottom (Library of Congress: LC-DIG-ppmsca-33352).

troops from the Valley—or even better—a great success by Hancock and Birney would put Richmond in great peril.[15]

The II and X Corps operation was a secret even to the men themselves as movements began on August 13. The men of II Corps boarded their transports. They believed, as Grant wanted Lee to, that they were headed for Washington, D.C. Similarly, the 39th thought they were headed to Mobile Bay where the United States had just taken control, or perhaps to their old stomping grounds in the Shenandoah Valley. The X Corps First Division, still under General Terry, was joined by a provisional division under Birney's brother, Brigadier General William Birney. The two divisions marched to the James River, and instead of boarding transports for either of their supposed destinations, the men crossed the long pontoon bridge. While the deception was well-intentioned, it caused the U.S. force its own problems. Many sick or injured men thought they were simply marching to board transports and claimed they were fit for duty. The long journey in the heat then caused many to fall out. Anchored five miles down the James and bivouacked in the woods near Confederate lines, the II and X Corps spent a hot, stale, mosquito-filled night awaiting the fighting they knew would soon come.

In the morning, Birney's Corps would attack the south-facing Confederate line guarding New Market Road, and Hancock would attack the line facing east.[16]

❖   ❖   ❖

General Terry's first division was in the lead on the morning of August 14, with the 39th and First Brigade, now led by Colonel Francis Pond as Howell was temporarily commanding Third Division, anchoring the left.[17] Just after the first hints of daylight, First and Third Brigades charged a line of Confederate skirmishers. The rebels were driven back to their picket line rifle pits, and an hour-long exchange of fire began. Spread too thin in their current arrangement, First Division's momentum was halted, and for the moment, things became quiet. The Confederate defenders had heard the movements over the pontoon bridge the previous day and had been ready and preparing for an attack.[18]

By 7:00 a.m., Terry was concerned the division had not covered more ground and that he was falling behind in the need to coordinate his attack with Hancock to the east. Terry brought Second Brigade up from the rear and deployed them to First Brigade's west. His full division now presented in a line of battle, Terry ordered them to advance at 7:15 a.m. On the Federal right, the Third Brigade cracked the entrenched Confederate picket line in front of them, then turned to the west, joining the 39th and Second Brigade, who were barreling forward in the Federal center. Together, the two brigades drove the pickets of three Confederate brigades back to their principal lines taking many prisoners along the way. Besides pushing back the rebels and taking prisoners, the advance had rendered some forward Confederate cannons undefended and unusable.[19]

First Division advanced towards Four Mile Creek and the foot of New Market Heights when they started trading fire with Confederates inside their main earthworks. Becoming concerned about the Confederate position's strength, Birney's decision was made for him when he received word from Hancock around 9:00 a.m. II Corps' travel had not gone as planned. The steamers had taken on water and ships bottomed out while trying to extend gangplanks to the shore. Only half of Hancock's men had disembarked when Birney's attack had begun, and the rest were not ashore until just before Hancock sent word to Birney. Once on land, II Corps' advance was slowed not only by Confederate skirmishers and cavalry but the insufferable heat. Heatstroke was creating more casualties than enemy fire, and men were dropping on the roads. The operation was suffering from starts and stops. Still, it had already merited some useful information: General Grant was made aware that prisoners taken in the early fighting confirmed Robert E. Lee had sent just one division to the Shenandoah Valley—meaning Sheridan was not outnumbered there.[20]

Now waiting for orders as II Corps caught up and got into position, X Corps suffered from both heat and enemy fire. The Confederate force had used the lull in the X Corps advance to reposition some artillery that had been left behind in the morning attacks, and the temperature was sending swaths of men to the rear. The 39th spent the rest of the day making positioning movements and acting as reinforcements but seeing little other action. In the early afternoon, Hancock ordered

Birney's Corps to move east and attack Confederate works. The U.S.S. *Agawam* delivered fire on Confederate positions to some effect, but General Grant soon arrived to meet with Birney and Terry. Viewing the Confederate works beyond New Market Road, Grant called off Birney's assault. Instead, elements of X Corps moved east, capturing some abandoned Confederate guns and creating a link to II Corps. As X Corps consolidated their position and rested, the II Corps advance continued to the east, facing strong resistance. Darkness ended the day's action, and the 39th went on picket duty.[21]

The day had been a mixed bag for the Federal force at Deep Bottom. Terry's Division of X Corps had achieved early success, consolidated its line, and captured enemy guns with minimal losses for the amount of fighting they did. Hancock was understandably unhappy with the delays and the inability to follow up on X Corps successes. However, the operations had forced Lee to cancel the movement of troops to the Shenandoah as Grant had sought, and the force was in place to follow-up the next day. The day had cost the Federal force approximately 600 battle casualties, but the heat continued to be what whittled the ranks. The night brought the first rain in some time, and while it was a relief, it made rest difficult and turned the dry bottom land into a mess. For the 39th and X Corps, however, it did not matter if rest would be difficult. They were roused from their sleep late in the evening and soon on the move.[22]

❖ ❖ ❖

Hancock believed X Corps could flank the Confederate left overnight, and in the very early morning hours of August 15, portions of Terry's division headed northeast while the bulk of X Corps, to include the 39th, withdrew back to the James. There they moved downstream and re-crossed at another location to move east and link up with II Corps. Movement was laborious, slowed by bottlenecks at the river crossings, the darkness, and the bottomland's muck. The weather was soon the issue again, however, as dawn came and the heat and humidity returned. The men rested in an area called Strawberry Plains, east of Deep Bottom, while cavalry reconnoitered the route. Resuming their advance mid-morning, the heat became the formidable opponent of the day. Butler had sent roughly 9,000 men from X Corps to be part of the Deep Bottom operations, and approximately 3,000 of them fell out as stragglers in the heat. The road was lined with men in all manner of horrific conditions from the heat, and the Corps did not reach its specified locations until mid-afternoon.[23]

The 39th spent the day supporting a battery exchanging fire with the rebels while sharpshooters and skirmishers exchanged fire along various portions of the Federal line. Mostly, however, the day was quiet as the difficulty and delays of the movement had forced Hancock to abandon any notion of attacking and would have to delay until the 16th. Taking the opportunity to position themselves, the Confederate force ignored the small number of X Corps infantry on their right and correctly assessed Hancock's intentions. By the end of the day on the 15th, 17,000 rebels were facing east to hold their line between Fussell's Mill and New Market Road. The 39th found themselves in the Federal center, with Gregg's cavalry to their right and the bulk of II Corps to the left. The next day, they would attack west and look to turn the Confederate left, or perhaps assault the principal works themselves.[24]

❖ ❖ ❖

The morning of August 16 brought no relief from the hot and humid conditions. Three days of brutal sun and a lack of adequate water took a toll on the entire Federal force. The morning report of the 39th Illinois showed that only 228 men were fit for duty after the recent losses of battle and removing the men struck down by the heat. Fifteen of those men had been kept at Bermuda Hundred to work on fortifications, and thus, the 39th Illinois would enter the day's assaults with 213 enlisted men and eleven officers. Other II and X Corps elements had the same issues, but after two days of missed opportunities, Hancock and Birney could wait no longer. The Confederates had been forced to divert men to the area, but they now needed to be kept there. The Federal force was only eight miles from Richmond and needed to strike before any more reinforcements could arrive.[25]

Around 6:00 a.m., Gregg's cavalry and a II Corps brigade moved forward as skirmishers on the Confederate line's extreme left. Within an hour, the advance had driven back Confederate pickets on the end of the line, and a further advance drove back additional pickets over a half-mile. By 10:30, Gregg's cavalry had moved far enough west that they were almost straight north of the Confederate works and controlled both sides of Charles City Road—severely threatening a Confederate retreat route towards Richmond. The Confederates soon counterattacked against Gregg's position, and he and the II Corps brigade spent the better part of the day in a back-and-forth stalemate.[26]

The 39th had been slowly moving forward since the sun came up, part of First Division leading X Corps into the fight. With Confederate forces near Charles City Road occupied, General Terry's aim was to attack the Confederate flank and works between Charles City and Darbytown Roads. Terry planned to snap the Confederate line in front of him, then wheel the entire division to the left, funneling retreating rebels towards II Corps. Confederate skirmishers and pickets were driven back to the principal works. Continuing to move forward, the advance ran off more Confederate pickets shortly after 9:00 a.m. and continued onward. As the advance continued—now only 200 yards from the Confederate entrenchments—the division was funneled into a ravine and took heavy fire from beyond a wooded area.[27]

Terry brought First Brigade forward to the division's right, less than 200 yards from the Confederate works. Under heavy fire, the brigade formed up inside a wooded area, eyeing the opening between them and the Confederate line full of slashed timber, tree stumps, and uneven ground. General Terry rode amongst the men telling them they were going to "charge those works" as Colonel Pond placed the 67th Ohio in front as skirmishers, with the 39th, 62nd Ohio and 85th Pennsylvania in the main battle line. Seven hundred and fifty soldiers of the "Western Brigade" were lined up in a double-column formation—each regiment formed up two companies wide and five deep. The 39th and 62nd would carry the works and wheel left. The 85th would move right. Third Brigade was to the left, and 2nd would follow them both. Aligned and ready, the men laid flat and hugged the earth while waiting for the word.[28] Speaking to his men, Company H commander Chauncey Williams, of Old Town, exclaimed, "[b]oys, we will go into those pits, or die!"[29]

Very near noon, the "forward" command was given, and the men moved out in a steady march but came under an immense amount of fire as soon as they stepped into the clearing—practically erasing the lead of each regiment. The 39th's color-bearer, Company G Private Henry Hardenbergh of Bremen Township, was hit in the shoulder, dropping the colors to the ground. Remembering what Colonel Osborn had long ago told them about their regiment's colors, Company E Lieutenant Norman Warner of Wilmington immediately reached for the flag. Hardenbergh, too, remembered Osborn's words and held on so tightly that a piece remained in his hands when Warner took it. The colors raised again, the brigade now charged ahead "with a regular western yell," wrote Homer Plimpton.[30]

Swaths of men were struck down crossing the open area, but the Western Brigade had moved so quickly that a second volley of Confederate fire could not be delivered. The brigade made it to the Confederate works, with Company K private James Latimer, of Marseilles, being said to have been the first man up and over.[31] A nasty fight ensued as shots were fired and bayonets were thrust. Lieutenant Warner was struck by a bullet in the leg, the Yates Phalanx colors falling again. "Another officer snatched them up and sprang upon the parapet," wrote Plimpton, "followed by scores of others, who leaped over right among the Johnnies."[32] "The Western Brigade swept over the parapet into the Confederate works like a tornado," recalled Colonel Pond.[33] Stabbing with their bayonets and using their muskets like "clubs," the men broke the line and began rounding up prisoners. Barreling down the line to the left, the brigade rounded up hundreds of Confederate prisoners and five of their colors.[34]

Twenty of the prisoners were taken by the 39th alone, and one flag was taken by none other than Henry Hardenbergh himself. After being shot and dropping the colors in the opening salvo, Hardenbergh had picked himself up, continued forward, and found himself in hand-to-hand combat with the 10th Alabama color-bearer—who now lay dead on the field. General Birney was so impressed with Hardenbergh's valor even after being wounded that he recommended him for appointment as an officer in the Corps' Thirty-Sixth United States Colored Troops and would be recommended for the Medal of Honor.[35]

While the 39th and First Brigade had made their charge, so too had Third Brigade to their left. Third Brigade also made it to the Confederate fortifications, and the two brigades linked-up inside the entrenchments. The Second Brigade soon followed up, and Terry's division had made a serious breakthrough that controlled the Confederate trenches from just north of Fussell's Mill stretching north of Darbytown Road. Terry twice attempted to expand the breakthrough while II Corps guarded the Federal flank, but Confederate reinforcements were rapidly arriving, and a Confederate counterattack re-took portions of their line. The Federal left soon in danger; they were forced to fall back under heavy fire to the east of Bailey's Creek. It was during this withdrawal that Homer Plimpton's brother Olin was wounded in the left arm and sent to the rear and then hospital. Plimpton would not see him for the rest of the war, but once again was unharmed himself. The day had cost over 1,500 casualties among the 7,200 engaged from the two corps—the Confederates had lost 900 out of 6,400.[36]

For the 39th, involved in its first significant offensive charge, the battle that would become known as Second Deep Bottom had been enormously costly. Of the 213 enlisted men and eleven officers that took part in the assault, 97 men and seven officers had become casualties. Anthony Taylor, who had been recently assigned as an orderly to Doctor Clark, wrote "such sights I never saw before and never want to again" and that there was a "pile of legs and arms nearly as big as a haystack."[37]

Captain Baker's leg was shattered by a bullet so severely as he led that charge that it required amputation—yet another regimental commander to fall in battle. Lieutenant Warner, who so nobly picked up the flag at the beginning of the assault, also would require his leg to be ampu- tated. Company A Lieuten- ant William Butterfield, of Wilmington, and Company D Lieutenant Horace Knapp, of Chicago, were also wounded. Butterfield would soon be fit for duty again, while Knapp required a ball to be cut out of his shoulder. Three Phalanx officers made the ultimate sacrifice on August 16. Company D Lieu- tenant John Frame of Paine's Point died alongside his men who made the brave charge, and Company I Lieutenant James Lemon, of Santa Anna, would die four days later from wounds. Captain Wil- liams' declaration proved to not be an either-or statement. His men took the rifle pits, but he gave his life in doing so. Twenty-four-year-old Company E Captain Lewis T. Whipple, of Rockville, was now the commanding officer of the 39th Illinois.[38]

Historical marker in front of ground the 39th Illi- nois charged at the Second Battle of Deep Bottom on August 16, 1864. Private Hardenbergh's Medal of Honor action is noted (author's photograph).

Even those still standing, and fit for duty, were realizing how delicate their lives were in the current fighting. Company G's Private Ransom Bedell wrote home to a cousin that "rebel bullets ventilated" his hat "uncomfortably near my head."[39] Joseph Ward would write later in October to his wife telling her he hadn't yet received a mark of any kind, even a bullet hole in his clothes, but added "I don't think there is another main in our company can say the same."[40]

The day was also full of bravery and meritorious service, however. Besides Hardenbergh's heroic actions as color bearer, Company K private Lewis Marsh, of Marseilles, had his arm shattered so badly it would require amputation, but was seen carrying a wounded man off the field. Others found redemption in the actions of the day. Company K private William Moxton, of Marseilles, had been a corporal but reduced to the ranks for a disagreement with an officer. Following his conduct in charging the works on August 16, however, he was promoted to Sergeant for meritorious conduct.[41]

❖   ❖   ❖

Tactically, the result of the battle had been a successful Confederate counterattack; but Lee had been forced to pull men from Petersburg and the Howlett line to meet Hancock and Birney's advance. Confident he had achieved his objective of using Deep Bottom to set the stage for other offensives, Grant shifted men of his own towards the Weldon and Petersburg railroad. Grant wanted Hancock and Birney to hold their position as long as possible but ordered a fleet of steamers towards Deep Bottom to act as if the force would soon withdraw. Skirmishing continued for the next few days, but Confederate attacks achieved nothing more than pushing in Federal pickets. As August 20 turned to the 21st, the 39th withdrew and returned to their Bermuda Hundred camp. Federal forces had suffered 2,901 casualties—1,678 from X Corps alone. The 39th returned to camp with only 116 enlisted men and four officers fit for duty. Confederate losses had been 1,250, and they had shown that—despite forcing Lee to reshuffle troops—Deep Bottom would not serve as a path to Richmond.[42]

HEADQUARTERS TENTH ARMY CORPS
Fussel's Mills, VA., August 19th, 1864.

GENERAL ORDERS

The Major-General commanding congratulates the Tenth Corps upon its success. It has on each occasion, when ordered, broken the enemy's strong lines. It has captured during this short campaign four siege guns protected by the most formidable works, six stands of colors, and many prisoners. It has proved itself worthy of its old Wagner and Sumter renown. Much fatigue, patience and heroism may yet be demanded of it; but the Major-General commanding is confident of the response.

(Signed)
MAJOR-GENERAL D.B. BIRNEY[43]

❖   ❖   ❖

The effort at Deep Bottom, however, was not made in vain. Sheridan arrived in the Valley during the Deep Bottom offensive and routed Confederate infantry

Chevaux-de-frise in front of the U.S. Army's Fort Sedgwick on the Petersburg line. Such forts were found up and down the line and represent the landscape the 39th found themselves in (Library of Congress: LC-DIG-cwbp-02618).

at the Battle of Guard Hill. Meanwhile, Grant's move of troops to the Weldon Railroad proved fruitful between August 18 and 21, destroying miles of track and garnering the Federal's first tactical victory of the Petersburg siege. Confederate forces at Petersburg were now forced to move supplies overland, going far out of the way, and had lost 2,300 men they could not spare. Early on the morning of the 24th, the 39th was on the move again, reinforcing the Petersburg front. The following day, upon withdrawing from Deep Bottom, II Corps engaged Confederates at Reams Station. While the engagement was a somewhat costly tactical defeat—II Corps lost 2,700 men—the rebels lost another 1,000, and more track was destroyed and disrupted. Grant's army may have "lost" two out of three of the engagements, but a strategy of attrition, supply disruption, and running the Confederates ragged was paying dividends—albeit at great cost.[44]

❖   ❖   ❖

The 39th made their new camp in a land of entrenchments with dirt mounds rising six feet above the ground, just northwest of Petersburg near the railroad.

Confederate shot and bullets flew day and night, and the toll the recent fighting had taken on the 39th would continue to rise. A reminder that no man was safe, on August 25, Henry Hardenbergh was struck by a shell fragment and killed. The man who had been shot, dropped the colors, rejoined the fight, and captured the enemy's colors was killed while merely resting in camp. His Lieutenant commission would arrive the next day, and he would never know he was awarded the Medal of Honor.[45]

Grant's August offensives had cost his army 9,922 soldiers, and while it had furthered the siege and protected Washington, Richmond was no closer to falling. As John Horn writes in *The Siege of Petersburg: The Battles for the Weldon Railroad, August 1864*, Grant "did not have forever to capture Richmond. He had only until November 8th, 1864."[46] Politicians and civilians at home did not see the strategy, only the tangible number of dead and wounded. The action at Reams Station highlighted the further toll on the once mighty Army of the Potomac. "I am going to be beaten," remarked Lincoln, "and unless some great change takes place *badly be*aten."[47] The tremendous loss of life would require tangible results to deliver Lincoln's election and save the Federal war effort. The first days of September would bring the "great changes" Lincoln so desperately needed.

16

Campaign Season

Joseph Hallett was born in Somersetshire, England in 1843 and moved to America with his parents in 1852. In 1861, he was working as a marble-cutting apprentice in Bloomington, Illinois and answered a call for volunteers to the 8th Illinois, traveling to Springfield to do so. At five feet two inches tall, and not yet 18 years of age; however, he was advised to "return home to his mother."

After the events of Bull Run; however, he enlisted in Company B of the 39th, serving in the company until March 1864 when he was detailed as the bugler, wounded while performing that duty on May 16, 1864 at Drewry's Bluff. In August 1864, when George Heritage was called to command the regiment, Hallet was made sergeant and often in command of Company B through the spring of 1865.[1]

SIEGE LIFE IN FRONT OF PETERSBURG was one of steady shelling and musket fire, surrounded by mounds of dirt while living in a dirty trench. Valentine Randolph, now only weeks away from his enlistment ending with many others, wrote that there were so many flies "a person can hardly eat or drink without swallowing them by the dozen."[2] The existence was a strange one. A constant fire was directed toward each line, and errant shells would crash into the few trees that hadn't been cut down with a tremendous noise. Men would be shot just for sticking their heads above the works or be wounded by a shell while resting in camp. Picket duty consisted of being crammed into a ditch with your comrades for a day or two at a time, bullets steadily whizzing back and forth, watching for enemy movements. Yet, there was also the bartering for goods inside no-man's-land—a normalcy during the war—yet strangely out of place in this current setting. Under white flags, men would meet and trade Union coffee for Confederate tobacco, or a Yankee pocketknife for a rebel newspaper. A man may trade with the enemy in the morning, only to be shot by him in the afternoon.[3]

The Confederate line in front of the 39th and the Federal line extended nearly forty miles from the Appomattox's left bank around Petersburg and to the James, then north and east towards Richmond. The Federal line was less fortified but improving daily and just as long. Grant's headquarters were still at City Point, and a railroad had been constructed that ran from there to the far left of the line. Men were busy placing guns, building parapets, and slashing timber in front of them to slow any advance. Throughout September, Federal engineers created elaborate defenses in front of City Point, reinforced those already at Bermuda Hundred, and ensured the men on the siege lines had all the protection they could get.[4]

❖   ❖   ❖

While there was nothing quiet or comfortable about siege life in the trenches, the beginning of September was an operationally still time for the 39th. On September 3, however, they received word that their tactically inconclusive action at Deep Bottom had indirectly contributed to a major victory. Near Atlanta, General Sherman had cut the last open railroad leading into the city. Confederate General John Bell Hood was forced to attack on August 30, but he was firmly repulsed without reinforcements from Petersburg. Sherman followed up the next day, and the result was a rout. Hood evacuated Atlanta, Sherman entered and raised the American flag, and cannons and church bells throughout northern lines and northern cities celebrated the victory. Just a few days prior, the Democrats had nominated George McClellan to oppose Lincoln on a platform of ending the war, asking only for union. A view the party would sell on account of Lincoln's mismanaged war that was costing so many lives with so little success. A platform that led the Confederacy to believe that they didn't have to win the military struggle; they just had to keep from losing it before November.[5]

After Sherman's victory, however, the Republicans were no longer the ones doing the in-fighting, and it was the Democrat's platform that was splintering. McClellan, in his desire to not tarnish the cause he had fought for or alienate the military, had written a bet-hedging acceptance letter. Waffling between acceptance of the anti-war stance while flirting with a war fought simply for peace and re-union; McClellan made nobody in his party happy while unifying Republicans and pro-war democrats. Sherman's victory had even brought a surge of new enlistments and calmed down the need for an expanded draft—another staple of anti-war sentiment. Sherman's success, and the taking of Mobile Bay in August, had "knocked the bottom out of the Chicago platform," wrote Secretary of State William Seward.[6] Most notably disappointed were the men in the Army of the Potomac who fought for him and now saw their former commander as denigrating their service and the sacrifices of their brethren.[7] In his memoirs, Grant would later note that Sherman's victory was the "first great political campaign for the Republicans in their canvass of 1864."[8]

The August offensives, and the sacrifices of the 39th, continued to reap rewards as the month went on. The attempted breakthrough to Richmond at Deep Bottom and the cutting of the Weldon Railroad had forced Lee to bring a division of men back from the Shenandoah to reinforce the lines and guard the ever-lengthening supply routes. After weeks of small but significant victories, Sheridan struck the Confederates at Winchester on September 19, scoring a tide-turning win in the Valley and putting Early on the defensive.[9] Again remarking in his memoirs, Grant commented on the addition of Sheridan's success to Sherman's that the two campaigns were more effective than "all the speeches, all the bonfires, and all the parading with banners and bands of music in the North," in getting Lincoln re-elected.[10] When Grant had taken command of all U.S. armies and developed his coordinated plan to prevent Confederates from reinforcing each other, Lincoln had told him "those not skinning could hold a leg."[11] While

Lincoln's metaphor had more than adequately described what happened, it had been Grant's forces at Petersburg "holding the leg."

❖   ❖   ❖

While the stump speeches of Sherman and Sheridan had only strengthened the 39th's support for Illinois' own President Lincoln and his cause, the Yates Phalanx was learning they would not receive the opportunity to add their votes to his tally. The regiment had long thought they might get the chance to take furloughs to vote, but the urgency of the military situation prevented it. While election officials from various states would soon arrive near the lines to take the army's votes, the Illinois legislature Yates had been battling saw fit to deny Illinois troops from voting unless it was in person. "Little Mac had but few friends in the army operating against Richmond," wrote Doctor Clark, adding that the 39th was "loud in expressing our condemnation of the Illinois Copperhead legislature in not permitting us to vote."[12] Rallying around this cause was a unifying morale boost for a regiment being ravaged by casualties and now losing the members who did not reenlist. While Colonel Osborn was doing his best to recruit in Illinois, his real impact had been the leadership and culture he instilled before being wounded. Despite all the losses and being on their sixth commander, the regiment remained a capable fighting force.

Like many other regiments were doing, the 39th sent a resolution to Illinois newspapers stating both their support for Lincoln's war and calling on men from home to enlist rather than subject the country to the embarrassment and decisiveness of the draft. Going further, Delaware, Indiana, Massachusetts, and New Jersey regiments joined the 39th in further condemnation of their state legislatures disenfranchisement of service members by denying absentee votes. Even those in the army who had been ardent supporters of McClellan, and were once inclined to agree with his politics, were disgusted by their former commander's alignment with the anti-war cause. The U.S. army, it seemed, was ready to attack the Confederacy not just with rifles and bayonets but with their voices or votes.[13]

❖   ❖   ❖

As Sheridan continued his success, Lee was forced to divert even more manpower to the Valley, and Grant decided upon another offensive. Once again, Grant set in motion a plan to make a vigorous complimentary effort by the Army of the James north of the James River and the Army of the Potomac closer to Petersburg. While similar to the August offensive, Butler would be in command north of the James, and Grant gave his commanders freedom to make their own plans within his intent: Butler should at the very least occupy the attention of Confederate troops north of the James, and not allow them to reinforce elsewhere. If Butler broke the line, he should enter Richmond. South of the James, Meade should further target the railroads, consolidate the expanding Federal line, and attack Petersburg if the opportunity presented itself. Both men's goal was to take control of roads and routes that forced the Confederate supply chain to lengthen even more.[14]

On September 25, the 39th received orders that it would soon move with the rest of the division across both rivers and towards Richmond. The men took all their extra baggage to the rear and were told to prepare to move in "light marching" order—gun, sixty rounds, and a haversack with five days of hardtack and pork or beef fat. After adding an overcoat, blanket, and canteen and cup, it was enough to "keep a man from flying," wrote Doctor Clark, but viewed as just the essentials.[15] The men were likely happy to escape life in the trenches; however, such an order was a sure sign that the coming movement would move quickly, never stop for long, and lead towards an assault.

Butler's plan was a two-pronged attack that Petersburg Campaign historian John Horn called "his best performance of the war."[16] Butler once again had both his corps at his command and Kautz's cavalry division and would bring his 26,000 men against 6,000 well dug-in rebels between Deep Bottom and Richmond. While previous Federal offensives in the area had sought to turn the Confederate left, Butler intended to go after the center and right. X Corps and the Black Division of XVIII Corps would attack New Market Heights to occupy the force there, while the cavalry hopefully exploited this distraction by heading up New Market Road to Richmond. The rest of XVIII Corps, now led by Major General Edward Ord after Smith had fallen ill, would cross at a place called Aiken's Landing. Ord's aim would be Richmond's long-standing outer line of defense in an area called Chaffin's Bluff or Chaffin's Farm, specifically Fort Harrison—the most vital portion of the line.[17] Successful efforts on the right and left would then allow the Army of the James to link up together and press north.

The march was a long, and hard one, made in the darkness of night with brief rest. Given the movement of two corps and multiple river crossings, there was no action until early September 29. The precaution of moving at night had not prevented the crossings from going completely undetected, however, and at sunrise that morning, Lee began moving men from Petersburg to the area. This was just what Butler wanted, though, and there was now the opportunity to achieve Grant's desire to pull troops from Petersburg but attack before they could arrive. Brigadier General Charles Paine's Division moved north from the Deep Bottom Crossing and headed for the New Market Line. The terrain was covered with timber slashing and many obstacles, but the division charged valiantly at a Texan brigade. A few men were able to make it onto the Confederate works, but the attack was repulsed. The defenders were well dug in, and the obstacles had left the attackers exposed to fire far too long.[18]

While initially unsuccessful, the assault had two very positive affects. First, was the brave fighting of the Black division. While the sentiment of the U.S. army had, on the whole, become one that supported Black troops, assaults like the one on the 29th proved there was no compromise in ability. Four Black soldiers were awarded the Medal of Honor for their actions.[19] Perhaps more importantly, the assault rattled the psyche of the Confederate troops. As Confederate numbers and supplies dwindled, The Union wasn't letting up throwing fresh men at them, and the symbolism of Black men fighting for a Union without slavery was not lost on anyone.

The attack had also occupied the Confederate troops at New Market Heights, while Ord simultaneously launched an XVIII Corps division, led by Brigadier General George Stannard, at Fort Harrison and the Richmond outer line to X Corps' west. Not expecting a direct attack on the line, especially considering the past Federal attempts to attack the Confederate left, Ord had the element of surprise. His men faced little resistance in the form of men, obstacles, or artillery as they blew by Confederate skirmishers and advanced within 100 yards of Fort Harrison. Confederate General John Gregg, in command of the line at New Market Heights, received word of Ord's attack, and perhaps because he had just repulsed an attack in his front, detached men to the aid of Fort Harrison. The Confederate reinforcements were now too late to stop XVIII Corps and had opened the door for X Corps at New Market Heights. Paine's men renewed their attack and broke the New Market Line, while XVIII Corps spilled into Fort Harrison.[20]

While XVIII Corps had the rebels on the run for their secondary lines, all three of Stannard's brigade commanders had been killed in the assault, and the assault stalled amidst a lack of leadership direction. Brigadier General Charles Heckerman's division became mired in a swamp near the James when called in reserve and came under assault from Confederate ironclads. Attempting to rally the men himself in the confusion, Ord was severely wounded. Heckerman, who had gotten lost at Drewry's Bluff and been captured before eventually being exchanged for, took command in the field but could not rally the assault. The Second Division of X Corps and a brigade led by William Birney attempted assaults to the north in the early afternoon, but the reinforcements from New Market, and others sent by Lee, proved too much to handle. With their forward momentum stopped, Major General Godfrey Weitzel took command of XVIII Corps and put his men to work reversing Fort Harrison.[21]

The 39th, and Alfred Terry's First Division, had moved up following the initial assault at New Market, and while they did not actively engage, their presence on the Confederate left had allowed for Paine's follow-on assault. Their position put the Army of the James in control from Chaffin's Bluff to New Market Road. This allowed Kautz's cavalry to raid down New Market and Darbytown Roads, harassing Richmond's defenses and holding Confederate troops in place. The 39th and X Corps were soon busy with their spades, fortifying their positions while Federal engineers made the new lines their own. General Meade had spent the day demonstrating at Petersburg to hold Confederate troops there, but Grant was concerned that Butler had not done enough to give Meade freedom of movement. As his men now raced to make the captured fortifications their own, Grant hoped that Lee would mass troops there in the morning.[22]

❖　❖　❖

General Lee obliged, and General Grant's men did not disappoint. By midday on the 30th, Lee had moved almost 10,000 troops and their batteries from Petersburg to north of the James. The Confederate strength now 16,000, Lee urged his commanders to use all of it to retake Fort Harrison and the outer line. General Butler's 21,000 men, however, had made significant progress in reversing the former Confederate stronghold and placed guns in sound positions. The Confederates attacked just before 2:00 p.m., but brigades advanced in stops and starts as they faced heavy Federal fire, never fully concentrating their assault or getting near their lost fort. The shrinking Confederate army wasn't just suffering from a lack of manpower, but a lack of experienced leadership. General Lee was personally on hand to witness the plan fall apart, as Confederate losses totaled roughly 1,200 men to Butler's approximately 250.[23]

Lee's movement of troops to retake Fort Harrison had failed while pulling 10,000 sorely needed men from the Petersburg line. After demonstrating with his force the previous day, Meade acted on the 30th. As Lee's Fort Harrison reinforcements marched away from Petersburg, V Corps, and a cavalry division marched for the vacated position near an area called Peebles Farm. V Corps broke a Confederate line and captured Fort Archer, while IX Corps headed for Boydton Plank Road, which was part of the circuitous supply route the Confederates were being forced to use. The operation had forced Lee to send one division back from Fort Harrison, and while this halted the IX Corps advance, it was an ominous sign for Lee and the game he now had to play. As the day ended, V and IX Corps consolidated their position, and Federal soldiers spent another night reversing captured territory and fortifying their positions.[24]

❖   ❖   ❖

As the calendar turned to October, the situations at Chaffin's and Peebles Farms changed very little. The Confederates launched an attack on the Federal right, which drove back some picket forces, but ultimately found V Corps well-entrenched and supported by guns. The rebels lost 400 men, and Meade sent reinforcements on Grant's newly constructed military railroad. At Chaffin's Farm, Lee turned his guns on his former stronghold at Fort Harrison to no avail and did not mount an attack. The 39th joined Terry's Division and Kautz's cavalry in a movement up Darbytown Road in a reconnaissance in force of the Richmond defenses, coming within two miles of the city. After leaving the Valley with the impression they'd march on Richmond in 1862, waiting for it with McClellan at Harrison's Landing, and thinking they would five months ago when arriving at Bermuda Hundred; the 39th came the closest to Richmond of any U.S. force since the war began. After skirmishing with forces manning the city's intermediate line, Terry's division withdrew back to New Market Heights. No Federal troops would get closer before the war's end.[25]

By the morning of the 2nd, Grant had ceased what many historians refer to as his Fifth Offensive. The combined operations at Chaffin's Bluff and Peebles Farm had cost Grant approximately 6,300 men to Lee's roughly 3,000—oddly split almost the same for both sides at both locations.[26] Lee had not withdrawn as many men from the Valley as Grant would have wished, and Richmond still stood, but Butler had taken Fort Harrison—just six miles south of Richmond, and the New Market Heights position that the Federals had attacked in vain twice before. Most notably, the success of the Army of the James had pried rebels away from Petersburg that could not be used for offensives against the Army of the

Potomac's position. Meade's attacks had put the Federals within striking distance to the South Side Railroad and the Confederate overland supply routes. Given the importance of the ground they had taken, Grant ordered Butler to hold the positions at Fort Harrison and New Market Heights. Butler was concerned his flank was exposed, but Grant wanted to force Lee to defend the longest front possible between the two cities and prevent him from attacking at Petersburg.[27]

The 39th had been pieces on the board to shape the battle and spent most of their effort with the spade rather than their rifles. Hot and dry conditions of summer had turned to the cool and wet weather of early fall, with the men sleeping on rubber blankets in the mud—at least with a daily ration of whiskey and quinine to keep sickness down. The changing of the seasons would see events that completely reversed the United States summer of desperation and all but assure Lincoln's reelection as the fall moved towards another winter. However, in service to the necessity of holding the newly won position, many of the 39th Illinois' remaining men wouldn't be around to see it.

17

Darbytown Road

George Heritage was born in Oxfordshire, England in 1834, and he and his father moved to Canada after his mother died while he was young. In 1856 he moved to Illinois seeking employment, then bouncing between Canada and the Midwest with no luck in finding work. In 1859 he found himself working in Bloomington but attempted to head west to capitalize on the growing number of mining towns but had no luck. Unable to make a go of it, and without the finances to return home, he took a job driving cattle that eventually brought him back to Bloomington.

Heritage joined the 8th Illinois Infantry—commanded by Richard Oglesby who became a Major General and post-war Illinois governor— for a three-month commitment. Heritage returned to Bloomington and took an active role in forming a company for the three-year service, eventually being named Orderly Sergeant of Company B, and ultimately one of its officers. Heritage was wounded by a shell fragment in August 1864 and in hospital for 20 days, but returned to the regiment, and by reason of seniority amidst all the death and injury, took command of the 39th.[1]

MORALE IN NORTHERN CITIES was on the rise in the first days of October, as news spread that besides Sherman and Sheridan's successes, Grant was closing the vise grip around Petersburg and Richmond. The 39th spent the days following the Chaffin's Farm engagements doing heavy fatigue duty fortifying the new positions while often being called to the trenches because of picket firing and skirmishing. On the whole, however, it was a quiet few days. The men's shelter tents and knapsacks came up from the Petersburg rear, and for the first time in over a week, they had fresh clothes and some cover at night.[2]

While the 39th had not been in heavy combat action since Deep Bottom, there had still been the slow but steady trickle of death, wounding, injury, and sickness. The biggest thief of manpower was not the enemy or disease, however, but expiring three-year enlistments. Since the beginning of September, the 39th had lost roughly 50 men who had not reenlisted the previous winter.[3] While the draft would hopefully provide men for the regiment, and Colonel Osborn was actively recruiting Illinois men near Chicago, losing 50 men was not an insignificant number when combined with all the other reasons men had been, and continued to be, lost. Especially significant was the ever-decreasing number of officers the regiment had. Besides those already lost to death, wounds, and resignation; the regiment had lost four officers to expiring terms or resignations in the last month. Five more were slated to muster out by the end of the year, including Captain Whipple, who had been in command, and Captain George Heritage who had been recovering from his wounds. This led to situations like Company G, where Homer Plimpton was one of only two officers, or Company I, where Samuel Gilmore of Champaign, who had been wounded at Drewry's Bluff, was given a commission in June so that the company would have an officer at all.[4] Through it all, the remaining men stayed loyal to their purpose and supported the men beside them as leaders continually stepped forward. Perhaps buoyed by a promise of reinforcements and the return of a recovering Osborn, the 39th soldiered on.

❖   ❖   ❖

Soldering on would soon be needed north of the James. General Lee decided an offensive was necessary to reduce the threat to Richmond and allow himself the chance for offensives at Petersburg. If Lee could roll up the right flank of X Corps, his troops could attempt to push the Federal troops back to the James. Shortly after sunup on October 7, Confederates opened-up with artillery near the X Corps right occupied by Terry's First Division. The men lined up to man the trenches as they saw smoke rising to the right. Confederate cavalry drove in the pickets, then made for Kautz's cavalry on Darbytown Road. A coordinated attack of cavalry and infantry soon became a lopsided affair. The Confederates brought up their own guns while capturing many of Kautz's, and the 39th's position was quickly under fire as Kautz retreated. Recently promoted Corporal Anthony Taylor wrote, "I never was under a hotter fire of artillery"[5] as Confederate infantry slowly advanced towards First Brigade's position holding the Division's right flank.

A confederate shell hit a caisson full of powder, causing a tremendous explosion near the 39th position. "[H]ad it been full of shells," wrote Taylor, "our whole [company] would have bit the dust."[6] Another Confederate shell slammed into the 39th's breastworks sending debris flying and hitting Homer Plimpton in the back of the head, but not seriously enough to injure him.[7]

First Brigade men got off what shots they could while Federal artillery got into place, and Terry called up his other brigades to reinforce the flank. Now answering with a battery of their own and the flank secured, the 39th and the rest of the brigade were better positioned to fight. Federal artillery targeted the rebels attempting to merge for a charge, and the attack became disjointed when one of the Confederate brigade commanders, John Gregg, was killed. The few who made it inside the artillery barrage came under heavy fire from First Brigade, not getting much closer than 100 yards from the Federal line. The rebels were soon in retreat, and Company A of the 39th was deployed with pursuing skirmishers, running the attackers completely off over the rest of the day. The retreat allowed Kautz to re-occupy his lost position on Darbytown Road, and Lee's attempt to break Butler's position had cost him 700 casualties with nothing gained.[8]

The October 7 battle of Darbytown and New Market Roads is a seldom discussed one, a minor footnote of Grant's Fifth Offensive if mentioned at all. The struggle was consequential, however, beyond just the story of the 39th. Lee had been forced into a decision to attack in a desperate attempt to rid himself of keeping so many men on the peninsula, and the attack had failed while costing him more men he couldn't afford to lose. While finally inflicting more losses than they suffered, the encounter had cost Butler approximately 430 men—split almost evenly between First Division and Kautz's cavalry.[9] Fifteen of those casualties came from the 39th Illinois. The only death was Ransom Bedell, who had not been as fortunate as he was at Deep Bottom.[10]

The result forced Lee not just to abandon other notions of offensive on the peninsula, but near Petersburg, and he focused on creating new defensive positions while deciding his next move. For the 39th specifically, the result of the day would affect them significantly in the coming week.

❖   ❖   ❖

As X Corps engineers went to work re-fortifying the right flank, the Confederates were busy creating a new line in front of Richmond. The growing consensus among the men was that the rebels would attempt to attack their position again. Others thought Lee would soon abandon his positions at Petersburg to reinforce Richmond and make a last stand at the capital. With the election less than a month away, it was thought perhaps Lee would launch a major attack in one last attempt to damage Lincoln's chances. The men completed their re-fortification efforts following the October 7 action, and a few days of quiet ensued. On October 10, the fall's first cold front came through, and minds thought about winter quarters and whether the year would see much more fighting.[11]

Perhaps preparing for defending winter lines, on October 11 Lee had ordered a new Confederate intermediate line constructed between the one the Federals had previously captured and the interior line just outside Richmond. Lee wanted to connect his army's various defensive positions, and by early morning on October 12, there was a noticeable earthwork on Darbytown Road noticed by Kautz's pickets. Alerting Butler, the information was passed to Grant. Alfred Terry, now a brevet Major General, had taken command of X Corps after Birney recently fell quite ill. Terry's command in the time since the Army of the James arrived on the peninsula had been excellent and was being recognized. In response to the news, and in anticipation of what may come next, he ordered his men ready to move at a moment's notice with three days rations.[12]

By midday, Grant had decided it a good idea to send a reconnaissance in force to study the new Confederate position, and if practicable, drive them off it. Butler ordered Terry to take First and Third Divisions, leaving Second Division—supported by XVIII Corps—to hold the Army of the James' line. First Division, now led by Adelbert Ames, who had led serious fighting at Gettysburg, would form north of Darbytown Road and look to turn the Confederate left. At the same time, William Birney's division would advance on the line. Kautz and his cavalry would cover the right flank. After leaving behind pickets, and men to help man the lines, First and Third Divisions would only have 3100 and 1600 men, respectively, facing about 6,000 partially dug in Confederates.[13]

Well before sunup on October 13, Terry's men set out towards the new

Confederate line. There was a fair amount of irritation among the men who were concerned the Confederate position was still too much of an unknown and that they were outnumbered against an entrenched position. The men marched for roughly a mile before the 39th, and First Division moved off to the right, north of Darbytown Road. Birney's division formed a line south of Darbytown Road, but the attack meant to come at sunrise was delayed while waiting for Kautz's cavalry division to arrive. The element of surprise now lost, both divisions, and the cavalry became engaged in heavy skirmishing. Companies A and I of the 39th were at one point sent out as skirmishers through thick timber, and came under heavy fire, forced to retreat as they saw Kautz's cavalry doing the same on their right.[14]

Ames' line was a half-mile long extending north from Darbytown Road and reported that the works in front of him were covered by over 100 yards of heavy slashing, rifle pits, and a well-placed battery. Birney also reported strong fortifications and artillery in front of Darbytown Road. General Lee had arrived on the field, and sensing a Federal attempt to flank his position, had ordered his commanders to reinforce the Confederate left. Learning all of this, Terry reported to Butler that he did not find an attack practicable and requested Butler's orders. Butler ordered Terry to hold in place while he referred the question to Grant. Shortly after noon, as artillery and skirmish fire continued, Grant advised Butler not to attack entrenched positions and considered it a successful reconnaissance for future operations. Butler sent word to Terry, ordering him not to attack the enemy in their entrenchments and to retire once the position was fully reconnoitered.[15]

However, Kautz reported to Terry that there was a location in front of him with no slashing and where the Confederates had not yet fully dug into their position. Perhaps interpreting that Grant intended to attack if possible, Terry ordered Ames' to extend his division to the right—the 39th being on the far right—and conferred with his commanders.[16] As the officers conferred, Company A color-sergeant George Yates of Wilmington took out all the letters he had from his pockets. Yates read over each of them, then tore them, and tossed them into the wind. Fearing the officers would choose to charge, and knowing their brigade was at the point where it would take place, Yates had resigned himself to the situation. "Boys," said Yates calling together the other color-bearers, "I shall in all likelihood fall. When the order is given to charge, let not one of you desert those colors. Save them, whether I am lost or not."[17]

Terry approved the assault, and Ames assigned the task to Pond and his First Brigade. Three miles from Richmond, the Confederate line just in front of them, the 39th would again charge a fortified position. The officers of the brigade had made their appeals to Pond and the division leadership, to no avail. Their duty was now to lead the men, who also knew the difficulty of what they were being asked to do. The assault would have to move through heavy underbrush, then out into the open. While there was no slashing immediately in front of the position, there was to each side, and the men would be funneled in with fire coming from both flanks. Just after 2:00 in the afternoon, Pond formed his 570 men in a tightly packed double column and sent them forward with 300 yards of the brush to clear before the charge could ensue. The most successful portion of the advance was before a shot was even fired. Movement through the heavy brush had flanked the Confederate position, but reinforcements had arrived during the advance. Reaching the clearing where the brush had been cleared, the Brigade found themselves under fire from three directions.[18]

"CHARGE!" went up the call, and the brigade leaped forward into the fire with the tremendous western yell. Bullets flew in all directions as Confederate artillery crashed down on the brigade. George Yates had barely an opportunity to lay his eyes on the goal in front of him when he was cut to the ground by four Confederate balls. As had happened before, ever mindful of Osborn's orders to never let the flag be lost, the colors had to be ripped from Yates' hands by Corporal John Kipp. At a reunion of the regiment in 1885, Company K's Sergeant David Slagle of Marseilles remembered that the air was full of "whizzing bullets, the scream of solid shot and shell, the rattle and sweep of grape and canister through our ranks."[19]

Some men, members of the 39th included, briefly reached the fortified works, but less than half made it the 800 yards back to safety.[20] The brigade had charged fearlessly but never had a chance. "Charge we must, and charge we did, and Death reaped a rich harvest as the result," wrote Homer Plimpton. "Our little regiment lost sixty brave men in less time than it takes to tell it. Our colors were completely riddled, and the color-guard all killed or wounded with the exception of three."[21] One of Corporal Kipp's arms had been shattered, but still he made his way off the field carrying both his gun and the flag in the other. When an officer offered to assist by taking the flag, Kipp replied that "if he was so anxious to assist that he might carry his gun; but the flag, never."[22]

Terry informed Butler of the debacle, and at 3:30 p.m., Ames ordered his division to fall back into a line of battle, leaving skirmishers forward in case of a Confederate counterattack. A Confederate line formed and briefly advanced, but Federal artillery pounded the position and ended the threat. Heads hung low, and the men returned to their lines around sundown—having lost much and gained nothing. On the day, Butler's losses were 437 men, with the Confederates suffering only 50 casualties and holding all their ground.[23]

One hundred eighty-one of the casualties came from First Brigade alone— 60 of those from the 39th Illinois.[24] Doctor Clark had established a field hospital quite near the action and was forced to take cover in an old corn crib as shells crashed around him. Wounded men were dressed and sent to the rear as fast as they could be. After the retreat, the doctor returned to the Corps' hospital and took better stock of the damage that had been done. Company H Lieutenant Charles Wilder of Chicago was the only man killed in the battle. Company F Lieutenant Nathan Davis, of Chicago, had a hand wounded so bad that it required major surgery. He was sent to a hospital where gangrene ravaged the wound and killed him a month later. Captain Heritage had a bullet lodge in his left shoulder that had damaged his spinal column. He would forever suffer from the wound, sustained in fighting he chose to do just four days before he was scheduled to muster out—believing it his duty to lead the regiment. Three men had amputations done, and 14 were captured—including George Yates and David Sla-gle. Slagle would recover from a wound and eventually be paroled. The Confeder-ates found Yates clutching a bloody piece of the regimental flag, so badly wounded they immediately paroled him. He would die two weeks later. The other bearer of Yates' flag, John Kipp, died of his wounds on November 5.[25]

Upon inspection the next day, the 39th Illinois had less than 300 men fit for duty and only three field officers.[26] One of those was Captain Whipple, who would muster out in less than two week's time, but for now, was the senior offi-cer fit for duty. The others were Company C First Lieutenant James Hannum of Rook's Creek and Lieutenant Plimpton. Regimental colors were brought out, tat-tered, but still in the regiment's possession.[27] The attack had been ill-advised, per-haps because of unclear guidance, miscommunicated intelligence, or over eager commanders in the field. While the grander history of operations in the area speaks little of it—merely a follow-on of the successes earlier in the month—the outcome was quite real and significant for the 39th Illinois.

The period between May 16–October 13, 1864, saw the 39th lose more men than any other stretch of their service during the war. Just over half the regiment's total deaths from being killed or wounded in battle occurred during the five-month stretch—along with eight in ten of its total wounded. Of the 118 men of the 39th that were taken prisoner during the war, 92 of them were taken that spring and fall. Their few leaders that remained would need to rally the men to close out the year's operations.[28]

❖   ❖   ❖

In the week following the 39th's battle at Darbytown Crossroads, two import-ant things solidified President Lincoln's chances of reelection. On October 15, John Bell Hood ceased his efforts to run Sherman out of Atlanta. With nothing good to come from Confederate forces in Georgia, and Lee's men in Petersburg all used up defending against Grant's Fifth Offensive, it was Jubal Early who was "left with the burden of persuading the Northern electorate to change administra-tions," wrote John Horn in *The Petersburg Campaign*.[29] Sheridan's forces had been tearing up the Shenandoah countryside to prevent food for men and livestock from making it to Petersburg. Lee sent Early an infantry division and cavalry bri-gade, and Early made plans to attack. While Sheridan was away in Washington meeting with U.S. high command, Early sprung a surprise attack near Winchester. Overnight between the 18th and 19th of October, Early struck two of Sheridan's divisions on the left flank at Cedar Creek. The early result was an absolute rout in the Confederates' favor.[30]

Still early in the day, however, VI Corps and the cavalry were intact, and Sheridan arrived on the field. In a genuine case of heroic battlefield leadership by a general, Sheridan quite literally led his men into battle with a strong counterat-tack. Celebrating their victory, many by feasting on Union food to quell their hun-ger, the Confederates were entirely unprepared for the renewed fight. Sheridan and his men sent the rebels running, capturing over a thousand prisoners while recapturing all their guns and then some. What could have been a disaster for

Federal momentum and Lincoln's reelection bid turned into a resounding victory with a hero story attached. The Federal batteries near Petersburg and Richmond delivered a 100-gun salute.[31]

The fighting quieted considerably following events on the 13th, and the men were mostly kept busy with inspections and improving the lines. A good deal of work was done constructing bomb proofs in the trenches. These were partially underground huts built up to shelter men during incoming artillery fire. Beyond that was the usual picket duty and the routine of camp life. The weather continued to grow colder, and the men drew extra clothes and winter gear to establish winter quarters.

General Grant was not quite ready for his armies to hibernate, however. On October 25, President Lincoln, along with Secretary of War Stanton, performed grand reviews of the men near Petersburg and Richmond. While reviewing X Corps, Doctor Clark noted that Lincoln was reviewing a substantially smaller First Division than he had six months prior. When passing the regiment bearing the flag of his friend Governor Yates, Lincoln would have seen only 225 men and three field officers bearing the 39th Illinois' colors. Indeed, still a "long ways from home."[32]

Sitting with Lincoln at his City Point headquarters during this visit, Grant likely told the President of his plans for a sixth offensive to follow up Sheridan's successes. Both men knew the cost/benefit of another offensive so close to the election. Continuing the current momentum could lock up the election for Lincoln. However, a defeat could cast doubt and leave little time for news of later success to reach voters. From a fighting perspective, Grant wanted to make one last attempt at extending and thinning Lee's lines—and possibly break through—before his remaining men returned from the Shenandoah and winter set in. Grant's sixth offensive would consist of demonstrations by the Army of the James on the peninsula, while the Army of the Potomac once again went after Boydton Plank Road and the Southside Railroad. On October 26, the 39th received orders to strike their tents and be ready to move with three days rations, 60 rounds, rubber blankets, and overcoats.[33]

❖   ❖   ❖

Before the sun on October 27, Lieutenant Hannum formed up the 39th and set off once again for the Confederate lines a few miles to the north. Having achieved his station in the U.S. army primarily because of political connections, General Butler knew keenly that capturing Richmond and a Lincoln reelection could finish the war. While the latter was in the voters' hands, Butler sought to take the former in his own. Butler would have XVIII Corps cross White Oak Swamp and attempt to turn the Confederate left near a place called Fair Oaks while X Corps demonstrated in the very spot they had looked to attack two weeks prior. Success on the left would allow XVIII Corps to press on the flank of the forces in front of X Corps, and the Army of the James could march into Richmond.[34]

Unknown to Butler; however, the Confederate line on the peninsula had recently received an upgrade. General James Longstreet, Lee's "Old War Horse," had returned to command after an injury during the Battle of the Wilderness. Often to the dismay of fellow commanders who preferred more aggressive tactics, Longstreet was a master of defensive strategy. As Butler's force began its movements, Longstreet went to work, preparing to counter the coming attack.[35]

While Meade began his operations south of the James at daybreak, X Corps demonstrated along a line stretching from New Market Road, over Darbytown Road, to Charles City Road—a distance of roughly two miles. Second Division centered the line on either side of Darbytown Road, with First Division, and the 39th, extending to the right. Lieutenant Hannum ordered Lieutenant Gillmore with four companies from the regiment's right to move forward as skirmishers and find out what was in front of them. The movement was through thick brush and slow going, but the regiment drove back Confederate pickets before receiving some fire in return. Division artillery quieted the Confederate fire. Regiments all along the X Corps line were encountering similar situations, and the cat-and-mouse game was kept up as XVIII Corps made their move forward. By early afternoon, XVIII Corps made it to 1862's Seven Pines battlefield near Fair Oaks Station and the Richmond and York River Railroad—two and a half miles east of the X Corps right.[36]

While lightly manned works were expected in front of XVIII Corps, Longstreet had changed that. Ever the expert on defensive operations, Longstreet had correctly assessed that Terry was not attacking on a two-mile-wide line, and the attack would instead come on his left. The XVIII Corps advance began at 3:30 p.m., but Longstreet had shifted veteran men to that position by that time. XVIII Corps elements came under heavy fire as their advance halted and casualties mounted. While some elements of the attack pushed back pickets and entered Confederate works, they could not hold them as the Confederate left could dispatch reinforcements. Longstreet's return to corps command had immediately bolstered the Confederate's Richmond defenses, and XVIII Corps could not turn the left.[37]

Butler sensed that if Longstreet had fully reinforced his left flank, then there must be a weakness somewhere on the Confederate center or right. Terry was ordered to advance the demonstration further. At 4:00 p.m., Lieutenant Hannum took four companies from the left and made a quick advance through heavy slashing to within 150 yards of the Confederate line. Slowed by the obstacles and taking heavy fire from the right, Hannum could advance no further and had his men dig in as best they could. The rest of X Corps met the same resistance, unable to get in position for any kind of legitimate attack. Only Second Division had any amount of success, capturing a few rifle pits but doing little else. Not wishing to repeat the events of October 13, and understanding he was only meant to demonstrate in force, Terry called off any further advance. Grant ordered Butler to have his men hold their positions overnight hoping to draw out the Confederates, but the defensive-minded Longstreet did not oblige. The Army of the James retired to their trenches early on the morning of the October 28.[38]

Butler's plan to break through to Richmond never became a serious threat to Longstreet's men, who suffered less than 100 casualties while inflicting 1,590. XVIII Corps alone suffered 1,064 casualties, and almost 700 of Butler's men were taken prisoner. Only five of the casualties came from the 39th, occurring as men were caught in the open during Gilmore and Hannum's advances.[39]

South of the James, things had gone only slightly better. Meade's men made progress in moving rebels off part of the Boydton Plank Road but encountered too much dug in resistance trying to advance on the South Side Railroad. In an effort to merge the three corps taking part in the attack, the Federal forces at one point became surrounded, but then made a successful counterattack that left Hancock's II Corps in control of the all-important Boydton Plank Road. Hancock's men were nearly out of ammunition, however, and the location did not support the movement of supplies or reinforcement. In a vulnerable position without what he needed to fight, Hancock elected to abandon the road with Meade's blessing. Losses south of the James were 1,758 from the Army of the Potomac and 1,300 Confederates.[40]

Losing over 3,000 men to gain absolutely nothing risked dragging down Lincoln's reelection chances after a series of successes. Not wanting to risk that, or allow a narrative that rebels were once again repelling offensives, Grant told Stanton the effort was a "reconnaissance" that never intended to be any kind of attack.[41] Stanton kept the matter quiet and continued his practice of reducing Federal losses by half before reporting them to the press.[42] However, the offensive had once again forced the Confederates to stretch their already thin lines that now ran 35 miles from east of Richmond to southwest of Petersburg. Informing Davis of such, Lee told the Confederate leader that he feared a "great calamity will befall us" if he didn't get reinforcements.[43]

❖   ❖   ❖

The 39th had suffered greatly but played an essential role through October to stress the Confederate defenses and maintain the momentum of Lincoln and his army. Significant operations in and around Petersburg ceased as October came to a close, and the constant shelling of the city—20,000 shells since mid–June— wound down as well.[44]

On picket duty the night of a frosty October 31, Anthony Taylor wrote that he only heard a few shots all night.[45] The loudest and most powerful shot of the current campaign would come in eight days' time.

18

A Final Winter

John Russell was born in Northfield in 1843 and spent his childhood working on his father's farm in the planting and harvest seasons and attending school in the winter. This routine continued until the age of 16 when he enrolled at Northwestern University, remaining there until the call for men to fight for the Union came about. Attempting to join a regiment just after the war began, he was rejected on account of his age. In August 1861, however, Russell had just turned 18 and joined Amasa Kennicott's company that eventually became Company F of the 39th Illinois.

Taking part in all the regiment's actions through the winter of '61–62, Russell was promoted to Corporal in February 1862, and also took on being his company's clerk—keeping their books and preparing their muster and pay rolls. When re-enlistment came up, Russell also played an active role in assisting Lieutenant Knapp in preparing paperwork to that effect. Russell was wounded slightly in a skirmish leading up to the Battle of Second Deep Bottom, but that did not prevent him from continuing to serve, and being promoted Sergeant in August 1864.

Over the winter of '64–'65, as the XXIV Corps was routinely drilled and inspected, Russell—in combination with his administrative work and fighting experience—was selected to represent the brigade in a competition of drilling, tests, and examinations. It was through this competition that Russell was selected to receive a commission as Second Lieutenant in the 38th U.S. Colored Troops Regiment. He left Company F and the 39th, but would not travel far from them.[1]

EARLY NOVEMBER SAW MEN in the 39th working earnestly on their winter quarters near the Federal lines at Chaffin's Farm. Logs were gathered, and—as soldiers develop an excellent knack for—the best possible shelters were constructed. Anthony Taylor called his a shanty, Homer Plimpton wrote that he had a "log house" like those we "sometimes see in the clearings of the west," and Joseph Ward was just happy to have a bench to sit on "beside a comfortable fire."[2]

Confederate deserters were becoming more and more frequent. While many probably envied the shelters and more abundant food and clothing supplies of the U.S. army, some were simply resigning themselves to the reality of the situation. After fighting to defeat McClellan early in the war, they now realized that a "Little Mac" victory was their only real hope. Conversely, U.S. soldiers who had once supported McClellan as their leader, or who had been democrats themselves, knew a McClellan victory meant their sacrifice would have been for nothing. Sure, the fighting may end, but with it would come dis-union, a continuation of slavery, and three and a half years of spilled blood and spent treasure for no gain.[3]

On November 8, 1864, soldiers from states allowing absentee ballots submitted their ballots to election judges sent to the front. Even though the night before had seen heavy skirmishing along the line as some Confederate soldiers taunted the Federal troops with cheers for McClellan, the day went off with no problems.[4] Writing to a friend, Homer Plimpton wrote that men were "dealing blows to the so-called Southern Confederacy" by dropping in ballots with the "fingers which they have pulled the trigger on many a battle field."[5] Even with soldier votes from New York, Connecticut, and Minnesota being sent home sealed and hard to track, the army reported 80 percent participation from soldiers eligible to vote.[6] The inability to cast votes left an unpleasant taste in men's mouths in the 39th Illinois and furthered their desire to see their Illinois president reelected. Writing in his diary on November 8, Anthony Taylor concluded the entry with "I hope they reinstate old Abe back in his old chair again where he belongs."[7]

Much like many of the strategic victories of 1864 that took time to bear their fruits, the election victory was not made known to the U.S. army near Petersburg until November 13, but was celebrated nonetheless. Soldier ballots were tabulated separately in twelve states that allowed them to vote absentee, and Lincoln carried that vote 119,754 to 34,291. This was a majority 25 percent higher than the civilian average in those states.[8] Up and down ballots for lower offices as well, Lincoln's Republican party had done well, in large part because of the army vote. While many states had tried to argue that an army shouldn't be voting to decide whether and how it was to be used, that battle was lost in most states and the soldiers let their voices be heard. While displays of partisan politics from the military are rightly discouraged and avoided in the modern military, the men fighting for the Union in 1864 found politics and the war as exactly the same. If they were fighting to save the Union, then they would vote to do so as well.

As it had gone throughout the war, the 39th's journey and experiences were once again dictated as much by outside forces as the results of their battles. Had Lincoln lost the election, he and Grant would have been forced to press the war as aggressively as ever to end it before McClellan took office. Knowing the Confederacy would need only to survive until March, the fighting near Petersburg and Richmond may have raged through the winter to capture the capital and destroy the Army of Northern Virginia. Lincoln's victory, however, was forcing the Confederacy to make plans for somehow lasting another four years. With cold weather and snow beginning in Virginia, however, Grant knew that a continued siege of the thinning, ill-supplied Confederate army throughout the winter would set him up to end the war come spring.

Sherman would depart Atlanta, march to the sea, finish off Georgia, then turn north. The Armies of the Potomac and James would reinforce their positions and ranks throughout the winter with VI Corps returning from the Shenandoah and new enlistees arriving regularly. Grant would bring it all to bear come spring and end the war once and for all. To go along with occasional raids on trenches and railroads around Petersburg and Richmond, the only significant battles that would occur before the end of the year happened in Franklin, Tennessee—a decisive Federal victory and one of the bloodiest battles of the war—at the end of

November, and Nashville in the middle of December. John Bell Hood led forces against Federal positions in Tennessee to distract Sherman and pull him away from sweeping to the coast then north to link with Grant. However, Sherman was undeterred in his attempt to snap the Confederacy in two and trap Lee between three U.S. armies.[9]

❖   ❖   ❖

November passed relatively quietly for the 39th Illinois. There was the occasional movement out of camp or "long roll" in the middle of the night to answer Confederate picket fire, but nothing more than the occasional skirmish or artillery exchange. More often than not, the Confederate fire was meaningless, intended only by their officers to keep the men busy and awake.[10] The men's time was spent mostly in picket duty, the occasional work on fortifications, and rotations manning the forts and trenches but mainly perfecting their winter homes. Men cut logs to make floors and walls, then used tents, pine branches, tarps, or anything else they could find to create a roof. Clay and mud were used to fill in space between the logs, and while a long way from first class, most of the shelters even had crudely constructed fireplaces. The men would have somewhere dry and warm to rest after duty in the cold.

The ground froze, and the calendar moved towards Thanksgiving. Generous donations from throughout the Union were made that army soldiers may have a good meal. On November 24 and 25, regimental bands played lively music. Anthony Taylor wrote that he helped carve up two turkeys, two chickens, one goose, one leg of mutton, two pounds of cheese, half a pound of sausage, half a pound of cake, and 66 apples. The food was divided up as best as possible, and every man in the regiment got a share of something. While Confederate troops manning their lines only miles away literally froze and starved, the Federal troops gave thanks and feasted.[11]

On December 2, the men of the 39th gathered and were delighted to have none other than Thomas Osborn there to speak to them. Still not fully recovered from his wounding nearly seven months prior, he was well enough to return to the front. His return to command of the regiment, however, was extremely brief. On December 3, a re-organization of the army took place. X and XVIII Corps were discontinued, and the White infantry troops of the two were merged to form the new XXIV Corps. The Black soldiers from XVIII Corps, and the larger Department of Virginia and North Carolina, created the new XXV Corps. Major General Edward Ord took command of XXIV Corps, and Major General Godfrey Weitzel took command of XXV Corps. The two Corps would still operate together as the Army of the James under Butler. Shortly after this, however, Grant dispatched XXV Corps and elements of XXIV to North Carolina. Butler would lead the elements to capture Fort Fisher—the last Confederate port that could run blockades.[12]

Realignment brought new division and brigade assignments, but the 39th was still in the First Brigade of First Division, now of XXIV Corps. The 39th was still in a brigade with the 62nd and 67th Ohio and the 85th Pennsylvania and

Winter quarters near Chaffin's Farm (reproduced from Clark, *History*).

newcomers of the 199th Pennsylvania. The officer now in command of First Brigade, First Division: Colonel Thomas Osborn. In command of the 39th, Illinois was the Northwestern graduate who had been teaching school in Sterling, Illinois, when the war broke out. The recently promoted Captain Homer Plimpton was now the senior officer of the regiment.[13]

Plimpton's rise through the ranks was both unusual and instructive. Before his time as Doctor Clark's steward, he saw some skirmishing action in the Shenandoah but was mostly used for his mind. A college degree would have been rare among any of the men, very well a private, and Plimpton's writing skills were put to use as a clerk. Plimpton would have been exposed to leadership decisions and officers in ways the other men were not during those two assignments. Combined with his most recent intimate experiences with battle, Plimpton was the most well-rounded leader the regiment had. The new regimental commander's first vital task was to replace the officers the regiment had shed since arriving at Bermuda Hundred seven months ago.

In dire need of officers was Plimpton's former Company G. The "Preacher's Company" had lost many respected officers, and one not so respected one. Slaughter had resigned, Captain Rudd was killed, and Captain Savage and Lieutenant James Harrington of Ottawa had recently mustered out—Savage because of deteriorating physical health.[14] Plimpton, who had considered becoming a minister and was quite devout himself, wrote often in his journey of God's blessing on the Union cause and of his own safety seemingly a miracle at times. While he did not have a preacher to put in charge of Company G, he performed his own miracle in giving them a new officer.

Neriah Kendall, who had been severely wounded in the head at the Battle of Drewry's Bluff, causing the letter to his mother be written announcing his probable death, and a funeral to be held at his home church. As Clark would later write in Kendall's roster entry, however, Kendall was "perhaps the only person in the regiment who had such a distinction ... dead, yet *alive*."[15] Nearly ready to throw him in a grave, a Confederate burial detail realized Kendall was barely alive, and he was taken to a prison. Suffering severely from his head wound, but recovering, he was paroled in August, and sent home to further recover. Kendall had apparently not had enough, however, and returned to the 39th in November, and was made First Sergeant. Plimpton now requested a commission for Kendall as a Lieutenant, writing that "the dead is alive and the lost found," adding the understatement that he was a "noble young man for all of that."[16]

❖   ❖   ❖

The weather turned even colder in the second week of December, as Butler and his men detached for duty in North Carolina set out on transports for Wilmington on December 8. Admiral David Porter had assembled 60 warships, plus transports for Butler's 6,500 men. As Butler and Porter's task force headed for Fort Fisher, Sherman and his army arrived on Savannah's doorstep, with the 10,000 Confederate soldiers defending it deciding to leave before being left with no escape. Sherman famously wired President Lincoln to present him a gift of "the city of Savannah, with 150 heavy guns and ... about 25,000 bales of cotton."[17] Meanwhile, in Tennessee, Major General George Thomas and his Army of the Cumberland soundly defeated Hood at the Battle of Nashville. By December 19, Sherman had completed his march to the sea. He was ready to turn north, Hood's army in Tennessee was virtually eliminated as a fighting force, and Sheridan was still destroying supplies in the Shenandoah. A victory by Butler at Fort Fisher would take away the final fledgling ability the Confederacy had to bring in supplies.[18]

Unfortunately, such a victory would not be added to the coming Christmas celebrations. Butler's plan for taking the fort was ill-conceived, and he had barely disembarked his troops on Christmas Eve when he called off the attack for fear of it having no chance at success. While the Fort was considered an incredibly strong one, and Lee had dispatched reinforcements that arrived the day before, Butler seemingly never gave his assault a chance. As James McPherson wrote in *Battle Cry of Freedom*, the "fiasco provided Grant with the excuse he had been looking for to get rid of Butler."[19] Butler's failure to achieve more than he did in the initial Bermuda Hundred landings, and mostly lackluster performance since, had long eaten at Grant. Forced by the election's political needs to bite his tongue and make do with the politically influential Butler, Grant could now relieve Butler with the election in the past. He was soon replaced by Major General Ord, which put Major General John Gibbon in command of XXIV Corps.[20]

Considering everything else, the failure at Fort Fisher did not put a damper on Christmas in the trenches for the 39th and the rest of the U.S. army near Petersburg and Richmond. The weather was still cold, alternating between snow and windy rain, but there was no real fighting, and Sherman's "gift" had put men in the holiday spirit. The Army of the James' miniature town behind the lines was decorated as best as conditions allowed, and families and aid groups sent food for the soldiers. Doctor Clark wrote that the regimental band played on Christmas Eve and that some dancing was done with women doing work in the earliest days of what would become the Red Cross. Most notably, a Miss Clara Barton. Clark added that Osborn and some other officers also enjoyed some eggnog made possible through the hens they kept for eggs.[21] Joseph Ward, now a Sergeant, wrote to his wife that the weather was nice on Christmas Day with little to do, and he expected to have some oysters for dinner. "I have a little whiskey," he added, "so I expect to have a bender."[22] As with Thanksgiving, all up and down the Federal lines, men celebrated the holiday with better than usual rations and festivity, while Confederate soldiers had barely a thing to eat—and very little to be festive about.

❖   ❖   ❖

The new year of 1865 was ushered in by the "coldest day of the winter," wrote Anthony Taylor.[23] It was the fourth New Year's Day of the war, and while they couldn't know for sure, the Union men likely expected it to be the last. The turn of the calendar brought no turns of the tide for the Confederacy as Sherman and his army turned north from Savannah, ready to barrel through the Carolinas. In response to pleas for protection at Charleston, more of Lee's men were peeled off.[24] To make matters even more dire for the Confederacy, Grant had put the increasingly successful Alfred Terry in charge of the troops at Wilmington, North Carolina, and added 1,500 soldiers. Working with the navy, Terry's force captured the fort and its 2,000 men. Nearly out of supplies on land and running impossibly long supply lines to move them, the Confederacy was now cut off from the sea.[25]

Confederate Vice President Alexander Stephens called the loss of Fort Fisher, "one of the greatest disasters that had befallen our Cause," as Confederate leaders lost hope and looked for a way out.[26] The cold and hungry soldiers were losing hope as well. Desertions soared, especially among soldiers from places like Georgia, Tennessee, and the Carolinas, as men left the lines for home to take care of their families. Others simply delivered themselves to Federal lines so they could get food and somewhere warm to sit. Anthony Taylor wrote in his diary that even before Fort Fisher's fall, 79 deserters came in on January 7, and another 25 on the 10th.[27] In one month-long stretch in the early part of 1865, Lee lost eight percent of his army to desertion.[28]

Becoming desperate, Confederate peace commissioners were sent to meet with Lincoln on a steamer near Grant's City Point Headquarters on February 3, but Lincoln's demand remained the same: Unconditional surrender, restoration of the Union, and the decisions on slavery were final. This last point was driven home by the House's recent passage of the Thirteenth Amendment—given an extra bit of satisfaction to Lincoln by the fact that Illinois had been the first of seven states to already ratify.[29]

As February began for the men on the Federal lines, the Confederates seemed on their last legs, and the notion grew that movement would soon be made. Camp life in winter quarters had grown routine, and almost comfortable, by wartime standards. However, inspections and drilling became more frequent as Captain Plimpton prepared his men for what he knew was to come. The commander of the 39th wasn't just keeping his veterans sharp after a long winter but training the new recruits and draftees that had been trickling in since fall and continued to do so. Joseph Ward wrote that Plimpton was improving in his drilling and "pays strict attention to his every duty."[30] The weather turned warm on February 4, and before a cycle of thawing and freezing began, Grant desired to take advantage of the conditions and exploit the sagging Confederate morale.[31]

On February 5, Federal cavalry set out to cut off and destroy Confederate wagon traffic on Boydton Plank Road, while II and V Corps kept Confederate infantry busy. The Federal force was initially successful and repelled a Confederate counterattack late on the 5th, but then were attacked and driven back on the 6th. On the 7th, V Corps launched a counter-attack that regained what was lost on the 6th fighting near a mill at Hatcher's Run.[32] Army of the Potomac losses were 1,539 to 1,000 Confederate losses, but Grant's lines were extended four miles to his left, and Lee's supply lines became even longer and more endangered.[33]

❖   ❖   ❖

The week of February 14, the 39th had four drill inspections, including ones at the brigade and division level as preparations for spring continued. On February 19, the failed peace conference and events at Hatcher's Run fresh in their minds, 250 Confederate soldiers accompanied by two colonels, and six captains made their way to the lines where the 39th was camped. The "Confederacy was built upon sand," wrote Doctor Clark, "and the tidal wave that Grant and Sherman were sending was fast crumbling the whole fabric of their superstructure."[34]

Grant's slow stranglehold on Petersburg and Richmond was tightening. Sherman made his way north through the Carolinas towards Virginia, and Sheridan was about to be unleashed one final time in the Shenandoah. The Confederacy was running on a bare minimum of supplies, and those they did have had impossible journeys to make it to the lines. Worse yet, Robert E. Lee's Army of Northern Virginia was shrinking by the day—and only minimally from battle. Nevertheless, for every Confederate politician, soldier, and citizen who felt all was lost, it seemed there were two as committed as ever to their cause. Jefferson Davis did what rallying he could around the argument of Lincoln's "degrading" and "humiliating" terms and pressed his people to fight on.[35]

❖   ❖   ❖

The American Civil War would not end without a last fight, and only a full military surrender was going to cease the hostilities. Captain Homer Plimpton's 39th Illinois, of Colonel Thomas Osborn's First Brigade of the First Division of XXIV Corps, would take a significant part in that fight in the very near future.

19

Once More to Petersburg

Henry Day was born in 1841 in Troy, New York, just north of Albany. Nothing is known of how Day came to reside in Illinois, but in August 1861 he enlisted in Company A of the 39th Illinois with so many other men from his hometown of Wilmington. The schoolteacher was promoted to Corporal in March 1862, and after re-enlisting, he took part in all the regiment's fighting during the brutal summer and fall of 1864.[1]

Abner Allen was born in 1839 in Woodford County, Illinois, just northwest of Bloomington. He enlisted with Company K of the 39th Illinois on September 2, 1861, and was promoted to Corporal in December 1863. Like Day, he re-enlisted and survived the 39th's time at Bermuda Hundred and Chaffin's Farm.[2]

Both Corporals were less than a month away from moments of valor that would follow them the rest of their lives—one way or another.

MARCH 1865 CAME IN LIKE A LION for Robert E. Lee and the Confederacy. Lee was sparsely manning a forty-mile defensive line with 56,000 troops, no supplies coming from the sea, little remaining railroad control, and an impossibly long overland wagon train. His counterpart, Lieutenant General Ulysses S. Grant, had twice as many men who were well supplied, well-fed, and had spent a winter as comfortably as an army can.[3] On March 2, Sheridan's force, specifically Brigadier General George Custer's division, destroyed what was remaining of Jubal Early's Shenandoah Confederates, then went to work destroying supply lines west of Richmond.[4] Sheridan would soon arrive to reunite with the Army of the Potomac, and Sherman and his 80,000 men were fast approaching from North Carolina. Lee might continue to hold out against Grant and Sheridan, a long shot to be sure, but Sherman's arrival would swallow the Confederate force.[5]

With Grant's noose tightening, Lee realized that staying put on the defensive was no longer an option. Lee decided his only chance was to abandon Petersburg and Richmond and escape to North Carolina, where he could link up with General Joseph Johnston. If he and Johnston could defeat Sherman, they could then turn back to the north and attack Grant. It was the longest of shots, but the only shot remaining. Almost as impossible would be withdrawing the Army of Northern Virginia from 40 miles of trenches that Grant had nearly locked down. To give himself a chance at pulling off his plan, Lee would need to break the lines somewhere, or at the very least, make an effort that caused Grant to rearrange troops that provided an opening. Lee and his corps commanders went to work looking for such a target.[6]

Grant called the period "one of the most anxious" for him during the war. Fearing Lee would try to escape as soon as he could, Grant wrote in his memoirs he feared "every morning that I would awake from my sleep to hear Lee had gone."[7] Grant wanted to act as soon as possible to prevent that move by taking the offensive at Petersburg himself, but the ongoing freeze-thaw cycle had rendered the roads useless for such a movement. Grant needed the weather to improve so he could launch the spring campaign all the men had been waiting for and end the war before Lee could move away and drag things out.[8]

The men in the U.S. camps continued their daily routines of picket duty, drilling, and being inspected as the anxiousness for a spring offensive continued to grow. On March 12, the 39th and the First Division and Second Division of XXIV Corps were reviewed by Grant. "It was the best thing I ever saw," wrote recently promoted Sergeant Anthony Taylor of the scene.[9] Five days later, Doctor Clark was at the Corps hospital when he stepped outside to meet an arriving officer. General Grant came forward alone, asking if there might be a suitable desk to write some dispatches. The commanding officer of all U.S. armies, who was about to finish a great Civil War, wore his coat unbuttoned, with no additional flourish or need for attendants or pomp. Demanding nothing from the men other than to ask for some water, Grant wrote at the desk for 30 minutes, asked where the telegraph station was and went on his way. A Few hours later, Grant accompanied Secretary of War Stanton for a review of the Army of the James.[10] Osborn told Plimpton that he "never saw the regiment look better."[11]

The freeze-thaw cycle stopped, and a series of warm days strung themselves together. Corduroy roads—a track of logs and timber—were placed on roads leading off the peninsula towards Petersburg. On March 20, the men received orders to turn over all their camp equipment and have everything ready to move at any moment beginning the next morning.[12] The men struck the winter camp that had been their home for some four months and prepared to be on the move. Sheridan would soon be back with the Army of the Potomac, and Sherman defeated Johnston at Bentonville, North Carolina, in a bloody three-day battle ending on March 21.[13] The U.S. army was ready to end the war, and General Robert E. Lee was about to play the last card he had.

❖   ❖   ❖

After Sherman defeated Johnston in North Carolina, Lee could no longer count on the Confederate general to slow down the Federal force. Lee planned to move his army as quickly as possible to the west, then south, swinging into North Carolina and unite with Johnston behind Sherman. The plan had already lost some luster after Johnston's force was severely weakened at Bentonville, and it still required the successful offensive diversion at Petersburg. For that portion of the plan, Lee's Second Corps commander John Brown Gordon had recommended an attack on Fort Stedman.[14]

Fort Stedman was a mile south of the Appomattox, in a location where only 200 yards separated the two armies and only 50 yards between pickets. Gordon planned to use men posing as deserters to dispatch the Federal pickets and then storm the fort while giving its defenders minimal time to prepare. Once the fort was captured, the Confederates could strike at Grant's supply lines and separate the Armies of the Potomac and James, which Lee assumed would force Federal troops to move to their left. This would give Lee his opening to remove to the west. Lee was convinced his men could take the fort but holding it would be another issue. To facilitate this, he moved men guarding Boydton Plank Road southwest of Petersburg. Gordon's assault was planned to begin in the early hours of March 25. As final preparations were being made, Sheridan arrived on the peninsula on March 24, and Grant issued orders for his own offensive. During the night, three divisions from the Army of the James, to include First Division of XXIV Corps and the 39th, began to quietly withdraw from their forward lines.[15]

Gordon's men advanced at 4:00 a.m., on the morning of March 25, and were initially successful in capturing the fort. The rebels cut through the Federal lines on either side of Fort Stedman, gained access from behind, and even fought off a counterattack. However, the teams designated to destroy Federal works and the railroads never made it that far. Darkness was an issue, and once nearby Federal artillery realized their men were no longer in the fort, they opened up on the Confederate attackers. Worse yet for Gordon, many of his men were so hungry and ill-equipped that they began searching the works for whatever food, clothing, and equipment they could. Fort Stedman's reserve division came forward and led a counterattack with IX Corps soon reinforcing. Before 9:00 a.m., a long line of Confederate prisoners was being marched away to the delight of President Lincoln, who had arrived in the area the night before. The attack had cost Lee between 3,000–4,000 men. Making the Confederate failure even worse, Federal forces had attacked and taken ground from where Lee had pulled men for the assault.[16]

On March 26, knowing their departure from the peninsula was imminent, XXIV Corps formed for a grand review. Waiting for almost two hours, the men wondered why General Grant needed to review them once again. However, when a large entourage escorted by cavalry finally arrived, it was not the commanding general but the Commander-in-Chief. Accompanied by Grant and Stanton, Anthony Taylor said that it was a "grand sight" but that the "old Gent looks as if he was about worn out."[17] The next day, aboard Lincoln's steamer, docked at City Point, the President's weariness was clear to Grant, Sherman, and Admiral David Porter. While Lincoln desperately hoped there could be an end to the bloodshed, Grant and Sherman convinced him that one more bloody offensive would need to be fought to end the war. Grant, however, would not wait for Sherman's army to arrive. With Johnston's Confederate force no longer a threat, Sherman would position his army to box Lee in, and Grant would launch his last offensive of the war.[18]

❖   ❖   ❖

The final offensive of the campaign around Petersburg would begin just as the first one had the previous summer—with a crossing of the James River. Late in the evening on March 27, the men of the 39th were ordered to fall in. At dark, the three divisions that had pulled from the lines set out on what would be a forty-mile march to the very left of the Army of the Potomac's lines in front of Petersburg. Nighttime movement, and the fact that Lee had needed to reposition so much cavalry, left the movement of Major General John Gibbon's XXIV Corps undetected. The men marched all night, carrying their knapsacks with 60 rounds, four days' rations, and a poncho. The march was silent, save for the sounds of gear rattling and boots on the ground, with the magnitude of the movement lost on no man as they crossed over the Deep Bottom pontoon in darkness. They were three divisions worth of United States soldiers marching off to bring an end to the Civil War. Just before daylight, they crossed the Appomattox and went another three miles before stopping to warm up coffee, force down some hardtack, and get what rest they could before continuing.[19]

As the Army of the James moved closer to the Federal left, II Corps and V Corps prepared to shift left. The divisions from the Army of the James would replace them as they extended the Federal lines to the left and reinforced Sheridan's efforts on Boydton Plank Road. Just after dark on March 28, the 39th stopped for the night and bivouacked after 27 hours of no sleep and only a few brief stops for food and coffee. Longstreet was still in the dark about the Federal forces that had left the peninsula as his cavalry was being used near Petersburg, at a place called Five Forks, to protect the railroad and monitor the Federal left. The undetected movement had allowed Grant to amass a singular force that none of his previous offensives had enjoyed. Further yet, Grant now brought the Army of the James' cavalry division over from the peninsula to the vicinity of Petersburg. As with the infantry, the lack of cavalry on Longstreet's part allowed the Federal movement to go undetected.[20]

The 39th and their XXIV Corps comrades were up well before the sun on March 29 for more coffee and hardtack and a five-mile march to the left. First Division reached Hatcher's Run, seven miles southwest of Petersburg, at 8:00 a.m. From a wooded location, the men were now looking at II Corps' entrenchments, as the Army of the Potomac men began their movement to the southwest. It was here that Major General John Gibbon's XXIV Corps took their place on the Federal line in front of Petersburg, in "plain sight of the rebel earthworks," wrote Anthony Taylor.[21] By this time, the movement was no longer going undetected by Lee and the Confederates. Lee concentrated what available forces he had to the west of Petersburg on his right flank, causing positions down the Confederate line to thin and spread out. His goal was to protect the roads he needed for supplies and an exit from Petersburg and Richmond.[22]

Grant's plan was to have II Corps wheel to the right, while V Corps moved forward on the far left of the Federal line. Further to the left, Sheridan's cavalry divisions would disrupt Lee's supply lines and communications. The plan gave Grant the option of either leaning in on the Confederate flank, and thus Petersburg itself, or if practicable, have most of the Federal line press forward leaving IX Corps to hold south of the James, and the rest of XXV Corps on the peninsula. Heavy rain began late on the 29th, making the decision. II Corps and V Corps movements were nearly unopposed, but Sheridan's actions were limited by the slow movement of wagons in the mud. Lee continued to shift forces to the right, to counter the threat, further thinning his line in other places. The 39th spent the day manning the trenches and doing shifts on picket duty. While the skirmish fire on their left caused them to fall in on a handful of occasions, they were never called into action, and the waiting game continued.[23]

The heavy rain of the 29th became the heavy rain of the 30th, further muddying the roads and flooding trenches and rifle pits. The day saw only minor skirmishing, as Sheridan's cavalry and V Corps positioned themselves per Grant's plan. II Corps began the right wheel and stretched the line to link up with V Corps. This brought XXIV Corps into action, as Gibbon brought his men up to fill the positions II Corps had occupied. Late in the afternoon, infantry and artillery fire was heard, and the 39th was in line with their arms. The Corps advanced some 400 yards and drove back Confederate pickets to cover the rest of the II Corps movement. Two men from Osborn's Brigade were wounded, to include one from the 39th. By the end of the day, The Federal force had solidified its position on the Boydton Plank Road and had connected a unified line that was now flanking the Confederate right. The 39th, and XXIV Corps, attempted to entrench their new position, but the soggy ground made the work useless. By the end of the day, Grant thought Sheridan's cavalry might turn the Confederate flank with help from V Corps. He was also considering a full-on assault by VI and IX Corps on the Petersburg front to distract from Sheridan's movements while forcing Lee to decide where to defend. Hoping that Lee would move men to his flank to protect his supply and escape routes, Grant told Meade to prepare for an attack at Petersburg.[24]

On March 31, however, Lee attempted to take the initiative for himself. Knowing the soggy ground would prevent any significant Federal movements, and mostly just out of any other options, Lee attacked. Lee ordered General Pickett to attack Sheridan's cavalry, then also sent four brigades towards V Corps' left flank that had not yet been solidified and was vulnerable to attack. Lee's plan was initially a success, in that it caught the U.S. generals by surprise and prevented Grant's plan for a March 31 assault. The four brigades sent after V Corps initially pushed back two divisions, and Pickett's force guarding a crossroads called Five Forks moved south and forced Sheridan off his position at Dinwiddie Courthouse. However, both Confederate advances were turned back by a resource the United States had plenty of and Lee had none of: Reserves. II Corps came to the aide of V Corps and pushed the rebels back to their entrenchments while cutting them off from Pickett. At Dinwiddie Courthouse, Major General George Custer's cavalry division arrived on the field and halted Pickett's gains.[25]

The Battles of White Oak and Dinwiddie Courthouse were Robert E. Lee's last offensives of the Civil War. While the action at Dinwiddie Courthouse had been a tactical victory for Pickett, the damage was limited from strategically harming the Federal cause, and II and V Corps victories at White Oak had cut the Confederates off from each other. Lee lost even more men he couldn't afford to, and the pieces on the board were now set in a way to end the Siege of Petersburg. As March came to a close, Lee sent word to Pickett to hold Five Forks "at all hazards" and keep the Federals from cutting off the railroad. Eager to resume his offensive, Grant sent orders to Sheridan that V Corps would join him, and they were to take Five Forks the next day.[26]

Very early on April 1, Pickett's men began a withdrawal from the area near Dinwiddie Court House towards Five Forks. Sheridan's cavalry followed the movement at a distance but did not pursue an engagement as V Corps disengaged and moved left. This caused II Corps to extend to the left, followed by XXIV Corps. Around the same time, Robert E. Lee was sending a note to Jefferson Davis stating the situation's dire nature and that he may need to evacuate his position near the James River. Needing to plug all holes at Petersburg and maintain his supply and exit routes, Lee moved men from his line at White Oak Road, which forced him to pull men from Longstreet on the peninsula to reinforce. Lee was choosing to thin his lines even more in front of Petersburg to protect this right flank—gambling that Grant would not attack before he could make his escape.[27]

As was the recent trend, however, Lee's gamble did not pay off, and April 1, 1865, became known as the "Waterloo of the Confederacy."[28] Early in the afternoon, Sheridan's two cavalry divisions demonstrated on the Confederate right while V Corps' 12,000 attacking infantry moved into position on the Confederate left. Shortly after 4:00 p.m., the V Corps movement to seek the Confederate flank required II and XXIV Corps to shift as well. As darkness approached, Thomas Osborn ordered his brigade to be ready to move with the rest of XXIV Corps. Homer Plimpton ordered the 39th to fall in and be prepared to move as quickly as possible. Men grabbed their rifles and slung their packs, now hearing firing going on from Sheridan's attack. The Confederate line was thinning and opening up, at various points, and the U.S. army was standing by to exploit the situation.[29]

The Battle of Five Forks was "one of the most crushing defeats" Lee suffered, wrote Earl Hess in his book *In the Trenches at Petersburg*.[30] Although a bit disorganized because of the rapidly giving way rebels and rapidly advancing Federal men, Sheridan's victory was a rout. The Federal force inflicted upwards of 4,000 casualties, suffering roughly 800.[31] Lee had all but lost his right flank, was forced to thin and extend his line everywhere, and the U.S. armies had unfettered accesses to the South Side Railroad. Pickett's force was no longer an effective fighting unit, and by extension, neither was the Army of Northern Virginia. As the fighting was going on, the 39th had moved three miles to the left and was placed in readiness to charge with the brigade. Word of the victory, and its implications, was spreading, and the men knew they would soon advance to end the war.[32]

❖   ❖   ❖

At 9:00 p.m., an aide from Sheridan arrived at Grant's headquarters to deliver the news from the Federal left. The aides surrounding Grant were briefly quiet as they processed what they were hearing before celebrating loudly as the head of all U.S. armies walked into his tent. Down the Federal line, the 39th, and Osborn's brigade, lay in wait in front of Confederate entrenchments straddling the Boydton Plank Road on a ridge just a few miles southwest of Petersburg. Late in the evening, Osborn sent six men forward to find out the "strength of the enemy" and "nature of the ground."[33] One of those men was the 39th's G Company Private William Howard—originally from New York who had reenlisted from Chicago, and the five others, advanced without arms that they may attempt to present themselves as deserters if caught. Taking some fire as they crossed in the open, the men were able to report back with the position of batteries on the left and right and two fortifications.[34]

Forts Gregg and Whitworth were mutually supportive works meant to protect the innermost Confederate line west of Petersburg should the outer line fail. The fortifications had been constructed in the fall of 1864 and were intended to hold the all-important position of Boydton Plank Road until reinforcements could arrive. Fort Gregg was the closer of the two and had tall earthen walls—over fifteen feet—surrounded by a flooded moat from the recent rain. The fort's rear was protected by thick logs set in a zigzag pattern roughly ten feet high. There was one narrow opening to enter the fort, and the logs were situated in such a way that defenders could fire from, but attackers could not reach for the same purpose.[35]

General Grant emerged from his tent and notified his aides he was ordering a general assault all along the line come morning. Shortly after 10:00 p.m., 150 Federal guns opened-up on Confederate positions as the men of the 39th moved forward silently, with only the sound of thumping cannon disturbing the darkness. The entire brigade moved forward to the picket line, massed for the morning. Shortly after 1:00 a.m., the shelling stopped, and the men lay down where they were and tried to get some sleep. The morning would bring a day they would never forget.[36]

20

Breakthrough and Fort Gregg

Michael Wetzel enlisted in Company I, 39th Illinois Infantry, on September 4, 1861, from Santa Anna, a township in DeWitt County in central Illinois. Wetzel was promoted to Corporal March 1, 1863, then Sergeant in February 1865.[1] As with many of the companies, Company I lost two officers in the Bermuda Hundred fighting, and as a Corporal, then Sergeant, Wetzel would have had a great deal of responsibility leading and organizing the enlisted men of the company. Sergeant Wetzel had his arm nearly severed by Confederate canister shot, and it was later amputated. He would later declare of April 2, 1865, "there is not a day of my whole life the events of which are preserved so vividly in my mind as those of that day."[2]

PRESIDENT LINCOLN AWOKE EARLY on April 2, unable to sleep after a night of cannonade, worries over ending the war, and a dream he couldn't shake that foretold his assassination. Around 7:00 a.m., the Commander-in-Chief was notified that a telegraph from Grant had arrived at City Point. VI Corps had broken the Confederate lines.[3] The President was delighted. At 10:45 a.m., the news got even better when Grant sent another message to President Lincoln and Secretary Stanton. Grant notified the two men that "everything has been carried" left of IX Corps. XI Corps had captured 3,000 men, and II and XXIV Corps had captured artillery and men. "We are now closing around the works of the line immediately enveloping Petersburg. All looks remarkably well."[4] The telegram also notified the men that Grant had moved his headquarters nearer the lines and that he was now on Boydton Plank Road, three miles southwest of Petersburg. Events were moving fast, and the commander of all U.S. armies wanted to witness them first-hand.

❖ ❖ ❖

Colonel Thomas Osborn was also situated roughly three miles southwest of Petersburg near Boydton Plank Road. As he sat atop his horse, looking on Fort Gregg, he likely reflected on the morning as he thought of the battle to come. His First Brigade of First Division had been up since 4:00 a.m., ready to support VI Corps. At 4:40, a lone Federal gun had fired, and 14,000 men from Major General Horatio Wright's VI Corps had picked themselves up off the ground and charged a thin portion of the Confederate line held by 2,800 men.[5] By 5:00 a.m., Osborn had sent Homer Plimpton, and his old regiment, ahead of their lines as skirmishers—bullets occasionally whizzing past them as XXIV Corps listened to VI Corps storm the Confederate defenders in a dark fog. Fifteen minutes later, VI Corps

THE BATTLE OF PETERSBURG Vᴬ APRIL 2ᴺᵈ 1865.

Currier and Ives depiction of the April 2, 1865, Battle of Petersburg (Library of Congress: LIC-DIG-pga-06140).

broke the Confederate line on Boydton Plank Road in what Earl Hess called the "most decisive breakthrough of a heavily fortified line" of the entire Civil War.[6] Working to exploit and expand the breakthrough, VI Corps momentum carried them further west towards Confederate positions near Hatcher's Run and north towards Petersburg, which brought Osborn to where he now was.

At 6:00 a.m., Osborn recalled the 39th to the brigade's line of battle as General Gibbon's XXIV Corps was about to be on the move. The light of day showed the flooded ground in front of Gibbon's men to be unsuitable for an attack—and II Corps was handling the retreating Confederate force near Hatcher's Run. Grant ordered General Ord's Army of the James to follow a reforming VI Corps and exploit the breakthrough. Gibbon sent most of General Robert Foster's First Division, and two of General John Turner's independent division brigades northeast, with various elements left in the Hatcher's Run vicinity to hold the ground and guard prisoners. Osborn wrote in his report that the distance to travel was between four and five miles, and the 39th, and his First Brigade, were the vanguard of the movement, running off remaining Confederate defenders on the Hatcher's Run line.[7]

After learning of the break in the line, Lee realized he must send word to his capital that Richmond should be evacuated, and the Army of Northern Virginia may need to retreat that night if they survived that long. As a messenger made his way down a Richmond church aisle to give the message to Jefferson Davis, XXIV

Corps was making its way northeast on Boydton Plank Road towards Petersburg. VI Corps had turned back from Hatcher's Run and was now positioned to the left and right of XXIV Corps. The only thing between the two U.S. army Corps and Petersburg's inner line was Forts Gregg and Whitworth. General Gibbon met with General Wright and suggested his troops take the lead as they were fresh. Wright's Corp had been under arms for 18 hours and had just finished multiple exhausting charges, and Wright agreed. Still in the lead of XXIV Corps, Osborn's men continued forward through the VI Corps lines.[8]

Around 8:30 a.m., as First Brigade was closing in on five miles of marching, Osborn began hearing firing up ahead where VI Corps had previously broken the line. As Osborn's men crossed the original broken outer line, he received word that a Confederate counterattack was underway. Osborn sent his men ahead on the "double quick," the 62nd Ohio in front, followed by the 39th straddling Boydton Plank Road, the 67th Ohio, and the 199th Pennsylvania from left to right.[9] The heat of a warmer than usual April day had already been getting to the men, as many had been casting off blankets and coats to lighten the load. Now covering a mile at the double-quick, Anthony Taylor wrote that his "breath [was] most gone" as the "Johnnies [began] to shell us."[10]

The advancing brigade of Illinois, Ohio, and Pennsylvania boys must have been a welcome sight to VI Corps brigade commander, Colonel Joseph Hamblin. He had only two regiments and was quickly being pushed back. At 9:00 a.m., Osborn ordered his men to charge the line of the Confederate counterattack. By 10:00, the Confederate line was in retreat, moving back to fill into the two forts. First Brigade took 25 prisoners and turned two artillery pieces onto the retreating rebels.[11]

Now, Osborn watched his men take their positions only 800 yards from Fort Gregg as rebels retreated across the swampy ground. His men would soon need to cross that ground; the task made even more difficult by the broad field of fire the Fort Gregg defenders would have. The lawyer from Chicago, whose regiment almost wasn't accepted for service, and had lost the use of his right arm at Drewry's Bluff, was now knocking on Petersburg's door with that same regiment in a brigade he commanded. After a leadership trial by fire holding off Stonewall Jackson, languishing at Harrison's Landing, resigned mostly to support at Charleston Harbor, and laying in a hospital while his regiment was cut up on the peninsula; Colonel Thomas Osborn—a brevet Brigadier General of volunteers—was about to lead the attack that could send Robert E. Lee's Army of Northern Virginia running for its life.[12]

Ensuring his men were ready for what was soon to come, Captain Homer Plimpton was just as likely to be reflective. Entering the regiment as a private, it was apparent throughout his wartime journal that he often questioned why some men led the way they did, and if he could do a better job. However, Plimpton did not let that impede his work and, after becoming a non-commissioned officer, took care of his fellow enlisted men, earning the respect of both them and the officers and earning a commission. The regiment had badly needed new leadership, and Plimpton not only rose to the task but pulled others up with him.

Kurz and Allison's "Fall of Petersburg" (Library of Congress: LC-DIG-pga-01904).

Taking nothing for granted, Plimpton drilled his regiment hard so that both he and they would be ready for this moment. Now, Plimpton and 150 Illinois men of the 39th—the rest of the regiment on picket duty along the captured Confederate lines—stood ready to put a nail in the coffin of the Confederacy.[13] The devout Methodist, and onetime almost preacher, could now look into Petersburg and see their many church spires on this second to last Sabbath Day of the war. There would be no peaceful worship, however, and not much need for drill tactics. Fort Gregg was going to be taken with an 800-yard frontal assault and a hand-to-hand battle of determined wills.

❖   ❖   ❖

Generals Grant, Ord, and Gibbon were unaware of how manned the Confederate line was and just how many men sat waiting inside the mutually supportive forts. Leaving nothing to chance, the other First Division Brigades were brought up, and the Third Brigade of Turner's independent division was placed west of Fort Whitworth. A mile away from his headquarters, Ulysses S. Grant watched Fort Gregg projectiles fall near Colonel's Osborn and George Dandy's First and Third Brigades of XXIV Corps' First Division. The commander of all U.S. armies was growing nervous and impatient, knowing what capture of the two forts meant. Still, all the leaders in the chain of command wanted reinforcements ready, defense against any counterattack in place, and troops ready in line of battle to exploit any openings. Eleven brigades were being positioned to storm the two forts, with three divisions of VI Corps flanking them.[14]

By 12:15 p.m., Dandy's Third Brigade composed of the 10th Connecticut, 11th Maine, and 100th New York formed on Osborn's left. The two brigades formed an arc bent away from the fort, with the 39th connecting First Brigade to Third. The 62nd Ohio had raced forward under fire to deploy as skirmishers, resting in the cover of a sunken portion of Boydton Plank Road only 80 yards from the fort. Fourth Brigade of First Division arrived from Hatcher's Run and took up a position to the west of the fort, able to be called into action at either location. Behind Foster's Division were two brigades of Turner's independent division—notably including the 23rd Illinois, which had arrived to XXIV Corps during the winter. Sergeant Wetzel couldn't fathom that the Confederate artillery wasn't tearing up the assault force assembling in full view of the fort or why they hadn't spent more rounds on the 62nd. While a few shots landed with some minor casualty numbers, Wetzel eventually realized that the defenders didn't have the ammunition to spare. Some men waiting for the assault, actually "stacked arms and ate lunch." At 1:00 p.m., VI Corps was finally in position. General Gibbon sent Foster the order to attack.[15]

❖   ❖   ❖

"Keep down men; keep down!" cried Confederate officers as Osborn's brigade moved forward.[16] Low on ammunition, the only chance Fort Gregg's roughly 350 defenders from A.P. Hill's III Corps had was to wait for more accurate shots, then use the formidable fort's defenses as best they could. Hearing of the breakthrough earlier in the morning, A.P. Hill had ridden out to assess the situation and been killed. The only thing Fort Gregg's defenders knew now was not to surrender, fight to the last man, and give Longstreet's Corps time to reinforce the Dimmock Line. Osborn's brigade was moving forward at quick time, advancing from the south and east while Dandy's brigade waited to the west. Roughly 200 yards in front of them was a marshy area that Osborn knew had to be cleared before a proper charge could occur. When the brigade cleared the "deep and difficult slough," Osborn gave the command to charge.[17]

The brigade gave a terrific yell and took off running up the ravine "under a terrible fire of grape, cannister, and minnie-balls tearing through the ranks," wrote Osborn.[18] Reaching the top of the ravine, the brigade could now again fully see the fort and the wide-open 300 yards in front of them. The only remaining shelter was the sunken portion of Boydton Plank Road over 200 yards away still—and on the charge continued. A confederate gun off to the east opened up, and the right flank of the charge, mainly the 199th Pennsylvania, was torn apart. Men were "falling on all sides," wrote Anthony Taylor. "It may be my turn text," he continued, but "forward ... like so many hungry wolves," the charge continued.[19] Dandy's brigade began their advance as Osborn's reached the roadbed, allowing for a brief gathering of one's wits, courage, and breath. Whether thoughts of the Union or just survival, were in their minds only they knew. The position did not provide cover from the cannon to the east; however, and the brigade went up from the roadbed, sprinting the final 80 yards towards the ditch surrounding the fort. Leading the way in front of the 39th Illinois was Company E Sergeant George Burton of Wilmington, carrying the colors.[20]

Modern-day view of the well-preserved remains of the Fort Gregg earthworks. The First Brigade's assault was from the right edge of the photograph moving left (author's photograph).

As Burton reached the ditch, his carrying of the colors made him a top target, and he was soon struck down, tumbling towards the moat as the first of seven color bearer casualties the 39th would suffer.[21] A "destructive fire of musketry and grape ... mowed down our men," wrote Plimpton, "but we faltered not."[22] "I could see our boys falling thick and fast," wrote Private Howard, recalling his arrival at the moat.[23] Nearby, Sergeant Wetzel took his last steps before jumping into the ditch when a piece of shrapnel struck his right arm. Wetzel gathered himself enough to continue forward and throw himself into the ditch—the first to reach it. Landing hard and losing blood, Wetzel felt himself losing consciousness and drug himself against the relative safety of the ditch's front wall as Howard and others piled in practically on top of him.[24]

Howard looked up to see a Confederate officer waving his hat and sword to encourage his men, and quickly stood up and fired a shot, dropping the officer. Before he could get back to the ditch's safety, however, he was struck in the neck by a rifle ball. Howard froze in disbelief that he had been shot in the neck and was unharmed. The shot had likely come from Fort Whitworth over 700 yards away and was, as Howard wrote, "a nearly-spent ball and did no great damage."[25] Meanwhile, someone, perhaps not even a member of the 39th, had taken the national colors from the fallen Burton and stuck them into the slope of the fort—a visual rallying cry for the brigade.[26]

❖　❖　❖

Men continued to dive into the ditch as First Brigade waded through waist, and often chest, deep water seeking the cover of the fort's wall. Third Brigade was now crashing into the fort's west side, and the wall and the defenders now firing at Dandy's advance briefly brought First Brigade some relief. Men were attempting to move up the wall, turned back by bullets and the slick mud. Company E Private Charles Ware, of Joliet, looked up to see a familiar face reaching out to him. His former regimental commander, Colonel Thomas Osborn, had jumped into the ditch and helped his four regiments struggling in the water. "MEN, WE MUST TAKE THIS FORT," he yelled as he boosted them up with his one good arm, "BEFORE THE ENEMY RECEIVES REINFORCEMENTS!"[27]

At the bottom of the wall, Sergeant Wetzel had regained consciousness only to realize he was "almost buried in loose dirt, kicked down by the men climbing up over me." Wetzel looked up in panicked desperation; he was losing blood and couldn't move. He grabbed at the nearest man's pants, and his friend Sergeant Ernest Tateburg, of Le Roy, looked down at him. Wetzel was "covered with blood and mud from head to foot," but his company mate recognized him. Tateburg cut Wetzel's pack and gear away from him and secured a handkerchief around the bleeding arm—saving Wetzel's life—before continuing up the wall.[28]

Looking down the remains of the Fort Gregg trench, and the wall the 39th fought to scale (author's photo).

As Wetzel helplessly laid against the wall watching men splash and flail in the ditch, things were even more vicious at the top. Men were using bayonets and swords to carve out footholds in their "frantic attempts to gain the top of the works," wrote Plimpton. "The enemy continued to fire grape and minnie balls at all who attempted to come to our assistance."[29] Slowly, some men made it near the parapet to find themselves face to face with the Confederate defenders. Rebels attempting to fire at the men below had first to knock attacking bayonets away. Private Ware raised his gun to shoot at a man only a rifle length away when he was struck by a bullet in the neck and knocked senseless. "When I came to my senses a dead man was laying across my back," wrote Ware.[30]

Men would continually reach the top of the wall only to be shot, struck by grapeshot, or knocked down by a rifle butt, rock, or just a shove from the defenders. Some fell dead into the water, some wounded, and some returned to the wall and began again. Company F Corporal William Stillhammer, of Bloomington, had recently returned to the 39th in a prisoner swap and found himself at the top of the wall. However, he was shot in the leg and, while attempting to crawl for cover, was hit again and killed, according to a letter home to his mother from Captain Reuben Bottsford.[31] The fighting was hand to hand and brutal. On the east side of the fort, the 67th and 199th tried to gain entry through the fort's rear, but the heavy door, deep water, and mass of defenders were making it difficult. Even with Dandy's Brigade gaining a foothold on the more stable west wall, Osborn's attack was stalling and in danger of failing.[32]

❖　❖　❖

It was now 2:00, and eight regiments were engaged in the brutal quagmire that was Fort Gregg. From General Robert Foster's vantage point on Boydton Plank Road, however, the attack was in danger of failing. Retreat was not an option because of the timeliness of the objective and the wide-open, marshy, casualty-ridden ground that his men would need to traverse to do so. As the First Division commander pondered all this, an aide on horseback came racing up to Foster. Colonel Dandy did not know why Osborn's men could not make more headway, but his men needed reinforcements. With his ultimate superior, General Grant, watching nearby, Foster threw Colonel Harrison Fairchild's Fourth Brigade into the fray. Crossing wide open ground and exposed to fire from Fort Whitworth, two regiments of Fairchild's brigade rocketed themselves into the moat from the west. The momentum of new bodies—both physically and mentally—propelled men to the top of the wall. Some even scrambled around back and began launching themselves into the wooden door, starting to splinter it.[33]

There were now Federal flags atop the west wall, encouraging all the men in blue. Fort Gregg's defenders were focusing all their fire on the Federal's left, and Osborn implored his men to take advantage and get to the top of the south and east walls. The situation had transformed in the fifteen minutes since Fairchild's men had joined the assault, and Major General Gibbon sensed an opportunity. Gibbon ordered two of General Turner's independent division brigades into the fight, to include the 23rd Illinois—nicknamed the "Western Irish Brigade." Beginning their charge from a third of a mile away, the third wave of assault took heavy fire, which again provided more breathing room to those already on the wall and brought the total number of attackers to over 4,000 men.[34]

The men already engaged in the fighting were happy to see regiments like the 23rd, and not just for the additional manpower. Many in the unit carried Henry repeating rifles, possibly resulting from their close work with Sheridan's cavalry in the Valley. Recognizing the men from his home state, Charles Ware marveled at the quick-firing rifles. "One fellow I remember especially, who was on his knees, about eight or ten feet distant from me, working the lever and sending the balls with such rapidity as to cause great havoc and commotion among

Modern-day view of the wall the 39th was assaulting from the defender's perspective "inside" the fort (author's photograph).

the Johnnies." Men on the west side planted colors atop the wall of Fort Gregg and rallied each other towards it. Near the northwest corner, Ware now saw Colonel Osborn pointing his sword at an officer of the 23rd Illinois. "I order you sir, to lead your men into the fort at once."[35]

Men soon discovered a ramp of dirt from an unfinished rifle pit that led them up towards the western wall, forcing Gregg's defenders to shift their fire and attention in that direction. The 39th, and First Brigade, had their opportunity. "The enemy's attention being turned to that point," remembered Ware, "our boys immediately jumped the walls and joined the conflict."[36] Captain Samuel Gillmore, who had recovered and been promoted since his serious injury at Drewry's Bluff, was first to reach the top with others soon behind.[37]

"We finally gained the top of the parapet," wrote Homer Plimpton. "The fighting became hand to hand." Bayonets, butts of guns, swords, fists, rocks, and anything else that could be found became weapons for the men of each side. Plimpton proudly watched Corporal Henry Day, a man of only five foot three inches, struggle to the top of the wall and plant the regiment's national colors before being struck in the chest. Corporal Abner Allen rushed to control the colors, where Plimpton now positioned himself. Rallying his men to their flag, the United States flag, he waved his sword in the air and drew his pistol, ready to defend the position. "It was the first time since entering the service that I ever thought it necessary to use my revolver in battle," he wrote to his aunt and uncle. Seemingly

XXIV Corps charging Fort Gregg (sketch for *Harper's Weekly* by Alfred Waud, Library of Congress: LC-DIG-ppmsca-21010).

ordained by God to lead his men at this moment, the former "Preacher's Company" private turned regimental commander willed his men over the wall and into Fort Gregg.[38]

Inside the fort, the men encountered a horrific scene. Dead and dying men were everywhere—some very old and very young—yet the rebels kept up the fight even as over 3,000 men surrounded and poured into the fort. Off to the east of the fighting, a group of Confederate officers watched the horror unfold but had just found out an element of Longstreet's Corps had arrived to man the inner line. The number of men would not be nearly enough to defend against the Federal force, which now had a free run into the city.[39]

Hundreds of Union men were now pouring into the Fort, shooting those who fought and rounding up prisoners with the defenders now out of ammunition, stamina, and able bodies. The defenders were defiant to the end, however as Federal soldiers approached an artilleryman holding the lanyard of a canister-filled gun. Ordering the man to drop it or be shot, he yelled, "Shoot and be dammed!" discharging the weapon and wounding many before being riddled with bullets.[40] More U.S. soldiers jumped into the fort, engaging in desperate hand to hand combat as the Confederate men held out until half the fort was in their enemy's possession.

At 3:15 p.m., two hours after the assault began, and 24 minutes after First Brigade gained the parapet, the air fell quiet. Mississippi Lieutenant Colonel James Duncan had turned his sword over to Captain W.A. Smiley of the 12th West Virginia. Injured himself, and nearly all his men dead or captured, Duncan merely surrendered to the nearest officer.[41] Years of frustration came out among many of the Union men who had seen so much suffering, and "it was with the greatest difficulty that we could prevent our infuriated soldiers from shooting down and braining all who survived," wrote Plimpton. Thankfully, cooler heads prevailed, and the officers got control of their men.[42] Fifty-five of Fort Gregg's defenders died inside the fort; every other man was wounded and or captured.[43]

❖   ❖   ❖

The Army of the James had long been considered by the Army of the Potomac as the junior varsity team of Federal forces operating near Petersburg and Richmond. "I wonder if those fellows will stand up to it," a VI Corps member yelled out as XXIV Corps men moved toward Fort Gregg earlier in the day.[44] The Army of the James, though, couldn't help that they hadn't been sent to fight at places like Gettysburg, or the Wilderness, and had been plagued by inexperienced political Generals—not their lack of fight. The Army of the James had gained a great deal of experience during the trials of 1864, and after a winter of training, reorganization, and new leadership, came ready to prove its mettle in the final offensives. Major General John Gibbon was a significant part of this transformation. Gibbon was a career army man who had taught tactics at West Point. He led the famed "Iron Brigade" at Antietam, commanded a division at Fredericksburg, and was wounded leading his men defending against Pickett's Charge at Gettysburg. After leading a division during Grant's Overland Campaign, he had been an obvious choice for Corps Command when the Army of the James reorganization occurred.

Given all the action Gibbon had seen in some of the war's bloodiest fighting, it is no small compliment when Gibbon wrote that "one of the bravest acts I ever witnessed in a body of men occurred at the capture of Fort Gregg."[45] XXIV Corps suffered 714 casualties on the day, 122 of them deaths. Ten officers lost their lives, and 27 were wounded, leading their men to the fort, through the moat, and up the wall.[46] Gibbon's report only accounted for the numbers in the immediate aftermath, however. As men later died after succumbing to their wounds, and initially minor wounds became more severe and took men out of action, the casualty number grew to 849.[47] "The slaughter was appalling," wrote a Confederate prisoner who was led through the field in front of the fort. He described that the dead began some 300 yards in front of the fort and increased in numbers closer to the fort until it was "simply fearful." Another added, "I never saw so many dead in so small a space lying just where they had fallen."[48]

Robert Foster's First Division had suffered the brunt of XXIV Corps' casualties with 512. A plurality of those came from Osborn's First Brigade at 241—a result of not just being the first wave but finding themselves assaulting the fort at such an inhospitable position. According to Osborn's report, Captain Homer Plimpton's 39th Illinois had struck the very front of the fort and suffered greatly in the brave struggle. Of the 150 men of the 39th Homer Plimpton led in charging the fort, 65 became casualties. Company F Lieutenant William Lamb, of Sandoval, had been wounded at Deep Bottom in August of the previous year, but returned to the regiment, earned a commission just the day prior, and gave his life leading 39th men into the Fort Gregg assault. According to Plimpton, 19 enlisted men were killed in action in addition to Lamb, and one officer and 44 men were wounded—six of them later dying.[49]

Such bloody and vital battles are always accompanied by reluctant recognition, awards, and promotions. Osborn sent Plimpton's name forward for a promotion to Major, and Osborn himself was recommended for full Brigadier General vice the brevet capacity he was serving in.[50] Fourteen United States soldiers were awarded the Congressional Medal of Honor for valor during the battle. The majority of them had either planted the national colors on the fort or captured those of the Confederate defenders. These men would later accompany Major General Gibbon to Washington, D.C., where they would present the captured Confederate flags to Secretary of War Stanton and receive the Medal of Honor.[51]

Corporal Henry Day was under the impression he had been awarded the Medal of Honor for planting the 39th's colors on the top of the fort but could not attend the ceremony because of his ongoing recovery in the hospital at Fort Monroe. Corporal Abner Allen, who is believed to have assumed control of the 39th's colors when Day fell, attended the ceremony and was awarded the Medal of Honor. Whether Allen was initially slated to receive the honor seems an unsolved mystery. Both Clark's history and the Adjutant General's report state Day planted the flag, was then severely wounded and was awarded the Medal of Honor. Given that Clark was not at the battle as he was stationed at the XXIV Corps hospital, it is likely that he pieced together reports of the battle from talking to officers and men as he did throughout his book—making the account of Day's actions very likely. It also seems likely, again based on Clark's report of Allen being honored for his service at Fort Gregg, that he was the one who picked up and guarded the flag when Day was shot. While Allen's actions in the fight were, without a doubt, brave and courageous, it's a historical disappointment that official records do not show Day was awarded the Medal of Honor. Day always believed he had been, however, and it was even noted on his gravestone when he died in 1899.[52]

For the 39th as a regiment, their efforts in the last offensive did not go unmarked. After the war ended in a grand review of XXIV Corps, General Gibbon presented a new flag standard to the regiment. Gibbon had ordered it himself, and it had a bronze eagle on top and was engraved to "Commemorate the Gallant Conduct of the Thirty-Ninth at the Assault on Fort Gregg, Va., April 2, 1865."[53]

❖ ❖ ❖

The fall of Fort Gregg had made the fall of Fort Whitworth a foregone conclusion. Before U.S. commanders could even begin to put reserve troops in motion towards the fort, Whitworth's defenders ran for the remaining inner defenses of Petersburg.[54] Following the battle, as the dead and dying were tended to, General Gibbon formed his men in an unbroken line in front of the remaining Confederates, linking XXIV Corps with VI Corps. "Ord was especially eager to lay out and dig protection for the artillery and men," wrote Earl Hess in *In the Trenches at Petersburg.*[55]

The daylight of April 2 was running low, and the Federal breakthrough of the morning, made worse by the loss of Forts Gregg and Whitworth, had put General Lee in an even more precarious position. He knew he needed to abandon Richmond and Petersburg, head west, and resupply before attempting to link up with Johnston, but he desperately wanted to wait until nightfall. Even though more of Longstreet's men were arriving to the Dimmock Line, another Federal push could breakthrough to Petersburg and Richmond, ruining final evacuations of those cities and risking capture of the entire Army of Northern Virginia.[56]

The Federals had lost 3,936 men on the day to Lee's 5,000 killed, wounded, and captured.[57] Darkness and exhausted troops were now the deciding factors in the Federals consolidating their newly gained positions rather than continuing the breakthrough. VI Corps had lost over 1,000 men in the space of fifteen minutes in the hard fighting of the initial breakthrough, then spent the rest of the day on the move, and XXIV Corps had done their marching and fighting as well. Both Corps had been under arms since daybreak and had not slept in 36 hours. IX Corps and II Corps had seen action and moved into new positions on the right and left, respectively, and Grant wanted V Corps and Sheridan's cavalry ready to press across the Appomattox at daybreak. That night, Grant wrote to his wife that "this has been one of the greatest victories of the war." He continued that this was true due to the regard the Confederacy had for Lee's Army. "We may have some more hard work but I hope not."[58] Going a step further, a private from Vermont wrote to his father that evening that April 2, 1865, "has been one of the greatest days in American history."[59]

Grant knew that hope was not a course of action, however, and planned for the worst. Not knowing how many reinforcements moved to the Dimmock Line, he had his commanders prepare for Lee's men to make a last stand in front of Petersburg instead of withdrawing. In his memoirs, Grant wrote that "our line was intrenched from the river above to the river below" and that he ordered an artillery bombardment for 5:00 a.m., the next morning, to be followed by an assault an hour later.[60]

Neither the barrage nor assault would be required, however. The Army of Northern Virginia, and government officials, began their retreats from Petersburg and Richmond at 8:00 in the evening. At 3:00 a.m., on April 3, Federal skirmishers discovered that the Confederate lines were emptied. If empty lines weren't enough sign, fires could be seen in both cities as the retreating rebels had sought to destroy records and anything of military value they couldn't take with them. After 11 months, 42,000 Federal casualties, and 28,000 Confederate casualties, the Siege of Petersburg was over.[61]

❖   ❖   ❖

The 39th Illinois Infantry was up at 5:00 a.m. on April 3, 1865, preparing to march. In Petersburg, VI and IX Corps elements were racing to be the first to plant their colors in the besieged city, and XXV Corps moved forward unopposed into the conquered Confederate capital. One of the first regiments into Richmond was the 38th USCT, led by former 39th Illinois Sergeant, and now Second Lieutenant, John Russell—the symbolism of a Black regiment marching into the Confederate capital lost on nobody. General Grant telegraphed President Lincoln with the news of the morning, then sent his horse and some guards to escort the President to his headquarters. The President who had once told the 39th Illinois they were a long way from home now came to Petersburg to see what they, and the brave men of the Union, had accomplished the day prior. Lincoln congratulated

FRANK LESLIE'S ILLUSTRATED NEWSPAPER.   [April 29, 1865.

President Lincoln visiting the late residence of Jefferson Davis in Richmond on April 4, 1865 (sketch by Joseph Becker, Library of Congress: LC-DIG-USZ62–6932).

his general, discussed the impending surrender, then visited Petersburg before heading upriver to visit Richmond the next day.[62]

There in the former Confederate capital, he sat in Jefferson Davis' study and then walked the streets, suddenly without a care in the world. Formerly enslaved Black men and women flocked to Lincoln, praising him and even kneeling before him. "Don't kneel to me," implored Lincoln—overcome by the moment—"kneel to God only, and thank Him for the liberty you will enjoy hereafter."[63]

❖   ❖   ❖

After Grant left Lincoln, he headed west to catch up with his armies. At 8:00 a.m., soon to be General Thomas Osborn formed up his brigade, led by soon to be Major Homer Plimpton's 39th Illinois, at the front of First Division, at the front of XXIV Corps of the Army of the James.[64] After three and a half years of service and 11 months near Petersburg and Richmond, the Yates Phalanx had played a significant part in what they'd hoped was about to happen so many times before. The regiment marched west along the Southside Railroad, "on after the Johnnies," wrote Anthony Taylor.[65] The 39th had six days, and 80 miles, left before they'd bring the war to an end.

To Appomattox

Samuel Gillmore was the epitome of an Illinois man committed to service in defense of the Union. Born in Ohio in July 1838, he moved to LeRoy, Illinois at 14. He lived on a farm until the age of 23 when he enlisted with Company I of the 39th just as the regiment was arriving at Benton Barracks in St. Louis. Gillmore rose from private to sergeant by June 1862, but fell ill that summer, like so much of the U.S. army at Harrison's landing, and was sent to a hospital in New York with typhoid pneumonia in August 1862.

Undeterred to serve, he rejoined the regiment at Suffolk in December 1862, and was later wounded through both thighs at Drewry's Bluff in May 1864. Saved from rebel pursuit, Gillmore was sent to hospital a second time.

Once again, however, Gillmore returned to his brothers-in-arms. In September 1864 he was back with Company I, and because of his own fine service, and losing men in those awful months, rose from Sergeant to Captain—and commander of Company I—by the end of the year.

Leading his men in the assault on Fort Gregg, Gillmore was the first to reach the parapet. Joining in October 1861 as a private, enduring multiple hardships, and rising to be a Company Commander in the regiment's most important battle; Gillmore embodied the 39th's journey. To top it all off, Gillmore was in command of the first men of the 39th to fire shots at Appomattox on the fateful morning of April 9, 1865.[1]

THE FEDERAL EFFORT OF April 2, 1865, had shrunk the Confederate forces at Petersburg and Richmond to 35,000 men and sent the splintered divisions scurrying west under cover of darkness. The men were starving, ill-equipped, many lacked shoes, and even the horses were hungry and tired. Lee's force was struggling to hang on while entrenched in place and now was on the move to regroup thirty-five miles to the west at Amelia Courthouse. After getting re-supplied, Lee's army would then make for Danville to link up with Johnston and begin a guerrilla war of sorts in the hinterland.[2] As Earl Hess writes in his conclusion of *In the Trenches at Petersburg* regarding Grant and Lee's eleven months of battle, "the tenor ... had now changed." After Grant's never-ending chess moves that ever so slightly shifted the board, it was now "literally a race," writes Hess, "in a desperate effort to escape the Army of the Potomac and the Army of the James."[3]

As Grant's army moved west in pursuit, the U.S. general decided that a direct pursuit was not the advised one. Assuming Lee would move along the Richmond and Danville Railroad, eventually needing to turn south to head towards North

Carolina, Grant ordered his commanders to remove that option. Southwest of Amelia Courthouse, and 20 miles west of Petersburg, was Burkeville junction—the town where the Richmond and Danville and South Side railroads crossed. On Lee's route through Amelia Courthouse, the distance to Burkeville was 55 miles; moving straight west mirroring the South Side Railroad, the distance was 36 miles—General Grant had his plan.[4]

The 39th Illinois covered 18 miles on April 3 while moving west with General Ord and the Army of the James. They bivouacked that evening roughly three miles beyond Sutherland Station. To the north, near Namozine Church, Sheridan's cavalry had swiped at the rear of Lee's movement, grabbing approximately 1,200 prisoners. Behind Sheridan was V Corps, II Corps, and VI Corps. Behind the Army of the James was IX Corps. In a position to continue the chase come morning were 76,000 Federal soldiers.[5] Grant noted in his memoirs that rations could not be brought up during the night, but "so elated by the reflection that at last they were following up a victory to its end," the men were happy to continue rather than run a "possible risk of letting the enemy elude them."[6]

❖   ❖   ❖

While Grant had an army so hungry for finishing the fight that they were willing to skip rations; Lee's starving army was hungry for actual food. On the morning of April 4, the Army of Northern Virginia opened train cars at Amelia Station to find not food but ammunition. A sizable supply of rations was supposed to have been sent from Richmond, but in the confusion of the retreat, the order had been mixed up. Lee was now forced to appeal to local citizens for whatever they could spare while requesting rations from Danville—a piece of information Sheridan had intercepted at the Jetersville telegraph office. While Lee was stalled at Amelia Courthouse playing quartermaster, the U.S. army continued pressing west with Sheridan's cavalry and V Corps entrenching at Jetersville, II and VI Corps close behind, and the Army of the James paralleling them to the south en route to Burkeville, stopping for the day at 4:00 p.m.[7]

In his memoirs, Grant wrote that many of Lee's men out foraging near Amelia Courthouse were taken prisoner by Federal elements—some of them by their choosing. He wrote to Secretary Stanton on the evening of the 4th, notifying him that Lee's path to turn south was blocked. He believed Lee would try to make for Farmville and a train of supplies that would allow him to get to Lynchburg for more substantial outfitting. Grant encouraged Sheridan to continue moving forces west to intercept Lee at Farmville.[8] "We had now no other objective than the Confederate armies," Grant wrote of his thoughts on the 4th, "I was anxious to close the thing up at once."[9]

❖   ❖   ❖

On April 5, Sheridan cut the railroad near Danville as elements of his force continued west towards Farmville, while also taking continued swipes at Lee's rearguard. II Corps had also now made it to the vicinity of Jetersville, and the Army of the James marched a tedious 28 miles to reach Burkeville, bringing their

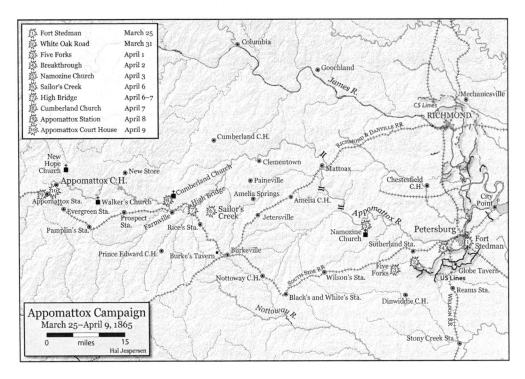

Fort Stedman	March 25	
White Oak Road	March 31	
Five Forks	April 1	
Breakthrough	April 2	
Namozine Church	April 3	
Sailor's Creek	April 6	
High Bridge	April 6–7	
Cumberland Church	April 7	
Appomattox Station	April 8	
Appomattox Court House	April 9	

Appomattox Campaign
March 25–April 9, 1865

0   miles   15
Hal Jespersen

Appomattox Campaign, April 2–9, 1865 (map by Hal Jespersen).

total since leaving Petersburg to 52 miles. The 39th had an especially grueling day as they had been detailed to guard the wagon train as it packed up and prepared to move and then had to march throughout the night to catch up with the brigade.[10] Of the situation that had developed, Lee would later state that his forced delay at Amelia Courthouse was "fatal and could not be retrieved."[11] Despite the long hard travel that the U.S. armies had done on April 5, Grant realized his moment to end the war was close at hand. He ordered Meade to move II and V Corps north towards Lee's position at Amelia Courthouse, Sheridan to take his cavalry west toward Deatonville, and Ord to move northwest towards Farmville to cut a railroad bridge over the Appomattox. The movements would bring about the most consequential day of the Appomattox Campaign and the final significant engagement between Grant and Lee.[12]

❖   ❖   ❖

After their long night of marching, the 39th was ordered to put up their tents in anticipation of staying a day or two, but "not half of them got poles for their tents," wrote Anthony Taylor when the regiment was ordered to fall in to march.[13] Osborn's First Brigade was on the move at 1:00 p.m. towards Rice's Station, arriving there to find forces under James Longstreet's command "in heavy force throwing up entrenchments at the station to oppose us."[14] The Army of Northern Virginia had moved west, under cover of darkness, attempting to get to Farmville as Grant suspected. Acting in concert with the rest of XXIV Corps, Osborn sent forward the 62nd Ohio and 199th Pennsylvania as skirmishers, with the 39th and 67th Ohio in line of battle moving behind them. Osborn's brigade advanced within one mile of the station under heavy shelling and musket fire from both sides, pushing the Confederate force back. Osborn's brigade lost two officers and 23 enlisted men in the skirmish, none of which were from the 39th.[15]

The 39th and First Brigade's action on April 6 was merely a fraction of the fighting on the day. The westward movement of the Army of Northern Virginia and the Army of the Potomac's pursuit brought the two armies together at Sailor's Creek, where a "heavy engagement took place, in which infantry, artillery, and cavalry were all brought into action," wrote Grant.[16] The day was a catastrophe for Lee's army, with the Federals not only having the numerical advantage, but advantages of terrain, attacking multiple flanks, and firing in the direction they were moving. The Battle of Sailor's Creek is often considered three separate battles occurring in the same vicinity—and they were three knockout punches. Reports show that six to eight Confederate generals were lost and over 7,700 men taken prisoner—one-fifth of Lee's remaining force.[17]

General Ord had thought it better to not press the engagement at Rice's Station any further, unsure of the size of Longstreet's force, and knowing Federal troops were behind him. Lee, however, had arrived at Rice's Station to confer with Longstreet, and realized the disaster that had unfolded at Sailor's Creek prompting his uttering to aides "my God, has the army dissolved?"[18]

As the 39th and Ord's Army of the James laid down to sleep on their arms in line of battle, Longstreet removed his forces under darkness towards Farmville.[19] Lee received a message from Jefferson Davis asking him if his army had an objective point, with Lee having to answer that he was "governed by each day's developments," and that a "few more Sailor's Creeks and it will be all over." General Grant, meanwhile, was trading messages of a very different tone with his President. Grant sent word to Lincoln at City Point that General Sheridan believed "if the thing is pressed I think that Lee will surrender." Lincoln's reply, likely his last strategic message to his general, reached Grant on the morning of the 7th: "Let the thing be pressed."[20]

❖ ❖ ❖

The war's conclusion was brought closer by engagements and battle on April 5 and 6 and would be brought into focus through movement and correspondence on April 7 and 8. The Army of the James was on the move early Friday the 7th, with the 39th and Osborn's brigade advancing on the Confederate positions at Rice's Station at 6:00 a.m. The works were empty, however, and skirmishers were sent forward in anticipation of following the retreating rebels. Advancing forward, the men were soon joined by some of Sheridan's cavalry who delivered the previous day's news. Moving along the road towards Farmville, Gibbon and XXIV Corps encountered the retreating enemy at the Bush River, two and a half miles southeast of Farmville. As Longstreet's rear attempted to cross and destroy the bridge, Sheridan's cavalry moved in, running off the rebels while extinguishing the flames, as the 39th and Osborn's brigade were part of a wave moving in the direction of the retreat. Unable to make a stand, or entirely destroy the bridges, the Confederate retreat continued with the U.S. army in close pursuit. The 39th arrived in Farmville near sundown and could finally get some rest.[21]

As Sheridan and Ord pressed the Confederates from the south, Meade was moving V Corps in from the north, and II Corps was driving straight towards Farmville from the east. Engaging rebels at Cumberland Church, II Corps took moderate casualties on the day, but slowed the Confederate retreat and kept them from their supplies. Arriving in Farmville, Grant received word from Sheridan that seven trains of supplies were waiting for Lee at Appomattox Station, and notified Grant of his intention to make a forced march with Ord, coordinating with V Corps. His objective was not only to reach the supplies before Lee but prevent him from moving south once he arrived. Earlier in the day, Grant had received word that a captured Confederate general had been speaking of the dire situation the Confederates found themselves navigating. On top of the supply and manpower issues, the Army of Northern Virginia no longer had an avenue of escape given the terrain and Federal forces' disposition. Taking all of this into account, Grant sent word to Lee that it was his "duty to shift from myself the responsibility of any further effusion of blood" and requested Lee's surrender.[22]

The 39th moved out from Farmville at 6:00 a.m., on April 8, with Sheridan's cavalry riding off ahead of them and V Corps joining them from the south during the day. II and VI Corps were advancing from the north. Noting the ferocity the army was moving with, Grant wrote in his memoirs that Sheridan's troops "moved with alacrity" and the infantry "marched about as rapidly as the cavalry could."[23] Marching on the sides of the road to allow cavalry, artillery, and wagons through, the 39th covered an astounding 37 miles on the day, calling themselves "Foster's Flying Infantry" in honor of their division commander.[24]

Motivation came from higher up as well, with General Ord mixing into the march at various points to encourage the men. "Legs will win this battle men." "It rests with us to head them off." "They can't escape if you will to keep it up."[25] Late in the day, the Army of the James heard firing in front of them, which would turn out to be Sheridan's cavalry capturing supply trains, cannon, wagons, and taking over 1,000 prisoners. The Army of the James finally stopped at midnight, and the 39th laid down for what would be a brief rest. Palm Sunday was the next day, and it would be their last of the war.[26]

◈　　◈　　◈

The final day of fighting for the 39th Illinois began after only three hours of rest and without food, but there was "not much grumbling," according to Anthony Taylor, "for we know they would not march us so for nothing."[27] "The call to fall in was sounded," wrote Doctor Clark, "stimulated by the reports that Sheridan's cavalry was in the front and flank of the enemy, and fighting desperately to arrest the progress of Lee's army."[28] Moving at a quick step for two and a half hours, the men stopped at 6:00 a.m., for coffee and hardtack, but heavy skirmishing was soon heard—only a mile away at Appomattox—and the stop was short-lived.[29]

Lee was attempting to move his Army of Northern Virginia southwest out of Appomattox then head west for Lynchburg. While aware of Sheridan's cavalry that had the trains, their situation was desperate, and the rebels attacked, believing there only to be Federal cavalry in the vicinity. As more of Lee's men were brought forward, Sheridan's cavalry was pushed back by a Confederate Corps led by General John Gordon. In what would be the final offensive move by Lee's army, the Confederates pushed back Sheridan's forces at Appomattox Station three-fourths of a mile.[30]

Moving with the tenacity of an army looking to end the war and determined not to have done 40 miles of forced march for nothing, General Gibbon was racing XXIV Corps towards the scene. Leading the way was General Foster's First Division, led by Thomas Osborn's First Brigade, "as usual," according to Anthony Taylor.[31] Covering over a mile at the double-quick, the brigade fell into lines of battle on the move, with six of Homer Plimpton's 39th Illinois companies being sent forward as skirmishers. Advancing through a strip of timber, XXIV Corps was met by the sound of increased fire and the coming and going of cavalry leaving and joining the fight.[32]

Osborn's brigade never slowed as they emerged from the woods to the Confederate force's total shock and the Federal cavalry's absolute delight. "With a deafening yell we rush forward," wrote Anthony Taylor.[33] "We emerged from the woods with a regular western yell," wrote Plimpton, "pouring a volley into the astonished rebels."[34] "The rebels were totally unaware of the presence of infantry, the timber which we were in hiding them from view," wrote Clark, "but they were soon apprised of the fact by hearing the unmistakable crack of the Springfield rifle, which was easily distinguished from the cavalry carbine."[35] The Confederate force was initially surprised by the appearance of Federal infantry but stood their ground for a brief period.

Company E private Martin Hademan of Wilmington was one of the last Federal men to be wounded in the engagement—one of seven wounded from the regiment, along with six killed and 44 wounded from the brigade.[36] Under heavy musket and artillery fire—Osborn's horse was shot out from under him—First Brigade sought refuge in a ravine and was soon joined by Colonel George Dandy's Third Brigade. With Dandy shoring up Osborn's left just like at Fort Gregg; XXIV Corps advanced once again, pushing the rebels back and capturing a piece of artillery. Soon Colonel Harrison Fairchild's Fourth Brigade joined on the right, and the advance continued with even more urgency. Major General John Turner's Independent Division soon joined the advance behind Foster's Division, with XXV Corps elements dotting the surrounding terrain. The Army of the James was now in Lee's front to the west, V Corps was quickly joining Sheridan's cavalry on Lee's southeast flank, and II and VI Corps were quickly advancing on the rear. There would be no final grand battle—Robert E. Lee was out of moves.[37]

Osborn called up a battery and fired three shots into the retreating Confederate column in front of him. "At one time," recalled Company E Corporal Charles Hudson of Wilmington, "we thought the rebels had gained an advantage and got in our rear, as we heard lively volleys of musketry."[38] However, what Hudson and the rest of the 39th Illinois heard was the celebration of one of XXV Corps' USCT regiments celebrating the news they had just received in the rear. Just before

"The Room in the McLean House, at Appomattox C.H., in which GEN. LEE surrendered to GEN. GRANT," Major and Knapp. Lee and Grant are seated, with General Sheridan between them and General Meade to Grant's right. Generals Gibbon and Ord are at the far left and right, respectively (Library of Congress: LC-DIG-pga-020–91).

10:00 a.m., Confederate couriers began racing along the lines with white flags. "I was passing the enemy's right when I was ordered to halt," wrote Osborn in his report, "word having been received that the Army of Northern Virginia had surrendered to the Armies of the United States."[39]

"[S]oon the welcome order 'cease firing!' came to us," concluded Corporal Hudson, "with the glad tidings that Lee was capitulating."[40] Standing in front of the 39th Illinois was its commander who had risen through the ranks to lead them in this climactic moment. No doubt exhausted, both physically and mentally, the usually eloquent Homer Plimpton had no words for the moment, even almost three weeks later. "It is useless for me to attempt a description of the scene that followed the tidings. The tears rushed to my eyes; my heart was too full for utterance."[41]

❖   ❖   ❖

Wild cheers went up along the 39th Illinois' line, joining the growing chorus of shouts and celebration. In town, negotiations would soon begin on the exact terms of surrender at the McLean House, with Grant and Lee meeting face to face. In the field, however, the men "finally comprehended what all this scene meant," wrote Doctor Clark. "It meant the war was practically at an end."[42] While

Johnston wouldn't surrender to Sherman until April 26, and the Confederate government wouldn't formally dissolve until May 5—the war was effectively over.[43]

The 39th Illinois left Chicago, 750 miles away, in October 1861. Three and a half years, 144 combat deaths, 25 deaths in Confederate prisons, 411 wounded, and nearly 100 lives lost to disease later, their struggle was over.[44] Chasing Stonewall Jackson through the Valley, grinding away in the heat near Fort Sumter, re-enlisting, the hard duty at Bermuda Hundred, the sacrifice at Fort Gregg, and the relentlessly hard marching towards Appomattox—all of it done by volunteers from Illinois in service to preserving a whole, and free, United States of America.

The Yates Phalanx journey from Chicago to Appomattox was complete.

Epilogue: "Muster Out"

Doctor Charles Clark rode out of the timber to see the enemy's wagons, surrounded by white flags on a small rise beyond the town. Grant and Lee were discussing the terms of surrender at the McLean house, and shortly after the official announcement around 4:00 p.m., Clark rode into Lee's camp. There he "mingled somewhat with the poorly-clad and emaciated rebels who had proved on many occasions foemen worth of our steel." Clark recalled that many Confederate officers were looking to sell their horses or other valuables to raise money to return home. Thomas Osborn bought one such horse, whose "Old Mack" had been shot out from him during the day's fight.[1]

The good doctor, and one-day history author, left for Richmond with the regiment on April 17—the same day they were informed of Lincoln's assassination. "A great sorrow passed our minds ... he whom we had so lately seen in health," Clark wrote. "A few days ago were the happiest of our lives, but now the most sorrowful."[2] In Richmond, Clark was named Chief Operating Surgeon of XXIV Army Corps by General Ord. In early September, he was then sent to Norfolk, Virginia, to be the Chief Medical Officer of the District and Surgeon of the post hospital there. In this capacity, he served until returning home to Illinois with the regiment. Clark married and began a medical practice, and in 1868 was appointed Surgeon to the Soldiers' Home in Chicago. Upon his wife's passing in 1872, he accepted an appointment to the regular army and returned to service at Forts Larned and Riley in Kansas, and then Fort Union, New Mexico. In 1880 he returned to Chicago and continued to practice medicine, ultimately being selected by a committee of 39th veterans to serve as the editor for their history published in 1889. Clark passed away four years later at the age of 69.[3]

❖ ❖ ❖

Sergeant Joseph Ward had missed all the action. Ward had been granted a furlough and left the winter camp on March 6 to travel home to Illinois. Home for nearly a month, Ward arrived back to City Point on April 5, where he saw his first sign of the Confederate evacuation, and no sign of his regiment, brigade, division, or corps. While he would never fully understand what had happened in his absence, he would gain a much better picture when he rejoined the regiment in early May and helped put up boards at the graves in front of Fort Gregg.[4]

Promoted to Second Lieutenant on October 16, 1865, but unable to muster because of the regimental strength, Ward was with the regiment until its final muster out in Springfield. Following the war, Ward and his wife farmed in Cook County until 1868, when they moved to Kansas. It was there he lived when Doctor Clark wrote the regimental history, remarking that Ward was "prospering and deserving of it."[5] Raising eight children, the couple farmed there until Ward was 57 and then moved to Oklahoma, where he spent the rest of his life—dying of cancer in 1912.[6]

❖ ❖ ❖

Sergeant Anthony Taylor closed his April 9 diary entry and opened that of April 10, 1865, remarking how "odd it seems to hear no firing" and how "calm everything is no firing and nothing going on."[7] While performing guard duty of surrendered war material with the rest of First Division of XXIV Corps until April 17, Taylor witnessed Confederate soldiers coming in to get their parole passes for safe passage home. It was the same day that duty ended, and the regiment began moving towards Richmond that they received the news of President Lincoln's assassination, and a salute of 100 guns was fired. "Cussed be the man that done this cowardly act," wrote Taylor.[8]

Taylor traveled through Richmond and home to Illinois with the rest of the regiment. He was promoted to Second Lieutenant on October 10 but could not muster due to regimental strength and mustered out as Sergeant. He lived the rest of his life in Illinois, and died in 1912, a year before his wife, and is buried in Custer Park.[9]

❖ ❖ ❖

Richard Yates was in Washington, D.C.—where he had just been seated as a U.S. Senator—when he heard of his dear friend and President's assassination. Yates had met with Lincoln early on the fateful Good Friday, April 14, to seek a colleague's appointment as a customs collector. The President even invited his Illinois friend to Ford's theater that evening, along with new Illinois governor Richard Oglesby who was in town to mark the end of the war, but both men ended up declining. However, Yates later changed his mind and went to the theater, rushing after the horrible event to deliver the news to his Illinois associates. Yates stood across the street from the Petersen House in the pouring rain early on the morning of the 15th as government officials came and went. Soon after, the various Illinois men in the nation's capital met in Yates' hotel room to plan Lincoln's return to Illinois—the one Lincoln was unsure he would ever make again. Yates served as one of the pall bearers for the funeral.[10]

Senator Yates served one term in the U.S. Senate, where he worked closely with notable anti-slavery Senator Charles Sumner on continuing progress for Blacks in America. While he worked on committees dealing with reconstruction and the newer territories, his most notable vote was likely the one he cast in favor of convicting impeached President Andrew Johnson.[11] Yates died two years after his term ended in 1873 at 58. Yates was remembered fondly by L.U. Reavis, an Illinois native, newspaperman, writer, and public speaker, in an 1881 speech before a session of the Illinois legislature. Remarking throughout on Yates' ardent anti-slavery and pro–Union views, his opening summed up the Illinois view of Yates. Putting him in company with great Illinois men of the era like Lincoln, Douglas, and Grant, Reavis said that "no children ever loved a fond parent better than the people of Illinois loved Richard Yates."[12]

❖   ❖   ❖

Valentine Randolph's last day as a soldier in the trenches had been September 17, 1864. The prolific writer who kept a habitual and thoughtful daily diary had completed his three-year enlistment and was headed home. Randolph was an interesting man to study, as he seemed to have a firm conviction in what he was doing and the rightness of the Union cause, yet never seemed to adapt to army life fully. As Stephen Wise wrote in an Epilogue to Randolph's published diary, "despite the pride in his service, Randolph apparently did not take part in postwar reunions." He points out that Clark's history says nothing more of him than what company he was in and when he mustered in and out.[13]

That being said, Randolph's published diary recounts the life and trials of the 39th Illinois through September 1864, and it is abundantly clear that Randolph believed in the cause with all his heart and served it as such. After the war, Randolph graduated from Ohio Wesleyan University in 1868, earned his Bachelor of Divinity in 1869, and became a Methodist minister. In 1870, he married and in 1881 was transferred from his ministering services in central Illinois to Nashville, Tennessee, returning to Illinois a couple of years later. In 1892 he was offered a position at Hedding College and eventually served as vice president at what later became Illinois Wesleyan University in the 1930s. Randolph eventually developed kidney-related health problems, perhaps due to malaria he suffered from in the service and died in January 1895.[14]

❖   ❖   ❖

Major Homer Plimpton had risen from a private to Major and commander of a regiment who fought against the surrendering Army of Northern Virginia at Appomattox Courthouse. Plimpton watched General Lee leave the McLean House and beamed with pride as a smiling General Grant tipped his hat to men of the 39th as he passed by. In the immediacy of the surrender, Plimpton had written of the regiment that "gratitude filled our hearts when we contemplated this grand result of all our toils, our hard marches, hard fightings and exposures." A few days later, however, he would learn of President Lincoln's assassination as the regiment marched back to Richmond. Writing of his "horrified" and mourning men, Plimpton wrote that they "never knew the depth of our love for that noble man until we heard of his cruel murder." Plimpton led his regiment back to Richmond, and on April 24. XXIV marched them through the main streets of the rebellion's former capital with their "tattered banners flying."[15]

Leading the regiment through the remainder of their service in Richmond and the surrounding area, Plimpton returned home to Illinois with the men he had served with the last four years. Over that time, Plimpton lost his father and two sisters and spent much time near the end of the war wondering if his brother was ok. In the words of Patrick Quinn, in a brief biography at the beginning of Plimpton's published journal, "[h]e had left Illinois in 1861 as a young, college-educated schoolteacher. He returned as a battle-tested veteran soldier."[16] Upon his return home, Plimpton married in 1868, worked for the IRS in Chicago until 1880, and later moved out west, serving as a mining company superintendent in Colorado and a cattle rancher in New Mexico. The deeply religious man, for whom the war had been just as much about Union as ending slavery, lived a full life—not only by the measure of days, but the extent of his deeds, and passed away in 1914 at age 76.[17]

❖   ❖   ❖

Thomas Osborn lived a lifetime inside a week between April 2 and April 9, 1865. On April 2, he led his brigade in the bloody fighting at Fort Gregg the day the Confederate line collapsed, then moved them roughly 80 miles west while skirmishing with the retreating foe. Commanding a brigade closing in on General Lee's forces in their waning moments, the closest thing we have to Osborn's thoughts on the week is his formally written official report. Following the surrender and return to Richmond, Osborn was made commander of the First Division of XXIV Corps until early July, then resigned from the army in late September 1865.[18]

Osborn returned to Chicago and his law practice, and in 1868 won election as the treasurer of Cook County by a large majority. When his term was up, he was appointed as a member of the board of the National Asylums for Disabled U.S. Soldiers—serving with General Butler and notable Illinois general and politician, John Logan. After serving in that capacity with one former superior, another former superior nominated him for a new job: President Ulysses S. Grant named Osborn Minister to the Argentine Republic in 1873. Osborn served in the role, to great distinction, under presidents Grant, Hayes, Garfield, and Arthur. Most notably, Osborn played an active role in mediating a border dispute between Argentina and Chile that averted war and brought tremendous accolade from the Argentine government. Upon leaving the position in 1884, he worked in the South American railroad business until returning home in 1890.[19]

The lawyer from Chicago, who formed a regiment to fight for the United States, led it east to fight the rebels, lost use of an arm in battle, then led its brigade on the two most fateful days of the war, died suddenly in Washington, D.C., in 1904 at 71 after a life of service to the Union. General Thomas Osborn is buried, along with other national heroes, at Arlington National Cemetery.[20]

❖   ❖   ❖

The 39th Illinois Infantry's return trip from Appomattox to Chicago began by retracing its steps from late in the war. On April 25, 1865, the First and Second Divisions of XXIV Corps marched between two lines of a "lustily cheering" Third Division that had been garrisoning the city. Clark points out in his *History* that without war correspondents on the march to Appomattox, much of the fame and glory of the surrender went to the Army of the Potomac, ignoring the Army of the James' hard march under Generals Ord and Gibbon. However, the men of XXIV Corps knew that the "First Brigade of the First Division of that Corps was entitled to the credit of being the first infantry to intercept the army of Lee, which was pushing on toward Lynchburg as fast as possible." Perhaps rubbing salt in the wound but doing their utmost to have pride in the Union, XXIV Corps received the Army of the Potomac on May 5 as it passed through to Washington for the grand review. On May 10, they did the same for General Sherman's army.[21]

Now Brevet Major General Alfred Terry had parlayed his success at Fort Fisher into command of the Department of Virginia and North Carolina, head-quartered at Richmond. Having been led by Terry in one capacity or another since the summer of 1863, the men of the 39th had tremendous respect for how he had done it. Homer Plimpton wrote that the men "would have gone through fire and flood" for Terry, and the General ensured they were well cared for in Rich-mond.[22] "The duties of the men at Richmond were not excessive or burdensome," wrote Doctor Clark.[23] In fact, they were rather enjoyable. A grand review was held where General Gibbon presented a new standard to the 39th with a bronze eagle, purchased by the corps commander himself, to commemorate the gallant conduct of the 39th at Fort Gregg. The time was even better for some individuals. The women of Richmond showed up after they realized the "Yankees did not wear horns, only drank them." Samuel Greenbaum, of Chicago, found a wife even.[24]

The regiment traveled to Norfolk in late July and had a wonderful reunion when reporting to the Southeastern District of Virginia commander: Brevet Brig-adier General Orrin Mann. After recovering from his wound suffered at Ware Bottom Church, Mann had been assigned as the pro-vost marshal and ulti-mately took command. On August 1, the XXIV Corps was deactivated, but some troops remained in Rich-mond to maintain order during the transfer to a new government. Accord-ing to Doctor Clark, "af-fairs were in the control" of the 39th, and they had a comfortable camp in the city square.[25]

When a Major General showed up to take com-mand on September 4, Mann was relieved of his duty and returning to the

Homer Plimpton, undated post war photograph (repro-duced from Clark, *History*).

regiment assumed command because of his seniority, Plimpton moving to number two. Captain Gillmore, his rise continuing, was serving as provost-marshal and was later appointed to the new commander's staff as Assistant General Inspector. Gillmore served on this, and other staffs in the region, remaining in the service until March of the following year.[26]

❖   ❖   ❖

The order to prepare to muster out came to the 39th on December 3, 1865. On December 6, after the military formality of paperwork and processing, the men boarded a steamer to take them to Baltimore. The next morning, they boarded a train for Chicago, enjoying comfortable accommodations, and celebrating the reality that their war was officially over. Upon arrival in Chicago, the Soldiers' Aid Commission once again came through, where a giant meal was laid out at Bryan Hall. The following morning, their last leg of travel marched them through Chicago, a third and final time, to the cheers of Chicagoans. One last time as a regiment, the 39th boarded a train—this time for Springfield.[27]

The regiment reached Springfield early on the morning of December 9 and proceeded to Camp Butler. Setting up camp one last time, the days were occupied by turning in equipment, finalizing discharge paperwork, and being paid one final time. On December 16, the regiment was formed as-for a parade, names were called off, and the men were "mustered out." The men then gathered in the chapel for a ceremony officiated by Adjutant General Isham Haynie, attended by the governor's staff and citizens from town.[28]

The regiment turned over their three flags, with General Mann telling their tales. One awarded by the State Agricultural Society for drill performance; the "prize" or "agricultural" flag, adorned with the inscribed eagle from General Gibbon. One the gift from then-Governor Yates, carried by the regiment's own *George* Yates, when it had to be ripped from his hands when he fell in battle. The third, the beautiful flag gifted to them before leaving Chicago in 1861. All of them "literally in ribbons, and bore incontrovertible evidence of the fiery ordeal through which they had passed." Never lost or surrendered as Osborn had bid them.[29]

General Haynie took possession of the flags, stating that "these old, tattered and riddled banners constituted the jewels of the State. They were made sacred by the blood which, they had been told, was shed upon them." Turning to the men and speaking for Governor Oglesby, the General offered his welcome home and gracious thanks for the "noble and heroic services they had rendered to the Nation." Haynie closed by offering that he hoped the men would maintain the spirit of their service in continuing to defend the Union and was met with applause and stirring music from a band. It was then time for General Mann to stand and deliver a final message to the men of the 39th Illinois.[30]

Soldiers: The period toward which your attention has been directed for a long time is at hand. Having served your country faithfully for nearly five years, you are today honorably discharged from the army of the United States. You will soon leave off your veteran garb of valiant blue, and putting on another suit, become honorable citizens of an honorable State—a state that has sent over two hundred and sixty thousand troops to the field, and give to the country a PRESIDENT who has fallen a martyr to that cause which, like the voice of God, called you from your homes to engage in the stern realities of fierce and bloody warfare. In parting with you, it is not necessary for me to remind you of the different departments in which you have served with distinction. The graves of your fallen but gallant comrades in Missouri, in Maryland, in the Carolinas, and in the Virginias, will keep them fresh in your memories. Nor need your commanding officer enumerate the many starry, moonless nights you have passed on picket, guarding your sleeping comrades from the midnight assaults of those who sought alike your lives and the life of your country—these will never be forgotten. The sanguinary fields which you have gallantly fought, and the frowning, formidable forts you have heroically stormed, you will always remember. Some of you will remember them by the wounds which are still fresh in your bodies, and by the limbs you have left to bleach on Southern soil, while on all your memories they are as deeply engraven as they are on your victorious old battle-flags, which you today turned over to the authorities of your State, unsullied by even an imaginary shade of dishonor.

The fortunes of war have been such as to prevent your commander from participating with you in the final campaign that crowned our common country with Victory and Peace. Yet from his post of duty elsewhere, he watched your interests with a jealous eye and heard of your deeds of valor with feelings of pride and regret. To your gallantry and efficiency in the fields is the largely indebted for his present rank and position, and he therefore most cheerfully embraces this last opportunity to thank you, one and all, for your soldierly bearing towards him, and for the promptness with which you have observed and executed his orders. He will ever regard it his sacred duty to contribute in any way to your individual prosperity, wherever he can, and bespeak for you that recognition of the glorious services you have rendered your country, and so nobly and dearly earned. Go to your homes, VETERAN SOLDIERS, and strive to perpetuate that peace, whose purchases was affected at so vast a price—which has made your once long lives short, and your full ranks thin. But should the emergency again arise, when either National honor must be compromised, or personal life laid on the altar of your country, let no member of the YATES PHALANX be slow in rushing to the conflict as a representative of the honored old THIRTY-NINTH.

Urging upon you, possibly for the last time, the vital importance of maintaining characters of honesty, integrity, industry, and stability, and hoping that again in the peaceful circles of home and friends you will leave far behind any habits contracted in the army that may tend to retard you in a manly career in the great campaign of life, your commander bids you, officers and men, one and all, an affectionate FAREWELL![31]

Homer Plimpton wrote that "for some moments a deep silence prevailed, but was soon broken by a burst of loud and prolonged cheering."[32]

❖   ❖   ❖

So many other stories could be told of 1,452 total men that served with the 39th Illinois at one time or another. Some did their three years and left, some re-enlisted, and some didn't join the service until late in the war. All three camps had men who served notably and heroically or simply did their jobs well and with little fuss.

For every Osborn or Mann, there was an officer who led his company to no great fanfare, but no dishonor, and returned home when their dutiful service was complete. Or for every Homer Plimpton or Samuel Gillmore who rose from private to an officer of great responsibility—or dead Corporal who returned to life to command a company—there was a private like Company A's Samuel Proud of

Channahon; who enlisted in 1861, was wounded at Ware Bottom Church, and killed in the heroic assault of Fort Gregg—never having been promoted.[33] Or men like G Company's Joseph McKee, from Bremen, who joined the regiment in the summer of 1862, and was then discharged for a disability that fall. Determined to serve, McKee re-enlisted in January 1864, was promoted to Corporal, wounded near Deep Bottom, and wounded again at Fort Gregg.[34]

Whether they made it through without a scratch on them or, like Company C's Hermann Girard of Long Point, were wounded three separate times between Drewry's Bluff and Fort Gregg—all who served honorably served the Union.[35] Most of the 144 men who lost their lives due to battle have no mention other than their name in the roster, but the significance of their sacrifice is not forgotten.

❖   ❖   ❖

Charles Clark closed his 1889 history of the regiment with a letter that will now close this history as well. Requesting any thoughts he could offer about a unit in his chain of command on so many occasions, Clark wrote to Major General Alfred Terry. Quite sick at the time with kidney disease, Terry stated that writing was a laborious task. Still, he offered heartfelt thoughts that so accurately and succinctly summarize the service of the 39th Illinois Volunteer Infantry.

> *NEW HAVEN, CONN.*
> *May 14th, 1889.*
>
> *My dear Doctor:*
>
> *You ask me to express my opinion about the "Old Thirty-Ninth Illinois." What can I Say about it—what can anyone say about it except that it was one of the most gallant of regiments and was as distinguished for its discipline and good order in camp and on the march as it was for its gallantry in action.*
>
> *Sum up all soldierly qualities and attribute them to the regiment, and you will do it no more than justice.*
>
> *Sincerely yours,*
> *Alfred H. Terry*[36]

Appendix: Roster of the 39th Illinois Infantry

The roster included here is adapted from Dr. Charles M. Clark's 1889 history of the regiment. Information of individuals is limited to their service between October of 1861 and the end of the war, with some notable exceptions. Clark's methodology for listing officer's and non-commissioned officers of regiments seemed to be by seniority/roles they served, and I've tried to replicate that. Another issue is that many men were told post Appomattox that they were being promoted, but they did not muster out with that rank. Finally, there are many men who were drafted and sent towards the unit, only to arrive after the end of the war. While they were assigned to the 39th, accounting for all of them is very difficult. In the interest of both clarity, and space, I have omitted draftees that joined the regiment after the surrender at Appomattox.

Cities and towns listed next to name denote from where the member mustered. While inaccuracies no doubt exist, I have done my best to check entries against the Adjutant General's report as required. When there is disagreement, however, I have chosen to go with Clark's History on spelling of men's names or accounts of their biography. The regiment initially all mustered in October 11, 1861, enlistment dates pre-dating that are provided if available. Draftees assigned to the regiment very late in the war have little in the way of biographical information and may or may not have been from Illinois. Those looking for specific details should research that report or consult the 39th Illinois' page on Illinois Gen Web's Civil War Project, or the National Archives. A great deal of information can also be found on ancestry websites with as little as a name. Errors in deciphering/transcribing rosters and records are my own.

Members who enlisted in 1861 reenlisted as veterans unless noted as mustering out in 1864.

*=mustered out with the regiment December 6, 1865
MO=Mustered out at completion of a service requirement prior to the end of the war
DD= disability discharge—whether the disability was related to combat or not is noted if known
KIA= Killed in action
WIA=Wounded in action
DS= Died in service—reason for death is noted if known.
POW=Prisoner of War—details are given if known

Field and Staff Officers

Light, Austin. Chicago, Colonel, received commission July 22, 1861; dismissed from service November 25, 1861

Osborn, Thomas O. Chicago, Lieutenant Colonel, Colonel, promoted vice Light; promoted to Brigadier General May 11, 1865; wounded May 14, 1864, at Drewry's Bluff while leading the regiment under fire; returned to service in winter of 1864 and assigned to command First Brigade, First Division, XXIV Corps through surrender at Appomattox Courthouse

Mann, Orrin, L. Chicago Major, Lieutenant Colonel, Colonel, promoted Brigadier General by brevet May 11, 1865; played a major role in initial recruitment of the regiment; wounded May 20, 1864, leading the regiment in a charge on enemy works; returned to service in January 1865 as Provost-Marshal of the Southeastern District of Virginia*

Plimpton, Homer A. Sterling, Major, Lieutenant Colonel (see Company G), promoted from Private to Sergeant following battles of May 16 and 20, 1864 to fill vacancies; thereafter detailed to act as Sergeant Major when Reese Bishop was taken prisoner; commissioned First Lieutenant vice Amos Savage promoted to Captain; promoted to Captain of Company G vice Savage discharged for a disability; took command of regiment by seniority*

Munn, Sylvester W. Wilimington, Major, promoted January 1862 vice Mann promoted to Lieutenant Colonel, resigned December 1862 due to disability

Linton, Samuel S. Willow Creek, Major, promoted vice Munn resignation, wounded through lung May 16, 1864, at Drewry's Bluff; MO November 10, 1864

Milliman, Minor W. Wilmington, Major, commissioned June 6, 1865, but unable to muster due to strength of regiment not warranting it (see Company E)*

Marshall, Frank B. Chicago, Adjutant, resigned July 15, 1862

Walker, Joseph D. Lockport, Adjutant, promoted from Sergeant Major vice Marshall resignation; planted the regimental flag at Fort Wagner; died of his wounds in Battle of Drewry's Bluff, May 16, 1865

Doud, Leroy. Bloomington, Adjutant, enlisted September 12, 1861; promoted vice Walker's death; served as regimental adjutant until January 1865; detailed to Osborn's staff as Assistant Adjutant General of First Brigade until its end as an organization; detailed by Major General Terry as Assistant Ordnance Officer of the South Department of Virginia at Norfolk; MO January 23, 1866

Cutler, Joseph A. Chicago, Quartermaster, discharged July 15, 1862

Linton, Jonathan, F. Lane, Quartermaster, commissioned June 12, 1862 (see Company D), received great credit for duties as quartermaster in clothing, equipping, and feeding the regiment; MO April 19, 1864

Hoffman, Stewart W. Sandoval, Quartermaster, promoted from Quartermaster Sergeant vice Linton (see Company F)*

Blake, Samuel, C. Chicago, Surgeon, resigned due to chronic illness, June 3, 1862

Clark, Charles M. Chicago, 1st Assistant Surgeon, Surgeon, promoted vice Blake, founding member of the regiment; Folly Island, S.C. Post Surgeon; Chief Operating Surgeon of XXIV Corps Hospital; author of 1889 regimental history*

Crozier, James. Waveland, IN, 1st Assistant Surgeon, commissioned December 6, 1862, joining the regiment in Suffolk, VA*

Woodward, William. Belvidere, 2nd Assistant Surgeon, commissioned December 9, 1862, joining the regiment at Suffolk; appointed Medical Purveyor of XXIV Corps in January 1865, transferred to 58th Illinois and commissioned Surgeon on April 11, 1865; MO April 1, 1866

De Normandie, Anthony. Gardner, 2nd Assistant Surgeon (see Company A), originally a hospital steward, after transfer of Woodward was recommended for commission which was granted due to meritorious service*

McReading, Charles S. Channahon, Chaplin, commissioned October 9, 1861, resigned August 9, 1862, due to poor health

Non-Commissioned Staff

Walker, Joseph D. Lockport, Sergeant Major, enlisted September 19, 1861; promoted Adjutant July 15, 1862

Bishop, Reese. Le Roy, Sergeant Major, enlisted October 18, 1861; taken prisoner during Battle of Drewry's Bluff on May 16, 1864; died while POW at Andersonville Prison, Georgia, November 7, 1864

Hawthorne, Ephraim, W. Fremont, Sergeant Major, promotion dated to February 9, 1864, when joined regiment as a recruit*

Clapp, Frederick. Chicago, Quartermaster Sergeant, enlisted August 5, 1861; MO September 9, 1864

Coursen, Christopher, E. Chicago, Quartermaster Sergeant, promoted August 5, 1864, vice Hoffman (see Company F)*

Johnson, Allen B. Wilmington, Commissary Sergeant, enlisted August 5, 1861, and appointed to position; promoted to 2nd Lieutenant of Company A (see Company A)

Wightman, James. Odell, Commissary Sergeant, appointed from position as sergeant in Company C vice Johnson promoted; promoted to 1st Lieutenant (see Company C)

Johnson, Abiram B. Commissary Sergeant; promoted vice Wightman (see Company I); MO September 12, 1864

Frisbie, Charles F. Worth, Commissary Sergeant, promoted January 1, 1864 (see Company G)*

Chief Musicians

Jones, Henry T. Pontiac, enlisted September 21, 1861; DD June 3, 1862

Hollowell, Robert C. Le Roy, enlisted September 18, 1861; MO September 18, 1864

Mott, Leander M. Chicago, enlisted August 15, 1862; MO June 20, 1865

Lace, Philip M. Pontiac, enlisted January 5, 1864.* (Lace had previously enlisted in September 1861 as leader of the regimental band, but was mustered out by order of the War Department, see story below under Regimental Band)

Fox, Franklin L. Chicago, enlisted January 1, 1864*

Regimental Band

The original band that left Chicago with the regiment in October 1861, was, by order of the War Department, mustered out of service June 4, 1862—as were all regimental bands that had been enlisted as such.

The second was organized by Philip Lace, who enlisted was placed on the non-commissioned staff as Principal Musician. The members were detailed from enlisted members of the regiment's companies. This was the band that left with the regiment from Chicago when returning from furlough. According to Clark, the band was considered the best in the Army of the James. During battle, it was the duty of the band's members to serve as stretcher bearers carrying wounded from the field.

Original Band

Bowman, N.B.
Hull, B.B.
Harrah, William C.
Hanning, William
Summers, Frank R.
Williams, Henry F.
Hannah, Calvin, taken prisoner at
    Strasburg, VA, May 1862; paroled
Lane, Edward H., taken prisoner at
    Strasburg, VA, May 1862; paroled

Pitcher, W.T.
Thaer, Andrew
Mears, D.C.
Towns, J.C.
Johnson, James, M.
Ladd, A.A.
Fisher, B.W.
Schermerhorn, Alford
Smith, C.E.

Band of 1864–1865

Lace, Philip M., Cornet
Hedge, Enoch C., Cornet
Wilson, James A., Cornet
Conley, Edward D., Cornet
Jones, Henry T., Alto,
McGregor, Charles A., Alto
Sackett, Edward A., Alto
Hull, Samuel, F., Baritone
Greenbaum, Samuel, Tenor

Butterfield, Frank L., Tenor
Brown, William H., Tenor
Lace, William C., Tuba
Pitcher, Theo, W., Tuba
Lewis, John, Cymbals
Johnson, James M., Cymbals
Cannon, Timothy, Small Drum
Hughes, William, Bass Drum
Fuller, M.H., Bass Drum

Company A
Will County—1860 Population: 29,321
Cook County—144,954

Killed in Battle	6
Died of Wounds	10
Died in Prison	2
Lost Limbs	6
Wounded	36

Taken Prisoner	12
Number Originally Enlisted	97
Mustered Out at Expiration of Service	21
Re-Enlisted as Veterans	26
Recruits	61
Mustered Out With Regiment	57

Elected Officers

Captain: Sylvester W. Munn
First Lieutenant: Joseph Richardson
Second Lieutenant: Leroy Baker

Company A was initially formed during April of 1861, and seemed destined to be part of the 20th Illinois Volunteer Infantry, but was replaced by a more completely formed company from Joliet. Remaining men who did not enlist with the 20th stuck together, and eventually traveled to Chicago to enlist and form the core of Company A, 39th Illinois Volunteers. The men forming, and overwhelmingly making up, Company A were from Wilmington, Illinois—a small town 60 miles southwest of Chicago. The regiment was made up primarily of farmers and farmers' sons.

Munn, Sylvester W. Wilmington, Captain, commissioned August 5, 1861; promoted to Major December 1, 1861 (see Field and Staff)

Baker, Leroy A. Wilmington, Captain, promoted from 1st Lieutenant vice Munn promoted; assisted in recruiting the company; during battle of Drewry's Bluff, May 16, 1864; took command of regiment after Linton was wounded and Phillips had been captured until relieved by Mann; took command again on May 20, 1864, after Mann wounded; retained command until August 16, 1864, when a wound required amputation of his leg; DD December 17, 1864

Parker, Horace B. Wilmington, Captain, promoted to 1st Sergeant December 1, 1861; promoted to 1st Lieutenant September 8, 1864, promoted to Captain December 17, 1864*

Richardson, Joseph W. 1st Lieutenant, assisted in raising the company; DS typhoid fever, November 17, 1861

Johnson, Allen B. Wilmington, 1st Lieutenant, promoted from 2nd Lieutenant December 1, 1861, vice Baker; DS yellow fever, September 1864 while detailed to Newbern, N.C., as ordnance officer

Herriott, John E. Wilmington, 1st Lieutenant, promoted from Corporal (enlisted October 1861) March 31, 1865, vice Parker*

Burrill, James. Wilmington, 2nd Lieutenant, promoted from 1st Sergeant December 1, 1861, vice Johnson promoted; wounded in camp on May 25, 1864; MO December 1864

Krauskup, George. Wilmington, Sergeant, enlisted August 5, 1861; DD February 5, 1862

Johnson, William H. Wilmington, Sergeant, enlisted August 5, 1862; transferred to Battery L, 4th U.S. Artillery, December 29, 1862

Smith, Henry G. Wilmington, Sergeant, enlisted August 5, 1861; while at Hancock MD in January 1862, Smith was detailed in command of a group of guards of an ammunition train; at the second battle of Bull Run he was ordered to burn the train, but succeeded in making it through to Washington, D.C.; was present at the battles of South Mountain and Antietam before rejoining the regiment at Suffolk in October 1862; wounded by shell fragment October 9, 1863, on Morris Island, S.C., wound required amputation of right leg, DD, date unlisted

Collinge, Alexander, J. Channahon, Sergeant enlisted September 12, 1861; promoted from Private on March 1, 1862; injured in railroad accident was on furlough in April 1864

Harris, William, J. Channahon Sergeant, enlisted August 19th, 1861; promoted from Corporal on March 1, 1862; KIA June 17, 1864, in skirmish near Chester Station, VA

Yates, George W. Wilmington, Sergeant, enlisted August 15, 1861; promoted to Corporal August 1, 1862; to Sergeant August 8, 1864; WIA at Darbytown Crossroads carrying the colors in the charge on October 13, 1864; taken POW but paroled; died of his wounds October 26, 1864; commission for him as a Captain of a USCT regiment arrived after his death

Taylor, Anthony G. Wilmington, Sergeant, enlisted August 5, 1861; promoted to Corporal September 10, 1864; to Sergeant March 1, 1865; to 2nd Lieutenant October 10, 1865*

Holter, John. Chicago, Sergeant, enlisted August 17, 1861; promoted from Private to Corporal March 1, 1862; WIA May 20, 1864, at Ware Bottom Church; promoted Sergeant April 1, 1865*

Keepers, William A. Wilmington, Sergeant, enlisted August 5, 1861; wounded at Fort Gregg, VA.; promoted from Corporal April 2, 1865*

Russell, William J. Wilmington, Corporal, enlisted August 15, 1861; DD August 15, 1862

Jones, William R. Chicago, Corporal, enlisted August 8, 1861; transferred to Battery L, 4th U.S. Artillery, December 29, 1862

Dorr, Michael. Wilmington, Corporal, enlisted August 5, 1861; MO September 10, 1864

Deline, Thomas. Channahon, Corporal, enlisted August 5, 1861; taken POW near Drewry's Bluff June 2, 1864; MO under General Order 77, War Department, October 1865

Day, Henry M. Wilmington, Corporal enlisted August 5, 1861; promoted from Private March 1, 1862; WIA planting the colors on Fort Gregg, VA, April 2, 1865; promoted to Sergeant June 1, 1865; DD July 3, 1865; all regimental accounts and the Adjutant General Report state Day was awarded the Medal of Honor for bravery in the Fort Gregg assault, but there is no official army record of such; see the account of Fort Gregg in chapter 20

Reed, William H. Wilmington, Corporal, enlisted August 15, 1861; promoted from Private March 1, 1863; taken POW June 2, 1864; MO August 15, 1865

Butterfield, William. Wilmington, Corporal, enlisted August 12, 1861; promoted from Private August 22, 1863; KIA August 16, 1864, at Second Deep Bottom as member of color guard

Holz, Earnest. Wilmington, Corporal, enlisted August 5, 1861; promoted from Private January 1, 1865; to Sergeant July 3, 1865*

Houghton, Herrick. Wilmington; Corporal, enlisted August 22, 1861; promoted from Private April 1, 1865*

PRIVATES

Abrams, Frank. Reed, enlisted January 4, 1864; taken POW May 20, 1864, at Ware Bottom Church*

Adams, Samuel. Channahon, enlisted August 5, 1861, DD June 1, 1862

Ahrens, Claus. Wilmington, enlisted August 5, 1861; wounded at Ware Bottom Church, May 20, 1864*

Armstrong, Patrick C. Chicago, enlisted November 1, 1861; DD August 6, 1863

Ashton, Daniel. Wilmington, enlisted August 5, 1861; taken POW at Drewry's Bluff May 16, 1864; MO under General Order 77, August 16, 1865

Atkins, William C. Wilmington, enlisted August 5, 1861; DD July 21, 1862

Bailey, Patrick. St. Louis, MO., enlisted October 14, 1861, transferred to Battery L, 4th U.S. Artillery, December 29, 1862

Baxter, William. Wilmington, enlisted August 5, 1861; wounded in shoulder at Battle of Drewry's Bluff, May 16, 1864*

Benton, Silas. Wilmington, enlisted August 12, 1861; transferred to Company E November 15, 1861

Burden, John. Channahon, enlisted August 17, 1861; KIA August 16, 1864, at Second Deep Bottom

Brooks, Lysander R. Wilmington, enlisted August 5, 1861; served 2 years as brigade postmaster*

Brucket, Florence. Wilmington, enlisted February 19, 1864; taken POW May 16, 1864, during battle of Drewry's Bluff, sent to Andersonville, no further record

Brown (Bowen in Adjutant General's Report)**, Henry.** Florence, enlisted December 26, 1863; wounded May 16, 1864, at Second Deep Bottom*

Brown, William H.R. Chicago, enlisted August 21, 1861; wounded in hand and finger amputated at Ware Bottom June 2, 1864; MO September 10, 1864

Calhoun, William W. Wilmington, enlisted August 15, 1861; DS February 23, 1862, at Patterson's Creek, VA

Cambellick, William. Guilford, enlisted October 8, 1864; WIA April 2, 1865, at Fort Gregg, VA; in hospital when regiment MO; survived

Carpenter, Adelbert, F. Wilmington, enlisted August 5, 1861, promoted to Corporal July 1, 1865*

Carpenter, Joseph M. Wilmington, enlisted August 5, 1861; DD February 16, 1862

Carter, Joseph. Wilmington, enlisted August 5, 1861; died of wounds received at Fort Wagner, SC on August 26, 1863

Carter, William C. Wilmington, DD November 15, 1862

Clapp, Frederick G. Chicago, enlisted August 5, 1861; promoted Quartermaster Master Sergeant December 31, 1861; MO September 10, 1864

Cochran, David M. Chicago, enlisted August 8, 1861; promoted Corporal May 15, 1865*

Conley, Edward D. Wesley, enlisted January 5, 1864; detailed to band; brother of John Conley, Company E*

Connell, Charles C. unknown, enlisted February 28, 1862; DD June 21, 1862

Conroy, Francis. Wilmington, enlisted October 1, 1861; DD May 25, 1862

Coons, Montreville. Wesley, enlisted February 20, 1864; WIA taken POW May 16, 1864, at Battle of Drewry's Bluff

Corrigan, Hugh. Wilmington, enlisted December 30, 1863; WIA May 16, 1864, at Drewry's Bluff; died of wounds June 3, 1864

Croop, George W. Gardner, enlisted September 16, 1861; DD July 21, 1862

Croop, Jonas F. Gardner, enlisted August 5, 1861; WIA August 16, 1864, at Deep Bottom; MO August 1, 1865

Curtis, Cyrus. Channahon, enlisted September 12, 1861; discharged September 2, 1865, under General Order 396

Dailey, Daniel. Wilmington, enlisted December 28, 1863; WIA May 20, 1864, at Ware Bottom Church; POW; died at Newbern N.C. March 26, 1865

Dobson, James. Wilmington, enlisted December 23, 1863; WIA May 20, 1864, at Ware Bottom Church; arm amputated; DD November 3, 1865

Douse, Casper. Wilmington, enlisted February 23, 1864; MO May 22, 1865, under General Order 77.

Dolan, Timothy. Channahon, enlisted December 26, 1863; WIA May 16, 1864, at Drewry's Bluff; transferred to Veteran Reserve Corps.

Farable, David E. Gardner, enlisted August 5, 1861; DS April 22, 1862

Fitzpatrick, Michael. St. Louis, MO, enlisted August 14, 1861; transferred to Battery L, 4th U.S. Artillery, December 29, 1862

Fuller, Myron C. Wesley, enlisted June 5, 1864; detailed to band*

Galherer, John. Wilmington, enlisted December 28, 1864; wounded in hand October 13, 1864; discharged under General Order 96 May 29, 1865

Hartman, William H. Gardner, enlisted August 8, 1861; DS February 6, 1862

Hedge, Enoch C. Wilmington, enlisted August 15, 1861; detached to band; took a rifle and fought at Drewry's Bluff*

Hennings, John. Wesley, enlisted February 18, 1864; WIA October 7, 1864, near Chaffin's Farm; taken POW and paroled April 7, 1865, at Appomattox*

Hicks, William. Wilmington, enlisted August 5, 1861; DS February 5, 1862

Hopkins, Joseph (James in Adjutant General's report). Chicago, enlisted February 29, 1864*

Howell, George. Wilmington, enlisted August 19, 1861; DD February 5, 1862

Hughes, William J. Chicago, enlisted February 24, 1864; detailed to band*

Hurlburt, Amos. Lockport, enlisted December 29, 1863; discharged February 16, 1865

Irish, Franklin. Wesley, enlisted February 19, 1864; WIA October 7, 1865, near Chaffin's Farm*

Johnson, Edmond. Wilmington, enlisted August 5, 1861; DD March 19, 1863

Killfoyl, James. Wilmington, enlisted September 10, 1861; deserted March 17, 1864

Knowles, Benjamin F. Chicago, enlisted August 22, 1861; DD July 22, 1862, as result of accident while in Cumberland, MD

Kyle, Joseph. Guilford, enlisted October 8, 1864*

Lawler, Michael. Channahon, enlisted September 16, 1861; DD July 1, 1862

Lynch John. St. Louis MO, enlisted October 31, 1861; MO October 30, 1864

Lyons George. Wilmington, enlisted August 5, 1861; DS February 23, 1863, at St. Helena Island, S.C.

Maher, John. Wilmington, enlisted September 10, 1861; DS January 16, 1862

Maloney, James. Wilmington, enlisted December 4, 1863*

Martin, James. Chicago, enlisted August 16, 1861*

McCarty, Peter. Wilmington, enlisted August 12, 1861; DS June 12, 1862

McCullum, Alexander. Wilmington, enlisted September 14, 1861; transferred from Company E November 16, 1861; promoted to Corporal October 15, 1865*

McCulloch, John. Chicago, enlisted August 15, 1861; MO September 10, 1864

McDonald, James. Chicago, enlisted September 10, 1861; MO September 10, 1864

McKendrick, Michael. Wesley, enlisted December 26, 1863; WIA skirmish near Chester station and taken POW June 16, 1864

McKnight, William. St. Louis, MO, enlisted October 22, 1861; MO October 22, 1864

Mott, George. Wilmington, enlisted August 5, 1861; DS February 2, 1862

Murphy, Orrin. Wilmington, enlisted September 10, 1861; DD September 4, 1863

Murray, James. Wilmington, enlisted January 16, 1864; WIA October 7, 1864, near Chaffin's Farm*

Nichols, Benjamin. Wilmington, enlisted December 24, 1863; promoted Corporal September 28, 1865*

Nichols, Ira. Wilmington, enlisted August 21, 1861; veteran; WIA May 20th 1864 at Ware Bottom; escaped but recaptured; died as POW at Florence S.C.

Osgood, Thomas. Wilmington, enlisted February 19, 1864; WIA August 16, 1864, at Second Deep Bottom; died in hospital September 28, 1864

Osgood, Jerry. Wilmington, enlisted February 19, 1864*

Ottenheimer, Solomon. Chicago, enlisted October 1, 1864; discharged June 21, 1865, under General Order 96

Pelton, Alsen D. Wilmington, enlisted August 5, 1861; taken POW at Strasburg, VA, May 1862; DD December 1, 1862

Phillips, James P. Chicago, enlisted August 13, 1861; DD June 8, 1863

Preston, William J. Chicago, enlisted March 8, 1864; MO January 21, 1865

Proud, Samuel F. Channahon, enlisted August 8, 1861; WIA May 20, 1864, at Ware Bottom Church; KIA April 2, 1865, in assault on Fort Gregg

Randall, Frank R. enlisted August 5, 1861; DD October 28, 1863

Rawlings, (listed A Rollins in Clark's History) **Lemon P.** Guilford, enlisted October 8, 1864; MO January 27, 1866

Rogers, Thomas. Bucyrus, Ohio, enlisted September 24, 1861; DD December 1, 1862

Rourke, Hugh. Chicago, enlisted August 20, 1861; KIA April 2, 1865, in assault on Fort Gregg

Ruppenthal, Henry. Bath, VA, enlisted January 1, 1862; WIA May 20, 1864, at Ware Bottom Church; arm required amputation; died in hospital June 18, 1864

Ryan, Thomas. Wilmington, enlisted August 25, 1863; orderly on Osborn's staff during spring offensive of 1865*

Scanlin, John. Chicago, enlisted August 5, 1861; wounded at Bermuda Hundred; MO November 20, 1864

Seybert, Andrew. Wilmington, enlisted August 8, 1861; veteran; taken POW May 16, 1864, at Drewry's Bluff, died a POW at Andersonville August 11, 1864

Sherman, Martin. Channahon, enlisted September 12, 1861*

Smith, Charles W. Wesley, enlisted February 25, 1864; deserted October 26, 1865

Smith, Nicholas. Chicago, enlisted August 21, 1861; WIA April 2, 1865, in assault on Fort Gregg; died of wounds April 4

Sovereign, Milton. Chicago, enlisted September 14, 1861, as musician; MO September 10, 1864

Starkweather, Henry. Wilmington, enlisted August 5, 1861; DS July 14, 1863, on Folly Island, SC.

Stewart, James,. Wilmington, enlisted August 5, 1861; DD August 4, 1862

Stumph, Michael. Wilmington, enlisted August 5, 1861; DD August 4, 1862

Sullivan, Michael,. Chicago, enlisted August 22, 1861; DD May 19, 1862

Taylor, Bufort. Florence, enlisted December 25, 1863; DS May 14, 1865, at Richmond, VA

Tewkey (Tewbey in Adjutant's report), **Edward.** Wilmington, enlisted August 14, 1861; MO September 10, 1864

Thewlis (Thulis in Adjutan't report), **William.** Wesley, enlisted February 19, 1864*

Tower, Franklin H. Wilmington; enlisted February 29, 1864*

Tracy, Harvey (Harry in Adjutant's report). Wilmington, enlisted August 19, 1861; taken POW May 16, 1864, at Drewry's Bluff and sent to Andersonville; MO April 20, 1865

Vowalt, Christian. Wilmington, enlisted February 24, 1864*

Walters, Charles. Channahon, enlisted October 10, 1861; taken POW May 16, 1864, at Drewry's Bluff; DS at Annapolis MD March 26, 1865

Watson, John M. Wilmington, enlisted August 5, 1861; DD May 16, 1863

Watts, Charles W. Wilmington, enlisted August 15, 1861; deserted October 22, 1865

Welch, William James. St. Louis, MO, enlisted October 14, 1861; transferred to Battery L, 4th U.S. Artillery, December 29, 1862

Weldon, Jacob M. Wilmington enlisted August 8, 1861*

Whitney, Henry P. Wilmington, enlisted August 5, 1861; wounded June 2, 1864, near Ware Bottom; right arm amputated; DD June 30, 1864

Wilcox, James M., Wilmington; enlisted August 19, 1861; WIA May 16, 1864, at Drewry's Bluff; DD June 30, 1865

Wilcox, William. Chicago, enlisted October 10, 1861; WIA May 16, 1864, at Drewry's Bluff; DD unknown date

Willard, Cornelius S. Channahon, enlisted September 17, 1861; WIA October 7, 1864, near Chaffin's Farm and April 2, 1865, in assault on Fort Gregg; DD August 17, 1865

Willard, William. Channahon, enlisted December 26, 1863; WIA May 16, 1864, at Drewry's Bluff and October 13, 1864, at Darbytown Crossroads; MO August 11, 1865

Wills (Wells in Adjutant's report), **Pomeroy.** Wilmington, enlisted August 22, 1861; DD May 25, 1862

Wirts (Wurtz in Adjutant's report), **George.** Wilmington, enlisted August 27, 1861; MO September 10, 1864

Wiser, Theodore. Wilmington, enlisted August 5, 1861; wounded June 2, 1864; MO September 10, 1864

Company B
McLean County—1860 Population: 28,772

Killed in Battle	6
Died of Wounds	5
Died in Prison	1
Lost Limbs	3
Wounded	34
Taken Prisoner	13
Number Originally Enlisted	94
Mustered Out at Expiration of Service	34
Re-Enlisted as Veterans	28
Recruits	56
Mustered Out With Regiment	45

Elected Officers
Captain: Isaiah W. Wilmarth
First Lieutenant: David F. Sellards
Second Lieutenant: James S. Haldeman

Company B was organized in Bloomington, Illinois—135 miles southwest of Chicago in the north-central part of the state. The population in 1860 was just over 7,000. Many of the founding members of the company served three month stints in Company K of the 8th Illinois infantry, and upon returning, recruited men mostly from Bloomington, and a dozen from nearby Le Roy, for the purpose of forming a company for the three-year enlistments in the 39th Illinois.

Willmarth, Isaiah W. Bloomington, Captain, commissioned August 12, 1861; resigned May 26, 1862

Sellards, David F. Bloomington, Captain, promoted from 1st Lieutenant vice Willmarth May 26, 1862; forced to resign due to poor health August 31, 1862

Heritage, George T. Bloomington, Captain, elected Orderly Sergeant during company formation; promoted 1st Lieutenant May 26, 1862; promoted August 31, 1862; assumed command of the regiment by seniority in September of 1864; WIA October 13, 1864, at Darbytown Crossroads; shot through both shoulders; returned to regiment after 9 weeks in hospital but unable to perform duties; MO December 7, 1864

Alsup, John F. Le Roy, Captain, enlisted August 12, 1861; promoted Sergeant May 26, 1862; to 1st Sergeant January 1, 1863; WIA August 16, 1864, at Deep Bottom, in skirmishing on May 22, 1864, and on April 2, 1865, in assault on Fort Gregg; promoted to Captain on April 11, 1865, but unable to muster as such due to regimental strength; DD as Sergeant September 24, 1865

Platt, Charles D. Bloomington, First Lieutenant, enlisted September 12, 1861; WIA May 20, 1864, at Ware Bottom Church; promoted Corporal August 27, 1864; WIA October 13, 1864, at Darbytown Crossroads; promoted 1st Lieutenant, April 11, 1865*

Kidder, Lesmore D. Bloomington, First Lieutenant, enlisted August 12, 1861; promoted 1st Lieutenant December 24, 1862; WIA May 16, 1864, while in command of ambulance train at Battle of Drewry's Bluff; escaped capture on horseback with a shattered leg; MO February 9, 1865

Sweetser, Al C. Bloomington, Second Lieutenant, played active role in recruiting company; enlisted August 12, 1861; promoted 2nd Lieutenant May 26, 1862; WIA June 2, 1864, near Ware Bottom; shot through both legs, one requiring amputation; overcame severe case of gangrene*

Haldeman, James S. Bloomington, Second Lieutenant, commissioned August 12, 1861; resigned May 26, 1862

Gibson, James. Bloomington, Second Lieutenant, enlisted August 12, 1861; promoted to 2nd Lieutenant May 26, 1862; resigned September 21, 1862

Alsup, James. Le Roy, Sergeant, enlisted August 12, 1861, taken POW at Blackwater, VA on October 24, 1862, paroled and exchanged; deserted January 1863

Carman, Archibald L. Bloomington, Sergeant, enlisted August 12, 1861; promoted from Corporal May 26, 1862; MO September 10, 1864

Martin, John. Bloomington; enlisted August 15, 1861; promoted corporal June 1, 1863; Sergeant September 1, 1863; KIA August 16, 1864, at Second Deep Bottom

Turrill, John T. Decatur, Sergeant, enlisted August 12, 1861; promoted Sergeant January 1, 1863; DS July 14, 1864, from disease

Vermillion, Charles W. Bloomington, enlisted August 12, 1861; promoted Corporal August 7, 1863; Sergeant sometime later in year; taken POW May 16, 1864, at Drewry's Bluff; MO July 15, 1864, as POW

Covey, James. Le Roy, Sergeant, enlisted September 19, 1861; promoted to Corporal October 31, 1863; wounded at Fort Wagner September 14, 1863; promoted to Sergeant August 27, 1864*

Hallett, Joseph. Bloomington, Sergeant, enlisted August 12, 1861; served as bugler for company; WIA May 16, 1864, at Drewry's Bluff; promoted Sergeant August 27, 1864; commanded the company in assault on Fort Gregg; promoted to 1st Sergeant September 24, 1865*

Stephenson, George W. Bloomington, Corporal, enlisted August 12, 1861; MO September 10, 1864

Anderson, Henry. Bloomington, Corporal, enlisted August 12, 1861; served as wagon master; MO September 10, 1864

Hill, Elliott. Wapella, Corporal, enlisted August 12, 1861; DD August 5, 1862

Johnson, Stephen. Bloomington, Corporal, enlisted August 12, 1861, DD July 22, 1862

Bailey, Harvey. Bloomington, Corporal, enlisted August 12, 1861; WIA May 20, 1864, at Ware Bottom Church; DS June 10, 1864, from wounds

Sparrow, Darwin M. Bloomington, Corporal, enlisted August 12, 1861; DD February 25, 1863

Gillen, James R. Bloomington, Corporal, enlisted August 12, 1861; promoted Corporal October 19, 1861; MO September 16, 1864

Hartry, Edmund. Bloomington, Corporal, enlisted August 12, 1861; promoted Corporal January 1, 1863; WIA May 16, 1864, at Drewry's Bluff; died at Andersonville June 24, 1864; veteran

Kennedy, Dennis. Chicago, Corporal, enlisted October 25, 1861; promoted Corporal January 1, 1863; KIA August 14, 1864, in skirmish at Deep Bottom

Wolcott, William H. Corporal, enlisted September 5, 1861; promoted Corporal January 1, 1863, MO September 10, 1864

Leibo, Arthur B. Bloomington, Corporal, enlisted August 12, 1861; promoted Corporal January 1, 1864; WIA May 20, 1864, at Ware Bottom Church; color guard member*

Gibbs, Elias. Bloomington, Corporal, enlisted August 12, 1861; promoted Corporal August 28, 1864; WIA August 16, 1864, at Second Deep Bottom and October 7, 1864; promoted Sergeant September 24, 1865*

Paul, Alexander. Bloomington, Corporal, enlisted September 26, 1861; WIA May 20, 1864, at Ware Bottom Church; promoted Corporal August 27, 1864; WIA October 13, 1864, at Darbytown Crossroads*

Miller, Eliott S. Chicago, Corporal enlisted August 12, 1861; wounded May 30, 1864; promoted Coproral September 15, 1864; Sergeant September 14, 1865*

PRIVATES

Alsup, Robert D. Le Roy, enlisted February 26, 1864*

Bailey, Robert. Bloomington, enlisted October 15, 1861; deserted February 28, 1864

Ball, John T. Bloomington, enlisted August 15, 1861; DD October 26, 1863

Barton, William H. Bloomington, enlisted August 12, 1861; DD December 12, 1863

Beckwith, Lester S. Bloomington, enlisted February 22, 1864; WIA May 16, 1864, at Drewry's Bluff and May 20, 1864, at Ware Bottom*

Beckwith, Walter J. Bloomington, enlisted August 12, 1861; promoted to Corporal October 31, 1863; reduced to ranks May 1, 1865*

Bender, Charles. Bloomington, enlisted August 30, 1861; DD June 16, 1862

Berry, Joseph. Bloomington, enlisted August 12, 1861; WIA August 16, 1864, at Second Deep Run; leg amputated; died from wounds September 4, 1864

Bierbower, Jonathan. Bloomington, enlisted February 6, 1864*

Blanchard, John. Bloomington, enlisted August 27, 1861; MO September 10, 1864

Blevins, Stanford H. Bloomington, enlisted August 25, 1861; DD September 25, 1862

Bowen, Marion D. Chicago, enlisted October 21, 1864; WIA April 2, 1865, in assault on Fort Gregg; died from wounds same day

Bowers, John. Bloomington, enlisted August 27, 1861; taken POW May 1, 1862, at Strasburg, VA; paroled and exchanged; WIA August 16, 1864, at Second Deep Bottom; MO October 13, 1864

Brown, Lewis. Draftee; enlisted February 25, 1865*

Burke, George. Bloomington, enlisted August 12, 1861; MO September 12, 1864

Burke, Gerhard. Bloomington; enlisted August 12, 1861; MO September 12, 1864

Burns, Daniel. Draftee, enlisted February 25, 1865*

Butler, Harrison. Bloomington, enlisted August 30, 1861; veteran severely wounded June 16, 1864, in skirmish and Chester Station and assumed taken POW

Cain, Christopher D. Bloomington, enlisted February 24, 1864; WIA August 16, 1864, at Second Deep Bottom; DS September 10, 1865

Call, Carlton. Bloomington, enlisted August 12, 1861; DD July 4, 1863

Campbell, William E. Bloomington, enlisted February 22, 1864*

Carl, Oliver C. Hayworth, enlisted August 12, 1861; deserted January 26, 1862

Cavett, John A. Bloomington, enlisted August 6, 1864; MO July 6, 1865

Clark, Henry. Chicago, enlisted August 27, 1861; taken POW at Strasburg, VA May 1, 1862; paroled and exchanged September 14, 1862*

Clark, John W.A. Bloomington, enlisted August 12, 1861; DD July 25, 1862

Conklin, Lafayette. Bloomington, enlisted February 6, 1864; DS August 9, 1865

Cook, Levi. Jacksonville, enlisted August 28, 1861; taken POW at Strasburg VA May 1, 1862; paroled and exchanged June 24, 1862; DS October 27, 1862

Cook, Methusaleh. Bloomington, enlisted August 27, 1861; DD August 12, 1862

Covey, Edmond. Le Roy, enlisted August 12, 1861; WIA June 16, 1864, at Chester Station and October 13, 1864, at Darbytown Crossroads*

Cole, William. Draftee, enlisted March 1, 1865*

Crandall, James. Bloomington, enlisted November 20, 1862; MO November 20, 1865

Cranston, Joseph H. Chicago, enlisted October 19, 1861; DD December 30, 1862

Crossley, John. Bloomington; enlisted August 12, 1861; DD October 26, 1863

Cullar, Benjamin. Bloomington; enlisted August 12, 1861; taken POW May 1, 1862, at Strasburg, VA; paroled and exchanged, discharged June 17, 1862

Dailey, John. Bloomington, enlisted August 23, 1861; DD December 1, 1862

Dake, John W. Bloomington, enlisted August 12, 1861; veteran, KIA August 16, 1864, at Second Deep Bottom

Davis, Barnet H. Le Roy, enlisted August 17, 1861; taken POW May 1, 1862, at Strasburg VA; paroled and exchanged, discharged April 11, 1863

Dillon, Orange W. Bloomington, enlisted October 28, 1861; DD December 1, 1862

Dillon, Asbury P. Bloomington, enlisted October 28, 1861; WIA May 20, 1864, at Ware Bottom Church*

Downey, John. Bloomington, enlisted August 12, 1861*

Duff, Robert. Bloomington, enlisted March 2, 1864; KIA June 16, 1864

Egidy, Frederick. Bloomington, enlisted October 23, 1861; DD July 22, 1862

Ellliott, John. Draftee, enlisted March 1, 1865*

Fagot, Jacob. Peoria, enlisted September 21, 1861; transferred to Battery L, 4th U.S. Artillery, November 28, 1862

Fagot, Matthias. Peoria, enlisted September 21, 1861; taken POW May 1, 1862, at Strasburg, VA; paroled and exchanged; DD June 18, 1862

Fallon, Michael. Chicago, enlisted October 3, 1864; MO October 9, 1865

Fisher, Lewis. Enfield, enlisted February 11, 1864; WIA August 16, 1864, at Second Deep Bottom; DD February 28, 1865

Foot, Jerome. Concord, enlisted February 24, 1864; promoted Corporal September 14, 1865*

Fordyce, John K. Bloomington, enlisted August 27, 1861; wounded September 12, 1863, at Fort Wagner; leg amputated; DD June 20, 1864

Frankberger, Lee J. Bloomington, enlisted February 20, 1864*

Franks, Jacob C. Bloomington; enlisted February 23, 1864; drowned in James River, May 20, 1864

Gibbs, Jeremiah. Bloomington, enlisted August 12, 1861; KIA August 16, 1864, at Second Deep Bottom

Goldsmith, Nicholas. Bloomington, enlisted February 29, 1864; WIA May 20, 1864, at Ware Bottom Church; DD October 6, 1864

Gordon, Henry. Bloomington, enlisted September 5, 1861; MO September 16, 1864

Graves, James H. Bloomington, enlisted August 12, 1861; DD December 20, 1862

Groves, Thomas. Bloomington, enlisted August 12, 1861; promoted Corporal October 30, 1865*

Hafer, John R. Bloomington, enlisted August 27, 1861; promoted Corporal September 1, 1864; KIA October 13, 1864, at Darbytown Crossroads; veteran

Haines, Clayborn L. Decatur, enlisted August 27, 1862; MO June 28, 1865

Hallett, William D. Bloomington, enlisted August 12, 1861; WIA May 20, 1864, at Ware Bottom Church; MO October 13, 1864

Hammock, Peter. Bloomington, enlisted February 13, 1864*

Hartry, Alfred. Bloomington, enlisted February 20, 1864; taken POW May 16, 1864, at Drewry's Bluff; MO July 7, 1865, as POW

Harty, James. Bloomington, enlisted August 27, 1861; WIA August 16, 1864, at Second Deep Run; MO October 19, 1864

Harvey, Levi. Pontiac, enlisted August 12, 1861; MO September 10, 1864

Haspel, Frederick. Bloomington, enlisted August 27, 1861; DD December 23, 1864

Hayes, James H. Bloomington, enlisted August 27, 1861*

Henner, John. Bloomington, enlisted August 12, 1861; DD August 27, 1863

Henschad, Theodore. Draftee; enlisted March 1, 1865; DD July 19, 1865

Hillman, Henry B. Draftee, enlisted March 1, 1865*

Hoisington, Henry. Bloomington, enlisted August 12, 1861; DS December 4, 1861, from disease

Hotchkiss, Charles B. Bloomington, enlisted August 26, 1861; MO September 10, 1864

Howard, Robert. Bloomington, enlisted August 12, 1861; deserted October 28, 1861

Hummell, Henry. Bloomington, enlisted August 12, 1861; promoted Corporal October 1, 1864; wounded in the hand August 14, 1864, near Petersburg; reduced to ranks April 30, 1865

Hutchinson, William. Bloomington, enlisted August 27, 1861*

Johnson, Alfred. Empire, enlisted June 25, 1862*

Johnson, Franklin. Le Roy, enlisted June 5, 1864*

Johnson, Isaac R. Bloomington, enlisted September 19, 1861; DD August 12, 1862

Johnson, James. Bloomington, enlisted August 27, 1861; DS October 26, 1864

Johnson, James M. Bloomington, enlisted September 19, 1861; promoted Corporal May 1, 1865*

Johnson, John. Bloomington, August 22, 1861; DD June 28, 1864

Kark, Frederick. Bloomington, enlisted August 5, 1861; DD March 3, 1863

Kelly, John A. Chicago, enlisted February 6, 1864; transferred to Veteran Reserve Corps

Lafferty, William S. Bloomington, enlisted February 24, 1864; on furlough at MO of reg't

Lane, William J. Bloomington, enlisted August 27, 1861; promoted Corporal May 1, 1865*

Lemon, George W. Bloomington, enlisted February 24, 1864; WIA May 16, 1864, at Drewry's Bluff*

Lewis, Herman F. Bloomington, enlisted September 25, 1861; DD February 10, 1863

Lynch, John. Draftee, enlisted March 2, 1865; DS March 30, 1865

Marrigold, Charles L. Chicago, enlisted August 3, 1861*

Merrifield, Samuel. Bloomington, enlisted August 12, 1861*

Miller, Anthony. Bloomington, enlisted September 18, 1861; MO October 18, 1864

Neal, John A. Bloomington, enlisted September 12, 1861; MO June 11, 1864

O'Connell, John. Bloomington, enlisted September 27, 1861; DD March 15, 1862

O'Conner, Patrick. Bloomington, enlisted October 28, 1862; MO October 30, 1865

Owen, Leonard J. Bloomington, enlisted September 12, 1861; discharged July 11, 1862

Rounds, John J. Bloomington, enlisted September 12, 1861; transferred to Battery L, 4th U.S. Artillery, November 28, 1862

Sellman, S.H.M.,Bloomington, enlisted September 12, 1861; DD October 26, 1863

Shea, James. Bloomington, enlisted September 20, 1861; WIA August 16, 1864, at Second Deep Bottom; MO September 10, 1864

Steinkulan, Peter. Draftee, enlisted March 11, 1865*

Stout, John. Bloomington, enlisted September 12, 1861; DD March 23, 1863

Tanner, Andrew, J. Bloomington, enlisted August 12, 1861; MO September 10, 1864

Van Dusen, John. Chicago, enlisted September 20, 1861; DS October 4, 1862, from disease

Wheeler, John. Draftee, enlisted February 28, 1865*

Williams, John W. Bloomington, enlisted August 12, 1861; WIA May 16, 1864, at Drewry's Bluff; MO October 18, 1864; promoted to Corporal unknown date

Wilson, William F. Bloomington, enlisted September 30, 1861; DD February 5, 1863

Wolcott, Edwin N. Bloomington, enlisted February 9, 1864; WIA May 20, 1864, at Ware Bottom Church*

Wooding, Alfred,. Decatur, enlisted August 12, 1861; WIA and taken POW June 16, 1864, near Chester Station; MO July 26, 1865, as POW

Worely, William F. Bloomington, enlisted August 12, 1861; deserted June 28, 1863

Company C
Livingston County—1860 Population: 11,637
Cook County: 144,954

Killed in Battle	7
Died of Wounds	2
Died in Prison	4
Lost Limbs	4
Wounded	32
Taken Prisoner	13
Number Originally Enlisted	89
Mustered Out at Expiration of Service	18
Re-Enlisted as Veterans	39
Recruits	51
Mustered Out With Regiment	62

Elected Officers

Captain: John Gray
First Lieutenant: Wallace Lord
Second Lieutenant: S.S. Brucker

Company C was organized in Pontiac, Illinois—a town of roughly 700 people 90 miles southwest of Chicago. The majority of men were from Pontiac and nearby towns, with some men being recruited from Chicago and surrounding when the regiment arrived there. Company C is notable for having a higher than average number of recent European immigrants.

Wightman, James W. Odell, Captain, enlisted August 12, 1861; promoted Commissary Sergeant November 28, 1861; promoted 1st Lieutenant January 24, 1862; promoted Captain May 26, 1862; KIA May 16, 1864, at Drewry's Bluff

Hannum, James. Cayuga, Captain, enlisted August 12, 1861; promoted from Sergeant to 1st Lieutenant April 20, 1864; promoted to Captain July 2, 1864*

Lord, Wallace. Pontiac, First Lieutenant, commissioned Aug 12, 1861; resigned January 24, 1862, due to poor health

Brucker, Simon. Pontiac, First Lieutenant, commissioned 2nd Lieutenant August 12, 1861; promoted 1st Lieutenant May 26, 1862; resigned April 20, 1864

Guisinger, Daniel. Rook's Creek, First Lieutenant, enlisted August 12, 1861, and made Corporal; promoted to Sergeant unknown date; promoted 1st Lieutenant March 31, 1865; resigned commission July 12, 1865; records are unclear and may have served as 2nd Lieutenant late in 1864

Henderson, James. Rook's Creek, Second Lieutenant, enlisted August 12, 1861, and made 1st Sergeant; commissioned 2nd Lieutenant May 26, 1862; resigned June 28, 1863

DeLong, Henry H. First Sergeant, Esmond, enlisted August 28, 1861; promoted Corporal May 29, 1863; WIA June 17, 1864, near Ware Bottom promoted Sergeant October 1, 1864; 1st Sergeant March 31, 1865; First Lieutenant October 1, 1865, but unable to muster as such due to regimental strength*

Johnson, William. Rook's Creek, Sergeant, enlisted August 12, 1861; reduced to ranks May 9, 1862; MO December 6, 1864

Ellinwood, Charles. Edmond, Sergeant, enlisted August 12, 1861; DD July 4, 1863

Guernsey, Augustus C. Esmond, Sergeant, enlisted August 12, 1861; promoted from Corporal September 24, 1861; DD May 4, 1862

Howden, Martin. Rook's Creek, Sergeant, enlisted August 12, 1861; promoted from Corporal May 12, 1862; WIA and taken POW May 16, 1864, at Drewry's Bluff; died at Florence, S.C., October 11, 1864

Chapman, Edward O. Cayuga, Sergeant, enlisted August 12, 1861; promoted from Corporal February 10, 1863; MO September 10, 1864

Gray, Walter. Rook's Creek, Sergeant, enlisted August 28, 1861; promoted from Corporal May 10, 1862; deserted February 1, 1863

Johnson, John H. Esmond, Sergeant, enlisted August 12, 1861; promoted Corporal unknown date; Sergeant July 2, 1864; WIA June 2, 1864, at Chester Station, VA; KIA October 13, 1864, at Darbytown Crossroads

Schafer, John L. Cayuga, Sergeant enlisted August 12, 1861; WIA May 16, 1864, at Drewry's Bluff; promoted Corporal August 1, 1864; Sergeant January 1, 1865*

Worth, William R. Esmond, Corporal, enlisted August 12, 1861; taken POW May 16, 1864, at Drewry's Bluff; paroled and discharged August 15, 1865, after being POW at Libby Prison, Richmond, and Andersonville, GA; veteran

Streeter, Charles. Odell, Corporal, enlisted August 12, 1861; DD June 5, 1862

Fellows, Albert A. Pontiac, enlisted August 1, 1861; taken POW March 22, 1862, near Winchester, VA; paroled and discharged May 1862

Fellows, Albert. Rook's Creek; August 12, 1861; promoted Corporal December 24, 1861; taken POW May 16, 1864, at Drewry's Bluff; MO February 19, 1865

(The above two Albert Fellows entries are listed separately in both records despite some similarities)

St. John, Seth. Ocoya, Corporal, enlisted September 6, 1861; promoted Corporal March 10, 1862; taken POW May 16, 1864, at Drewry's Bluff and sent to Florence S.C.; died January 23, 1865

Johnson, Stephen. Ocoya, Corporal, enlisted September 19, 1861; promoted May 10, 1862; KIA May 20, 1864, at Ware Bottom Church

Long, William P. Pontiac, enlisted August 12, 1861; promoted Corporal May 10, 1862; DD July 4, 1863

Kendall, John. Ocoya, Corporal, enlisted August 28, 1861; promoted Corporal September 1, 1863; MO September 10, 1864

Malone, Andrew J. Rook's Creek, Corporal enlisted August 22, 1861; promoted Corporal September 4, 1864; Sergeant May 1, 1865*

Scott, Wesley. Pontiac, Corporal, enlisted August 16, 1861; WIA May 20, 1864, at Ware Bottom Church; promoted Corporal September 4, 1864; WIA and taken POW October 13, 1864, at Darbytown Crossroads; paroled and died in parole camp at Annapolis, MD November 10, 1864

Moore, Anderson L. Indian Grove, Corporal, enlisted August 28, 1861; promoted September 26, 1864; KIA April 2, 1865, in assault on Fort Gregg

Girard, Hermann. Long Point, Corporal, enlisted August 28, 1861; WIA October 9, 1863, at Fort Wagner; WIA May 16, 1864, at Drewry's Bluff; promoted Corporal November 1, 1864; WIA April 2, 1865, in assault on Fort Gregg; promoted Sergeant September 1, 1865

Jenkins, Issac R. Cayuga, Corporal, enlisted August 19, 1861; WIA May 20, 1864, at Ware Bottom Church; promoted Corporal January 1, 1865; Sergeant May 1, 1865*

PRIVATES

Akehurst, Henry. Pontiac, enlisted August 12, 1861; DD October 11, 1863

Akehurst, James. Pontiac, enlisted August 12, 1861; WIA May 20, 1864, at Ware Bottom Church; arm amputated; died from wounds May 28, 1864

Allen, Andrew C. Esmond; enlisted August 12, 1861; taken POW May 16, 1864, at Drewry's Bluff; died in Charleston, South Carolina prison September 25, 1864

Argubright, Caleb A. Livingston County, enlisted February 10, 1864; promoted Corporal July 1, 1865*

Armstrong, William. Chicago, enlisted February 26, 1864*

Atwater, H.J. Esmond, enlisted September 5, 1861; wounded August 20, 1863, near Fort Wagner; MO September 10, 1864

Baer, Joseph. Rook's Creek, enlisted August 12, 1861; WIA April 2, 1865, in assault on Fort Gregg*

Baker, Thornton. Sandwich, enlisted February 2, 1864; DD March 28, 1865

Bell, John. Draftee, enlisted August 29, 1864*

Brown, O.P. Esmond, enlisted August 25, 1861; DD October 28, 1861

Burnham, Foreman. Pontiac, enlisted August 12, 1861; DD June 26, 1862

Carroll, Harrison. Chicago, enlisted February 22, 1864*

Converse, Charles. Ocoya, enlisted August 21, 1861; WIA May 16, 1864, at Drewry's Bluff; MO September 10, 1864

Converse, Melvin. Ocoya, enlisted September 6, 1861; Clark history says MO December 27, 1864; Adjutant's report says MO May 18, 1865, as POW

Cooper, William S. Fairbury, enlisted August 28, 1861; taken POW May 26, 1862, at Strasburg, VA; paroled and discharged December 12, 1863

Davidson, James. Chicago, enlisted August 20, 1861; DD September 27, 1862

Dean, Adam. Draftee, enlisted March 1, 1865; DD August 9, 1865

DePuy, Hulburt. Chicago, enlisted February 17, 1864*

Douglas, Edward. Draftee, enlisted February 16, 1865*

Drake, Jasper N. Fairbury, enlisted August 20, 1861; DD June 18, 1862

Dunn, Adam. Draftee; enlisted February 1, 1865; WIA April 2, 1865, in assault on Fort Gregg*

Eaton, Lasson W. Long Point, enlisted February 14, 1864; promoted Corporal September 1, 1865*

Eggenberger, Gallus. Odell, enlisted August 12, 1861; transferred to Veterans Reserve Corps September 26, 1863

Fenlison, William H. St. Louis, MO, enlisted September 19, 1861; WIA October 13, 1864, at Darbytown Crossroads*

Gamble, Harvey. Rook's Creek, enlisted August 12, 1861*

Gardner, Oscar. Efford's Point, enlisted October 24, 1861; WIA May 20, 1864, at Ware Bottom Church; MO October 14, 1864

Gorbett, George W. Rook's Creek, enlisted August 12, 1861; DS April 17, 1864

Gorbett, Henry. Rook's Creek; enlisted August 12, 1861*

Gorbett, Quincy A. Rook's Creek, enlisted August 12, 1861; DD August 6, 1862

Gorton, Silas. Draftee, enlisted March 22, 1865*

Gott, Henry. Rook's Creek, enlisted August 28, 1861; taken POW June 2, 1864, at Hatcher's Run, VA; died at Andersonville June 15, 1865

Graham, William. Draftee, enlisted February 15, 1865*

Hamilton, Lester. Esmond, enlisted October 28, 1861; KIA May 20, 1864, at Ware Bottom Church

Haney, James. Nebraska, enlisted August 28, 1861; WIA October 13, 1864, at Darbytown Crossroads; MO December 6, 1864

Haney, John. Chicago, enlisted March 4, 1864; WIA May 20, 1864, at Ware Bottom Church*

Haney, Matthews. Nebraska, enlisted August 12, 1861; DD August 21, 1862

Headley, William M. Chicago, enlisted August 28, 1861; taken POW March 23, 1862, at Winchester, VA; discharged May 21, 1862

Hillsted, Errick. Chicago, enlisted September 24, 1864; MO June 20, 1865

Howden, Ephraim. Rook's Creek, enlisted September 6, 1861; WIA May 20, 1864, at Ware Bottom Church; promoted Corporal July 1, 1865*

Hughes, Edward. Pontiac, enlisted August 12, 1861; DD unknown date

Jenkins, William H. Esmond, enlisted December 30, 1863; WIA May 15, 1864, at Drewry's Bluff, and October 13, 1864, at Darbytown Crossroads with the latter requiring an amputated limb; DD May 18, 1865

Johnson, Samuel B. Pontiac, enlisted September 20, 1863; DS June 30, 1864, from disease at Bermuda Hundred

Kallsthoff, Henry. Chicago, enlisted September 6, 1861; taken POW May 23, 1862, near Warrenton Junction, VA; paroled and exchanged; again captured May 30, 1862; paroled and exchanged, MO December 6, 1864

Kearney, Michael. Chicago, enlisted February 24, 1864*

Kennedy, William P. New Michigan, enlisted August 12, 1861; DD unknown date

Kinsie, Franklin. Chicago, enlisted August 20, 1861; deserted December 3, 1861

Larkins, John M. Esmond, enlisted August 22, 1861; WIA October 13, 1864, at Darbytown Crossraods; DD June 19, 1865

Lilly, James (Joseph in Adjutant's Report). Rook's Creek; enlisted August 22, 1861; WIA May 16, 1864, at Drewry's Bluff; MO October 11, 1864

Malone, William H. Rook's Creek, enlisted August 22, 1861; WIA June 18, 1864, near Chester Station, VA; MO October 18, 1864

McElfreet, James. Chicago, enlisted February 16, 1864*

McGregor, Alonzo. Pontiac, enlisted August 22, 1861; MO September 10, 1864

McGregor, Charles. Chicago, enlisted February 22, 1864, and detailed to band*

McClaime, William, J. Draftee, enlisted February 28, 1865; KIA April 2, 1865, in assault on Fort Gregg

McNally, Michael. Pontiac, enlisted August 29, 1861; WIA May 16, 1864, near Ware Bottom Church; DD April 25, 1865

Miller, G.D. Pontiac, enlisted September 29, 1861; deserted February 24, 1862

Miner, John. Draftee, enlisted February 17, 1865; deserted June 15, 1865

Morgan, William M. Chicago, enlisted January 21, 1864; KIA June 2, 1864, near Ware Bottom Church

Murphy, David. Pontiac, enlisted September 18, 1861; DD December 12, 1863

Myers, Theodore. Chicago, enlisted August 6, 1861; deserted February 4, 1862

Myers, Thomas W. Draftee, enlisted March 22, 1865*

Nash, L.N. Fairbury, enlisted September 21, 1861; DD July 25, 1862

Palmer, Gersham. Pontiac, enlisted August 19, 1861; DS February 21, 1863

Pembroke, Jerry. Pontiac, enlisted August 12, 1861; DD January 31, 1862

Pernet, Joseph. Odell, enlisted September 9, 1864; MO September 10, 1864

Perry, William H. Esmond, enlisted August 12, 1861; DS February 25, 1862

Porter, John. Le Roy, enlisted March,1862; absent sick at MO of reg't

Potter, William. Rook's Creek, enlisted August 28, 1861; DS February 20, 1863

Raney, Samuel. Cayuga, enlisted August 12, 1861; taken POW June 2, 1864, near Ware Bottom Church; paroled and exchanged, DD September 26, 1865

Reese, Isaac C. Joliet, enlisted September 14, 1861; MO September 12, 1864

Reid, Henry H. Esmond, enlisted August 25, 1861; DS December 25, 1861

Relae, George. Clark, enlisted September 4, 1861; WIA and taken POW May 16, 1864, at Drewry's Bluff; paroled and exchanged; WIA April 2, 1865, in assault on Fort Gregg; arm amputated; DD June 17, 1865

Richardson, Jerry. Sunbury, enlisted August 21, 1861; WIA and taken POW May 20, 1864, near Ware Bottom Church; paroled and exchanged; MO June 24, 1865

Riley, Thomas. Rook's Creek, enlisted August 12, 1861; DD May 9, 1863

Robinson, William E. Rook's Creek, enlisted August 23, 1861; DD March 8, 1863

Schlweis, Jacob. Chicago, enlisted January 25, 1864; WIA April 2, 1865, in assault on Fort Gregg; DD July 20, 1865

Sellman, John. Rook's Creek, enlisted August 18, 1861; MO September 10, 1864

Sellman, Marion. Ocoya, unknown enlistment; mustered in October 11, 1861; promoted Corporal unknown date*

Sellman, Melvyn B. Chicago, enlisted February 22, 1864; promoted Corporal July 1, 1865*

Marion Sellman does not appear in Clark's roster, but does appear on the Adjutant Report. Clark lists Melvyn Sellman as being from Ocoya, whereas the report lists Chicago—all other dates are the same however.

Shultz, Valentine. Nebraska, enlisted August 12, 1861; WIA April 4, 1862, at Woodstock, VA; DD June 18, 1862

Smith, John. Chicago, enlisted March 14, 1864*

Springer, Reason. Amity, enlisted August 12, 1861; DD July 21, 1862

Starkey, Orlando. Amity, enlisted February 10, 1864; WIA August 16, 1864, at Second Deep Run; promoted Corporal May 1, 1865*

Stephenson, Albert A. Nebraska, enlisted August 27, 1861; taken POW May 16, 1864, at Drewry's Bluff and sent to Florence S.C.; died October 11, 1864

Strong, Ambrose. Draftee, enlisted February 17, 1865*

Unrine, Oscar. Esmond, enlisted August 28, 1861; promoted Corporal May 1, 1865*

Urick, Samuel. Chicago, enlisted December 22, 1864*

Van Valkinberg, E.P. Odell, enlisted August 30, 1861; WIA April 2, 1865, in assault on Fort Gregg; DD July 18, 1865

Vieux, John. Odell, enlisted September 10, 1861; KIA May 16, 1864, at Drewry's Bluff; veteran

Vieux, Casimir. Fairbury, enlisted August 16, 1861; DD December 16, 1862

Wagle, John. Monroe, draftee, enlisted February 28, 1865*

Watson, John. New Michigan, enlisted September 29, 1861; DD May 1862

Weidman, W.M. (Uriah in Adjutant's report). Rook's Creek; enlisted September 16, 1861; taken POW May 16, 1864, at Drewry's Bluff; paroled and exchanged; DS December 21, 1864

Wemick, William draftee, enlisted February 27, 1865; deserted June 26, 1865

Wilson, James A. Chicago, enlisted March 14, 1864*

Wood, Samuel C., Schaumberg, enlisted January 11, 1865; deserted August 12, 1865

Company D
Ogle County—1860 Population: 22,888
DeWitt County: 10,820

Killed in Battle	10
Died of Wounds	6
Died in Prison	2
Lost Limbs	2
Wounded	42
Taken Prisoner	15
Number Originally Enlisted	88
Mustered Out at Expiration of Service	12
Re-Enlisted as Veterans	43
Recruits	60
Mustered Out With Regiment	67

Elected Officers
Captain: Samuel S. Linton
First Lieutenant: J.F. Linton
Second Lieutenant: Austin Towner

Company D was organized by Samuel S. Linton in Rochelle, Illinois—a town of roughly 1,000 people in 1860, 80 miles west of Chicago. While formed in Rochelle, the majority of the men came from the nearby northern Illinois small towns of Oregon, Willow Creek, and Lindenwood—the majority of whom were farmers and farmers' sons. Of note, the Company D roster is very incomplete and has many mismatches between the Adjutant General's report and Clark's history.

Linton, Samuel S. Willow Creek, Captain, commissioned August 9, 1861; promoted Major January 13, 1863, vice Munn resigned; see Field and Staff Officers

Snowden, George O. Oregon, Captain, enlisted August 12, 1861, and became 1st Sergeant; commissioned First Lieutenant June 12, 1862, vice Linton promoted; promoted Captain January 13, 1863; WIA at Bermuda Hundred June 3, 1864; suffered gangrene infection in hospital; MO November 10, 1864

Linton, Jonathan F. Willow Creek, First Lieutenant, commissioned August 11, 1861; promoted Regimental Quartermaster June 12, 1862, vice Cutler resigning; see Field and Staff Officers

Knapp, Cyrus F. Chicago, First Lieutenant, enlisted August 12, 1861, and made Sergeant; commissioned 2nd Lieutenant September 4, 1862; promoted 1st Lieutenant September 11, 1862, vice Snowden promotion; WIA August 16, 1864, at Second Deep Bottom; MO December 17, 1864

Ferren, William H. Paine's Point, First Lieutenant, enlisted August 9, 1861; promoted Sergeant March 1, 1863; commissioned 2nd Lieutenant January 31, 1865; 1st Lieutenant March 31, 1865; August 16, 1865

Thayer, Edmond J. Lindenwood, First Lieutenant, enlisted August 21, 1861; WIA June 18, 1864, and October 7, 1864, promoted Sergeant August 21, 1865; promoted 1st Lieutenant September 15, 1865*

Towner, Austin. Lane, Second Lieutenant, commissioned August 9, 1861; resigned September 4, 1862

Frane, John. Paine's Point, Second Lieutenant, enlisted August 9, 1861, and made Sergeant; promoted 2nd Lieutenant January 13, 1863; KIA August 16, 1864, at Second Deep Bottom

Gitchell, John W. Paine's Point, Sergeant, enlisted August 9, 1861; reduced to ranks May 10, 1862; DS June 22, 1862

York, John L. Paine's Point, Sergeant enlisted August 9, 1861, and made Sergeant; DS October 18, 1861, in St. Louis

Collins, David. Paine's Point, Sergeant; promoted from Private to Corporal December 7, 1861; to Sergeant July 1, 1862; MO September 10, 1864

Johnson, Ezra E. Willow Creek, Sergeant, enlisted September 4, 1861; promoted from Corporal May 11, 1862; MO September 10, 1864

Hopkins, Thomas. Hennepin, Sergeant, enlisted August 22, 1861; promoted from Corporal October 4, 1862; KIA May 20, 1864, at Ware Bottom Church; veteran

Sawin, Royal E. Lane, Sergeant, enlisted August 12, 1861; promoted Sergeant May 20, 1864; KIA August 16, 1864, at Second Deep Bottom; veteran

Lynn, George W. Lane, Sergeant, enlisted September 21, 1861; promoted Corporal November 1, 1862; WIA June 2, 1864, and May 20, 1864, at Ware Bottom Church; promoted Sergeant September 1, 1864; WIA April 2, 1865, in assault on Fort Gregg*

Gaul, Cornelius D. Dwight, Sergeant, enlisted September 21, 1861; WIA August 16, 1864, at Second Deep Bottom; promoted from Corporal December 5, 1864*

Reese, John. Lane, enlisted August 9, 1861; promoted Corporal September 1, 1863; Sergeant April 1, 1865; deserted August 5, 1865

Gregory, Samuel. Aurora, Sergeant, enlisted August 16, 1861; promoted Corporal September 11, 1863; sergeant August 4, 1865

Wells, George W. Lane, Sergeant, enlisted September 12, 1861; promoted Corporal September 5, 1864; WIA October 13, 1864, at Darbytown Crossroads; promoted Sergeant September 20, 1865*

Miles, Charles. Lindenwood, Corporal, enlisted August 31, 1861; DD May 30, 1862

Horn, Gottlieb. Lindenwood, Corporal, enlisted August 12, 1861; reduced to ranks and made regimental bugler at his own request; WIA May 20, 1864*

Waite, Malden E. Oregon, Corporal enlisted August 9, 1861; reduced to ranks December 7, 1861; taken POW January 3, 1862, at Bath, VA; paroled; WIA June 16, 1864; DS July 2, 1864, from wounds

Beach, William H. Oregon, Corporal, enlisted September 5, 1861; DD May 30, 1862

Fuller, George L. Oregon, Corporal, enlisted August 22, 1861; promoted November 1, 1862; reduced to ranks July 15, 1864; MO September 10, 1864

Guyott, Frank. Willow Creek; Corporal, enlisted August 15, 1861; promoted November 22, 1862; deserted March 9, 1864

Cutler, George O. Dwight, Corporal enlisted August 28, 1861; transferred to and discharged with original in 1862; re-enlisted; wounded in head at Fort Wagner; December 15, 1862; DS September 11, 1863, from disease

Nason, Adam C. Rockford, Corporal enlisted November 19, 1861; taken POW March 28, 1862, at Winchester, VA; promoted Corporal September 1, 1864; WIA October 13, 1864, at Darbytown Crossroads; DD January 16, 1865, from wounds

Wurdeman, John H. Lindenwood, Corporal, enlisted August 28, 1861; promoted September 1, 1864; WIA October 13, 1864, at Darbytown Crossroads*

McCarnley, Frederick S. Lane, Corporal, enlisted August 21, 1861; taken POW January 3, 1862, at Bath, VA; promoted September 5, 1864; WIA October 13, 1864, at Darbytown Crossroads*

Hunt, Loam J. Peru, Corporal, enlisted August 9, 1861; WIA August 16, 1864, at Drewry's Bluff; promoted Corporal March 1, 1865; WIA April 2, 1865, in assault on Fort Gregg; deserted August 3, 1865

Fuller, Mahlon T. Oregon, Corporal enlisted August 21, 1861; WIA May 20, 1864, at Ware Bottom Church; promoted April 1, 1865*

Privates

Armstrong, Thomas. Willow Creek, unknown enlistment; mustered October 11, 1861; DD June 1862

Atkinson, Edward. Willow Creek, enlisted September 9, 1861; DD June 1862

Atwood, Joseph S. Paine's Point, enlisted August 12, 1861; WIA May 20, 1864, at Ware Bottom Church*

Birkenbuel, Henry. Peru, unknown enlistment; mustered January 25, 1864*

Bowden, Ferdinand. Oregon, unknown enlistment; mustered October 11, 1861*

Boyce, Hiram. Oregon, unknown enlistment; mustered October 11, 1861*

Bullis, Newman. Lane, unknown enlistment; mustered October 11, 1861; DD September 10, 1864

Cannon, Patrick. Oregon, enlisted February 25, 1864; WIA May 16, 1864, at Drewry's Bluff and October 13, 1864, at Darbytown Crossroads; DS October 22, 1864, from wounds

Chasm, Thomas. Oregon, enlisted August 21, 1861; DS August 18, 1862

Chicester, Sanford H. Hennepin, enlisted August 23, 1861; DD March 31, 1862

Core, Robert. Draftee, enlisted February 22, 1865; WIA April 2, 1865, in assault on Fort Gregg*

Corsant, Henry. Oregon, enlisted September 5, 1861; taken POW May 26, 1862, at Strasburg, VA; DD October 16, 1862

Crum, Gabriel. Oregon, enlisted September 5, 1861; DD June 27, 1862

Crum, William W. Oregon, enlisted September 5, 1861; taken POW January 3, 1862, at Bath, VA; DD June 6, 1862

Cummings, William S. Chicago, enlisted September 4, 1861; DD June 6, 1862

Dresser, Lewis. Lane, enlisted August 29, 1861; WIA October 13, 1864, at Darbytown Crossroads; DS October 16, 1864, of wounds; veteran

Dagnan, John. Schaumberg, enlisted September 26, 1864; DD June 10, 1865

Dietz, Augustus. Draftee, enlisted February 23, 1865*

Doran, James. Pontiac, enlisted November 22, 1863; DD June 23, 1864

Doyle, John. Chicago, February 9, 1864; WIA May 16, 1864, at Drewry's Bluff and taken POW; paroled unknown date

Ellis, Dwight D. Dwight, enlisted December 17, 1862; KIA August 16, 1864, at Second Deep Bottom

Farbel, Joseph D., Oregon, enlisted September 1, 1861; DD August 13, 1862

Farley, Patrick. Oregon, enlisted August 12, 1861; WIA May 16, 1864, at Drewry's Bluff; transferred to Veteran Reserve Corps May 15, 1865

Ferrell, Jesse A. Oregon, enlisted August 9, 1861; WIA and taken POW October 27, 1864; died in Florence S.C. prison recorded on same day; veteran

Folsom, William F. Hennepin, enlisted August 21, 1861; DD May 31, 1862

Fuller, Leander C. Oregon, enlisted August 29, 1861; DD June 14, 1863

Fuller, Thomas A. Rockvale, enlisted March 1, 1865*

Garrett, James. Chicago, enlisted October 9, 1861; WIA April 2, 1865, in assault on Fort Gregg; deserted August 3, 1865

Gaurley, Alexander. Dwight, enlisted September 21, 1861; MO May 6, 1865

Godfrey, Isaac W. Lane, enlisted August 21, 1861; WIA August 16, 1864, at Second Deep Bottom; DD June 20, 1865, from wounds

Grant, James L. Paine's Point, enlisted August 12, 1861; taken POW January 3, 1862, at Bath, VA; DD June 6, 1862

Green, Ira. Marion, enlisted February 27, 1864; WIA May 16, 1864, at Drewry's Bluff*

Griffith, George. Lane, enlisted August 21, 1861; wounded August 26, 1863, at Fort Wagner; DS August 31, 1863, from wounds

Harding, Eugene H. Dement, enlisted August 5, 1861; WIA August 16, 1864, at Second Deep Bottom; DD June 13, 1865

Hare, John. Lane, enlisted August 9, 1861; DD March 5, 1862

Harman, Thomas. unknown, enlisted September 10, 1864; discharged January 10, 1865

Hewitt, Frank E. Lane, enlisted August 6, 1861; taken POW January 3, 1862, at Bath, VA; DD January 9, 1863

Hummell, Robert N. Lane, enlisted August 16, 1861; WIA May 16, 1864, at Drewry's Bluff; KIA April 2, 1865, in assault on Fort Gregg

Jacobs, Bernard. Draftee, enlisted February 21, 1865*

Jones, William H. Lane, enlisted September 3, 1861; WIA October 13, 1864, at Darbytown Crossroads; DD May 26, 1865

Kinnaw, Thomas. Oregon, enlisted September 21, 1861; WIA August 16, 1864, at Second Deep Bottom*

Kinney, Barney. Draftee, enlisted February 22, 1865*

Kinney, Patrick. Oregon, enlisted September 22, 1861; WIA January 3, 1862, at Bath, VA; DD unknown date; re-enlisted February 25, 1864; taken POW May 16, 1864, at Drewry's Bluff; paroled and exchanged; KIA August 16, 1864, at Second Deep Bottom; Kinney's re-enlistment is not accounted for in the Adjutant's Report

Lacey, James L. Oregon, enlisted September 21, 1861; taken POW January 3, 1862, at Bath, VA; DD June 6, 1862

Ladd, Atticus A. Joliet, enlisted October 27, 1862; MO October 27, 1865

Lankenaw, Henry. Lane, unknown enlistment date; mustered October 11, 1861; KIA August 16 1864 at Second Deep Bottom; veteran

Lawson, Thomas. Lane, enlisted September 19, 1861; taken POW January 2, 1862, at Bath, VA; paroled and exchanged; promoted Corporal September 2, 1865*

Lee, Jefferson. Lindenwood, enlisted September 30, 1861; MO September 30, 1864

Low, Richard. Draftee, enlisted February 23, 1865*

Lyons, John. Lane, enlisted September 27, 1861; promoted Corporal April 1, 1865*

Martin, Albert. Springfield, enlisted December 17, 1862*

Martin, John. Lane, enlisted August 21, 1861; taken POW January 3, 1862, at Bath, VA; DD June 6, 1862

Martuze, John. Chicago, enlisted September 13, 1861; WIA May 20, 1864, at Ware Bottom Church*

McLain, M. Draftee, enlisted January 6, 1865; DS July 3, 1865

McLain, William. Draftee, enlisted January 6, 1865*

McLaughlin, John. Lane, enlisted September 3, 1861; transferred to Battery B, 5th U.S. Artillery December 5, 1862

McMiller, James. Draftee, enlisted February 22, 1865*

McTravis, John. Draftee, enlisted January 6, 1865*

Miller, John. Lane, enlisted August 28, 1861; WIA April 2, 1865, in assault on Fort Gregg; DD July 15, 1865, from wounds

Moore, Richard. Draftee, enlisted January 5, 1865; DD June 23, 1865

Moore, William. Lane, enlisted August 26, 1861; MO September 10, 1864

Morgan, Thomas J. Draftee, enlisted February 25, 1865*

Morgan, William H. Chicago, enlisted February 29, 1864; WIA October 13, 1864, at Darbytown Crossroads; DD September 1, 1865, from wounds

Myers, Joseph. Martinsburg, enlisted February 20, 1861; DS September 15, 1864

Nye, Edward. Lane, enlisted September 3, 1861; MO October 12, 1864

Odell, John L. Oregon, enlisted September 12, 1861; WIA June 2, 1864, near Ware Bottom Church; arm amputated; DS June 29, 1864, from wounds; veteran

Patterson, William A. Oregon, enlisted August 28, 1861; wounded October 1, 1863, at Fort Gregg, S.C., MO September 10, 1864

Peterson, Ole C. Lake View, enlisted September 22, 1864; discharged June 10, 1865

Poffenberger, James. Oregon, enlisted August 28, 1861; DD December 15, 1862

Postel, William S. Lindenwood, enlisted August 21, 1861; transferred to Veteran Reserve Corps June 20, 1864

Purck, Henry. Draftee, enlisted March 2, 1865; WIA April 2, 1865, in assault on Fort Gregg; DS April 4, 1865, of wounds

Robinson, George H. Hedgeville, VA, enlisted March 1, 1862; WIA May 20, 1864, at Ware Bottom Church; leg amputated; DS May 25, 1864, from wounds

Root, Charles. Lane, enlisted August 21, 1861; killed near Petersburg September 9, 1864; veteran

Root, Luther J. Santa Anna, enlisted April 10, 1864*

Rost, Lewis J. Dwight, enlisted September 21, 1861; WIA August 16, 1864, at Second Deep Bottom; DD September 21, 1864

Schuman, Charles F. Lindenwood, enlisted September 29, 1861; MO September 30, 1864

Schwab, Jacob. Willow Creek, enlisted August 9, 1861*

Shields, Peter. Draftee, enlisted February 20, 1865*

Smith, Michael. Lane, enlisted August 21, 1861; WIA May 16, 1864, at Drewry's Bluff*

Spinnings, Clark. Dwight, enlisted September 3, 1861; DD June 22, 1863

Staley, Abner. Dwight, enlisted December 17, 1862*

Stillyer, John. Willow Creek, enlisted August 9, 1861*

Taggart, John. Chicago, enlisted December 29, 1864; deserted August 3, 1865

Tindale, Daniel A. Chicago, enlisted November 19, 1863; WIA August 16, 1864, at Second Deep Bottom; deserted August 3, 1865

Tobias, Nathaniel. Lane, enlisted August 29, 1861; KIA May 16, 1864, at Drewry's Bluff

Vaughn, William D. Draftee, enlisted February 23, 1865; KIA April 2, 1865, in assault on Fort Gregg

Walls, Nelson. Willow Creek, enlisted August 20, 1861; taken POW January 3, 1862, at Bath, VA; Adjutant's report lists that he deserted, but Clark states that he went into the gunboat service in March 1864 and served until the end of the war

Willis, Frederick. Chicago, enlisted February 29, 1864; MIA, assumed POW after August 16, 1864, at Second Deep Run

Wills, Elmore. Draftee, enlisted March 23, 1865; DS June 16, 1865

Wise, Christian. Lindenwood, enlisted August 21, 1861; both Clark and the Adjutant's report state almost identically that on April 18, 1862, Wise wandered from camp in a "state of insanity"

Company E
Will County—1860 Population: 29,321
Cook County—144,954

Killed in Battle	11
Died of Wounds	5
Died in Prison	3
Lost Limbs	7
Wounded	41
Taken Prisoner	13
Number Originally Enlisted	58
Mustered Out at Expiration of Service	4
Re-Enlisted as Veterans	42
Recruits	78
Mustered Out With Regiment	59

Elected Officers
Captain: James H. Hooker
First Lieutenant: Lewis T. Whipple
Second Lieutenant: Norman C. Warner

Company E took shape in May of 1861 when a group of men from Wesley Township, Illinois were inspired by Stephen Douglas' speeches in support of the Union. Wesley Township is five miles southeast of Wilmington, and the men met at a schoolhouse in Florence Township, just to the north, to learn drill from Lewis Whipple—calling themselves the "Florence Rifles." Many of the men were from Wilmington, and the company's choice of joining the 39th Illinois was influenced by Company A being made up of Wilmington men. Even with receiving a great deal of individuals from around the state once they arrived in Chicago, and Lieutenant Warner leaving St. Louis to do recruiting back home, the company numbered barely 50 men when the regiment arrived at Benton Barracks, and did not fill their ranks until after the veteran furlough.

Hooker, James H. Wilmington, Captain, commissioned August 12, 1861; resigned May 26, 1862, due to poor health

Whipple, Lewis T. Rockville, Captain, mustered as 1st Lieutenant; promoted Captain May 26, 1862, vice Hooker's resignation; MO October 25, 1864

Milliman, Minor W. Wesley, Captain, enlisted September 12, 1861; promoted Sergeant May 26, 1862; First Sergeant January 1, 1863; Captain December 9, 1864, vice Whipple mustering out*

Ripple, John L. Orbisonia, PA, First Lieutenant, enlisted October 28, 1861; promoted to Sergeant January 16, 1862; taken POW May 9, 1862, near Columbia Bridge, VA; taken to Libby Prison in Richmond; paroled September 13, 1862; taken POW again May 16, 1864, at Drewry's Bluff and sent to Andersonville, GA; paroled at Savannah November 19, 1864; promoted First Lieutenant December 15, 1864, vice Warner mustering out

Warner, Norman C. Wilmington, First Lieutenant, mustered in as 2nd Lieutenant; promoted First Lieutenant May 26, 1862, vice Whipple's promotion; took the colors from the wounded Sergeant Henry Hardenburgh on August 16, 1864, at the Battle of Second Deep Bottom and was severely wounded requiring amputation of a leg; was breveted Major of Volunteers for meritorious conduct and DD December 15, 1864

Conley, John. Wilmington, Second Lieutenant, enlisted September 12, 1861; promoted Corporal then 1st Sergeant unknown dates; commissioned Second Lieutenant May 26, 1862, vice Warner's promotion; resigned August 8, 1862, due to severe lung issues that left him bedridden for his final four years of life

Kingsbury, Elisha. Wilmington, Second Lieutenant, mustered in as private; no information on any other enlisted promotions; commissioned 2nd Lieutenant August 8, 1862; WIA May 16, 1864, at Drewry's Bluff shattering an arm that required amputation; DD October 16, 1864; veteran

Baxter, William. Wilmington, First Sergeant, enlisted September 12, 1861; mustered as Corporal; WIA May 16, 1864, at Drewry's Bluff and taken POW; exchanged August 13, 1864; promoted Sergeant November 1, 1864; First Sergeant January 1, 1865*

Clark, George A. Sheldon, Sergeant, enlisted September 28, 1861; promoted Corporal February 25, 1863; Sergeant January 1, 1865*

Steele, William E. Chicago, Sergeant, enlisted October 2, 1861; promoted January 16, 1862, from Private; KIA October 13, 1864, at Darbytown Crossroads

Hanson, David M. Wilmington, Sergeant enlisted September 12, 1861; promoted from Private January 16, 1862; taken POW May 16, 1864, at Drewry's Bluff; died at Andersonville, GA from wounds in a railway accident October 22, 1864

Gronigal, Theodore D. Wilmington, Sergeant, enlisted September 12, 1861; promoted from Corporal May 9, 1863; WIA and taken POW May 16, 1864, at Drewry's Bluff; died June 9, 1864, in Petersburg from wounds; veteran

Burton, George W. Wilmington, Sergeant, enlisted September 20, 1861; WIA in both legs August 16, 1864, at Second Deep Bottom; promoted from Corporal November 1, 1864; KIA April 2, 1865, in assault on Fort Gregg

Kelley, William T. Wesley, Sergeant, enlisted November 13, 1861; promoted Corporal May 1, 1863; Sergeant March 1, 1865*

Evans, Joseph S. Wesley, Sergeant, enlisted December 21, 1863; WIA August 16 1864 at Second Deep Bottom; promoted Corporal January 1, 1865; Sergeant May 31, 1865; detailed as acting Commissary Sergeant and acting Sergeant Major*

Porter, Orson C. Wilmington, enlisted October 2, 1861; WIA May 20, 1864, at Ware Bottom Church; promoted Corporal August 16, 1864; WIA October 13, 1864, at Darbytown Crossroads; promoted Sergeant June 1, 1865*

Brown, William. Chicago, Corporal, enlisted September 27, 1861; detailed to regimental band*

Sartell, Henry E. Wilmington, enlisted October 27, 1861; promoted May 1, 1863; WIA August 16, 1864, at Second Deep Bottom; DD March 30, 1865

Whitman, John W. Concord, Corporal, enlisted September 28, 1861; unknown promotion date to Corporal; MO September 27, 1864

Kelly, John M. Orbisonia, PA, Corporal, enlisted February 12, 1862; promoted January 1, 1864; WIA June 17, 1864, and August 16, 1864, at Second Deep Bottom; died of wounds October 31, 1864

Merrill, Almon. Florence, Corporal, enlisted September 12, 1861; promoted March 4, 1864; WIA May 16, 1864, at Drewry's Bluff; died of wounds July 16, 1864; veteran

Hudson, Charles C. Corporal Wilmington, enlisted September 17, 1861; promoted Corporal unknown date in 1864*

Milks, Hermann. Gardner, Corporal, enlisted September 12, 1861; promoted March 1, 1865*

Axtell, Theodore F. Wesley, Corporal enlisted February 27, 1864; WIA August 16, 1864, at Second Deep Bottom and October 13, 1864, at Darbytown Crossroads; promoted April 1, 1865*

Morey, Oscar R. Florence, Corporal, enlisted February 24, 1864; promoted Corporal May 16, 1865*

Vandebogart, James. Florence, Corporal, enlisted February 22, 1864; promoted August 1, 1865*

Nelson, James W. Wilmington, Corporal, enlisted September 12, 1861; promoted Corporal, November 1, 1865*

Ware, Charles W. Joliet, Corporal, enlisted September 14, 1861; promoted Corporal November 20, 1865*

Privates

Anderson, Alexander. Draftee, enlisted February 23, 1865; KIA April 2, 1865, in assault on Fort Gregg

Andreas, William. Wesley, enlisted September 1, 1861; wounded October 3, 1863, at Fort Wagner; DD May 16, 1864

Babcock, Ralph. Chicago, enlisted March 8, 1864; WIA October 7, 1864, near Chaffin's Farm; KIA April 2, 1865, in assault on Fort Gregg

Baker, Lawrence. Durham, enlisted September 18, 1861; WIA and taken POW May 16, 1864, at Drewry's Bluff; died June 9, 1864, in Richmond; veteran

Baldwin, Charles. Chicago, enlisted September 28, 1861, under Charles Creamer to elude his guardian; DD September 18, 1862

Barton, Samuel A. Bloomington, enlisted December 16, 1862; DD July 4, 1863

Batchelder, Samuel C. Wilmington, enlisted December 21, 1863; discharged June 3, 1865

Benton, Silas. Wilmington, enlisted August 12, 1861; KIA May 14, 1864, at Drewry's Bluff; veteran

Bogart, Walter. Wilmington, enlisted September 17, 1861; killed October 12, 1863, at Fort Gregg, S.C.

Bohmler, William. Chicago, enlisted September 26, 1864; MO June 20, 1865

Button, Lorenz. Wilmington, enlisted October 2, 1861; DD date unknown

Cannon, John. Wilmington, enlisted October 21, 1865; DD November 20, 1865

Casey, John. Wilmington, enlisted March 11, 1864*

Clark, James H. Channahon, enlisted December 22, 1863; KIA August 16 1864 at Second Deep Bottom

Corbett, Frank M. Florence, enlisted February 24, 1864; WIA May 20, 1864, at Ware Bottom Church*

Dagan, Patrick. Wilmington, enlisted September 25, 1861; KIA October 13, 1864, at Darbytown Crossroads

Dannable, William J. Wesley, enlisted March 2, 1864; WIA August 16, 1864, at Second Deep Run; MO June 3, 1865

Dunn, George H. Rockville, enlisted October 6, 1861; WIA May 20, 1864, at Ware Bottom Church; absent from company after that date; veteran

Elick, Joseph. Draft substitute, enlisted February 25, 1865*

Ely, William W. Concord, enlisted September 28, 1861; transferred to Company F as musician January 1, 1864

Flowers, Lewis. Draft substitute, enlisted October 17, 1864; MO October 18, 1865

Flynn, William. Chicago, enlisted September 28, 1861; DS January 10, 1864, at Beaufort, S.C.

Gillett, Henry. Wesley, enlisted November 13, 1861; DS February, 1862 in Cumberland, MD hospital

Gillett, James. Wesley, enlisted November 13, 1861; WIA May 16, 1864, at Drewry's Bluff; died of wounds August 17, 1864

Gray, Alexander. Wilmington enlisted October 6, 1861; WIA August 16, 1864, at Second Deep Bottom*

Grice, Daniel S. Rockville, enlisted October 15, 1861; discharged, unknown date; imperfect record

Hademan, Martin V. Wilmington, enlisted November 13, 1861; WIA June 2, 1864, near Ware Bottom Church; and April 9, 1865, at Appomattox Court House—one of last to be wounded by the enemy*

Harsh, J.O. Rockville, enlisted September 27, 1861; MO September 27, 1864

Hartman, George. Draft substitute, enlisted February 22, 1865; MO May 3, 1865

Hawath, John. Chicago, enlisted October 2, 1861; deserted February, 1862

Hayworth, George. Draft substitute, enlisted February 22, 1865; taken POW April 9, 1865, at Appomattox Courthouse and paroled same day; one of last men to be captured by Army of Northern Virginia*

Hazzard, Monroe. Chicago, enlisted March 24, 1864; detached for service as orderly to Osborn and other staff*

Hertzog, Charles W. Rockville, enlisted September 20, 1861; transferred to Veteran Reserve Corps November 16, 1864

Hertzog, William F. Rockville, enlisted September 20, 1861; WIA May 20, 1864, at Ware Bottom Church; KIDA June 18, 1864, near same; veteran

Houghton, Azor. Wilmington, unknown enlistment date; mustered December 31, 1863; MO June 2, 1865

Howe, Calvin H. St. Louis, MO, enlisted October 2, 1861; deserted January 30, 1862

Howe, Hermann H. St. Louis, MO, enlisted October 2, 1861; deserted January 30, 1862

Howell, Daniel. Wilmington, enlisted October 2, 1861; DD unknown date

Howell, George. Wesley, enlisted December 31, 1863; WIA October 13, 1864, at Darbytown Crossroads requiring a hand to be amputated; DD March 30, 1865

Hull, Samuel F. Chicago, enlisted February 27, 1864; detailed to reg't band*

Ingleman, Augustus. Cicero, enlisted March 7, 1864*

Jackson, Charles A. Florence, enlisted February 28, 1864; WIA August 16, 1864, at Second Deep Bottom requiring amputation of arm; DD November 7, 1864

Jewett, William O.L. Wesley, enlisted September 12, 1861; one of first to arrive in Camp Mather in Chicago and was sent home on recruiting duty; in July 1862 was sent to hospital in very poor health and never returned to active service; DD June 6, 1863

Johnson, James M. Chicago, enlisted February 26, 1864; detailed to reg't band*

Johnston, Howard. Channahon, enlisted March 9, 1864; WIA May 16, 1864, at Drewry's Bluff requiring amputation of an arm; DD November 21, 1864

Kahler, Lloyd W. Florence, enlisted February 24, 1864*

Karr, Elisha. Sheldon, enlisted October 25, 1861; KIA May 14, 1864, at Drewry's Bluff

Kelly, William. Draft substitute, enlisted February 21, 1865*

Kelsey, Albert C. Draft substitute, enlisted March 30, 1865*

Kinney, Thomas. Wilmington, enlisted October 2, 1861; WIA August 16, 1864, at Second Deep Bottom; DD June 20, 1865

Lansing, John W. Draft substitute, enlisted February 26, 1865; deserted August 5, 1865

Laughlin, John. Huntington, PA, enlisted February 1, 1862; DS February 11, 1862, of typhoid fever

Lee, Ditson. Essex, enlisted February 24, 1864; taken POW May 16, 1864, at Drewry's Bluff; paroled at Savannah, GA November 19, 1864*

Levally, Charles T. Chicago, enlisted March 14, 1864; severely wounded September 10, 1864, near Petersburg, transferred to Veteran's Reserve Corps November 3, 1865

Lyons, Sydney. Florence, enlisted September 12, 1861; WIA October 13, 1864, at Darbytown Crossroads*

Mahan, John. Pittsburgh, PA, enlisted February 24, 1861; deserted April 20, 1862

Mallett, Cyran. Chicago, enlisted March 24, 1864; WIA October 13, 1864, at Darbytown Crossroads*

Martin, William. Chicago, enlisted March 8, 1864*

Mayer, Moses. Florence, enlisted September 21, 1861; WIA at Ware Bottom Church on unknown date*

McCollum, Alexander. Gardner, enlisted September 14, 1861; transferred to Co. A

McMaster, James. Wilmington, enlisted October 6, 1861; DS December 9, 1861

Meyher, Caleb. Unknown, enlisted January 13, 1864; WIA June 18, 1864, near Ware Bottom Church*

Miller, William C. Draft substitute, enlisted February 24, 1865*

Monroe, James. Florence, enlisted September 17, 1861; WIA May 16, 1864, at Drewry's Bluff*

Monroe, John. Florence, enlisted February 22, 1864; WIA May 20, 1864, at Ware Bottom Church; taken POW and paroled on same day April 9, 1865, at Appomattox Courthouse; MO July 26, 1865

Morgan, George M. Sheldon, enlisted September 25, 1861; WIA and taken POW May 16, 1864, at Drewry's Bluff; paroled and exchanged; MO February 2, 1865

Musselman, Ephraim. Pittsburgh, PA, enlisted October 28, 1861; DS October 16, 1864, of typhoid fever

Nobles, James R. Wilmington, enlisted February 23, 1864*

O'Harra, Henry. Wesley, enlisted March 1, 1864*

Ohlhues, Henry. Florence, enlisted February 23, 1864; WIA May 20, 1864, at Ware Bottom Church; KIA April 2, 1865, in assault on Fort Gregg

Pennington, William H. Evanston, enlisted March 15, 1864; detailed as musician; company bugler during time at Bermuda Hundred*

Raleigh, Thomas. Wilmington, enlisted September 17, 1861*

Riley, Newton. Morris, enlisted February 21, 1865*

Ripple, William B. Orbisonia, PA, enlisted February 1, 1861; DS August 18, 1862, of fever

Rogers, Alpheus W. Wesley, enlisted December 31, 1863; WIA May 14, 1864, at Drewry's Bluff requiring amputation of arm; DD October 20, 1864

Sackett, Edward A. Chicago, enlisted October 10, 1861; detailed to reg't band*

Shade, Abraham. Orbisonia, PA, enlisted February 12, 1862; deserted September, 1862

Sheffler, M.F. Rockville, enlisted September 27, 1861; wounded August 16, 1863, at Fort Wagner; MO September 27, 1864

Slayton, Reuben. Chicago, enlisted March 27, 1864; WIA May 20, 1864; absent after that date

Smith, Charles M. Wilmington, enlisted September 20, 1861; DD February 14, 1863

Smith, Samuel. Draft substitute, enlisted February 25, 1865*

Snee, Hugh R. Rockville, enlisted September 27, 1861; WIA and taken POW May 16, 1864, at Drewry's Bluff; escaped from Andersonville September 22, 1864*

Stanton, William. Rockville, enlisted February 24, 1864*

Stearns (listed as **Stephens** in Adjutant's report) **F.L.** Wilmington, enlisted September 27, 1861; taken POW May 26, 1862, at Strasburg, VA; discharged unknown date

Stewart, Thomas. Wilmington, enlisted September 20, 1861; WIA and taken POW October 13, 1864, at Darbytown Crossroads; paroled and died in hospital at Annapolis, MD on October 30, 1864; veteran

Stoval, Eden. Draft substitute, enlisted February 25, 1865; WIA April 9, 1865, at Appomattox Courthouse*

Thayer, George. Wilmington, enlisted September 17, 1861*

Walrath, William. Chicago, enlisted March 24, 1864*

Wayne, Thomas. Chicago, enlisted March 9, 1864*

Webber, George A. Chicago, enlisted March 8, 1864; WIA October 7, 1864, losing a finger; DD August 21, 1865

Weiner (**Winn** in Adjutant's report), **John.** Wilmington, enlisted October 6, 1861; DD November 20, 1865

White, G.G. Wilmington, unknown enlistment date; mustered October 11, 1861; DD September 27, 1864; not listed in Clark history

Whiteman, John W. Concord, enlisted September 28, 1861; DD September 27, 1864

Company F
Cook County—1860 Population: 144,954
Lake County: 18,257

Killed in Battle	10
Died of Wounds	9
Died in Prison	4
Lost Limbs	2
Wounded	42
Taken Prisoner	12
Number Originally Enlisted	75
Mustered Out at Expiration of Service	8
Re-Enlisted as Veterans	40
Recruits	69
Mustered Out With Regiment	45

Elected Officers
Captain: Amasa Kennicott
First Lieutenant: John W. McIntosh
Second Lieutenant: Pat Seary

Company F had its core founded by Orrin Mann, then handed it off to Amasa Kennicott when he sought to be the regiment's Major. Then men primarily came from Chicago and Cook County, on account of Mann founding its beginnings, but also included men from areas near Waukegan—a town of 3,000 and the county seat of Lake County—35 miles north of Chicago.

Kennicott, Amasa. The Grove, Captain, commissioned August 27, 1861; resigned August 7, 1862

McIntosh, John W. Bloomington, Captain, commissioned 1st Lieutenant August 7, 1861; promoted Captain August 7, 1862, vice Kennicott's resignation; dismissed from service May 30, 1863

Hoffman, Adolphus B. Sandoval, Captain, enlisted August 12, 1861, and made 1st Sergeant; promoted 2nd Lieutenant August 1, 1862; promoted Captain March 30, 1863, vice McIntosh dismissal; MO December 30, 1864

Botsford, Reuben S. Waukegan, Captain; offered commission as 2nd Lieutenant if he recruited 25 men for Company F; accomplished this and mustered into regiment February 1, 1864; WIA June 20, 1864, at Ware Bottom; promoted 1st Lieutenant August 13, 1864; promoted Captain March 31, 1865, vice Hoffman mustering out*

Seary, Patrick. Sandoval, First Lieutenant, enlisted August 15, 1861, and made Sergeant; commissioned 2nd Lieutenant November 15, 1861; promoted 1st Lieutenant August 7, 1862, vice McIntosh promotion; resigned July 8, 1863

Lamb, William W. Sandoval, First Lieutenant, enlisted August 15, 1861, and made Corporal; promoted Sergeant February 13, 1862; WIA August 16, 1864, at Second Deep Bottom; promoted 1st Lieutenant April 1, 1865; KIA April 2, 1865, in assault on Fort Gregg

Davis, Nathan E. Chicago, Second Lieutenant, enlisted August 22, 1861, and made Corporal; promoted Sergeant November 1, 1862; promoted 2nd Lieutenant August 5, 1864; WIA October 13, 1864, at Darbytown Crossroads; died of wounds November 16, 1864

Abbott, William J. Sandoval, Sergeant, enlisted August 12, 1861, and made Sergeant; DD August 27, 1862

Mulvaney, Barney. Sandoval, Sergeant, enlisted August 13, 1861, and made Sergeant; DD July 27, 1862

Ballard, John P. Bloomington, Sergeant, enlisted August 12, 1861, and made Sergeant, reduced to ranks April 1, 1864*

Coursen, Christopher E. Sandoval, enlisted August 16, 1861, and made Corporal; promoted Sergeant August 30, 1862; made Quartermaster Sergeant (see Field and Staff Officers)

Loughram, Ownen. Sandoval, Sergeant enlisted August 15, 1861; promoted Corporal December 7, 1861; Sergeant February 1, 1864; KIA October 13, 1864, at Darbytown Crossroads

Preston, Dwight. Centralia, Sergeant, enlisted August 15, 1861, and made Corporal; promoted Sergeant December 7, 1862; WIA May 20, 1864, at Ware Bottom Church; DD June 1, 1865

Moore, William T. Chicago, Sergeant, enlisted September 27, 1861; promoted Corporal October 20, 1861; Sergeant August 5, 1864; WIA June 5, 1864, near Petersburg; promoted 1st Lieutenant May 9, 1865, but unable to muster*

Russell, John H. Northfield, enlisted August 13, 1861; promoted Corporal February 16, 1862; Sergeant August 23, 1864; discharged to commission as a Lieutenant in the 38th USCT Regiment, led troops into Richmond on April 3, 1865

Moore, Thomas. Chicago, Sergeant, enlisted August 22, 1861; promoted Corporal, November 1, 1862; WIA August 16, 1864, at Second Deep Bottom; promoted Sergeant March 6, 1865; later promoted to Lieutenant but unable to muster*

Morse, Ebenezer J. Centralia, Sergeant, enlisted August 15, 1861; promoted Corporal August 16, 1864; Sergeant April 1, 1865*

Underwood, George Melvin. Chicago, Sergeant, enlisted September 4, 1861; promoted Corporal January 1, 1865; Sergeant June 2, 1865*

Hoffman, Stewart W. Sandoval, Corporal, enlisted August 27, 1861; promoted to Quartermaster Sergeant then Regimental Quartermaster (see Field and Staff officers)

Bias, John A. Centralia, Corporal, promoted February 16, 1862; WIA May 20, 1864, at Ware Bottom Church; August 16, 1864, at Second Deep Bottom*

Crandall, David G. Chicago, Corporal, enlisted August 24, 1861; promoted November 1, 1862; WIA May 16, 1864, at Drewry's Bluff; WIA August 16, 1864, at Second Deep Bottom and died same day of wounds

McIntosh, James. Bloomington, Corporal, enlisted August 27, 1861; promoted November 1, 1862*

Washburn, George W. Chicago, Corporal, enlisted August 28, 1861; promoted November 19, 1862; DD August 5, 1863

Peters, Martin Van Buren. Elgin, Corporal, enlisted September 4, 1861; promoted February 1, 1864; WIA June 18, 1864; transferred to Veteran Reserve Corps March 17, 1865

Lake, David. Chicago, Corporal, enlisted September 28, 1861; promoted October 4, 1864; WIA April 2, 1865, in assault on Fort Gregg; DD July 18, 1865

Drake, John C. Avon, Corporal, enlisted February 23, 1864; promoted March 1, 1865*

Melody, Patrick H. Waukegan, Corporal, enlisted January 21, 1864; promoted March 15, 1865*

Robinson, William H. Chicago, Corporal, enlisted February 29, 1864; promoted Corporal June 2, 1865, for meritorious service in the assault on Fort Gregg and at Appomattox Courthouse*

Joyce, Patrick F. Waukegan, Corporal, enlisted January 21, 1864; promoted June 7, 1865*

Burdick, Charles L. Antioch, Corporal, enlisted February 13, 1864; promoted August 1, 1865*

Isbester, John. Waukegan, enlisted January 25, 1864; promoted Corporal August 1, 1865*

Privates

Arlt, Otto. Chicago, enlisted August 6, 1861; MO September 10, 1864

Bailey, Robert. Chicago, enlisted August 22, 1861*

Barron, Dallas. Chicago, enlisted December 29, 1863*

Babbitt, George M. Centralia, enlisted August 13, 1861; MO September 10, 1864

Babbitt, Joseph. Chicago, enlisted September 4, 1861*

Baur, Henry. Elgin, enlisted September 4, 1861; DD January,1862

Brogan, Daniel. Benton, MO, enlisted October 15, 1861; DD December 18, 1861

Brown, George. Sandoval, enlisted August 15, 1861; deserted April 18, 1862

Burdick, John H. Antioch, enlisted February 13, 1864*

Callahan, Calvin. Bloomington, enlisted August 10, 1861; taken POW May 16, 1864, at Drewry's Bluff; died of wounds August 21, 1864, at Andersonville; veteran

Campbell, Samuel. Chicago, enlisted January 14, 1864; WIA June 18, 1864*

Carpenter, Charles. Chicago, enlisted September 17, 1861; WIA June 18, 1864; DD December 8, 1864, from wounds; veteran

Casey, James. Unknown, enlisted September 20, 1861; DD October 22, 1862

Claire, Hippolyte. Northfield, enlisted February 29, 1864; WIA August 16, 1864, at Second Deep Run*

Cole, Preston. Cook County, enlisted August 15, 1861; DS January 4, 1862

Conner, Charles. Northfield, enlisted August 3, 1861; wounded August 5, 1864; taken POW August 16, 1864, at Second Deep Run; died in parole camp February,1865; veteran

Curry, James. Bloomington, unknown enlistment date; mustered October 11, 1861; DD unknown date

Dabner, Leonard. Fremont, enlisted January 28, 1864; taken POW May 16, 1864, at Drewry's Bluff; paroled and DS December 12, 1864, from disease

Danely, Henry. Waukegan, enlisted February 23, 1864; WIA October 13, 1864, at Darbytown Crossroads; DD May 27, 1865

Davis, Charles O. Joliet, enlisted December 17, 1863*

Denline, John Jr. Fremont, enlisted February 29, 1864*

Denline, John Sr. Fremont, enlisted February 29, 1864*

Deviney, Philip S. St. Louis, MO, enlisted October 28, 1861; KIA April 2, 1865, in assault on Fort Gregg

Dewey, Thomas. Northfield, enlisted August 15, 1861; KIA April 2, 1865, in assault on Fort Gregg

Dickinson, Joseph W. Chicago, enlisted August 5, 1861; served as clerk in regimental adjutant's office until December 1861, then set to Chicago to recruit; returned while regiment was on Morris Island and served on the staffs of Generals Vogdes, Terry and Seymour; re-enlisted, then given commission as a Captain of the 21st USCT Regiment in April 1864

Dobner, Henry. Fremont, enlisted February 29, 1864; MO June 16, 1865

Douglas, Aaron C. Waukegan, enlisted February 23, 1864; wounded September 16, 1864, and October 7, 1864; died May 11, 1865, from wounds

Eigner, Lewis. Chicago, enlisted August 28, 1861; MO September 10, 1864

Ellis, William. Chicago, enlisted September 10, 1861; MO September 10, 1864

Ely, William W. Chicago, enlisted September 28, 1861; transferred from Company E December 1864*

Fiddler, Henry. Waukegan, enlisted January 24, 1864; KIA August 16, 1864, at Second Deep Bottom

Fisch, James. Chicago, enlisted February 27, 1864*

Gosan, Christopher. Waukegan, enlisted February 12, 1864; DD September 16, 1864

Gosan, Jacob. Waukegan, enlisted February 12, 1864*

Hagan, Francis. Waukegan, enlisted February 12, 1864; WIA May 20, 1864, at Ware Bottom Church; died of wounds June 16, 1864

Hall, Joseph. Chicago, enlisted August 22, 1861; DD July,1862

Hamilton, Chester W. Goodale, enlisted February 4, 1864; WIA August 14, 1864, near Deep Bottom*

Harrison, John. Sandoval, enlisted September 6, 1861; WIA May 16, 1864, at Drewry's Bluff; died July 1, 1864, of wounds

Harvey, Henry. Avon, enlisted February 29, 1864; DD July 17, 1865

Harvey, Louis. Bloomington, enlisted August 14, 1861; WIA August 16, 1864, at Second Deep Bottom requiring amputation of arm; DD October 14, 1864, for wounds; veteran

Hauglebrock, William. Unknown, enlisted September 2, 1864; MIA and supposed captured October 13, 1864, at Darbytown Crossroads; no further information; not listed in adjutant's report

Hayes, John B. Chicago, enlisted August 15, 1861; deserted February 1864 and died in his home March 1864; veteran

Hayes, Stephen. Chicago, enlisted August 5, 1861; deserted unknown date 1862

Heirsagle, Joseph. Fremont, enlisted January 28, 1864; Clark history says deserted July 17, 1864; adjutant's report says died of wounds July 1, 1864

Herrick, M.B. Unknown, enlisted August 22, 1861; DD August 5, 1863; not listed in adjutant's report

Hewitt, Charles. Waukegan, enlisted January 9, 1864*

Hopkins, Benjamin B. Chicago, enlisted March 27, 1864; KIA August 16, 1864, at Second Deep Run

Hutchings, John A. Northfield, Corporal, enlisted August 21, 1861; promoted January 1, 1864; WIA May 20, 1864, at Ware Bottom Church; reduced to ranks at his own request*

Johnson, Frederick. Waukegan, enlisted February 4, 1864; WIA August 16, 1864, at Second Deep Bottom; died August 24, 1864, from wounds

Johnson, George. Chicago, enlisted August 5, 1861; DD October 15, 1861

Kame, Dennis. Sandoval, enlisted August 15, 1861; DS November 1, 1861, in Pittsburgh

Kame, James M. Chicago, enlisted August 22, 1861; taken POW May 1, 1862, at Strasburg, VA; DS September 23, 1862, in Annapolis

Kelly, John. Waukegan, enlisted February 12, 1864; WIA October 28, 1864, in skirmish near Darbytown Crossroads; MO July 15, 1865

Kemph, Charles H. Unknown, unknown enlistment date, mustered September 21, 1864; not in Clark's history*

Kemph, Frederick. Chicago, enlisted September 28, 1861; WIA May 16, 1864, at Drewry's Bluff*

Kemph, William. Lockport, enlisted August 22, 1861*

Kennedy, Thomas W. Antioch, enlisted February 22, 1864; WIA August 16, 1864, at Second Deep Bottom and taken POW; died shortly after in Richmond from wounds

Kramer, Jacob. Bloomington, enlisted September 8, 1861; DS June 14, 1864, from wounds of unknown origin

Larrett, Charles. Chicago, enlisted September 29, 1861; KIA April 2, 1865, in assault on Fort Gregg

Litwiller, Charles. Avon, enlisted February 29, 1864; WIA May 20, 1864, at Ware Bottom Church*

Lott, Theodore. Waukegan, enlisted, February 24, 1864; died suddenly on June 5, 1864; while returning from picket duty under fire, reached the intrenchments and fell dead; autopsy revealed heart disease

Loughram, John. Chicago, enlisted September 6, 1861; DD May 8, 1863

Lusk, Palmer. Avon, enlisted February 2, 1864; WIA and taken POW May 16, 1864, at Drewry's Bluff; died June 5, 1864, at Andersonville

Manzer, James M. Waukegan, enlisted January 25, 1864; WIA May 16, 1864, at Drewry's Bluff; DD June 22, 1865, from wounds

Marshall, Peter. Homer, enlisted February 27, 1864; WIA October 13, 1864, at Darbytown Crossroads*

McAree, Francis. Waukegan, enlisted January 28, 1864*

McCurley, Michael. Northfield, enlisted February 9, 1864*

McIntosh, Joseph. Bloomington, enlisted October 5, 1861; DD June,1862

McLarkey, Hugh. Chicago, enlisted September 16, 1861; DD August 25, 1862

McLaughlin, Dennis. Chicago, enlisted September 1, 1861; DD January,1862

Miller, Nichols. Chicago, enlisted September 16, 1861; deserted August,1862

Miltmore, Alonzo. Avon, enlisted February 29, 1864; DS March 23, 1864, of fever

Mooney, John. Bloomington, enlisted August 19, 1861; WIA August 16, 1864, at Second Deep Bottom*

Morris, James. Bloomington, enlisted August 10, 1861; WIA May 20, 1864, at Ware Bottom Church requiring amputation of leg; died July 9, 1864, of wounds in Philadelphia; veteran

Morse, Jacob. Chicago, enlisted September 4, 1861; deserted unknown date 1862

Nelson, James. Sandoval, enlisted August 15, 1861; wounded September 7, 1863, at Fort Wagner; MO September 10, 1864

Nevil, Richard. Bloomington, enlisted August 20, 1861*

Notmyer, Henry. Fremont, enlisted February 8, 1864*

O'Brien, Patrick. Bloomington, enlisted August 20, 1861; WIA and taken POW August 16, 1864, at Second Deep Bottom; died August 31, 1864, at Annapolis MD from wounds; veteran

Peck, William. Homer, enlisted February 22, 1864; WIA June 18, 1864, in skirmish near Ware Bottom Church; WIA August 16, 1864, at Second Deep Bottom; no discharge info available

Pike, Alpheus H. Bloomington, enlisted August 28, 1861; taken POW May 16, 1864, at Drewry's Bluff and sent to Andersonville; paroled, exchanged, and discharged February 21, 1865

Plowman, James. Chicago, enlisted September 15, 1861; WIA June 2, 1864; DS November 14, 1864, from wounds; veteran

Rarrick, Nathan. Chicago, unknown enlistment date, mustered October 11, 1861; DD August 5, 1863; not listed in Clark's history

Scoville, John. Chicago, enlisted December 4, 1864; transferred to Veteran Reserve Corps April 17, 1865

Scoville, William. Waukegan, enlisted February 4, 1864; WIA May 20, 1864, at Ware Bottom Church; DD Jan 7, 1865

Seltzer, Peter. Northfield, enlisted August 5, 1861*

Sheets, Eli. Chicago, enlisted September 27, 1861; transferred to Veteran Reserve Corps July 1, 1863

Sherwood, Daniel. Waukegan, enlisted January 25, 1864; KIA October 28, 1864, near Darbytown Crossroads

Siggs, Francis. Bloomington, enlisted August 19, 1861; WIA June 18, 1864; died of wounds June 21, 1864; veteran

Smith, Asahel. Avon, enlisted February 2, 1864; DD May 6, 1865

Snyder, Gottlieb. Bloomington, enlisted August 28, 1861; DD October 13, 1862

Springer, Samuel. Chicago, enlisted August 24, 1861; DD September 11, 1862

Stanton, Albert. Centralia, enlisted August 13, 1861*

Starr, Lucius. Newport, enlisted February 13, 1864*

Stillhamer, William. Bloomington, enlisted March 9, 1864; taken POW May 16, 1864, at Drewry's Bluff; paroled; KIA April 2, 1865, in assault on Fort Gregg

Stout, James. Centralia, enlisted August 14, 1861; WIA May 20, 1864, at Ware Bottom Church; DD October 3, 1864; veteran

Stroban, George. Waukegan, enlisted February 26, 1864*

Sullivan, George. Libertyville, enlisted February 26, 1864; WIA May 16, 1864, at Drewry's Bluff*

Trapp, Augustus. Northfield, enlisted August 22, 1861; DD August 20, 1862

Van Buskirk, John. Chicago, enlisted September 1, 1861; DD July 1, 1863

Vancourt, Rufus. Chicago, enlisted September 12, 1861; DD May 9, 1863

Van Patten, Adelbert. Antioch, enlisted January 28, 1864; WIA and taken POW August 16, 1864, at Second Deep Bottom; died of wounds

Webb, Daniel. Antioch, enlisted February 16, 1864*

Webb, Wallace H. Antioch, enlisted February 16, 1864; WIA June 18, 1864, in skirmish near Ware Bottom Church*

Weible, Nicholas. Chicago, enlisted October 4, 1861; MO October 4, 1864

Williams, Harry (adjutant's report lists **Henry**). unknown, enlisted February 25, 1864; adjutant's report says deserted August 13, 1864; Clark history states wounded October 13, 1864, at Darbytown Crossroads; no discharge date in Clark history

Woore, Henry. Northfield, enlisted August 5, 1861; MO September 10, 1864

Company G—"Preacher's Company"
Will County—1860 Population: 29,321
Cook County—144,954

Killed in Battle	11
Died of Wounds	6
Died in Prison	2
Lost Limbs	2
Wounded	50
Taken Prisoner	6
Number Originally Enlisted	101
Mustered Out at Expiration of Service	25
Re-Enlisted as Veterans	41
Recruits	68
Mustered Out With Regiment	52

Elected Officers
Captain: William B. Slaughter
First Lieutenant: Oscar F. Rudd
Second Lieutenant: Amos Savage

Company G was recruited and formed in Chicago in August of 1861 by a Methodist Episcopal reverend, William Slaughter, working closely with Oscar Rudd and Amos Savage. Nicknamed the "Preacher Company," on account of Slaughter promising to form a company of God-fearing men, the company was made up primarily of men from Chicago, Cook County, and areas of what would now be considered the southwest Chicago suburbs. However, the company did have men from Sterling, 100 miles to the west of Chicago, a handful of men from bordering Midwest states, and even men from Kansas and Philadelphia. Company G produced some of the regiment's most notable characters and took part in some of its most notable fighting.

Slaughter, William B. Blue Island, Captain, commissioned August 5, 1861; resigned July 20, 1862, while at Harrison's Landing

Rudd, Oscar F. Blue Island, Captain, commissioned 1st Lieutenant August 5, 1861; promoted Captain July 20, 1862, vice Slaughter's resignation; wounded June 16, 1864, in skirmish near Chester Station; died July 11, 1864, at Fort Monroe

Savage, Amos. Homer, First Lieutenant, commissioned 2nd Lieutenant August 5, 1861; promoted 1st Lieutenant July 20, 1862, vice Rudd's promotion; promoted Captain July 11, 1864, vice Rudd's death but did not muster; DD October 28, 1864, from loss of vision

Plimpton, Homer. Sterling, Captain, enlisted August 14, 1861; promoted from Private to Sergeant May 20, 1864; slightly wounded October 7, 1864, from shell fragments; promoted 1st Lieutenant October 28, 1864; Captain December 5, 1864; assumed command of regiment (See Field and Staff Officers)

Kendall, Neriah B. Joliet, Captain, enlisted August 9, 1861; promoted Corporal January 1, 1862; WIA May 16, 1864; reported as killed but had been taken POW and returned to regiment; promoted Sergeant August 15, 1864; 1st Sergeant November 1, 1864; commissioned as officer unclear date in winter of 1864–1865; promoted Captain April 12, 1865, vice Plimpton promotion*

West, James B. Homer, First Lieutenant, enlisted August 13, 1861; promoted Sergeant September 10, 1864; 1st Sergeant January 1, 1865; 2nd Lieutenant April 29, 1865; 1st Lieutenant May 10, 1865* (adjutant's report is very unclear on West and lists the same name as two different entries denoting the promotions but stating he mustered out as private)

Harrington, James M. Palos, Second Lieutenant, enlisted August 9, 1861, and made Sergeant; promoted Second Lieutenant July 20, 1862; MO October 17, 1864

Ward, Joseph R. Jr. Bremen, First Sergeant, enlisted November 29, 1861; promoted Corporal October 10, 1864; Sergeant November 1, 1864; Second Lieutenant October 16, 1865, but unable to muster*

Brink, Samuel H. Sterling, Sergeant, enlisted August 15, 1861, and made Sergeant; promoted 1st Sergeant January 1, 1864; DS September 22, 1864, of typhoid fever

Crowin, Horace T. Homer, Sergeant, enlisted August 16, 1861, and made Sergeant; WIA May 20, 1864, at Ware Bottom Church; MO September 20, 1864

Harrington, Stephen L. Palos, Sergeant, enlisted August 9, 1861, and made Sergeant, KIA May 16, 1864, at Drewry's Bluff; veteran

Spencer, W.W. Bainbridge, MN, Sergeant, enlisted August 15, 1861; promoted Sergeant July 2, 1862; wounded June 1, 1864, in Bermuda Hundred trenches; died of wounds July 5, 1864, in Philadelphia

Cox, Camillus. Blue Island, Sergeant, enlisted August 13, 1861; promoted Corporal April 13, 1864; Sergeant July 5, 1864; WIA October 27, 1864, in skirmish near Darbytown Crossroads; DD June 8, 1865, from wounds

Prior, James. Lockport, Sergeant, enlisted August 13, 1861, and made Corporal; WIA both legs June 2, 1864; promoted Sergeant November 1, 1864; transferred and commissioned 2nd Lieutenant in 122 USCT Regiment March 10, 1865

Herzog, Adam J. Lafayette, IN, Sergeant, enlisted August 15, 1861; WIA May 20, 1864, at Ware Bottom Church; promoted Corporal October 10, 1864; Sergeant January 1, 1865*

Klump, Jacob B. Peoria, Sergeant, enlisted September 4, 1861; promoted Corporal October 12, 1864; Sergeant May 1, 1865*

Katillinek, Albert. Thornton, Sergeant, enlisted August 15, 1861; promoted Corporal March 1, 1865; Sergeant July 1, 1865*

Gillett, Abner. Homer, Corporal, enlisted August 29, 1861, and made Corporal; MO September 10, 1864

Boughton, Jehial. Palos, Corporal, enlisted August 9, 1861, and made Corporal; DS April 12, 1864, from unlisted disease; veteran

Hawkins, John J. Palos, Corporal, enlisted August 18, 1861, and was made Corporal; commanded the company for 30 days when Rudd was in hospital; Harrington sick and Savage temporarily in command of Company C; MO September 10, 1864

McKee, Joseph. Bremen, Corporal, enlisted August 13, 1862; DD November 25, 1862; re-enlisted January 4, 1864; WIA August 14, 1864, in skirmish near Deep Bottom; promoted Corporal January 1, 1865; WIA April 2, 1865, in assault on Fort Gregg; DD July 22, 1865, from wounds

Crawford, John. La Salle, Corporal, enlisted August 14, 1861, and made Corporal; DD September 23, 1862

Chatfield, Jesse. Palos, Corporal, enlisted August 9, 1861; promoted September 24, 1862; WIA June 17, 1864, in skirmish; MO September 10, 1864

Grose, John. La Salle, Corporal, enlisted August 14, 1861, and made Corporal; DD February 10, 1863

Gregory, Orgro. Bremen, Corporal, enlisted August 19, 1861, and made Corporal; reduced to ranks January 1, 1862; DS August 13, 1863, at Morris Island, SC

Sherwood, Frank O. Shabbona, Corporal, enlisted August 26, 1861; promoted May 1, 1863; MO September 10, 1864

Colbert, William J. Chicago, Corporal, enlisted February 27, 1864; promoted October 10, 1864; died April 15, 1865, while on furlough

Deeming, Thomas. Homer, Corporal, enlisted August 15, 1861; WIA March 23, 1862, at Kernstown; promoted November 1, 1864*

Hammond, William. Homer, Corporal, enlisted August 27, 1861; promoted November 1, 1864*

Howard, William H. Lysander, NY, Corporal, enlisted August 14, 1861; WIA April 2, 1865, in assault on Fort Gregg; promoted April 3, 1865*

Meyers, John. Thorton, Corporal, enlisted August 26, 1861; WIA June 2, 1864, near Ware Bottom Church requiring a bullet to be cut out of his tonsil; WIA April 2, 1865, in assault on Fort Gregg; promoted May 1, 1865*

Shafer, John N. Scranton, PA, Corporal, enlisted September 19, 1861; promoted May 1, 1865*

Warren, Richard. Bremen, Corporal, enlisted September 5, 1861; taken POW June 2, 1864, near Ware Bottom Church and sent to Andersonville; paroled; promoted May 10, 1865*

Green, Henry. Ottawa, Corporal, enlisted August 19, 1861, and made 1st Sergeant, reduced to ranks July 28, 1864, WIA August 20, 1864, at Ware Bottom Church and

October 13, 1864, at Darbytown Crossroads; promoted Corporal July 1, 1865, and MO as such*

Privates

Agney, Washington. Freeport, enlisted February 29, 1864; KIA October 13, 1864, at Darbytown Crossroads

Ahishlager, Carl G. New Lenox, enlisted September 7, 1861; MO September 10, 1864

Allison, John H. New Genesee, enlisted August 28, 1861; DS September 28, 1862, by falling tree while building intrenchments at Suffolk

Andrews, Isaac B. Hartford, MI, enlisted September 10, 1861; KIA May 16, 1864, at Drewry's Bluff

Angel, William. Homer, enlisted August 19, 1861*

Anthony, Herbert. Bedford, MI, enlisted August 23, 1861; KIA May 16, 1864, at Drewry's Bluff*

Armstrong, Edward. Chicago, enlisted February 16, 1864*

Aurand, Robert D. Berryman, enlisted March 15, 1865*

Barron, William. Orland, enlisted February 1, 1865*

Bedell, Ransom. Cook County, enlisted August 15, 1861; KIA October 12, 1864, in skirmish near Chaffin's Farm; veteran

Beeler, Leonard. Wood's Grove, enlisted February 22, 1865*

Blake, Robert W. Chicago, enlisted September 9, 1861; WIA June 17, 1864, and August 16, 1864, at Second Deep Bottom; MO September 16, 1864

Borchers, Hermanus. Peoria, enlisted August 30, 1861; DS February 13, 1862, from disease

Bosworth, Isaac D. Manteno, enlisted August 30, 1861; MO September 10, 1864

Breninger, Benjamin. Wood's Grove, enlisted February 27, 1865*

Breninger, David. Hopkins, enlisted March 29, 1865*

Breninger, John. Freeport, enlisted February 27, 1864; WIA October 7, 1864, in skirmish near Chaffin's Farm*

Brink, Albert. Sterling, enlisted February 28, 1864*

Brown, George W.L. Orland, enlisted February 29, 1864; WIA April 2, 1865, in assault on Fort Gregg; DD July 19, 1865, for wounds

Brusch, Frederick. Palos, enlisted February 15, 1864; WIA April 2, 1865, in assault on Fort Gregg; DD November 18, 1865, from wounds

Bullen, David. Farmington, enlisted September 9, 1861; DD June 2, 1862

Bushnell, Albert. Palos, enlisted February 27, 1864*

Callanan, Theodore. Philadelphia, PA, enlisted August 28, 1861; MO September 10, 1864

Campbell, Merlin. Newport, MI, enlisted August 29, 1861; MO September 10, 1864

Campbell, William. Draft substitute, enlisted February 14, 1865; deserted May 12, 1865

Carl, John. Homer, enlisted August 16, 1861; MO September 10, 1864

Case, Henry N. Thornton, enlisted February 28, 1864; died February 13, 1865, while on furlough

Chapin, Caleb F. Atlanta, enlisted October 28, 1861; WIA June 2, 1864, near Hatcher's Run and died of wounds; veteran

Clark, Charles. Fremont, enlisted February 12, 1864; died April 8, 1864, in Chicago

Clifford, James. Draft substitute, enlisted October 15, 1864; MO November 25, 1865

Cook, Ezra A., Wheaton, enlisted September 2, 1861; WIA May 16, 1864, at Drewry's Bluff; MO September 10, 1864

Crandall, Christopher C. Joliet, enlisted October 14, 1862; WIA May 20, 1864, at Ware Bottom Church and October 7, 1864; MO October 13, 1865

Crews, Harrison H. Joliet, enlisted August 9, 1861; discharged February 19, 1864, by reason of commission to 2nd Lieutenant in 64th Illinois; entered regular army after war

Decker, Lester B. Orland, enlisted February 23, 1864; WIA May 16, 1864, at Drewry's Bluff and October 7, 1864*

Dilno, Aaron. Bellevue, MI, enlisted October 1, 1861; DS February 13, 1862, of disease

Dilno, Henry. Bellevue, MI, enlisted September 5, 1861; DD September 28, 1862

Dunham, Hiram G. Hartford, MI, enlisted August 19, 1861; DS February 23, 1865, of typhoid

Fitt, William. Bremen, enlisted February 29, 1864; WIA June 2, 1864, in skirmish near Ware Bottom Church; WIA April 9, 1865, at Appomattox Courthouse*

Flannigan, Rollin O. Thornton, enlisted March 14, 1864; DD June 3, 1865

Frank, Henry. New Lenox, enlisted September 22, 1861; WIA May 16, 1864, at Drewry's Bluff; MO September 22, 1864

Frisbie, Charles F. Worth, enlisted August 13, 1861; promoted to Commissary Sergeant October 1, 1864 (see Field and Staff Officers)

Fudor, Lewis. Palos, enlisted May 7, 1864*

Gallup, George. Worth, enlisted February 23, 1864*

Gardner, Charles H. Thornton, enlisted February 28, 1864*

Gibson, Hiram. Bremen, enlisted February 23, 1864; WIA October 13, 1864, at Darbytown Crossroads; died of wounds October 27, 1864

Goebel, John. Chicago, enlisted December 26, 1863; WIA May 20, 1864, at Ware Bottom Church; WIA April 2, 1865, in assault on Fort Gregg*

Goodman, Thomas. Lockport, enlisted December 29, 1863*

Groesbeck, William D. Wood's Grove, enlisted February 22, 1865*

Gurrand, Francis L. Chicago, enlisted December 21, 1863; taken POW May 20, 1864, at Ware Bottom Church; paroled*

Hahn, Christian. Homer, enlisted August 13, 1861; transferred to Veteran Reserve Corps April 10, 1864

Hamilton, James G. Bremen, enlisted February 26, 1864; WIA October 13, 1864, at Darbytown Crossroads requiring leg amputation; DD June 3, 1865

Handy, Austin A. Shabbona, enlisted September 9, 1861; MO September 10, 1864

Hanson, Edward P. Orland, enlisted August 29, 1861; DD September 3, 1862

Hardenburgh, Henry M. Bremen, enlisted August 15, 1861; WIA August 16, 1864, while performing meritorious action on the field of battle at Second Deep Bottom for which he was awarded the Medal of Honor; received a promotion to 1st Lieutenant of a USCT regiment but was killed by a shell in front of Petersburg on August 28, 1864, before commissioning

Hawkins, Edwin. Chicago, enlisted September 4, 1861; DD June 2, 1862

Helm, Willis N. Shabbona, enlisted August 26, 1861; DS April 10, 1862, of typhoid fever

Howland, Adelbert. Genesee, enlisted August 14, 1861; KIA August 16, 1864, at Second Deep Bottom

Humphrey, Thomas. Orland, enlisted August 29, 1861; KIA May 20, 1864, at Ware Bottom Church

Inglehart, Charles. Bremen, enlisted February 27, 1864; wounded June 17, 1864, near Ware Bottom Church; WIA April 2, 1865, in assault on Fort Gregg; DD October 30, 1865, from wounds

Jenkins, Robert T. Coloma, enlisted August 14, 1861; DD June 27, 1862

Jenks, George W. Orland, enlisted August 19, 1861; DD January 16, 1863

Klumpp, William. Peoria, unknown enlistment date; mustered October 11, 1861; died at Morris Island S.C., October 2, 1863; not listed in Clark's history

Lambert, William J. Unknown, enlisted October 23, 1863; MO April,1864

Lewis, Andrew J. Amboy, enlisted August 9, 1861; DS July 4, 1863, on Folly Island S.C. of typhoid

Lewis, John. Amboy, enlisted August 19, 1861; DD December 21, 1862

Livingstone, Kilsyth. Chicago, enlisted March 12, 1864; deserted October 2, 1865

Love, James. Draft substitute, enlisted February 8, 1865*

Luscomb, Albert. Bellevue, MI, enlisted August 15, 1861; WIA and taken POW May 16, 1864, at Drewy's Bluff; died from wounds June 26, 1864, in Petersburg prison

Magee, William T. Macomb, enlisted September 5, 1861; detailed for majority of service as hospital cook*

May, William H. Genesee, enlisted August 28, 1861; KIA May 16, 1864, at Drewry's Bluff

McCracken, Solomon. Thornton, enlisted February 13, 1865*

McLaughlin, Dennis. Bremen, enlisted September 15, 1861; transferred to Company F October 1, 1861

McLaughlin, Patrick. Bremen, enlisted September 5, 1861; transferred to Company F October 1, 1861

Moran, John. Draft substitute, enlisted October 12, 1864; deserted August 16, 1865

Morrison, William. Draft substitute, enlisted January 23, 1865; deserted April 2, 1865

Muller, John B. Pekin, enlisted August 30, 1861; DD July 4, 1863

Murray, Levi. Berryman, enlisted March 15, 1865*

Norris, Henry D. Chicago, enlisted August 6, 1861; DD June 1, 1862

Nutting, Harrison. Champaign County, enlisted August 14, 1861; WIA June 2, 1864, near Ware Bottom Church; died of wounds November 27, 1864, at Fort Monroe

Ogle, Daniel. Sterling, enlisted February 13, 1864*

Onsoig, Frederick. Chicago, enlisted February 17, 1864*

Pacey, John. Brimfield, enlisted September 24, 1861; WIA and taken POW May 16, 1864, at Drewry's Bluff; died of wounds July 26, 1864, in Richmond prison

Pacey, Richard. Brimfield, enlisted September 24, 1861; transferred to Veteran Reserve Corps unknown date

Parrish, Harrison. New Genesee, enlisted August 14, 1861; WIA June 2, 1864, in skirmish near Ware Bottom Church; MO September 10, 1864

Parrish, Watson. New Genesee, enlisted August 14, 1861; WIA May 16, 1864, at Drewry's Bluff; MO September 10, 1864

Parrish, William C. New Genesee, enlisted August 14, 1861; DS November 29, 1861, of heart disease

Parkhurst, Henry S. Le Roy, PA, enlisted August 20, 1861; DD June 29, 1863

Parkinson, Isaac W. Wood's Grove, enlisted February 22, 1865*

Paul, Jacob. Draft substitute, enlisted May 23, 1864*

Pettijohn, James. Orland, enlisted February 23, 1864; WIA May 14, 1864, in skirmish near Drewry's Bluff; DD May 23, 1865, from wounds

Pitzer, Henry. Orland, enlisted March 12, 1864; WIA October 13, 1864, at Darbytown Crossroads*

Plimpton, Olin. Sterling, no enlistment date; mustered October 11, 1861; DD November 21, 1864; surprisingly not mentioned in Clark's history given that he is Homer Plimpton's brother; Homer Plimpton mentions him infrequently in his journal

Pond, Henry D. New Genesee, enlisted August 21, 1861; MO September 10, 1864

Potter, Isaac. Johnson County, KS, enlisted August 19, 1861; DS February 1, 1862, from unknown disease

Pratt, James. Orland, enlisted February 27, 1864; DS May 28, 1864, of scarlet fever

Price, William. Draft substitute, enlisted February 16, 1865; deserted August 14, 1865

Rayner, Sylvester. West Bend, WI, enlisted September 9, 1861; MO September 10, 1864

Reed, Stephen C. Palos, enlisted December 31, 1863*

Reeves, Joseph H. Palos, enlisted February 29, 1864; WIA May 16, 1864, at Drewry's Bluff requiring amputation of limb; DD March 18, 1865

Riche, William. Chicago, enlisted December 31, 1863; WIA October 13, 1864, at Darbytown Crossroads;*

Riley, John. Draft substitute, enlisted December 14, 1864*

Roberts, Charles H.L. New Genesee, enlisted August 28, 1861; wounded September,1863 at Fort Wagner; WIA May 20, 1864, at Ware Bottom Church; MO October 21, 1864

Root, Pilny F. Greenwich, MA, enlisted August 6, 1861; DS December 31, 1863, of chronic diarrhea in Hilton Head, SC

Ross, George. Homer, enlisted August 13, 1861; DD June 27, 1862

Rowley, Charles. Homer, enlisted September 10, 1861; DS February 20, 1862, of typhoid fever

Rumsey, Girard. Manteno, enlisted September 25, 1861; discharged for commission as 1st Lieutenant 5th USCT regiment August 15, 1864; veteran

Schermerhorn, Almon L. Worth, enlisted August 6, 1861; WIA May 16, 1864, at Drewry's Bluff; was unfit for duty with the company after wounding but served as an orderly*

Shipley, Thomas. Draftee, enlisted January 3, 1865; DD July 15, 1865

Smith, Robert W. Sterling, enlisted August 9, 1861; DD September 9, 1864

Spicer, Daniel W. Thornton, enlisted February 29, 1864; DS April 14, 1864, in Washington, D.C.

Turney, Daniel W. Orland, enlisted March 7, 1864; WIA August 16, 1864, at Second Deep Bottom*

Tyler, James. Lockport, enlisted August 13, 1861; DD June 2, 1862

Wadhams, Mortimer C. Joliet, enlisted October 14, 1862; DS February 19, 1865, of smallpox

Wagonrod, Henry. Bremen, enlisted September 12, 1861; DS November 10, 1863, on Folly Island

Walker, John W. Lockport, enlisted December 29, 1863; wounded October 7, 1864*

Warren, William. Lyons, IA, enlisted September 3, 1861; WIA May 16, 1864, at Drewry's Bluff; MO September 10, 1864

Wells, Matthew. Orland, enlisted March 9, 1864; WIA and taken POW May 16, 1864, at Drewry's Bluff; discharged May 30, 1865

Weston, Perry E. Shabbona, enlisted September 16, 1861; MO September 16, 1864

Williams, Henry W. Neoga, enlisted October 28, 1861; DD February 26, 1862

Williams, John. Draft substitute, enlisted February 7, 1865; deserted August 14, 1865

Williams, William C.W. Palos, enlisted February 29, 1864; DD May 19, 1865

Winder, Joseph K. Lamoille, enlisted August 29, 1861; KIA August 16, 1864, at Second Deep Run

Winder, Lorenzo. Lamoille, enlisted August 29, 1861; DD October 23, 1862

Wolfe, William. Wood's Grove, enlisted February 27, 1865*

Company H
Cook County—1860 Population: 144,954

Killed in Battle	5
Died of Wounds	5
Died in Prison	1

Lost Limbs	3
Wounded	29
Taken Prisoner	8
Number Originally Enlisted	77
Mustered Out at Expiration of Service	32
Re-Enlisted as Veterans	13
Recruits	55
Mustered Out With Regiment	51

Elected Officers

Captain: Chauncey Williams
First Lieutenant: Charles J. Wilder
Second Lieutenant: George Searing

Company H began to be formed in 1861, but then many of the members left for other regiments when Thomas Osborn's first attempt to raise a regiment was denied. When the 39th did eventually form, all the other companies were accounted for, except H who had too few members to muster. When men from the 39th were sent to Illinois to recruit in the spring of 1862, however, a group of men began to be recruited and found their way to Camp Butler in Chicago as a "lost company." When Chauncey Williams, from Company I, arrived in Chicago to recruit in June, he was well liked and told the men he would deliver them to the regiment—an exciting promise given the regiment was currently at Harrison's Landing, VA seemingly to march on Richmond. Williams was elected as their Captain, and the final company of the 39th mustered into service on July 11, 1862, arriving to the regiment on the 24th.

Williams, Chauncey. Old Town, Captain, commissioned July 11, 1862; KIA August 16, 1864, leading the charge on the enemy works at Deep Bottom

Downs, Williams. Downs, Captain, enlisted April 1, 1862, and made Sergeant; WIA August 16, 1864, at Second Deep Bottom; promoted 1st Lieutenant October 13, 1864; Captain March 31, 1865*

Wilder, Charles J. Chicago, First Lieutenant commissioned March 22, 1862; KIA October 13, 1864, at Darbytown Crossroads; buried under the tree he fell near

Harrison, William H. Kingston Mines, First Lieutenant, enlisted February 16, 1862, and made Sergeant; promoted 1st Lieutenant March 31, 1865*

Searing, George. Chicago, Second Lieutenant, commissioned July 10, 1862; resigned September 10, 1864

Harrington, Walter. Pecatonica, First Sergeant, enlisted February 1, 1862, and made 1st Sergeant; WIA May 20, 1864, at Ware Bottom Church; WIA August 16, 1864, at Second Deep Bottom; DD April 4, 1865, from wounds

Mitchell, William C. Wilmington, Sergeant, enlisted April 5, 1862, and made Sergeant; MO May 9, 1865

Smith, James J. Pecatonica, Sergeant, enlisted March 17, 1862, and made Sergeant; MO March 23, 1865

Wilson, Elias H. Santa Anna, Sergeant, enlisted April 14, 1862, and made Corporal; promoted Sergeant January 1, 1865; MO May 9, 1865

Wilkins, Zephaniah M. Le Roy, Sergeant, enlisted April 14, 1862, and made Corporal, WIA August 16, 1864, at Second Deep Bottom; promoted Sergeant January, 1865; MO May 9, 1865

Gairon, Ulmer. Kingston Mines, enlisted February 27, 1862; promoted Corporal November 4, 1864; Sergeant April 2, 1865*

Brown, Ebenezer. Downs, Sergeant, enlisted March 1, 1862; promoted Corporal April 16, 1865; Sergeant June 20, 1865*

Brown, John J. Downs, Sergeant, enlisted March 1, 1862; promoted Corporal May 16, 1865; Sergeant June 20, 1865*

Jared, Thomas. Draft substitute, Sergeant enlisted March 3, 1865; promoted Corporal May 10, 1865; Sergeant September 1, 1865*

Potts, Frederick. Randolph, Sergeant, enlisted March 1, 1862; promoted Corporal January 13, 1865; Sergeant March 20, 1865*

Wilson, John S. Santa Anna, Sergeant, enlisted August 20, 1861; transferred from Company I September 1, 1862; promoted Corporal May 1, 1863; DD as Sergeant— promotion date unknown—July 7, 1865

Mendenhall, Absalom. Wilmington, Corporal, enlisted March 15, 1862, and made Corporal; WIA August 16, 1864, at Second Deep Bottom; MO April 14, 1865

Cain, William B. Wilmington, enlisted March 13, 1862, and made Corporal; reduced to ranks May 1, 1863; MO March 23, 1865

Berry, Charles. Kingston Mines, Corporal, enlisted February 1, 1862, and made Corporal; WIA May 20, 1864, at Ware Bottom Church; died June 17, 1864, from wounds; veteran

Crotts, Silas. Le Roy, Corporal, enlisted February 13, 1862, and made Corporal; killed September 23, 1863, at Fort Gregg S.C.

Edminston, Miles B. Wapella, Corporal, enlisted February 13, 1862, and made Corporal; DD October 9, 1862

Whittaker, Alvin. Le Roy, Corporal, enlisted February 13, 1862, and made Corporal; WIA and taken POW May 16, 1864, at Drewry's Bluff; paroled; MO July 15, 1865

Lewis, Jacob L. Le Roy, Corporal, enlisted May 10, 1862, and made Corporal; WIA October 13, 1864, at Darbytown Crossroads; MO March 23, 1865

McNally, John. Le Roy, Corporal, enlisted February 6, 1861; promoted Corporal July 24, 1862; reduced to ranks November 3, 1862; transferred to 4th U.S. Artillery December 5, 1862

Armstrong, James. Unknown, Corporal, enlisted July 14, 1862, and made Corporal, reduced to ranks May 19, 1863; wounded August 15, 1863, at Fort Wagner requiring amputation of foot; DD November 3, 1864, for wounds

Boyd, Hiram C. Old Town, Corporal, enlisted February 12, 1862; promoted Corporal March 20, 1863; WIA June 2, 1864, near Ware Bottom Church; MO March 3, 1865

Twigger, George. Chicago, Corporal, enlisted March 25, 1862; promoted Corporal unknown date—likely at enlistment*

Calbeck, William. Draft substitute, Corporal, enlisted February 28, 1865; promoted May 10, 1865*

Lucas, Henry. Randolph, Corporal, enlisted March 1, 1862; WIA October 13, 1864, at Darbytown Crossroads; promoted Corporal May 10, 1865; DD June 24, 1865

Campbell, Alexander. Draft substitute, Corporal, enlisted March 3, 1865; promoted Corporal May 14, 1865*

Valentine, William. Draft substitute, enlisted March 4, 1865; promoted Corporal June 28, 1865*

Gardner, Mahlon. Le Roy, Corporal, enlisted September 11, 1861; transferred from Company I August 1, 1862; promoted Corporal September 1, 1865*

Lakey, James A. Draft substitute, Corporal, enlisted March 3, 1865; promoted Corporal September 1, 1865*

Privates

Aldridge, Lawson. Draft substitute, enlisted February 22, 1865*

Allahan, William S. Polo, enlisted February 1, 1862; DD March 3, 1863

Allen, John W. Chicago, enlisted April 10, 1862; deserted October 30, 1862

Bartlett, Asher. Draft substitute, enlisted March 4, 1865; DD November 22, 1865

Beachy, Josiah F. Kingston Mines, enlisted February 1, 1862; WIA June 2, 1864, near Ware Bottom Church requiring arm amputation; MO March 3, 1865

Birch, William. Ashmore, enlisted February 2, 1862; WIA June 2, 1862, near Ware Bottom Church; WIA April 2, 1865, in assault on Fort Gregg; MO June 2, 1865

Brennan, Thomas S. Chicago, enlisted March 29, 1864; WIA May 20, 1864; died June 22, 1864, from wounds

Breckenberg, Charles. Draft substitute, enlisted March 2, 1865*

Brightman, William. Unknown, enlisted March 1, 1862; DS December 19, 1863, in St Augustine, FL hospital

Carr, Henry. Le Roy, enlisted February 13, 1862; transferred to Company I August 1, 1862

Casey, Edward. Chicago, enlisted February 28, 1862; taken POW October 13, 1864; paroled and exchanged*

Cherry, Luke. Chicago, enlisted February 1, 1862; WIA and taken POW August 16, 1864, at Second Deep Bottom; released at end of war*

Clayton, Francis. Draft substitute, enlisted March 3, 1865*

Clifford, George A. Chicago, enlisted February 4, 1864; discharged July 7, 1864

Cochlin, David. Fairbury, enlisted February 18, 1862; WIA August 16, 1864, at Second Deep Bottom; died August 20, 1864, from wounds; veteran

Conlin, Owen. Chicago, enlisted March 24, 1864*

Corrigan, William. Mt. Pleasant, enlisted June 21, 1862; deserted August 3, 1865

Davis, Isaac T. Monticello, enlisted June 28, 1862; deserted October 13, 1863

Derrick, Albert. Padua, enlisted February 12, 1864; WIA October 13, 1864, at Darbytown Crossroads; DD July 25, 1865

Dickison, James. Pittsfield, enlisted April 5, 1862; MO May 9, 1865

Dickson, John. Point, enlisted April 8, 1864*

Donahue, Patrick. Draft substitute, enlisted April 8, 1864*

Donald, George. Draft substitute, enlisted February 24, 1865, under the name of John O'Brien to elude his guardians and get into the service*

Eastman, James P. Pecatonica, enlisted May 1, 1862; wounded June 7, 1864; MO May 9, 1865

Everett, Eli J. Le Roy, enlisted February 6, 1862; transferred to Company I August 1, 1862

Gardner, John W. Delta, enlisted September 11, 1861; transferred from Company F August 1, 1862; MO September 10, 1864

Goff, James O. Pecatonica, enlisted March 17, 1862; MO March 25, 1865

Hager, James D.B. Pecatonica, enlisted March 18, 1862; MO March 23, 1865

Hagins, Daniel. Springfield, enlisted August 14, 1862; WIA May 20, 1864, at Ware Bottom Church; MO June 20, 1865

Hornberger, George. Vermillion, enlisted June 21, 1862; WIA April 2, 1865, in assault on Fort Gregg; MO June 20, 1865; not listed in adjutant's report

Howell, William. Cerro Gordo, enlisted June 28, 1862; KIA August 16, 1864, at Second Deep Bottom

Johnson, William. Hitesville, enlisted June 16, 1862; WIA August 16, 1864, at Second Deep Bottom; MO June 20, 1865

Kautz, George. Lemont, enlisted March 31, 1865*

Kimbler, Charles W. Downs, enlisted May 28, 1862; WIA and taken POW August 16, 1864, at Second Deep Bottom; paroled and exchanged; MO June 28, 1865

King, George B. Le Roy, enlisted March 4, 1862; DS August 7, 1863, of disease at Hilton Head

Kohn, John. Draft substitute, enlisted March 3, 1865*

Lace, Philip M. Pontiac, enlisted January 5, 1864; promoted Principal Musician (see band)

Lattimer, Louis. Draft substitute, enlisted February 15, 1865; DD May 27, 1865

Lawrence, Daniel W. Draft substitute, enlisted March 1, 1865*

Lewis, Lorenzo. Clark, enlisted June 26, 1862; MO June 20, 1865

Maloney, Richard. Wilmington, enlisted March 13, 1862; MO March 23, 1865

Martin, Daniel J.J. Santa Anna, enlisted June 13, 1862; MO June 20, 1865

McGinnis, William G. Kingston Mines, enlisted February 1, 1862; deserted July 4, 1862

Morgan, E.A. Paris, enlisted June 28, 1862; DS April 1, 1865, cause unknown

Morley, William R. Santa Anna, enlisted April 13, 1862; MO May 9, 1865

Morris, William M. Draft substitute, enlisted February 13, 1865; MO December 6, 1865

Mott, William J. Chicago, enlisted March 1, 1862; transferred to the U.S. Signal Corps April 23, 1863

Needham, Washington. Draftee, Spring Point, enlisted March 31, 1865*

Newport, Henry. Paris, enlisted June 19, 1862; WIA August 16, 1864, at Second Deep Bottom; MO June 20, 1865

O'Harra, James. Springfield, enlisted April 5, 1862; DD November 1, 1862

Phillips, Gideon. Chicago, enlisted February 12, 1864; KIA August 16, 1864, at Second Deep Bottom

Pickens, Samuel. Paris, enlisted June 17, 1862; transferred to 4th U.S. Artillery November 4, 1862

Porter, James H. Bloomington, enlisted March 16, 1862; wounded November 1, 1863, on Morris Island; deserted August 3, 1865

Porter, John S. Le Roy, enlisted March, 1862; transferred to Company C April 1, 1863

Potts, Edward. Randolph, enlisted March 31, 1862; MO May 9, 1865

Preeler, Frank J. Chicago, enlisted February 1, 1862; WIA and taken POW October 13, 1864, at Darbytown Crossroads; leg amputated; paroled and exchanged; MO October 17, 1865, for disability

Reese, Amos B. Le Roy, enlisted February 24, 1862; wounded May 23, 1864, near Hatcher's Run; died from wounds June 22, 1864

Robinson, Hiram. Fairbury, enlisted March 29, 1862; wounded September 7, 1864, near Petersburg; MO May 9, 1865

Rose, Henry C. Pittsfield, enlisted April 5, 1862; taken POW January 5, 1863; died September 27, 1864, at Andersonville

Rush, James. Springfield, enlisted April 5, 1862; DS August 8, 1862, from disease

Russell, Edward. Chicago, enlisted April 5, 1862; transferred to 4th U.S. Artillery November 24, 1862

Schaefer, Frank. Chicago, enlisted March 31, 1864; taken POW October 2, 1864; no known information post captured and assumed to have died in prison

Seymour, William H. Thornton, enlisted March 12, 1862; deserted May 12, 1863

Shackley, Joseph. Le Roy, enlisted April 7, 1862; MO May 9, 1865

Shoudorf, Ferdinand. Draft substitute, enlisted February 27, 1865; deserted June 22, 1865

Smith, Isaac. Bloomington, enlisted February 25, 1864; WIA May 20, 1864, at Ware Bottom Church; WIA August 16, 1864, at Second Deep Bottom; transferred to Veteran Reserve Corps April 17, 1865

Smith, William. Bloomington, enlisted February 25, 1864; DS September, 1864 of disease

Spong, Augustus. Kingston Mines, enlisted February 27, 1862; DD May 27, 1863

Spong, John. Kingston Mines, enlisted February 27, 1862; discharged June 26, 1865; veteran

Sweiger, Jacob. Draft substitute, enlisted February 25, 1865*

Taylor, John. Springfield, enlisted February 1, 1862; MO June 20, 1865

Tovera, Thomas, J. Bloomington, enlisted July 1, 1862; MO June 20, 1865

Trumble, George. Le Roy, enlisted March 1, 1862; WIA October 13, 1864, at Darbytown Crossroads and died shortly after

VanSchoick, John. Le Roy, enlisted April 8, 1862; transferred to Company I September, 1862

Wardram, Charles A. Chicago, enlisted March 4, 1862; WIA August 16, 1864, at Second Deep Bottom; MO March 23, 1865

Wardrum, R.S.C. Chicago, enlisted March 4, 1862; MO March 23, 1865

Weston, James D. Draft substitute, enlisted March 4, 1865*

Wyatt, Edward. Springfield, enlisted April 8, 1862; MO July 13, 1865

Company I
DeWitt County—1860 Population: 10,820
Boone County: 11,678

Killed in Battle	9
Died of Wounds	7
Died in Prison	3
Lost Limbs	3
Wounded	48
Taken Prisoner	16
Number Originally Enlisted	85
Mustered Out at Expiration of Service	23
Re-Enlisted as Veterans	41
Recruits	54
Mustered Out With Regiment	41

Elected Officers
Captain: Hiram M. Phillips
First Lieutenant: Emory L. Waller
Second Lieutenant: Albert M. Fellows

Company I was recruited in September of 1861 by Hiram Phillips, a Mexican American War veteran, of Le Roy, Illinois—a town of 650 people in the central portion of the state. At 39 years of age, Phillips would have easily qualified as the "old man" in the regiment. The majority of the men were from Le Roy and nearby Santa Anna Township, but also included men from nearby areas surrounding Champaign and Bloomington, as well as Boone County in the most northern reach of the state.

Phillips, Hiram M. Le Roy, Captain, commissioned September 6, 1861; WIA and taken POW May 16, 1864, at Drewry's Bluff; sent to Libby Prison in Richmond and paroled after 3 months; MO December 5, 1864, by reason of disability

Gillmore, Samuel. Champaign, Captain, enlisted October 16, 1861, and made

Corporal shortly after; promoted Sergeant June 27, 1862; WIA May 16, 1864, at Drewry's Bluff; promoted 2nd Lieutenant June 2, 1864; promoted 1st Lieutenant September 5, 1864, vice Lemon's death; promoted Captain August 20, 1864, vice Phillips mustering out; remained in service on various high ranking staffs in Virginia until March 20, 1866

Waller, Emory L. Santa Anna, First Lieutenant, commissioned September 6, 1861; resigned January 4, 1862

Lemon, James D. Santa Anna, First Lieutenant, enlisted September 4, 1861, and made Sergeant; promoted 1st Lieutenant June 14, 1862; WIA August 16, 1864, at Second Deep Bottom; died of wounds August 20, 1864

Neal, Joseph W. Santa Anna, First Lieutenant, enlisted September 4, 1861, and made Corporal; WIA June 16, 1864; promoted 1st Sergeant September 5, 1864; promoted 1st Lieutenant December 6, 1864; WIA April 2, 1865, in assault on Fort Gregg requiring amputation of arm; served on various staffs in time after losing arm until end of service*

Fellows, Albert M. Santa Anna, Second Lieutenant, commissioned September 6, 1861; KIA June 2, 1864, in skirmish near Ware Bottom Church

Robinson, Noah L. Le Roy, First Sergeant, enlisted September 4, 1861, and made Corporal; promoted 1st Sergeant February 7, 1865; and 2nd Lieutenant October 4, 1865, but unable to muster; MO as 1st Sergeant*

Parks, L.H. Le Roy, First Sergeant, enlisted September 4, 1861, and made 1st Sergeant; reduced to ranks June 27, 1862; MO September 10, 1864

Nelson, O.P. Le Roy, Sergeant, enlisted September 14, 1861, and made Sergeant; taken POW May 26, 1862; paroled and exchanged; taken POW again May 16, 1864, at Drewry's Bluff; died October 24, 1864, at Andersonville

McMurray, William C. Santa Anna, enlisted September 4, 1861, and made Sergeant; taken POW May 16, 1864, at Drewry's Bluff; paroled and exchanged; MO March 16, 1865

Creager, James B. Le Roy, Sergeant, enlisted October 6, 1861; promoted Sergeant June 27, 1862; WIA October 13, 1864, at Darbytown Crossroads; DD July 8, 1865, from wounds

McKinney, Charles A. Le Roy, Sergeant, enlisted October 13, 1861; promoted Corporal January 1, 1863; WIA May 16, 1864, at Drewry's Bluff; WIA April 2, 1865, in assault on Fort Gregg; promoted Sergeant August 1, 1865; discharged October 1, 1865

Hoover, Columbus. Santa Anna, Sergeant, enlisted September 21, 1861; promoted Corporal May 11, 1862; Sergeant October 10, 1865*

Johnson, Thomas J. Santa Anna, Sergeant enlisted September 4, 1861, and made Corporal; promoted Sergeant January 1, 1865*

Wetzell, Michael. Santa Anna, Sergeant, enlisted September 4, 1861; promoted Corporal March 1, 1863; Sergeant February 7, 1865; WIA April 2, 1865, in assault on Fort Gregg requiring amputation of arm; DD June 17, 1865, for wounds

Brennan, James. Santa Anna, Sergeant, enlisted September 4, 1861; promoted Corporal September 1, 1864; Sergeant April 2, 1865*

Spencer, William J. Le Roy, Sergeant, enlisted September 22, 1861; wounded June 17, 1864; promoted Corporal September 18, 1864; promoted Sergeant August 1, 1865*

Tateburg, Ernest W. Le Roy, enlisted September 18, 1861; promoted Corporal May 16, 1865; Sergeant October 28, 1865

Kimbler, Franklin. Le Roy, Corporal, enlisted September 4, 1861, and made Corporal; reduced to ranks March 6, 1862; MO September 11, 1864

Bean, John A. Santa Anna, Corporal, enlisted September 4, 1861, and made Corporal; reduced to ranks March 6, 1862; KIA October 27, 1864, in skirmish near Darbytown Crossroads

Keith, E.H. Le Roy, Corporal, enlisted September 4, 1861, and made Corporal; transferred and promoted Hospital Steward in the regular army September 2, 1862

Lyon, William W. Le Roy, Corporal, enlisted September 4, 1861, and made Corporal; DD July 7, 1862

Clearwater, C.W. Santa Anna, Corporal, enlisted September 4, 1861, and made Corporal; DD July 4, 1863

Riddle, George. Le Roy, enlisted September 17, 1861; promoted Corporal June 27, 1862; MO September 17, 1864

Weedman, John W. Mount Pleasant, Corporal, enlisted September 4, 1861; promoted June 27, 1862; taken POW May 16, 1864, at Drewry's Bluff; died November 15, 1864, at Andersonville

Richards, Dudley. Le Roy, Corporal, enlisted October 6, 1861; promoted March 1, 1863; KIA August 16, 1864, at Second Deep Run

Tomlinson, Andrew J. Le Roy, Corporal, enlisted September 4, 1861; promoted March 1, 1863; WIA August 16, 1864, at Second Deep Bottom requiring amputation of leg; died of wounds September 14, 1864

Coss, Alexander. Le Roy, Corporal, enlisted September 23, 1861; promoted Corporal May 1, 1864; WIA May 16, 1864, at Drewry's Bluff; DD August 5, 1865, from wounds

Carr, James. Le Roy, Corporal, enlisted September 4, 1861; promoted Corporal September 5, 1864*

Johnson, Joshua H. Le Roy, Corporal, enlisted September 4, 1861; wounded May 16, 1864, at Drewry's Bluff; promoted Corporal April 2, 1865*

Davis, James M. Le Roy, Corporal, enlisted February 22, 1864; WIA October 13, 1864, at Darbytown Crossroads; promoted Corporal April 4, 1865*

Shinkle, Thomas W. Le Roy, Corporal, enlisted September 4, 1861; promoted June 1, 1864; wounded August 28, 1864; KIA April 2, 1865, in assault on Fort Gregg

Marcellious, Jacob S. Delta, Corporal, enlisted September 14, 1861; WIA October 13, 1864, at Darbytown Crossroads; promoted Corporal August 1, 1865

Weedman, Norman A. Mount Pleasant, Corporal, enlisted February 17, 1864; promoted August 1, 1865*

Charleston, Richard C. Le Roy, Corporal, enlisted October 13, 1861; taken POW May 26, 1862, at Strasburg, VA; paroled and exchanged; promoted Corporal October 9, 1865*

Grooms, Irwin. Le Roy, Corporal, enlisted September 17, 1861; promoted Corporal October 24, 1865*

Dunlap, Lewis. Cheney's Grove, Corporal, enlisted September 4, 1861; promoted Corporal October 27, 1865*

Woodard, Edward. Santa Anna, Corporal, enlisted October 2, 1861; WIA August 16, 1864, at Second Deep Run; promoted Corporal, unknown date in 1865*

Privates

Bailey, David. Le Roy, enlisted September 4, 1861; KIA April 2, 1865, in assault on Fort Gregg

Bailey, Perry. Le Roy, enlisted September 4, 1861; DD July 4, 1863

Baker, Israel. Le Roy, enlisted September 18, 1861; drowned May 30, 1863, on Folly Island

Baker, James W. Le Roy, enlisted February 28, 1864; WIA May 16, 1864, at Drewry's Bluff*

Bean, B.L. Le Roy, enlisted September 4, 1861; DD November 1, 1862

Beard, John P.S. Le Roy, enlisted February 13, 1864; WIA June 2, 1864, near Ware Bottom Church; DS February 1, 1865, of disease

Berry, John. Santa Anna, enlisted September 4, 1861; WIA May 16, 1864, at Drewry's Bluff; MO October 18, 1864

Bishop, Reese. Le Roy, enlisted October 18, 1861; promoted Sergeant Major and transferred to regimental staff July 15, 1862 (see Field and Staff Officers)

Blandin, John K. Santa Anna, enlisted February 16, 1864; WIA April 2, 1865, in assault on Fort Gregg; discharged May 31, 1865

Bowen, James R. Champaign, enlisted October 3, 1861; taken POW May 20, 1864, at Ware Bottom Church; no further information

Brown, John F. McLean County, enlisted September 4, 1861; wounded June 16, 1864; MO September 10, 1864

Canady, Calvin. Le Roy, enlisted February 26, 1864*

Canady, George W. Le Roy, enlisted February 26, 1864*

Carr, Henry. Le Roy, enlisted October 13, 1862*

Clark, Lake. Santa Anna, enlisted September 14, 1861; DD June 28, 1862

Clark, Marion. Champaign, enlisted October 16, 1861; DD May 31, 1862

Collins, James. New York, NY, enlisted August 28, 1861*

Craig, John. Le Roy, enlisted October 18, 1861; DS November 22, 1863, of disease on Folly Island

Craig, L.E.W. Delta, enlisted September 4, 1861; taken POW May 20, 1862, at Strasburg, VA; DD June 28, 1862

Don Carlos, Thomas. Le Roy, enlisted December 28, 1863; DD September 1, 1864

Draper, Abraham. Mahomet, enlisted September 14, 1861; WIA October 13, 1864, at Darbytown Crossroads; died from wounds October 15, 1864; veteran

Everett, Eli J. Le Roy, enlisted February 6, 1862; WIA May 16, 1864*

Everett, Thomas. Le Roy, enlisted October 1, 1861; MO October 8, 1864

Ford, Newton J. Santa Anna, enlisted September 9, 1861; WIA and taken POW May 16, 1864, at Drewry's Bluff; died October 15, 1864, at Andersonville

Gardner, John W. Delta, enlisted September 17, 1861; transferred to Company H August 1, 1862

Gardner, Mahlon. Le Roy, enlisted September 17, 1861; transferred to Company H August 1, 1862

Gesford, William. Santa Anna, enlisted September 19, 1861; DD July 18, 1862

Gibbs, Simeon. Le Roy, enlisted October 4, 1861; DD October 14, 1862

Goltra, Joseph W. Lincoln, enlisted October 19, 1861; transferred to Veteran Reserve Corps November 15, 1863

Goodin, Hiram. DeWitt, enlisted February 4, 1861; WIA May 16, 1864, at Drewry's Bluff; MO July 22, 1864

Green, Martin R. Le Roy, enlisted January 1, 1864; deserted September 24, 1864

Griffith, Daniel. Bloomington, enlisted November 10, 1862; WIA August 16, 1864, at Drewry's Bluff; MO November 10, 1865

Grooms, John W. Le Roy, enlisted September 4, 1861; taken POW May 26, 1862, at Strasburg, VA; paroled and exchanged*

Grooms, Martin V. Le Roy, enlisted September 22, 1861; taken POW May 26, 1862, at Strasburg, VA; paroled and exchanged; DD July 4, 1863

Haggard, Lemuel J. Bloomington, unknown enlistment date; mustered February 29, 1864; not listed in Clark history*

Halloway, Philip M. Santa Anna, enlisted September 4, 1861; MO September 10, 1864

Hallowell, John E.W. Le Roy, enlisted September 18, 1861; taken POW May 16, 1864, at Drewry's Bluff; DD June 29, 1865

Hallowell, Robert C. Le Roy, enlisted September 18, 1861; promoted Principal Musician September 1, 1863*

Hancock, Erastus B. Randolph, enlisted March 1, 1864; WIA April 2, 1865, in assault on Fort Gregg; MO June 15, 1865, for wound

Hand, John M. Santa Anna, enlisted September 20, 1861; MO September 20, 1864

Hashman, Lewis. Springfield, enlisted December 30, 1862; WIA May 20, 1864, at Ware Bottom Church; DD June 15, 1865, from wounds

Hirst, James. Champaign, enlisted October 2, 1861; DD July 4, 1863, for disability originating from fording the icy Potomac on January 4, 1862

Hoover, John. Santa Anna, enlisted September 4, 1861; wounded August 18, 1863, at Fort Wagner; taken POW May 16, 1864, at Drewry's Bluff; presumed died in prison

Hoover, Theodore. Santa Anna, enlisted February 18, 1864; WIA May 16, 1864, at Drewry's Bluff; MO June 15, 1865

Hurley, Lewis. Santa Anna, enlisted September 4, 1861; KIA May 16, 1864, at Drewry's Bluff; veteran

Hurst, Edward. Santa Anna, enlisted September 6, 1861; KIA August 16, 1864, at Second Deep Bottom

Igsa, Henry. Le Roy, enlisted September 24, 1861; WIA May 16, 1864, at Drewry's Bluff; WIA October 7, 1864*

Jackson, James. Bloomington, enlisted February 12, 1864*

Johnson, Abiram B. Le Roy, enlisted September 12, 1861; promoted Commissary Sergeant January 24, 1862 (see Field and Staff Officers)

Johnson, George W.B. Empire, enlisted January 1, 1864; WIA October 13, 1864, at Darbytown Crossroads; discharged May 2, 1865

Johnson, Joel B. Santa Anna, enlisted March 10, 1864; WIA May 16, 1864, at Drewry's Bluff; DD June 2, 1864

Johnson, John S. Santa Anna, enlisted September 4, 1861; DD July 1, 1862

Kimbler, Benjamin E. Le Roy, enlisted September 18, 1861; DD September 12, 1862

Kimbler, William. Le Roy, enlisted September 4, 1861; MO September 13, 1864

Kirby, John W. Santa Anna, enlisted September 4, 1861; WIA May 20, 1864, at Ware Bottom Church; DD April 13, 1865, from wounds

Lamb, Matthew W. Le Roy, enlisted October 13, 1861; WIA May 20, 1864, at Ware Bottom Church; died from wounds October 29, 1864; veteran

Lemon, Richard A. Le Roy, enlisted February 26, 1864; discharged June 1, 1864

Littleton, Van Buren. Bloomington, enlisted September 24, 1864; discharged June 21, 1865

Littleton, William S. Mahomet, enlisted September 4, 1861; DS February 25, 1862, of disease

Lonebarger, George. Le Roy, enlisted September 4, 1861; WIA May 16, 1864, at Drewry's Bluff*

Lyon, Martin V. Le Roy, enlisted September 4, 1861; DS January 18, 1862, of disease

Lysle, John. Le Roy, enlisted September 20, 1861; transferred to Veteran Reserve Corps; MO September 20, 1864

Marcellious, John J. Delta, enlisted February 15, 1864; DD May 2, 1864

McCoy, Orlando. Le Roy, enlisted February 23, 1864*

McGrade, James. McLean County, enlisted October 8, 1861; MO October 8, 1864

Miller, Albert. Le Roy, enlisted February 16, 1864; taken POW May 16, 1864, at Drewry's Bluff*

Neal, Amos. Santa Anna, enlisted February 28, 1864; discharged June 22, 1865

Neal, Henry T. Le Roy, enlisted September 14, 1861; DD June 28, 1862

Neal, Silas. Le Roy, enlisted September 4, 1861*

Parks, Benjamin F. Le Roy, enlisted September 4, 1861; WIA August 16, 1864, at Second Deep Bottom; MO October 8, 1864

Patton, Francis M. Empire, enlisted February 10, 1864; wounded in trenches before Petersburg August 30, 1864*

Perry, Arthur. Waukegan, enlisted February 10, 1864; DD August 20, 1864

Poff, Henry M. Santa Anna, enlisted September 21, 1861; DD July 4, 1863

Pratt, T.J. Le Roy, enlisted February 23, 1864*

Prey, Nelson. Le Roy, enlisted September 4, 1861; DD April 30, 1863; not listed in adjutant's report

Randolph, Valentine C. Lincoln, enlisted September 16, 1861; MO September 17, 1864

Rapp, John W. Le Roy, enlisted September 4, 1861; killed August 29, 1864, in trenches before Petersburg; veteran; listed as Popp in adjutant's report

Reams, Adam. Le Roy, enlisted September 25, 1861; wounded June 18, 1864, near Ware Bottom Church*

Reams, Samuel. Le Roy, enlisted September 25, 1861; taken POW May 16, 1864, at Drewry's Bluff; paroled and exchanged*

Robertson, George P. Santa Anna, enlisted September 4, 1861; DD November 3, 1863

Rowley, James. Le Roy, enlisted September 14, 1861; DS October 11, 1864, in Newbern N.C. hospital

Rue, John A. Mount Pleasant, enlisted March 8, 1864; WIA August 16, 1864, at Second Deep Run; died of wounds October 18, 1864

Runyan, George W. Le Roy, enlisted October 6, 1861; DD July 4, 1863

Sproul, William. Le Roy, enlisted September 4, 1861; taken POW June,1862; paroled and exchanged; discharged March 22, 1865

Thomas, James M. Franklin County, enlisted September 4, 1861; MO September 4, 1864

Van Winkle, Willitt. Enfield, enlisted February 16, 1864; WIA October 13, 1864, at Darbytown Crossroads; discharged May 27, 1865

Vanschoyck, John. Le Roy, enlisted April 7, 1862; taken POW May 16, 1864, at Drewry's Bluff; discharged May 7, 1865

Veta, Osta. Bloomington, enlisted November 10, 1862; sent from Folly Island to Beaufort S.C. and failed to report, supposed to have drownded

Wagoner, William. Le Roy, enlisted January 1, 1864; WIA and taken POW May 16, 1864, at Drewry's Bluff; discharged July 3, 1865

Weedman, Jacob F. Santa Anna, enlisted February 11, 1864; discharged June 2, 1865

Weedman, John B. Santa Anna, enlisted September 26, 1861; MO September 28, 1864

West, George W. Draftee, Hunter, enlisted March 23, 1865; DD July 15, 1865

Westfall, Rueben. Le Roy, enlisted February 13, 1864; WIA April 2, 1865, in assault on Fort Gregg; DD June 10, 1865, for wounds

White, William D. Santa Anna, enlisted September 4, 1861; WIA May 16, 1864, at Drewry's Bluff; DD June 16, 1865, for wounds

Wilhoite, Willis F. Le Roy, enlisted October 2, 1861; WIA May 16, 1864, at Drewry's Bluff; DD May 4, 1865, for wounds

Wilson, John S. Le Roy, enlisted October 20, 1861; transferred to Company H August 1, 1862

Wilson, William S. Delta, enlisted September 4, 1861; DD September 12, 1864

Woodward, William B. Bloomington, enlisted February 12, 1864; WIA May 16, 1864, at Drewry's Bluff; WIA October 13, 1864, at Darbytown Crossroads*

Wren, Asa. Le Roy, enlisted February 13, 1864; discharged July 20, 1865

Company K
LaSalle County—1860 Population: 48,332
McLean County: 28,772
Cook County: 144,954

Killed in Battle	7*
Died of Wounds	6
Died in Prison	2*
Lost Limbs	2
Wounded	54
Taken Prisoner	10
Number Originally Enlisted	80
Mustered Out at Expiration of Service	14
Re-Enlisted as Veterans	37
Recruits	56
Mustered Out With Regiment	14

The author's great-great-great-great uncle Cicero Barber was killed at the battle of Ware Bottom Church, and Cicero's brother Alden was wounded at Drewry's Bluff, and died in a Confederate prison.

Elected Officers
Captain: Joseph Woodruff
First Lieutenant: Frank B. Marshall
Second Lieutenant: Donald A. Nicholson

Company K was recruited by Frank Marshall, who traveled from Chicago to Marseilles, Illinois—a town of less than 700, just down the road from Ottawa which had hosted one of the Lincoln-Douglas debates. Marshall met with Joseph Woodruff, a Marseilles native and Mexican American War veteran. Marshall told Woodruff, and others, that they could elect their own officers if they could raise a company to join the 39th Illinois. A good deal of the original men came from Marseilles and surrounding small towns and townships in the area 60–70 miles southwest of Chicago. Upon arriving in Chicago, a good deal of men from Bloomington and McLean County who had originally attempted to join Company H were assigned to K, as well as a handful of men from Cook County. The divide of hometown, and initial company, loyalties initially divided the company, but was quickly overcome. The men were primarily farmers, as well as some from the Marseilles area who would have performed work associated with moving goods on the river.

Woodruff, Joseph. Marseilles, commissioned August 24, 1861; mortally wounded by a shell fragment near Fort Gregg, SC September 23, 1863, and died the same day

Wheeler, Andrew W. Marseilles, Captain, enlisted August 14, 1861, and made 1st Sergeant; commissioned 2nd Lieutenant March 15, 1862; promoted 1st Lieutenant June 14, 1862, vice Nicholson resignation; promoted Captain September 23, 1863, vice Woodruff's death; WIA October 13, 1864, at Darbytown Crossroads; MO October 24, 1864

Myers, Ebanis C. Bloomington, Captain, enlisted August 14, 1861, and made Sergeant; promoted 1st Sergeant June 14, 1862; commissioned 1st Lieutenant October 24, 1864; promoted Captain December 7, 1864, vice Wheeler mustering out*

Belcher, Oscar S. Bloomington, First Lieutenant, commissioned August 20, 1861; resigned May 11, 1862; served 3 months as a Corporal in 8th IL Infantry before his time in the 39th; enlisted in the 16th Illinois Cavalry in May 1863 serving until August of 1865

Nicholson, Donald A. Marseilles, First Lieutenant, commissioned 2nd Lieutenant fall of 1861; promoted 1st Lieutenant March 15, 1862; resigned June 14, 1862, due to rheumatism resulting from fording the frozen Potomac on January 4, 1862

Butterfield, Marion L. Marseilles, First Lieutenant, enlisted August 17, 1861, and made Sergeant; commissioned 2nd Lieutenant June 14, 1862; promoted 1st Lieutenant September 23, 1863; WIA August 16, 1864, at Second Deep Run; MO December 7, 1864

Smouse, Daniel. Bloomington, First Lieutenant, enlisted August 19, 1861, and made Corporal; promoted Sergeant September 1, 1862; commissioned 2nd Lieutenant October 24, 1864; promoted 1st Lieutenant December 7, 1864; in command of the company at Appomattox Courthouse*

Guntz, Emile. Chicago, First Sergeant, enlisted August 6, 1861, and made Corporal; promoted Sergeant October 1, 1863; WIA and taken POW May 16, 1864; paroled from Andersonville in November 1864 and returned to regiment; promoted 1st Sergeant September 1, 1865; 2nd Lieutenant October 4, 1865, but unable to muster due to regimental strength*

Slagle, David H. Marseilles, First Sergeant; enlisted August 27, 1861, and made Sergeant; WIA and taken POW October 13, 1864, at Darbytown Crossroads; paroled and exchanged; DD May 22, 1865

Fuller, Henry. Marseilles, Sergeant, enlisted August 19, 1861, and made Sergeant; taken POW January 4, 1862, near Bath, VA; paroled; DD Jan 23, 1862

Hewitt, James W. Wayne County, enlisted October 8, 1861; promoted Sergeant April 15, 1862; DD July 23, 1862

Terrell, William H. Bloomington, Sergeant, enlisted August 18, 1861, and made Corporal; promoted Sergeant June 14, 1862, but reduced to ranks August 22, 1863; DD July 25, 1864

Sanborn, James. Marseilles, Sergeant, enlisted August 19, 1861; promoted Sergeant September 1, 1862; KIA August 16, 1864, at Second Deep Bottom

Pollock, George. Marseilles, Corporal, enlisted September 3, 1861, and made Corporal; DD July 18, 1863

Moxton, William. Marseilles, Sergeant, enlisted August 6, 1861, and made Corporal; was reduced to ranks at one point but recommended for promotion to Sergeant following meritorious service during the charge at Deep Bottom on August 16, 1864*

Allen, James K. Bloomington, Sergeant, enlisted September 2, 1861; promoted Corporal December 1, 1864; Sergeant January 1, 1865*

Latimer, James A. Marseilles, enlisted August 14, 1861; promoted Corporal September 6, 1862; WIA May 20, 1864, at Ware Bottom Church; promoted Sergeant unknown date*

Stebbins, Emory. Marseilles, Corporal, enlisted August 19, 1861, and made Corporal; taken POW January 4, 1862, near Bath, VA; DD June 3, 1862

Begnail, O.B. Marseilles, Corporal enlisted September 3, 1861, and made Corporal; DD August 11, 1862

Craig, William. Bloomington, Corporal, enlisted August 14, 1861; promoted Corporal September 6, 1862; DD December 4, 1863

Cordell, Alex C. Bloomington, Corporal, enlisted October 10, 1861; promoted Corporal August 1, 1863; wounded August 26, 1863, on Morris Island*

Kipp, John. Marseilles, Corporal, enlisted August 14, 1861; promoted Corporal August 1, 1863; WIA October 13, 1864, at Darbytown Crossroads; died November 5, 1864, of wounds; veteran

Welcome, James A. Bloomington, enlisted October 10, 1861; promoted Corporal August 1, 1863; killed by explosion of enemy shell August 26, 1863, near Fort Wagner, SC

Thomas, Francis Marion. Bloomington, Corporal, enlisted August 14, 1861; promoted Corporal October 1, 1863; KIA June 17, 1864, near Hatcher's Run, VA

Allen, Abner P. Bloomington, Corporal, enlisted September 2, 1861; promoted Corporal December 1, 1863; accompanied General John Gibbon to Washington, D.C., with captured colors from April 2, 1865, and was awarded the Medal of Honor for his valor in the assault on Fort Gregg (see discussion in Chapter 20)*

Burns, James D. Marseilles, Corporal, enlisted August 14, 1861; promoted Corporal December 1, 1863*

Adams, Thomas J. Chicago, enlisted August 27, 1861; promoted Corporal December 1, 1863; MO September 10, 1864

Nichols, Joseph T. Marseilles, Corporal, enlisted August 14, 1861; promoted Corporal August 16, 1864; WIA April 2, 1865, in assault on Fort Gregg; died May 19, 1865, of wounds

Putnam, John S. Bloomington, Corporal, enlisted October 3, 1861; WIA June 2, 1864, near Ware Bottom Church; promoted Corporal May 1, 1865*

Webster, Levi C. Chicago, enlisted February 6, 1864; promoted Corporal May 1, 1865*

Churchill, John. Marseilles, Corporal, enlisted September 18, 1861; promoted Corporal May 2, 1865; reduced to ranks September 27, 1865*

Garrett, Willis. Unknown, Corporal, enlisted December 23, 1862; WIA August 16, 1864, at Second Deep Bottom; promoted Corporal unknown date 1865

Moore, James. Marseilles, Corporal, enlisted September 3, 1861; promoted Corporal unknown date*

Shaw, James B. Marseilles, musician, enlisted August 14, 1861; played the fife; DD June 1862

Cannon, Timothy. Troy, WI, musician, enlisted September 27, 1861; drummer detailed to band*

Privates

Austin, Charles. Chicago, enlisted September 16, 1861; DD unknown date in 1862

Barber, Alden. Marseilles, enlisted February 6, 1864; WIA and taken POW May 16, 1864, at Drewry's Bluff; died June 18, 1864, from wounds in Richmond's Libby Prison

Barber, Cicero. Marseilles, enlisted August 16, 1861; KIA May 20, 1864, at Ware Bottom Church

Beamish, Thomas. Elwood, enlisted September 10, 1861*

Bedford, Peter. Marseilles, enlisted February 24, 1864; DS April 9, 1864, of disease

Bedford, Wallace. Marseilles, enlisted August 14, 1861; wounded August 26, 1863, on Morris Island; WIA October 13, 1864, at Darbytown Crossroads*

Bess, James F. Draft substitute, enlisted February 14, 1865; DS September 18, 1865

Birge, Andreas. Bloomington, enlisted August 18, 1861*

Broughton, Charles. Morris, enlisted August 14, 1861; DD unknown date 1862

Brower, August. Bloomington, enlisted September 5, 1861; DD June 18, 1862

Brown, George P. Bloomington, enlisted October 17, 1861; WIA October 13, 1864, at Darbytown Crossroads; absent-wounded at regiment's mustering out

Burget, Lawrence. Marseilles, enlisted August 27, 1861; DD August 17, 1863

Butterfield, Augustus. Marseilles, enlisted December 16, 1863; taken POW May 16, 1864, at Drewry's Bluff; prisoner at Andersonville; paroled*

Butterfield, Francis L. Marseilles, enlisted February 4, 1864; entered for service in band; detailed as nurse to care for Osborn, Mann, and Linton while in hospital in 1864; discharged as musician May 30, 1865

Caddigan, John. Unknown, enlisted February 16, 1864; WIA May 20, 1864, at Ware Bottom Church; died November 14, 1864, from wounds

Clear, Peter. Bloomington, enlisted September 3, 1861; DS July 11, 1862

Clement, Frank. Chicago, enlisted October 10, 1861; MO October 10, 1864

Cole, James. Belleville, enlisted October 11, 1861; DS November 24, 1865

Coleman, James. Draft substitute, enlisted February 13, 1865*

Collins, George. Marseilles, enlisted August 19, 1861; DS July 14, 1862

Craig, Henry. Bloomington, enlisted September 5, 1861*

Drake, George. Marseilles, enlisted August 11, 1862; DS July 20, 1862, from lung problems

Farrance, Anthony. Ottawa, enlisted August 23, 1862; wounded October 6, 1863, at Fort Wagner; MO June 20, 1865

Flory, Thomas W. Bloomington, enlisted September 19, 1861; taken POW August 16, 1864, at Second Deep Bottom; MO June 2, 1865

Fowler, Jessie W. Bloomington, enlisted October 10, 1861; DD June,1862

Fowler, Josiah. Bloomington, enlisted October 10, 1861; wounded June 11, 1863, on Folly Island; MO October 8, 1864

Franks, E.S. Seneca, enlisted August 14, 1862; DD November 10, 1862

Frink, Marcellus. Marseilles, enlisted August 19, 1861; taken POW January 4, 1862, at Sir John's Run near Bath, VA; paroled and discharged June 23, 1862

Gaddis, James I. White Oak, enlisted February 22, 1864; WIA August 16, 1864, at Second Deep Bottom; DD August 7, 1865, from wounds

Garrison, John R. Manilus, enlisted February 20, 1864; discharged June 8, 1865

Guntz, Francis P. Chicago, enlisted March 12, 1864; WIA August 16, 1864, at Second Deep Bottom*

Hagan, Henry. Draft substitute, enlisted February 14, 1865*

Halligan, Thomas. Marseilles, enlisted August 6, 1861*

Hayward, Stephen K. Bloomington, enlisted August 14, 1861; MO March 13, 1864

Hendricks, James S. St. Clair County, enlisted August 23, 1862; MO June 29, 1865

Hicks, Milton. Chicago, enlisted September 4, 1861*

Hubbard, Albert. Marseilles, enlisted August 14, 1861; MO October 10, 1864

Hummell, Lewis J. Chicago, enlisted September 10, 1861; MO September 10, 1864

Jones, William T. Bloomington, enlisted October 19, 1861; MO October 26, 1864

Kilmer, Egbert. Marseilles, enlisted August 14, 1861; MO October 26, 1864

Kirkman, William G. Marengo, enlisted August 19, 1861; was a telegraph operator before the war, and after helping erect a line in Charleston in the summer of 1863, spent the rest of his enlistment on telegraphic duty; MO August 19, 1864

Kockinkiniper, Francis. Draft substitute, enlisted February 14, 1865; DS July 8, 1865, in Richmond

Lammy, Lewis H. Chicago, enlisted August 6, 1861; DD October 5, 1863

Lee, Orville. Marseilles, enlisted February 27, 1864; WIA August 16, 1864, at Second Deep Bottom*

Lewis, John. Pontiac, enlisted January 5, 1864; taken POW May 16, 1864, at Drewry's Bluff; died June,1864 at Andersonville

Linton, George A. Bloomington, enlisted September 21, 1861; MO September 21, 1864

Maher, John. Chicago, enlisted February 6, 1864; WIA May 20, 1864, at Ware Bottom Church*

Marsh, Lewis. Marseilles, enlisted August 6, 1861; WIA August 16, 1864, at Second Deep Bottom requiring arm amputation; DD November 19, 1864

Massey, Langdon S. Marseilles, unknown enlistment date; mustered February 15, 1864; not listed in Clark history*

McDowell, George. Draft substitute, enlisted March 3, 1865; deserted May 23, 1865

McDowell, Riley. Draft substitute, enlisted February 13, 1865*

Mick, Parker. Marseilles, enlisted September 10, 1861; DS November 24, 1863, of illness; adjutant's report lists him as Nick Parker

Miller, Jacob. Draft substitute, enlisted February 21, 1865*

Mitchell, William R. Draft substitute, enlisted February 13, 1865*

Morgan, Charles. Marseilles, enlisted August 27, 1861; DD August 26, 1862

Myers, Alden. Bloomington, enlisted September 3, 1861; WIA August 16, 1864, at Second Deep Bottom; MO September 3, 1864

Neal, Daniel. Marseilles; enlisted September 3, 1861; seriously injured falling from a bridge during regiment's travel from St. Louis to Maryland; DD November 1, 1862, after not being expected to recover; enlisted in 8th Illinois Cavalry February 4, 1864

Oleson, Jacob. Marseilles, enlisted September 25, 1861; WIA and taken POW May 16, 1864, at Drewry's Bluff; paroled August,1864; transferred to Company A Veteran Reserve Corps and discharged November 13, 1865

Olmstead, Clinton. Chicago, enlisted March 5, 1864; discharged December 2, 1864

Olmstead, Orlando. Marseilles, enlisted August 19, 1861; WIA August 16, 1864*

Pitcher, Theodore W. Marseilles, enlisted October 27, 1861, as musician; MO in 1862 by order of War Department discontinuing regimental bands; re-enlisted March 5, 1864, and detailed to band*

Prebles, Edward. Draft substitute, enlisted February 13, 1865; WIA April 2, 1865, in assault on Fort Gregg*

Price, Michael. St. Louis, MO, enlisted August 21, 1861; taken POW January 4, 1862, near Bath, VA; paroled; WIA April 2, 1865, in assault on Fort Gregg*

Reed, John A. Marseilles, enlisted August 19, 1861*

Sauers, Peter. Bloomington, enlisted August 14, 1861; KIA April 2, 1865, in assault on Fort Gregg

Scullion, William. Marseilles, enlisted August 14, 1861; DD July 18, 1863

Seaman, Allen M. Marseilles, enlisted September 15, 1861; DS June,1862 while on sick furlough

Selleck, Hiram. Marseilles, enlisted September 21, 1861; DD November 10, 1862

Shero, Martin. Chicago, enlisted August 6, 1861; WIA October 13, 1864, at Darbytown Crossroads*

Simpson, Charles. Bloomington, enlisted March 4, 1864*

Slagle, James. Marseilles, enlisted December 16, 1861; WIA October 13, 1864, at Darbytown Crossroads; absent-wounded at muster out of regiment

Slater, George. Marseilles, enlisted August 27, 1861; DD September 25, 1862

Slater, William. Marseilles, enlisted September 10, 1861*

Sparks, Ely. Marseilles, enlisted August 6, 1861; taken POW May,1862 near Woodstock, VA; paroled and MO May 21, 1862

Sparks, John B. Marseilles, enlisted February 28, 1861; DD September 25, 1862

Stephenson, John D. Marseilles, enlisted September 3, 1861; DD unknown date 1862

Stokes, Stephen N. Bloomington, enlisted August 25, 1861; taken POW May 17, 1862; paroled October 1862; taken pow June 6, 1863; paroled October 1863; deserted August 25, 1864

Sweeny, Edward. Draft substitute, enlisted February 15, 1865*

Thomas, George N. Bloomington, enlisted September 3, 1861*

Thompson, Henry V. Marseilles, enlisted August 27, 1861; DD unknown date 1862

Thompson, James. Chicago, enlisted February 12, 1864; WIA May 20, 1864, at Ware Bottom Church; DD July 18, 1865

Thornell, Jackson. Marseilles, enlisted October 4, 1861; DD March 7, 1863

Timm, Christopher. Marseilles, enlisted December 16, 1863*

Van Slet, Samuel. Marseilles, enlisted September 17, 1861; DD November 10, 1862

Van Wermer, Chester. Belleville, enlisted October 14, 1861; taken POW in Shenandoah Valley and MO as POW

Washburne, Charles. Morris, enlisted August 27, 1861; DD unknown date early 1862

Werner, John. Bloomington, enlisted October 10, 1861; KIA May 16, 1864, at Drewry's Bluff; veteran

White, James R. Bloomington, enlisted September 19, 1861; discharged in 1862; re-enlisted March 4, 1864*

Wright, Richard. Marseilles, enlisted October 6, 1861; MO October 8, 1864

Overall Summary

Killed In Battle	83
Died of Wounds	61
Died of Disease	90
Died in Prison	25
Wounded	411
Drowned	4
Taken Prisoner	118
Discharged for Disability	293
Deserted	97
Men Who Had Limbs Amputated	34
Mustered Out at Expiration of Service	191
Enlisted in 1861	844
Re-Enlisted as Veterans	350
Recruits Received During War	608
Enlisted Men who Commissioned	34
Mustered Out at End of War	525
Miles Traveled by Rail and Water	5,038
Miles Marched	1,425
Total Miles Traveled	6,463

Source: Clark, History, 549.

Notes

Preface

1. Clark, Charles M. *The History of the 39th Regiment Illinois Volunteer Veteran Infantry in The War of Rebellion*. Chicago: Published under the auspices of the Veteran Association of the Regiment, 1889, 549.
2. Hicken, Victor. *Illinois in the Civil War*. Urbana: University of Illinois Press, 1991, ix.
3. *Ibid.*
4. Clark, *History*, 549.
5. *Ibid.*, vi–vii.

Introduction

1. "Kansas-Nebraska Act. [1854]." In *Encyclopedia Britannica*, July 31, 2019. https://www.britannica.com/topic/Kansas-Nebraska-Act. Originally crafted by Douglas, the Kansas-Nebraska Act repealed the Missouri Compromise. Instead of slavery being outlawed above the 36–30 line, except Missouri, slavery in a territory would now be decided by popular sovereignty. The law's passage led to violence in Kansas and the rise of the anti-slavery Republican party.
2. "House Divided Speech." Speeches and Writings. Abraham Lincoln Online. http://www.abrahamlincolnonline.org/lincoln/speeches/house.htm. State legislatures picked Senators at this time, and therefore, Lincoln and Douglas were campaigning for their parties to win seats in the congressional districts.
3. My own ancestry research revealed a newspaper clipping detailing that mygreat-great-great grandfather, John Barber, did attend the Ottawa debate.
4. Urofsky, Melvin I. "Dred Scott Decision—Reception and Significance." In *Encyclopædia Britannica*, September 10, 2020. https://www.britannica.com/event/Dred-Scott-decision/Reception-and-significance.
5. Beschloss, Michael R. *Presidents of War*. New York: Crown, 2018, 159.
6. Engle, Stephen Douglas. *Gathering to Save a Nation: Lincoln and the Union's War Governors*. Chapel Hill: University of North Carolina Press, 2016, 9.
7. Bohn, Richard E. "Richard Yates: An Appraisal of His Value as the Civil War Governor of Illinois." *Journal of the Illinois State Historical Society*, Civil War Sesquicentennial Issue, 104, no. 1/2 (2011), 19.
8. Jackson, Holly. *American Radicals: How Nineteenth-Century Protest Shaped the Nation*. New York: Crown, 2019, 214–216.
9. *Ibid.*, 229.
10. *Ibid.*, 219.
11. "Farewell Address." Speeches and Writings. Abraham Lincoln Online. http://www.abrahamlincolnonline.org/lincoln/speeches/farewell.htm.

Part I

1. Clark, *History*, 84.

Chapter 1

1. Clark, *History*, 380.
2. Reavis, L.U. *The Life and Public Services of Richard Yates, The War Governor of Illinois: A Lecture to the Illinois House of Representatives*. St Louis: J.H. Chambers & Co., 1881, 18.
3. Bohn, *Richard Yates*, 19.
4. Reavis, *Life and Public Services*, 23.
5. Hicken, *Illinois in the Civil War*, 13.
6. *Ibid.*, 1.
7. Bohn, *Richard Yates*, 18.
8. *Ibid.*, 21.
9. Clark, *History*, 368. Swansburg, John. "The Incredible Life of Lew Wallace, Civil War General and Author of Ben-Hur." Slate.com. March 26, 2013. http://www.slate.com/articles/life/history/2013/03/ben_hur_and_lew_wallace_how_the_scapegoat_of_shiloh_became_one_of_the_best.html.
10. Quote is from Clark, *History*, 1.
11. Quote is from Hicken, *Illinois in the Civil War*, 2.
12. A term from ancient Greek warfare, a phalanx was a massed block of heavy infantry with spears and spikes. The phalanx would move together tightly, defending and attacking as one. Fans of the movie *300* would be familiar.
13. While Edward Stanton is associated in history as the Secretary of War at this time, he did not hold the position until January of 1862.
14. The first major battle of the war, Union forces were defeated in a costly battle for both

sides that proved the conflict would not be brief as many expected.

15. Randolph, Valentine C., David D. Roe, and Stephen R. Wise. *A Civil War Soldier's Diary: Valentine C. Randolph, 39th Illinois Regiment*. DeKalb: Northern Illinois University Press, 2006, 10.

16. Ward, Joseph Richardson, D. Duane Cummins, and Daryl Hohweiler. *An Enlisted Soldier's View of the Civil War: The Wartime Papers of Joseph Richardson Ward, Jr.* West Lafayette, IN: Belle Publications, 1981, xix.

17. Plimpton, Homer A., and John L. Dodson. *The Civil War Journals of Col. Homer A. Plimpton: 1861–1865*. Bloomington: Trafford, 2012, vii, xi.

18. Guntz, Emile. "*Narrative of Emile Guntz, First Sergeant Company K*," contained in Clark, *History*, 340–341.

19. Clark, *History*, 441, 534.

20. Osborn was made the Lt. Colonel, and Orrin Mann was voted as Major as a reward for his recruiting efforts.

21. Clark, *History*, 3.

22. *Ibid.*

23. *Ibid.*, 4.

24. *Ibid.*, 4–5.

25. Company H was not present as it was finalizing recruiting efforts, ultimately joining up in Virginia later in the war.

26. Clark, *History*, 6–7.

Chapter 2

1. Stanley, Charles, "A Brief Biography of Valentine C. Randolph," contained in Roe, *A Civil War Soldier's Diary*, 243. Clark, *History*, 511.

2. The western theater consisted of operations in Alabama, Florida, Georgia, Kentucky, Mississippi, North Carolina, South Carolina, and Tennessee.

3. Yates letter to Lamon, February 1, 1862, http://www.chroniclingillinois.org/items/show/3020.

4. Randolph diary entry of November 10, 1861, 27.

5. *Ibid.*

6. Clark, *History*, 25.

7. Plimpton journal entry in November 1865 entry recalling events prior to beginning his journal, 7.

8. Randolph's diary entry of December 3rd, 33, discusses that the men learned the accusations leveled against Colonel Light were indeed true, and that the men accepted his fate then with no further strife.

Chapter 3

1. Clark, *History*, 490–491.

2. Cozzens, Peter. *Shenandoah 1862: Stonewall Jackson's Valley Campaign*. Chapel Hill: University of North Carolina Press, 2013, 71.

3. Clark, *History*, 27–28.

4. *Ibid.*, 29–31.

5. Plimpton journal entry of January 2, 1862, 10.

6. Cozzens, *Shenandoah 1862*, 69–71.

7. Clark, *History*, 30.

8. Cozzens, *Shenandoah* 1862, 72. Clark, *History*, 31–32.

9. *Ibid.*

10. Plimpton journal entry of January 3, 1862, 11.

11. Cozzens, *Shenandoah 1862*, 72. Clark, *History*, 32.

12. *Ibid.*

13. *Ibid.*

14. Clark, *History*, 32.

15. Cozzens, *Shenandoah 1862*, 72–73.

16. *Ibid.*, 72. Clark, *History*, 35.

17. Cozzens, *Shenandoah 1862*, 74–75.

18. Randolph diary entry of January 3, 1862, 45.

19. Plimpton journal entry of January 3, 1862, 11.

20. Plimpton journal entry of January 4, 1862, 11.

21. Osborn report to General Lander of January 8, 1862, included in Clark, *History*, 34. Cozzens, *Shenandoah 1862*, 76.

22. Plimpton journal entry of January 4, 1862, 11.

23. Cozzens, *Shenandoah 1862*, 76–78. Osborn report, in Clark, *History*, 36.

24. Myers, Elbanis, "*The Last to Cross the River at Sir John's Run*," contained in Clark, *History*, 326–327.

25. Clark, *History*, 41.

26. *Ibid.*, 42.

27. *Ibid.*, 43.

28. Plimpton journal entry of January 11, 1862, 19.

29. Clark, *History*, 44.

30. Randolph diary entry of January 4, 1862, 46.

31. Clark, *History*, 44.

32. Peters, Martin V.B. "*Narrative of Martin Van Buren Peters, Company F*," contained within Clark, *History*, 335–336.

33. Plimpton journal entry of January 4, 1862, 12. Osborn report, in Clark, *History*, 36. Cozzens, *Shenandoah 1862*, 76.

34. Jewett, William O.L. "*Bury Me Where I Lay, Boys!*" contained within Clark, *History*, 296.

35. *Ibid.*, 297.

36. Plimpton journal entry of January 4, 1862, 13.

37. Plimpton journal entry of January 8, 1862, 16.

38. Cook, Ezra, "*Reminiscences of Ezra A. Cook, Company G*," contained in Clark, *History*, 311–315.

39. Cozzens, *Shenandoah 1862*, 78–79.

40. Osborn report, in Clark, *History*, 36.

41. Cozzens, *Shenandoah 1862*, 80.

42. *Ibid.*

43. Clark, *History*, 46.

44. *Ibid.*, 46–47. Cozzens, *Shenandoah 1862*, 80–81.

45. *Ibid.*

46. Clark, *History*, 47–48. Cozzens, *Shenandoah 1862*, 81.

47. *Ibid.*, 49–50. Cozzens, *Shenandoah 1862*, 73.

48. Clark, *History*, 49.

CHAPTER 4

1. Clark, *History*, 372.

2. While waiting in Cumberland for the balance of the regiment, Homer Plimpton recounted in his diary that men there gave high praise to the 39th IL performance. "Some of the soldiers belonging to other regiments who were in the fight with our boys at Bath and Alpine say that the Illinois boys fought like regulars." Plimpton journal entry of January 9, 1862, 17.

3. Clark, *History*, 51.

4. *Ibid.*, 51–56.

5. *Ibid.*

6. *Ibid.*, 56.

7. Plimpton journal entry of February 5, 1862, 37–38.

8. Lander replaced General Kelley shortly after the events at Bath.

9. Clark, *History*, 58. A vital fort on the Tennessee/Kentucky border, Union control of Fort Donelson opened up the Cumberland River and a route into the south.

10. Clark, *History*, 521.

11. Cozzens, Peter. "Shenandoah Valley Campaign of 1862." Encyclopedia Virginia, November 29, 2012. https://www.encyclopediavirginia.org/Shenandoah_Valley_Campaign_of_1862.

12. *Ibid.* McPherson, James M. *Battle Cry of Freedom.* New York,: Oxford University Press, 1988, 423–425.

13. Clark, *History*, 297–298.

14. *Ibid.*, 59.

15. *Ibid.*, 59–60, 62, 65.

16. *Ibid.*, 59.

17. Shields' life is fascinating and worth its own exploration. He once challenged Abraham Lincoln to a duel before becoming friends with him, is the only man to be a Senator from 3 different states and is one of Illinois' two statues in the U.S. Capitol. See Castle, Henry A. *General James Shields, Soldier, Orator, Statesman.* Available online https://archive.org/stream/generaljamesshie00castrich#page/n5/mode/2up.

18. Randolph diary entry of March 10, 1862, 59.

19. Cozzens, *Shenandoah 1862*, 138–140, 144–145.

20. Cozzens, "Shenandoah Valley Campaign."

21. *Ibid.* Clark, *History*, 66. Cozzens, "Shenandoah Valley Campaign."

22. Cozzens, "Shenandoah Valley Campaign." Cozzens, *Shenandoah 1862*, 145.

23. Clark, *History*, 69. Cozzens, *Shenandoah 1862*, 140–144.

24. Clark, *History*, 69.

25. Randolph diary entry of March 18, 1862, 66.

26. Plimpton journal entry of March 18, 1862, 59. Cozzens, *Shenandoah 1862*, 148–151.

27. Clark, *History*, 69. Cozzens, *Shenandoah 1862*, 149–150.

28. Clark, *History*, 71. Cozzens, *Shenandoah 1862*, 150–151.

29. Cozzens, *Shenandoah 1862*, 151–152.

CHAPTER 5

1. Clark, *History*, 425.

2. Cozzens, *Shenandoah 1862*, 153.

3. Brucker, *"How Lieutenant S.S. Brucker Opened the Battle of Winchester (Kernstown),"* contained within Clark, *History*, 288–289.

4. *Ibid.*, 289. Cozzens, *Shenandoah 1862*, 153–154.

5. Brucker, in Clark, *History*, 289.

6. Cozzens, *Shenandoah 1862*, 154.

7. Brucker, in Clark, *History*, 290.

8. *Ibid.*

9. Cozzens, *Shenandoah 1862*, 154–155.

10. Clark, *History*, 73–74. Cozzens, *Shenandoah 1862*, 155–156.

11. Cozzens, *Shenandoah 1862*, 153, 156–158, 167.

12. *Ibid.*, 167–168.

13. Randolph diary entry of March 23, 1862, 68.

14. Cozzens, *Shenandoah 1862*, 169–171, 177.

15. Plimpton journal entry of March 23, 1862, 63.

16. Randolph diary entry of March 23, 1862, 68–69.

17. Cozzens, *Shenandoah 1862*, 178–179.

18. Plimpton journal entry of March 23, 1862, 63.

19. *Ibid.*

20. Cozzens, *Shenandoah 1862*, 175.

21. *Ibid.*, 191–192.

22. Plimpton journal entry of March 23, 1862, 63.

23. Numbers of killed, wounded and taken prisoner from the National Park Service summary of the battle. https://www.nps.gov/cebe/learn/historyculture/first-battle-of-kernstown.htm. Cozzens lists similar numbers with 737 killed, wounded, captured, or missing Confederates and 574 Union men, *Shenandoah 1862*, 215.

24. Cozzens, *Shenandoah 1862*, 209. Kimball received high praise for his performance at Kernstown and was made a General soon after. He successfully commanded a brigade at Antietam, a division during the Vicksburg Campaign. He was the only Union commander of the war who could say he defeated both Stonewall Jackson and Robert E. Lee in battle.

25. Randolph diary, March 23, 1862, 69.

26. Cozzens, *Shenandoah 1862*, 215–216.
27. Clark, *History*, 75–76.
28. Ibid., 76–77.

Chapter 6

1. Cummins, *An Enlisted Soldier's View of the Civil War*, xix.
2. Clark, *History*, 78.
3. Plimpton journal entry of April 12, 1862, 74–75.
4. Randolph diary entry of March 23, 1862, 69.
5. Cozzens, *Shenandoah 1862*, 228–229. Tanner, Robert G. *Stonewall in the Valley: Thomas J. "Stonewall" Jackson's Shenandoah Valley Campaign, Spring 1862.* Mechanicsburg, PA: Stackpole Books, 2002, 139–141.
6. Cozzens, "Shenandoah Valley Campaign of 1862."
7. McPherson, James M. *Battle Cry of Freedom.* New York: Oxford University Press, 1988, 425.
8. Joseph Ward letter to his parents dated April 27, 1862, contained in his wartime papers, 10–12.
9. Cozzens, *Shenandoah 1862*, 237. Cozzens, "Shenandoah Valley Campaign of 1862."
10. Clark, *History*, 79.
11. *Ibid.*, 79–80.
12. *Ibid.*, 81.
13. Cozzens, "Shenandoah Valley Campaign of 1862." Cozzens, *Shenandoah 1862*, 245–246.
14. Clark, *History*, 82.
15. Joseph Ward letter to his parents dated April 27, 1862, contained in his wartime papers, 10–12.
16. Clark, *History*, 82.
17. Ward letter to his parents, May 9, 1862, contained in his wartime papers, 12–13.
18. McPherson, *Battle Cry of Freedom*, 454.
19. The account of Lincoln's interaction with the regiment comes from Clark's *History*, 85–86.
20. Cozzens, *Shenandoah 1862*, 255–258.
21. *Ibid.*, 264–273, 276. Cozzens, "Shenandoah Valley Campaign of 1862."
22. Cozzens, "Shenandoah Valley Campaign of 1862." Cozzens, *Shenandoah 1862*, 276.
23. Cozzens, "Shenandoah Valley Campaign of 1862." Cozzens, *Shenandoah 1862*, 288.
24. Cozzens, *Shenandoah 1862*, 294–295, 307.
25. Cozzens, "Shenandoah Valley Campaign of 1862."
26. *Ibid.* McPherson, *Battle Cry of Freedom*, 457. Cozzens, *Shenandoah 1862*, 345.
27. McPherson, *Battle Cry of Freedom*, 457.
28. *Ibid.*, 458.
29. Cozzens, *Shenandoah 1862*, 435–440, 442–451, 456–476.
30. *Ibid.*, 512–513. Clark, *History*, 88.
31. Clark, *History*, 88.

Chapter 7

1. Clark, *History*, 484.
2. McFarland, Kenneth M. "James River During the Civil War." Encyclopedia Virginia, October 27, 2015. https://www.encyclopediavirginia.org/James_River_During_the_Civil_War. "Peninsula Campaign." Battlefields.org. December 13, 2016. https://www.battlefields.org/learn/civil-war/peninsula-campaign.
3. On top of his frustration at the numerous instances of losing troops to the Shenandoah, McClellan continually overestimated Confederate numbers. See McPherson, *Battle Cry of Freedom* 464.
4. Clark, *History*, 87–88.
5. McPherson, *Battle Cry of Freedom*, 466–467.
6. "The Battle of Gaines' Mill." February 26, 2015, Nps.gov. https://www.nps.gov/rich/learn/historyculture/gainesmillbull.htm.
7. McPherson, *Battle Cry of Freedom*, 469.
8. *Ibid.*
9. Fry, Zachery A. *A Republic in the Ranks: Loyalty and Dissent in the Army of the Potomac.* Chapel Hill: University of North Carolina Press, 2020, 36.
10. McPherson, *Battle Cry of Freedom*, 471.
11. Randolph diary entry of July 1, 1862, 90.
12. Plimpton journal of July 3, 1862, 116.
13. Clark, *History*, 89.
14. Randolph diary entry of July 23, 1862, 99.
15. Ward letter to his parents from early July,1862, contained in his wartime papers, 34–35.
16. Plimpton journal entries of July 7, 10, 1862, 119, 121.
17. Coffey, Walter. 2017. "Lincoln Visits the Virginia Peninsula." Civilwarmonths.com. July 8, 2017. https://civilwarmonths.com/2017/07/08/lincoln-visits-the-virginia-peninsula/.
18. Randolph diary entry of July 23, 1862, 99.
19. Ward letter to his parents dated February 4, 1862, contained in his wartime papers, 5–6.
20. Cook, "*Reminiscences of Ezra A. Cook,*" contained in Clark, *History*, 317–318.
21. Clark, *History*, 90.
22. Randolph diary entry of July 25, 1862, 99.
23. Engle, *Gathering to Save a Nation*, 189.
24. *Ibid.*, 193.
25. McPherson, *Battle Cry of Freedom*, 505.
26. *Ibid.*, 491.
27. Bohn, *Civil War Governor of Illinois*, 18, 24. Engle, *Gathering to Save a Nation*, 154–155, 167, Hicken, *Illinois in the Civil War*, 69.
28. Engle, *Gathering to Save a Nation*, 294.
29. Hicken, *Illinois in the Civil War*, 4.
30. McPherson, *Battle Cry of Freedom*, 502–504.
31. Randolph diary entry of August 4, 1862, 101.
32. Randolph diary entry of August 13, 1862, 102–103.
33. Plimpton journal entry of July 4, 1862, 118.
34. Ward letter to his parents dated September 1, 1862, contained in his wartime papers, 36–38.
35. Fry, *A Republic in the Ranks*, 1.
36. *Ibid.*, 2–3.
37. *Ibid.*, 34.

38. Clark, *History*, 92.

39. Randolph diary entry of August 17, 1862, 105.

40. McPherson, *Battle Cry of Freedom*, 501.

41. *Ibid.*, 113.

42. McPherson, *Battle Cry of Freedom*, 489.

43. Randolph diary entry of September 6, 1862, 114.

44. Clark, *History*, 97.

45. "Second Manassas." 2009. Battlefields.org. January 14, 2009. https://www.battlefields.org/learn/civil-war/battles/second-manassas. "Chantilly." 2009. Battlefields.org. January 14, 2009. https://www.battlefields.org/learn/civil-war/battles/chantilly.

46. McPherson, *Battle Cry of Freedom*, 532–534.

47. Randolph diary entry of September 10, 1862, 115.

48. Clark, *History*, 97.

49. McPherson, *Battle Cry of Freedom*, 535.

50. Ward letter to his parents dated October 10, 1862, contained in his wartime papers, 39–41.

51. McPherson, *Battle Cry of Freedom*, 544.

52. "Antietam." Battlefields.org. January 12, 2009. https://www.battlefields.org/learn/articles/antietam.

53. Ward letter to his parents dated October 10, 1862, contained in his wartime papers, 39–41.

54. Randolph diary entry of October 19, 1862, 122.

55. Hicken, *Illinois in the Civil War*, 128–129.

56. Engle, *Gathering to Save a Nation*, 264–265.

57. Fry, *A Republic in the Ranks*, 2.

58. Hicken, *Illinois in the Civil War*, 132–133.

59. Ward, *An Enlisted Soldier's View of the Civil War*, 40. See also Plimpton journal entry of October 18, 1862, 144.

60. Clark, *History*, 97–98.

61. Plimpton journal entry of November 6, 1862, 152.

62. *Ibid.*, 154.

63. *Ibid.*, 160.

64. Plimpton journal entry of November 17, 1862, 153.

65. McPherson, *Battle Cry of Freedom*, 574.

66. Randolph diary entry of December 25, 1862, 129.

67. Plimpton journal entry of December 25, 1862, 162.

68. Clark, *History*, 99.

PART II

1. Clark, *History*, 124–125.

CHAPTER 8

1. *Ibid.*, 370–371.

2. (1) Gettysburg, July 1–3: 51,000 casualties. (2) Chickamauga, September 19–20: 34,624 casualties. (5) Chancellorsville, May 1–4: 24,000 casualties. Antietam, in September 1862, was the bloodiest single day: 23,100 casualties.

3. Wise, Stephen R. *Gate of Hell: Campaign for Charleston Harbor, 1863*. Columbia: University of South Carolina Press, 2011, 1.

4. Clark, *History*, 102. Randolph diary entry of January 14, 1863, 135.

5. Clark, *History*, 106.

6. Wise, *Gate of Hell*, 23–27.

7. Plimpton journal entry of January 18, 1863, 177.

8. Clark *History*, 103.

9. Fry, *A Republic in the Ranks*, 70.

10. Engle, *Gathering to Save a Nation*, 286.

11. Fry, *A Republic in the Ranks*, 70.

12. Clark, *History*, 103–104. Randolph diary entries of January 28–29, 1862, 137.

13. Clark, *History*, 105.

14. *Ibid.*, 106.

15. Plimpton journal entry of February 1, 1863, 183.

16. Plimpton journal entry of February 4, 1863, 184.

17. Coffey, Walter. "The Army of the Potomac: Hooker Takes Command." Civilwarmonths.com. January 26, 2018. https://civilwarmonths.com/2018/01/26/the-army-of-the-potomac-hooker-takes-command/.

18. Clark, *History*, 106–107. Randolph diary entry of February 8, 1863, 140.

19. Wise, *Gate of Hell*, 25–27.

20. *Ibid.*, 23.

21. *Ibid.*, 26–27.

22. *Ibid.*, 27, Plimpton journal entry of February 17, 1863, 191. Randolph diary entry of February 15, 1863, 144.

23. Plimpton journal entry of February 23, 1863, 193.

24. Clark, *History*, 108.

25. Randolph diary entry of March 1, 1863, 147.

26. Plimpton journal entry of March 3, 1863, 195–196.

27. Engle, *Gathering to Save a Nation*, 286.

28. Fry, *A Republic in the Ranks*, 70.

29. Randolph diary entry of March 3, 1863, 147.

30. Plimpton journal entry of March 3, 1863, 196.

31. Randolph diary entry of March 3, 1863, 147.

32. Wise, *Gate of Hell*, 46.

33. *Ibid.*, 47.

34. Plimpton journal entry of March 8, 1863, 199.

35. Plimpton journal entry of March 14, 1863, 201.

36. Wise, *Gate of Hell*, 28.

37. Plimpton journal entries of April 2–3, 1863, 208. Randolph diary entry of April 2, 1863, 153.

38. *Ibid.*, 29.

39. Plimpton journal entry of April 3, 1863, 209.

40. Wise, *Gate of Hell*, 27.

41. Randolph diary entry of April 7, 1863, 155.

42. Plimpton journal entry of April 4, 1863, 210.

43. Clark, *History*, 111.
44. Wise, *Gate of Hell*, 29.
45. *Ibid.*, 30.
46. Randolph diary entry of April 7, 1863, 155.
47. Plimpton journal of April 9, 1863, 212.
48. Wise, *Gate of Hell*, 30. (Wise's book is phenomenal for those interested in the details and engineering of Charleston's defenses.)
49. Randolph diary entry of April 7, 1863, 155.
50. Wise, *Gate of Hell*, 31–32.
51. *Ibid.*, 31.
52. Randolph diary entry of April 11, 1863, 156.
53. Wise, *Gate of Hell*, 32.
54. Randolph diary entry of April 17, 1863, 157.

Chapter 9

1. Clark, *History*, 527.
2. McPherson, *Battle Cry of Freedom*, 639–645.
3. Clark, *History*, 125.
4. Wise, *Gate of Hell*, 33.
5. *Ibid.*, 34.
6. *Ibid.*, 38–39.
7. Clark, *History*, 118–119.
8. *Ibid.*, 125.
9. *Ibid.*, 125–128.
10. *Ibid.*, 128.
11. Randolph diary entry of June 14, 1863, 162.
12. Wise, *Gate of Hell*, 39.
13. Randolph diary entries of late June, 162–164. Clark, *History*, 132–133.
14. Clark, *History*, 132.
15. Wise, *Gate of Hell*, 43.
16. Randolph diary entry of July 4, 1863, 165. Clark, *History*, 133. Wise, *Gate of Hell*, 55.
17. Wise, *Gate of Hell*, 55.
18. Plimpton journal entry of June 26, 1863, 241.
19. Wise, *Gate of Hell*, 57–61.
20. Plimpton journal entry of July 8, 1863, 245.
21. Randolph diary entry of July 9, 1863, 165.
22. Wise, *Gate of Hell*, 67.
23. Valentine diary entry of July 10, 1863, 166.
24. Wise, *Gate of Hell*, 68.
25. *Ibid.*, 69–70.
26. *Ibid.*, 71.
27. Clark, *History*, 135.
28. Wise, *Gate of Hell*, 78.
29. Randolph diary entry of July 11, 1863, 166.
30. Wise, *Gate of Hell*, 80.
31. Randolph diary entry of July 16, 1863, 167–168.
32. Wise, *Gate of Hell*, 101.
33. Plimpton journal entry of July 19, 1863, 248.
34. Wise, *Gate of Hell*, 95.
35. Randolph diary entry of July 18, 1863, 169.
36. *Ibid.* Plimpton journal entry of July 19, 1863, 249. Pohanka, Brian C. "Fort Wagner and the 54th Massachusetts Volunteer Infantry." Battlefields.org. February 4, 2009. https://www.battlefields.org/learn/articles/fort-wagner-and-54th-massachusetts-volunteer-infantry.

37. Wise, *Gate of Hell*, 114. Randolph diary entry of July 18, 1863, 169.
38. Wise, *Gate of Hell*, 114.
39. Randolph diary entry of July 18, 1863, 168–169.
40. Wise, *Gate of Hell*, 139. Clark, *History*, 142–143.
41. Wise, *Gate of Hell*, 139–141.
42. Clark, *History*, 143–144.
43. Wise, *Gate of Hell*, 139.
44. Clark, *History*, 144.
45. Plimpton journal entries of August 15, 21, 1863, 253–260.
46. Wise, *Gate of Hell*, 156–158.
47. Clark, *History*, 143–144.
48. Wise, *Gate of Hell*, 148–150.
49. Clark, *History*, 151.
50. *Ibid.*, 150. Wise, *Gate of Hell*, 169–172.
51. Plimpton journal entry of August 26, 1863, 267.
52. Plimpton journal entry of August 25, 1863, 263. Wise, *Gate of Hell*, 173.
53. *Ibid.*, 263–264, Wise, *Gate of Hell*, 175, Randolph diary entry of August 26, 1863, 174–175. *Clark, History*, 145.
54. Clark, *History*, 145.
55. Randolph diary entry of August 26, 1863, 174. Plimpton journal entry of August 26, 1863, 265.
56. Wise, *Gate of Hell*, 202. Clark, *History*, 145.
57. Clark, *History*, 145–148.
58. *Ibid.* 147. Wise, *Gate of Hell*, 203.
59. Clark, *History*, 151–153.
60. Plimpton journal entries of September 9–11, 1863, 276–277.
61. Plimpton journal entry of September 25, 1863, 279.
62. Randolph diary entry of September 23, 1863, 182.

Chapter 10

1. Clark, *History*, 436.
2. Randolph diary entries of October 6–18, 1863, 184–185.
3. Randolph diary entry of October 28, 1863, 186.
4. "Operations against the Defenses of Charleston." Battlefields.org. February 21, 2017. https://www.battlefields.org/learn/civil-war/operations-against-defenses-charleston.
5. McPherson, *Battle Cry of Freedom*, 687.
6. "Chickamauga." Battlefields.org. January 14, 2009. https://www.battlefields.org/learn/articles/chickamauga.
7. Botts, Joshua. "'Brilliant and Important Victories'—Research—History of the Foreign Relations Series—Historical Documents—Office of the Historian." State.gov, July 3, 2013. https://history.state.gov/historicaldocuments/frus-history/research/brilliant-and-important-victories.
8. Plimpton journal entry of November 6, 1863, 291.

9. Fry, *A Republic in the Ranks*, 130.

10. Randolph diary entries of December 26–29, 1863, 189.

11. *Ibid.*

12. McPherson, *For Cause and Comrades*, 172.

13. Plimpton journal entry of January 23, 1864, 308.

14. Fry, *A Republic in the Ranks*, 124–126.

15. *Ibid.*, 125–126.

16. Plimpton journal entry of January 23, 1864, 308.

17. *Ibid.*

18. *Ibid.*, 308–309.

19. Clark *History*, 157.

20. *Ibid.*, 161. Plimpton journal entry of February 2, 1864, 310.

21. Clark, *History*, 162.

22. *Ibid.*, 163. Perfect numbers, especially at exact dates, are difficult to ascertain. While most accounts and records agree to the point of close approximations, deaths, injuries, sickness, and precise dates of when men left or came into the regiment were not always kept as perfect records. The record-keeping was actually quite good given the time and its circumstances.

23. *Ibid.*, 164.

24. *Ibid.*, 165.

25. *Ibid.*, 167.

26. *Ibid.*, 168.

PART III

1. Hicken, Victor. *Illinois in the Civil War.* Urbana: University of Illinois Press, 1966, 334.

CHAPTER 11

1. Clark, *History*, 392–394.

2. McPherson, *Battle Cry of Freedom*, 858.

3. Grant, Ulysses S., and Elizabeth D. Samet. *The Annotated Memoirs of Ulysses S. Grant.* New York: Liveright Publishing Corporation, 2019, 614. Robertson, William Glenn. *Back Door to Richmond: The Bermuda Hundred Campaign, April-June 1864.* Baton Rouge: Louisiana State University Press, 1991, 14.

4. Grant, *Annotated Memoirs*, 615.

5. Clark, *History*, 172.

6. Brown, Bambi Rae. *Haystacks of Limbs: The Siege of Petersburg, Virginia—1864–1865: The Civil War Diary of Anthony Gaveston Taylor, 39th Illinois Regiment—Company A—Volunteer Veteran Infantry.* Parker, CO: Outskirts Press, 2017, 24–25.

7. Robertson, *Back Door to Richmond*, 28–29, 35.

8. *Ibid.*, 256.

9. *Ibid.*, 36.

10. *Ibid.*, 38. Grant, *Annotated Memoirs*, 615.

11. Clark, *History*, 176.

12. Robertson, *Back Door to Richmond*, 59.

13. Grant, *Annotated Memoirs*, 615.

14. Clark, *History*, 309.

15. *Ibid.*, 309–310.

16. Robertson, *Back Door to Richmond*, 77.

17. Clark, *History*, 178.

18. Robertson, *Back Door to Richmond*, 72.

19. *Ibid.*, 82–83.

20. *Ibid.*, 83. Quote is from Ward letter to his wife dated May 7, 1864, contained in his wartime papers 107–108.

21. Robertson, *Back Door to Richmond*, 89.

22. Grant, *Annotated Memoirs*, 615.

23. Robertson, *Back Door to Richmond*, 109.

24. *Ibid.*, 110.

25. *Ibid.*, 110–115.

26. *Ibid.*, 119–121.

27. Randolph diary entry of May 9–10, 1864, 203.

28. Randolph diary entry of May 10, 1864, 203.

29. Robertson, *Back Door to Richmond*, 127.

30. *Ibid.*, 128, 139–142.

CHAPTER 12

1. Clark, *History*, 511–512.

2. Robertson, *Back Door to Richmond*, 142–143.

3. *Ibid.*

4. *Ibid.*, 145.

5. Randolph diary of May 13, 1864, 204.

6. Robertson, *Back Door to Richmond*, 147.

7. *Ibid.*, 147–148.

8. *Ibid.*, 148–149.

9. Plimpton journal, undated May 1864 entry, 317. Randolph diary entry of May 14, 1864, 204. Clark, *History*, 178.

10. Robertson, *Back Door to Richmond*, 150–151.

11. *Ibid.*, 151.

12. *Ibid.*, 151–153.

13. *Ibid.*, 154.

14. *Ibid.*, 154. Randolph Diary of May 14, 1864, 204. Plimpton journal, undated May 1864 entry 318.

15. Plimpton journal, undated May 1864 entry, 318. Randolph diary entry of May 14, 1864, 204. Clark, *History*, 178–179.

16. Clark, *History*, 178–179.

17. Robertson, *Back Door to Richmond*, 154. Randolph diary entry of May 14, 1864, 204–205.

18. Robertson, *Back Door to Richmond*, 155. Grant, *Annotated Memoirs*, 681.

19. Taylor diary entry of May 15, 1864, 33.

20. Plimpton journal, undated May 1864 entry, 318–319.

21. Robertson, *Back Door to Richmond*, 171.

22. *Ibid.*, 173. Grant was still tied up in terrible fighting in the two-week Battle of Spotsylvania Courthouse. Not only would Grant not arrive at Richmond on Butler's perceived timeline, but it would be the end of the month before Grant was anywhere close. As the old cautionary adage of military planning goes: "The enemy gets a vote."

23. *Ibid.*, 170–172.

24. *Ibid.*, 174–175. Plimpton journal, undated

May 1864 entry, 318–319. Randolph diary entry of May 15, 1864, 205.

25. Robertson, *Back Door to Richmond*, 175. Clark, *History*, 180–181.

26. Robertson, *Back Door to Richmond*, 178–179.

27. Clark, *History*, 181.

28. Robertson, *Back Door to Richmond*, 182–184.

29. *Ibid.*, 184–185.

30. *Ibid.*, 185.

31. *Ibid.*, 185–187.

32. *Ibid.*, 187.

33. *Ibid.*, 188–89.

34. *Ibid.*, 189–191, 198.

35. *Ibid.*, 199–200.

36. *Ibid.*, 200. Plimpton journal, undated May 1864 entry, 319. Randolph diary entry of May 20, 1864, 205.

37. Robertson, *Back Door to Richmond*, 200–201. Plimpton journal, 319–320. Randolph diary, 205–206.

38. Robertson, *Back Door to Richmond*, 201.

39. Plimpton journal, undated May 1864 entry, 320. Randolph diary entry of May 20, 1864, 206.

40. Robertson, *Back Door to Richmond*, 203.

41. Randolph diary entry of May 20, 1864, 206. Letter from Linton to Clark, December 1887, Clark, *History*, 186–187. Plimpton journal, undated May1864 entry, 320.

42. *Ibid.* Clark, *History*, 424.

43. Cook, *Reminiscences of Ezra A. Cook, Company G.*, contained in Clark, *History*, 320.

44. Plimpton journal, undated May 1864 entry, 320–321. Randolph diary entry of May 20, 1864, 206.

45. Cook, *Reminiscences of Ezra A. Cook, Company G*, contained in Clark, *History*, 320–321. Cook survived, eventually made it back to camp, and surgeons were able to save his hand by cutting out infection. However, he did not regain full use of it and was discharged in August.

46. Clark, *History*, 410.

47. Riddle, George, *George Riddle, Company I, Tells Some of His Experiences*, contained in Clark, *History*, 334–335.

48. Guntz, *Narrative of Emile Guntz*, contained in Clark, *History*, 341–342. Plimpton journal, 325. The official roster of the 39th Illinois reports that Bishop died at Andersonville Prison on November 7, 1864, Clark's roster of Company E lists Snee's escape, Clark, *History*, 462.

49. Clark, *History*, 187–188, 190, 512. Reece, J.N. *Report of the Adjutant General of the State of Illinois*, Vol. 3. "History of the Thirty-Ninth Infantry." Springfield, IL, Phillips Brothers State Printers, 141. The Adjutant General's report lists "almost 200" casualties. However, Homer Plimpton's journal gives a specific 119, Anthony Taylor states 114, and Valentine Randolph says, "about 120 men." Precise numbers were made difficult by not just field condition record keeping, but if a man was wounded on the 20th, and died a week later, they were simply listed as having died from wounds on that date.

50. Clark, *History*, 190, 456.

51. *Adjutant General*, 141.

52. Stanley, Charles. "When Duty Calls." *Chicago Tribune*, November 15, 1998. https://www.chicagotribune.com/news/ct-xpm-1998–11–15–9811150154-story.html.

Chapter 13

1. Clark, *History*, 410–411.

2. Robertson, *Back Door to Richmond*, 204–*Ibid.*, 217–220. Plimpton journal, undated May 1864 entry, 321. Randolph diary entry of May 17, 1864, 207.

4. Robertson, *Back Door to Richmond*, 219–220. Grant, *Annotated Memoirs*, 615–617.

5. Robertson, *Back Door to Richmond*, 205–206, 210–215, 217–218.

6. *Ibid.*, 217–218. Randolph diary entry of May 17, 1864, 207.

7. Robertson, *Back Door to Richmond*, 218–220 Plimpton journal, undated May 1864 entry, 321. Randolph diary entry of May 18–19, 1864, 207–208.

8. Robertson, *Back Door to Richmond*, 219–221.

9. *Ibid.*, 221. Plimpton journal undated May 1864 entry, 321–322. Randolph diary entries of May 19–20, 1864, 208. Clark, *History*, 191–192.

10. Howell Official Report to General Terry, May 21, 1864, contained in Clark, *History*, 192–194. O.L. Mann's Account of the Battle, contained in Clark, *History*, 195–197.

11. *Ibid.* Valentine Randolph diary entry of May 20, 1864, 208–209.

12. *Ibid.*

13. Mann's Account of the Battle, contained in Clark, *History*, 196.

14. Howell Official Report to General Terry, May 21, 1864, contained in Clark, *History*, 192–194. O.L. Mann's Account of the Battle, contained in Clark, History, 195–197. Randolph diary of May 20, 1864, 208–209.

15. Doctor Clark lists 70 and 300 on page 195 of his history, while Randolph states 68 regimental casualties in his diary of May 20. Colonel Howell's report to General Terry says 149 men were lost in the effort to re-take the rifle pits, and 300 casualties were suffered in the brigade during the day. The total casualty count comes from Robertson, *Back Door to Richmond*, 222.

16. Plimpton journal undated May 1864 entry, 326–327.

17. Robertson, *Back Door to Richmond*, 222–223.

18. Grant, *Annotated Memoirs*, 615.

19. Robertson, *Back Door to Richmond*, 225.

20. *Ibid.*, 230.

21. McPherson, *Battle Cry of Freedom*, 734–735.

22. *Ibid.*, 230–234. Clark, *History*, 200–201.

23. Robertson, *Back Door to Richmond*, 235–237.

24. Valentine Randolph diary entry of June 1, 1864, 217–218. Clark, *History*, 201.

25. Randolph diary entry of June 2, 1864, 218. Clark, *History*, 201–202. Robertson, *Back Door to Richmond*, 237–238.

26. Clark, *History*, 201–202.

27. Recounting of Andersonville by Richard Warren to Homer Plimpton, Plimpton journal entry of December 16, 1865. Clark, *History*, 549–551. "Documenting Prisoners of War Held at Andersonville." Nps.gov. https://www.nps.gov/ande/learn/historyculture/documenting_union_pows.htm.

28. Randolph diary entry of June 3, 1864, 219.

29. Clark, *History*, 441–442. Gaurley mustered out with the regiment in 1865 and was still living at age 95 when Clark wrote the regimental history in 1889.

30. Robertson, *Back Door to Richmond*, 238–240.

31. Grant, *Annotated Memoirs*, 712.

32. *Ibid.*, 715. Robertson, *Back Door to Richmond*, 241.

33. McPherson, *Battle Cry of Freedom*, 723–724. Robertson, *Back Door to Richmond*, 246–249.

34. Grant, *Annotated Memoirs*, 617.

35. Clark, *History*, 470. The story of the Barber family is from the author's ancestry records.

CHAPTER 14

1. Clark, *History*, 480, 483–484.

2. A variety of modern sources put the estimate anywhere from 40,000 to as many as 65,000.

3. Grant, *Annotated Memoirs*, 617.

4. Fry, *A Republic in the Ranks*, 155–157. Horn, John. *The Petersburg Campaign: June 1864-April 1865*. New York: Da Capo Press, 1999, 30, 35. Grant, *Annotated Memoirs*, 617.

5. Hess, Earl J. *In the Trenches at Petersburg: Field Fortifications & Confederate Defeat*. Chapel Hill: University of North Carolina Press, 2009, xiii.

6. *Ibid.*, 53. Hess, *In the Trenches at Petersburg*, 9. Bowery, Charles R., Ethan S. Rafuse, and Steven Stanley. *Guide to the Richmond-Petersburg Campaign*. Lawrence: University Press of Kansas, 2014, 10–12.

7. Horn, *The Petersburg Campaign*, 52. Hess, *In the Trenches at Petersburg*, 16.

8. Hess, *In the Trenches at Petersburg*, 11, 18. Robertson, *Back Door to Richmond*, 241. Horn, *The Petersburg Campaign*, 54.

9. Hess, *In the Trenches at Petersburg*, 18–19. Robertson, *Back Door to Richmond*, 241. Horn, *The Petersburg Campaign*, 55–58.

10. Hess, *In the Trenches at Petersburg*, 19–20. Robertson, *Back Door to Richmond*, 241–242. Horn, *The Petersburg Campaign*, 58–60. Bowery and Rafuse, *Guide to the Richmond-Petersburg Campaign*, 28–31.

11. *Ibid.*

12. Clark, *History*, 204. Horn, *The Petersburg Campaign*, 46, 60. Hess, *In the Trenches at Petersburg*, 23.

13. Horn, *The Petersburg Campaign*, 60. Hess, *In the Trenches at Petersburg*, 23.

14. *Ibid.* Plimpton journal undated May 1864 entry, 328–329.

15. Horn, *The Petersburg Campaign*, 61. Hess, *In the Trenches at Petersburg*, 23. Plimpton journal undated May 1864 entry, 329.

16. *Ibid.* Valentine Randolph Diary entry of June 16, 1864, 220. Clark, *History*, 204. OR XL P1 #251: Report of Captain Leroy A. Baker, 39th IL June 16, 1864, *The War of the Rebellion: A Compilation of the Official Records of the Union and Confederate Armies*, Volume XL, Part 1 (Serial Number 80), 687, accessed at www.beyondthecrater.com/resources/ors/vol-xl/part-1/-sn-80/or-xl-p1–251-l-a-baker-39-il-jun-16/.

17. *Ibid.* Taylor diary entry of June 16, 1864, 38.

18. Horn, *The Petersburg Campaign*, 60–62. Hess, *In the Trenches at Petersburg*, 21–25.

19. Randolph diary entry of June 17, 1864, 221.

20. Clark, *History*, 205. Plimpton journal entry of June 17, 1864, 330.

21. Horn, *The Petersburg Campaign*, 62. Hess, *In the Trenches at Petersburg*, 25–26.

22. Hess, *In the Trenches at Petersburg*, 26–27.

23. Horn, *The Petersburg Campaign*, 62. Plimpton journal entry of June 17, 1864, 330. Clark, *History*, 205. Randolph diary entry of June 17, 1864, 221.

24. Horn, *The Petersburg Campaign*, 62–63. Hess, *In the Trenches at Petersburg*, 27. Clark, *History*, 205. Plimpton journal of June 17, 1864, 330. Randolph diary entry of June 17, 1864, 221. Taylor diary entry of June 17, 1864, 39.

25. Horn, *The Petersburg Campaign*, 63–65. Hess, *In the Trenches at Petersburg*, 27–29. Bowery and Rafuse, *Guide to the Richmond-Petersburg Campaign*, 38–39.

26. Horn, *The Petersburg Campaign*, 64–65. Hess, *In the Trenches at Petersburg*, 29–30.

27. Horn, *The Petersburg Campaign*, 65–68. Hess, *In the Trenches at Petersburg*, 29–35. Bowery and Rafuse, *Guide to the Richmond-Petersburg Campaign*, 49.

28. Randolph diary entry of June 19, 1864, 222.

29. Plimpton journal entries of June 18–19, 1864, 330–331. Randolph diary entry of June 18, 1864, 221–222.

30. Hess, *In the Trenches at Petersburg*, 35.

31. Horn, *The Petersburg Campaign*, 68. Hess, *In the Trenches at Petersburg*, 35–37.

32. Clark, *History*, 205. Taylor diary entry of June 22, 1864, 39. Fry, *A Republic in the Ranks*, 155–158.

CHAPTER 15

1. Clark, *History*, 450.

2. Hess, *In the Trenches at Petersburg*, 38–41.

3. *Ibid.*, 41. Hess' book is a fantastic account

of the A-Z story of trench warfare at Petersburg for those interested in the battles beyond what the 39th took part in.

4. "P.G.T. Beauregard." Battlefields.org. December 19, 2008. https://www.battlefields.org/learn/biographies/p-g-t-beauregard.

5. Plimpton journal entry of June 30, 1864, 334.

6. Clark, *History*, 206–207.

7. Horn, John. *The Siege of Petersburg: The Battles for the Weldon Railroad, August 1864*. El Dorado Hills, CA: Savas Beatie, 2015, 1–2. "The Battle of Monocacy—July 9, 1864." *American Battlefield Trust*, 16 Oct. 2020, www.battlefields.org/learn/maps/battle-monocacy-july-9-1864.

8. Horn, *The Siege of Petersburg*, 2–3.

9. *Ibid.*, 3–4. Hess, *In the Trenches at Petersburg*, 43.

10. Horn, *The Siege of Petersburg*, 4–5.

11. Horn, *The Petersburg Campaign*, 102, 105, 109–118.

12. Plimpton journal entries of July 12, 1864, and August 2, 1864, 341–43, 346–47.

13. Plimpton journal entry of August 8, 1864, 348.

14. Randolph diary entries of July 24, 28, 1864, 226.

15. Horn, *The Siege of Petersburg*, 10, 16–17. Hess, *In the Trenches at Petersburg*, 124.

16. Hess, *In the Trenches at Petersburg*, 124–125. Horn, *The Siege of Petersburg*, 20–22.

17. Colonel Howell, the 85th Pennsylvania commander and long time First Brigade commander was killed in a non-combat accident in mid-September.

18. Horn, *The Siege of Petersburg*, 23.

19. *Ibid.*, 24–26.

20. *Ibid.*, 26–28. Hess, *In the Trenches at Petersburg*, 125.

21. Horn, *The Siege of Petersburg*, 33–45. "OR XLII P1 #257: Report of Capt. Lewis T. Whipple, 39th IL, August 13–20, 1864," *The War of the Rebellion: A Compilation of the Official Records of the Union and Confederate Armies*, Volume XLII, Part 1 (Serial Number 87), 692, accessed at http://www.beyondthecrater.com/resources/ors/vol-xlii/part-1-sn-87/or-xlii-p1-257-l-t-whipple-39-il-aug-13-20/.

22. Horn, *The Siege of Petersburg*, 45–48. Whipple Report, *Official Records*.

23. Horn, *The Siege of Petersburg*, 49–52.

24. *Ibid.*, 58–60. Hess, *In the Trenches at Petersburg*, 125–127. Whipple Report, *Official Records*.

25. Clark, *History*, 212.

26. Horn, *The Siege of Petersburg*, 61–67.

27. Horn, *The Siege of Petersburg*, 67–69. Homer Plimpton's Account of the Battle of Deep Run, contained in Clark, *History*, 210–211.

28. Horn, *The Siege of Petersburg*, 69–71. Plimpton's account, *History*,211.

29. Clark, *History*, 501.

30. Horn, *The Siege of Petersburg*, 75–76. Plimpton's account, *History*, 211.

31. Clark, *History*, 541–542.

32. Plimpton's account, *History*, 211.

33. Horn, *The Siege of Petersburg*, 76.

34. Plimpton's account, *History*, 211.

35. *Ibid.* "Colored Troops," it should be noted, was the nomenclature of the times and not a term I use by choice. "Henry M. Hardenbergh: U.S. Civil War: U.S. Army: Medal of Honor Recipient." Congressional Medal of Honor Society, n.d. https://www.cmohs.org/recipients/henry-m-hardenbergh.

36. Plimpton's account, *History*, 212. Hess, *In the Trenches at Petersburg*, 128. Plimpton journal entry of September 6, 1864, 351–352. Whipple Report, *Official Records*.

37. Taylor diary entry of August 16, 1864, 47.

38. Clark, *History*, 212–213. Whipple Report, *Official Records*.

39. Ransom Bedell letter to his cousin dated August 24, 1864, Flotow, Mark. *In Their Letters, In Their Words: Illinois Civil War Soldiers Write Home*. Carbondale: Southern Illinois University Press, 2019, 111.

40. Joseph Ward letter to his wife dated October 16, 1864, contained in his wartime papers, 171.

41. Clark, *History*, 542, 533.

42. Hess, *In the Trenches at Petersburg*, 128. Horn, *The Siege of Petersburg*, 104–105, 112–113. Clark, *History*, 212. Whipple Report, *Official Records*.

43. Birney general orders issued to X Corps, Clark, *History*, 216.

44. Hess, *In the Trenches at Petersburg*, 133–135, 140–141.

45. Clark, *History*, 218. Plimpton journal entry of September 6, 1864, 351.

46. Horn, *The Siege of Petersburg*, 310.

47. McPherson, *Battle Cry of Freedom*, 771.

CHAPTER 16

1. Clark, *History*, 412.

2. Valentine Randolph diary entry of August 25, 1864, 231.

3. *Ibid.*, Randolph's diary entries of August 25–29 vividly detail the 39th's transition to the siege lines, 230–231.

4. Clark, *History*, 218–219.

5. McPherson, *Battle Cry of Freedom*, 772–775. Horn, *The Siege of Petersburg*, 311.

6. Seward quoted in McPherson, *Battle Cry of Freedom*, originally in Lewis Lloyd, *Sherman: Fighting Prophet*, New York: Harcourt, Brace, 1932, 409.

7. McPherson, *Battle Cry of Freedom*, 775–776. Horn, *The Siege of Petersburg*, 312.

8. Grant, *Annotated Memoirs*, 637.

9. McPherson, *Battle Cry of Freedom*, 777. Horn, *The Siege of Petersburg*, 310–311.

10. Grant, *Annotated Memoirs*, 637.

11. McPherson, *Battle Cry of Freedom*, 722.

12. Clark, *History*, 224.

13. *Ibid.* Fry, *A Republic in the Ranks*, 161, 171.

14. Hess, *In the Trenches at Petersburg*, 160. Horn, *The Petersburg Campaign*, 158.

15. Clark, *History*, 224.

16. Horn, *The Petersburg Campaign*, 159.

17. Hess, *In the Trenches at Petersburg*, 160. Horn, *The Petersburg Campaign*, 158–159.

18. Hess, *In the Trenches at Petersburg*, 160–161. Horn, *The Petersburg Campaign*, 158–159.

19. Christian Fleetwood seized his regiments fallen colors as the assault neared the Confederate works. Along with another man, Charles Veale, Fleetwood rallied his men on the two flags he now held and continued the attack before it could falter. Fleetwood was awarded the Medal of Honor on April 6, 1865, with the citation reading "Seized the colors after 2 color bearers had been shot down, and bore them nobly through the fight."

20. Hess, *In the Trenches at Petersburg*, 161–162. Horn, *The Siege of Petersburg*, 159.

21. "Reversing" a fort was the act of fortifying it for attack from the north when it was previously set up for attack from the south. Horn, *The Petersburg Campaign*, 159–161. Hess, *In the Trenches at Petersburg*, 163.

22. Horn, *The Petersburg Campaign*, 161–162. Hess, *In the Trenches at Petersburg*, 163.

23. Horn, *The Petersburg Campaign*, 163–165. Hess, *In the Trenches at Petersburg*, 164.

24. Horn, *The Petersburg Campaign*, 162–166. Hess, *In the Trenches at Petersburg*, 164.

25. Horn, *The Petersburg Campaign*, 166–167. Hess, *In the Trenches at Petersburg*, 165–166.

26. Horn puts losses on the Peninsula at 3,327 for the Union to 1,700 Confederates. His numbers south of the James list 2,889 Union soldiers lost to 1,300 Confederates, 167 Hess' breakdowns of the same are 3,350 and 1,700 north of the James and 3,000 and 1,310 south of it, 166.

27. Horn, *The Petersburg Campaign*, 167–168. Hess, *In the Trenches at Petersburg*, 168.

Chapter 17

1. Clark, *History*, 409.

2. Taylor diary entries of October 2–6, 1864, 57–58.

3. 39th Illinois Infantry's consolidated rosters from the Adjutant General's report, located at https://civilwar.illinoisgenweb.org/reg_html/039_reg.html.

4. *Ibid.*

5. Taylor diary entry of October 7, 1864, 59.

6. *Ibid.*

7. Plimpton diary entry of October 12, 1864, 358.

8. *Ibid.*, 59–60. Horn, *The Petersburg Campaign*, 168–169.

9. Horn, *The Petersburg Campaign*, 169. *Official Records*, Volume XLII, Part 1 (Serial Number 87), 144–146.

10. *Official Records*, Volume XLII, Part 1 (Serial

Number 87), 144. Company G Roster, https://civilwar.illinoisgenweb.org/r050/039-g-in.html.

11. Taylor diary entry of October 10, 1864, 60.

12. Horn, *The Petersburg Campaign*, 169. Suderow, Bryce, "'An Ugly Looking Chance for a Charge': The Battle of Darbytown Road, October 13, 1864," February 1, 2015. https://www.beyondthecrater.com/news-and-notes/research/battles/an-ugly-looking-chance-for-a-charge-the-battle-of-darbytown-road-october-13–1864-by-bryce-suderow/.

13. *Ibid.*

14. Suderow, "An Ugly Looking Chance for a Charge," Taylor diary entry of October 13, 1864, 61.

15. *Ibid.*, Horn, *The Petersburg Campaign*, 170.

16. Suderow, "An Ugly Looking Chance for a Charge," Horn, *The Petersburg Campaign*, 170.

17. Homer Plimpton's account of the Battle of Darbytown Crossroads, contained in Clark, *History*, 226.

18. Suderow, *"An Ugly Looking Chance for a Charge,"* Horn, *The Petersburg Campaign*, 170.

19. Clark, *History*, 228,534.

20. Horn, *The Petersburg Campaign*, 170.

21. Plimpton's account, contained in Clark, *History*, 226.

22. Clark, *History*, 534.

23. Suderow, "An Ugly Looking Chance for a Charge," Horn, *The Petersburg Campaign*, 170.

24. *Official Records*, Volume XLII, Part 1 (Serial Number 87), 146.

25. Clark, *History*, 230–231, 534.

26. The 39th had more than three officers at this time, but field officers were those serving at the regiment level and not as company leaders. As the war carried on, promotions did not keep up with the need for regimental leaders, and the senior-most officers were pulled from companies while ensuring each company had at least one officer.

27. Plimpton account, contained in Clark, *History*, 226.

28. Regimental totals for killed, wounded, and captured come from Clark, *History*, 549. Totals for the five-month period in 1864 come from an undated reproduction of the 39th's Annual Reunion sometime in the winter of 1889, and are compared against the adjutant's report, and the consolidated roster at 39th Illinois Infantry Regiment (illinoisgenweb.org).

29. Horn, *The Petersburg Campaign*, 175.

30. *Ibid.* McPherson, *Battle Cry of Freedom*, 779–780.

31. *Ibid.*

32. Clark, *History*, 234.

33. *Ibid.* Taylor diary entry of October 26, 1864, 65. Horn, *The Petersburg Campaign*, 175–176.

34. Clark, *History*, 234. Horn, *The Petersburg Campaign*, 177.

35. Horn, *The Petersburg Campaign*, 177. Longstreet is a fascinating Confederate leader

worth further study. He spent most of the war arguing the Confederate army should be fighting defensively to preserve their limited manpower and supplies and put the onus on the Union. Seemingly never a believer in the Confederate "cause" and only wishing to defend his native South Carolina, Longstreet worked with Grant in the post-war years and supported Republican causes. Distancing himself from notions of the Confederacy, Longstreet became reviled by those with southern sympathies, and thus, is rarely mentioned with the likes of Jackson and Lee.

36. Horn, *The Petersburg Campaign,* 180. Taylor diary entry of October 27, 1864, 66. "OR XLII P1 #258: Report of Lieut. James Hannum, 39th IL, October 27–28, 1864," *The War of the Rebellion: A Compilation of the Official Records of the Union and Confederate Armies,* Volume XLII, Part 1 (Serial Number 87), 692–693, accessed at http://www.beyondthecrater.com/resources/ors/vol-xlii/part-1-sn-87/or-xlii-p1-258-j-hannum-39-il-oct-27-28/.

37. Horn, *The Petersburg Campaign,* 180.

38. *Ibid.,* 180–181. Hannum Report, *Official Records.* Hess, *In the Trenches at Petersburg,* 195–196.

39. Army of the James losses from *Official Records,* Volume XLII, Part 1 (Serial Number 87), 148–152. Confederate losses from Hess, *In the Trenches at Petersburg,* 196. Hannum Report, *Official Records.*

40. Hess, *In the Trenches at Petersburg,* 192–194.

41. Grant to Stanton, October 27, 1864, cited in Horn, *The Siege of Petersburg,* 313.

42. Horn, *The Petersburg Campaign,* 185.

43. Lee to Davis, quoted in McPherson, *Battle Cry of Freedom,* 780.

44. Hess, *In the Trenches at Petersburg,* 198.

45. Taylor diary entry of October 31, 1864, 67–68.

Chapter 18

1. Clark, *History,* 475–476.

2. Taylor diary entry of November 9–10, 1864, 69. Homer Plimpton letter to a friend of November 8, 1864, included in his journal, 360. Joseph Ward's letter to his wife of November 17, 1864, contained in his wartime papers, 174–175.

3. McPherson, *Battle Cry of Freedom,* 803.

4. Fry, *A Republic in the Ranks,* 177.

5. Homer Plimpton's letter to a friend of November 8, 1864, included in his journal, 360.

6. Fry, *A Republic in the Ranks,* 178.

7. Taylor diary entry of November 8, 1864, 69.

8. McPherson, *Battle Cry of Freedom,* 804.

9. *Ibid.,* 806–815.

10. Hess, *In the Trenches at Petersburg,* 211.

11. Taylor diary entry of November 24–25, 1864, 73–74.

12. Bowery and Rafuse, *Guide to the Richmond-Petersburg Campaign,* 291–292. Clark,

History, 288–289. McPherson, *Battle Cry of Freedom,* 819.

13. Horn, *The Petersburg Campaign,* 279. Homer Plimpton letter to a friend of December 12, 1864, included in his journal, 367.

14. Savage returned home to his family farm, having lost his vision but not his penchant for service. He served on the Board of Supervisors, became a member of the state legislature, then retired to farm once more, Clark, *History,* 484.

15. *Ibid.,* 485.

16. Stanley, Charles, *The Preacher's Company,* included in Plimpton's journal, xiv. Plimpton letter to a friend of December 12, 1864, included in his journal, 367. Stanley, "When Duty Calls."

17. McPherson, *Battle Cry of Freedom,* 820. Sherman telegraph to Lincoln quoted in McPherson, *Battle Cry of Freedom,* 811.

18. McPherson, *Battle Cry of Freedom,* 813–815.

19. *Ibid.,* 820.

20. *Ibid.* Bowery and Rafuse, *Guide to the Richmond-Petersburg Campaign,* 291–292.

21. Clark, *History,* 242.

22. Joseph Ward's letter to his wife of December 25, 1864, contained in his wartime papers, 190.

23. Taylor diary entry of January 1, 1865, 82.

24. Horn, *The Petersburg Campaign,* 199.

25. *Ibid.* McPherson, *Battle Cry of Freedom,* 820.

26. Stephens' writing is quoted in McPherson, *Battle Cry of Freedom,* 821.

27. Taylor diary entries of January 8, 10, 1865, 84–85.

28. McPherson, *Battle Cry of Freedom,* 821.

29. *Ibid.,* 822–823.

30. Ward diary entry of January 5, 1865, contained in his wartime papers, 195.

31. Hess, *In the Trenches at Petersburg,* 229. Horn, *The Petersburg Campaign,* 200.

32. Hess, *In the Trenches at Petersburg,* 229–232. Horn, *The Petersburg Campaign,* 200–201, 203, 206.

33. Hess, *In the Trenches at Petersburg,* 232. Horn, *The Petersburg Campaign,* 206.

34. Clark, *History,* 246–247.

35. McPherson, *Battle Cry of Freedom,* 824.

Chapter 19

1. Stanley, Charles. "Henry Day, 39th Illinois Infantry Company A." Illinoisgenweb.org. https://civilwar.illinoisgenweb.org/scrapbk/039-a-mh.htm. Clark, *History,* 399.

2. "Abner P. Allen." Congressional Medal of Honor Society. https://www.cmohs.org/recipients/abner-p-allen. Clark, *History,* 535.

3. Fox, John J. *The Confederate Alamo: Bloodbath at Petersburg's Fort Gregg on April 2, 1865.* Winchester, VA: Angle Valley Press, 2010, 1–2.

4. Horn, *The Petersburg Campaign,* 209.

5. *Ibid.,* 211. Alexander, Edward S. *Dawn of*

Victory: Breakthrough at Petersburg, March 25–April 2, 1865. El Dorado Hills, CA: Savas Beatie, 2015, 23. Fox, *The Confederate Alamo*, 2.

6. Alexander, *Dawn of Victory*, 23–24. Bowery and Rafuse, *Guide to the Richmond-Petersburg Campaign*, 71.

7. Grant, *Annotated Memoirs*, 834.

8. Alexander, *Dawn of Victory*, 23. Fox, *The Confederate Alamo*, 3–4.

9. Taylor diary entry of March 12, 1865, 94.

10. Clark, *History*, 249–251.

11. Plimpton letter to a friend included in his March 17, 1865, journal entry, 374.

12. *Ibid.*, 252. Taylor diary entries of March 15, 20, 1865, 95, 97.

13. Horn, *The Petersburg Campaign*, 211.

14. *Ibid.*, 211–212. Alexander, *Dawn of Victory*, 24.

15. Horn, *The Petersburg Campaign*, 212–213. Alexander, *Dawn of Victory*, 24–25.

16. Horn, *The Petersburg Campaign*, 212–216. Alexander, *Dawn of Victory*, 25–26.

17. Taylor diary entry of March 26, 1865, 98–99.

18. Alexander, *Dawn of Victory*, 34. Horn, *The Petersburg Campaign*, 219. Fox, *The Confederate Alamo*, 4.

19. Fox, *The Confederate Alamo*, 4–7. Horn, *The Petersburg Campaign*, 219. Alexander, *Dawn of Victory*, 37. Diary entries of Anthony Taylor on March 27–28, 1865, 99. Homer Plimpton journal entry of March 27, 1865, 376.

20. Fox, *The Confederate Alamo*, 7. Horn, *The Petersburg Campaign*, 220. Alexander, *Dawn of Victory*, 37.

21. Fox, *The Confederate Alamo*, 7–8. Horn, *The Petersburg Campaign*, 220. Alexander, *Dawn of Victory*, 37. Quote from Anthony Taylor diary entry of March 29, 1865, 99.

22. Fox, *The Confederate Alamo*, 9–10. Horn, *The Petersburg Campaign*, 220. Alexander, *Dawn of Victory*, 37.

23. Fox, *The Confederate Alamo*, 8–10. Horn, *The Petersburg Campaign*, 220–222. Alexander, *Dawn of Victory*, 39–40. Hess, *In the Trenches at Petersburg*, 255–57.

24. Alexander, *Dawn of Victory*, 40–42. Hess, *In the Trenches at Petersburg*, 257–258. "OR XLVI P1 #222: Report of Colonel Thomas O. Osborn, 39th IL, Commanding 1/1/XXIV/AotJ, March 27–April 9, 1865," *The War of the Rebellion: A Compilation of the Official Records of the Union and Confederate Armies*, Volume XLVI, Part 1 (Serial Number 95), 1185–1188, accessed from http://www.beyondthecrater.com/resources/ors/vol-xlvi/part-1-sn-95/appomattox-campaign-reports-95/or-xlvi-p1-app-222-t-o-osborn-1-1-xxiv-aotj-mar-27-apr-9/.

25. Alexander, *Dawn of Victory*, 42–44. Hess, *In the Trenches at Petersburg*, 258–259. Fox, *The Confederate Alamo*, 10–11.

26. *Ibid.*

27. Alexander, *Dawn of Victory*, 49. Hess, *In the Trenches at Petersburg*, 260. Fox, *The Confederate Alamo*, 13–14.

28. Bowery and Rafuse, *Guide to the Richmond-Petersburg Campaign*, 389.

29. Hess, *In the Trenches at Petersburg*, 260–261. Alexander, *Dawn of Victory*, 49–50. Osborn Report, *Official Records*. Taylor diary entry of April 1, 1865, 100.

30. Hess, *In the Trenches at Petersburg*, 263.

31. *Ibid.* Alexander, *Dawn of Victory*, 51.

32. Hess, *In the Trenches at Petersburg*, 263. Alexander, *Dawn of Victory*, 51. Fox, *The Confederate Alamo*, 12. Osborn Report, *Official Records*.

33. Osborn Report, *Official Records*.

34. Howard, William, *"Narrative of William H. Howard, Company G,"* contained in Clark, *History*, 339. Fox, *The Confederate Alamo*, 15–19.

35. Fox, *The Confederate Alamo*, 15–19.

36. Alexander, *Dawn of Victory*, 52. Fox, *The Confederate Alamo*, 21. Hess, *In the Trenches at Petersburg*, 264.

Chapter 20

1. Clark, *History*, 523.

2. Fox, *The Confederate Alamo*, xi.

3. Fox, *The Confederate Alamo*, 69–70.

4. General Grant telegram to Lincoln and Stanton on the morning of April 2, 1865. *The War of the Rebellion: A Compilation of the Official Records of the Union and Confederate Armies*, Volume XLVI, Part 1 (Serial Number 97), 447.

5. Alexander, *Dawn of Victory*, 65. Hess, *In the Trenches at Petersburg*, 272.

6. Hess, *In the Trenches at Petersburg*, 273.

7. Fox, *The Confederate Alamo*, 52–55, 70. Alexander, *Dawn of Victory*, 99. Osborn Report, *Official Records*.

8. Fox, *The Confederate Alamo*, 55. Alexander, *Dawn of Victory*, 104–105. Horn, *The Petersburg Campaign*, 243–244.

9. Osborn Report, *Official Records*.

10. Anthony Taylor diary entry of April 2, 1865, 101.

11. Fox, *The Confederate Alamo*, 56–57. Alexander, *Dawn of Victory*, 105–106. Horn, *The Petersburg Campaign*, 244. Osborn Report, *Official Records*. Homer Plimpton letter dated April 28, 1865, included in Clark, *History*, 253.

12. Fox, *The Confederate Alamo*, 70, 72.

13. Plimpton letter, contained in Clark, *History*, 255.

14. Fox, *The Confederate Alamo*, 75–76, 93. Alexander, *Dawn of Victory*, 108.

15. Osborn Report, *Official Records*. Fox, *The Confederate Alamo*, 93–94, 97–98. Alexander, *Dawn of Victory*, 108. Wetzel quote from Wetzel, Michael. "Fort Gregg: A One-Armed Comrade's Description of Its Capture." *National Tribune*, August 21, 1890.

16. Alexander, *Dawn of Victory*, 108.

17. Quotation is from Osborn Report, *Official*

Records, 1185. Alexander, *Dawn of Victory*, 108. Fox, *The Confederate Alamo*, 99. Hess, *In the Trenches at Petersburg*, 274.

18. Osborn Report, *Official Records*.

19. Taylor April 2, 1865, diary entry, 102.

20. Fox, *The Confederate Alamo*, 100–103, 105. Alexander, *Dawn of Victory*, 109. Osborn Report, *Official Records*. Plimpton letter, in Clark, *History*, 253.

21. *Adjutant General*, 142.

22. Plimpton letter, in Clark, *History*, 253.

23. "*Narrative of William H. Howard*," in Clark, *History*, 339.

24. Wetzel, "Fort Gregg."

25. "*Narrative of William H. Howard*," in Clark, *History*, 339–340.

26. Fox, *The Confederate Alamo*, 107.

27. Ware, Charles W. "Fort Gregg Again! A Voice from Illinois Regarding Its Capture," *National Tribune*, February 19, 1891.

28. Wetzel, *Fort Gregg*.

29. Plimpton letter, in Clark, *History*, 253.

30. Ware, "Fort Gregg Again!"

31. Fox, *The Confederate Alamo*, 111.

32. *Ibid.*, 111–113.

33. *Ibid.*, 145–147.

34. *Ibid.*, 149–153. Hess, *In the Trenches at Petersburg*, 275.

35. Ware, "Fort Gregg Again!"

36. *Ibid.*

37. Clark, *History*, 513.

38. Plimpton letter, in Clark, *History*, 253. Corporal Day planting the flag is mentioned in Clark, *History*, 399, and the Adjutant General's Report, 143.

39. Fox, *The Confederate Alamo*, 175, 185.

40. Alexander, *Dawn of Victory*, 111–112.

41. Fox, *The Confederate Alamo*, 185. Both Osborn's report and Plimpton's letter explicitly state the battle lasted 24 minutes from the time they gained the parapet.

42. Plimpton letter, contained in Clark, *History*, 255.

43. From Major General John Gibbon's report, cited in Fox, *The Confederate Alamo*, 201–202.

44. Fox, *The Confederate Alamo*, 163–164.

45. *Ibid.*, 174.

46. Gibbon's report of the battle, quoted in Bowery and Rafuse, *Guide to the Richmond Petersburg Campaign*, 451–452.

47. Fox, *The Confederate Alamo*, 202.

48. Letters of Confederate soldiers quoted in Hess, *In the Trenches at Petersburg*, 276.

49. Fox, *The Confederate Alamo*, 230. Osborn Report, *Official Records*. Plimpton letter, quoted in Clark, *History*, 255. Fox lists two officer deaths from the 39th, but Osborn only mentions Lamb, with Lieutenant Joseph Neal being wounded. The Illinois Adjutant General report shows that Neal mustered out in December of 1865. Plimpton also only lists 16 enlisted men killed but mentions the six who later died from wounds. Officers wrote these reports many days later, as the army was on the move the very next morning, and mistakes are to be understood. I have chosen to go with Osborn's numbers.

50. Clark, *History*, 271.

51. Fox, *The Confederate Alamo*, 250.

52. Clark, *History*, 399, 535. *Adjutant General*,143. Plimpton letter, contained in his journal, 380. See also Fox, John. *Medal of Honor—Or Not—for 39th Illinois' Corporal Henry M. Day? John Fox Books* (blog). July 30, 2011. https://www.johnfoxbooks.com/post-12-medal-of-honor-or-not-for-39th-illinois-corporal-henry-m-day/. Stanley, Charles. "In Search of Honor." *Chicago Tribune*, July 8, 1996. https://www.chicagotribune.com/news/ct-xpm-1996-07-08-9607080172-story.html.

53. Clark, *History*, 275.

54. Alexander, *Dawn of Victory*, 112–113.

55. Hess, *In the Trenches at Petersburg*, 276–277.

56. Alexander, *Dawn of Victory*, 118. Fox, *The Confederate Alamo*, 201.

57. Hess, *In the Trenches at Petersburg*, 279. Alexander, *Dawn of Victory*, 123.

58. Grant to his wife Julia on April 2, 1865, quoted in Hess, *In the Trenches at Petersburg*, 279.

59. Alexander, *Dawn of Victory*, 219.

60. Grant, *Annotated Memoirs*, 854.

61. Hess, *In The Trenches at Petersburg*, 279–280. Fox, *The Confederate Alamo*, 205. Horn, *The Petersburg Campaign*, 246–248. Alexander, *Dawn of Victory*, 126–127.

62. Alexander, *Dawn of Victory*, 126–129. Grant, *Annotated Memoirs*, 858–861. McPherson, *Battle Cry of Freedom*, 846–847.

63. McPherson, *Battle Cry of Freedom*, 847.

64. Osborn Report, *Official Records*.

65. Taylor diary entry of April 3, 1865, 103.

CHAPTER 21

1. Clark, *History*, 513.

2. McPherson, *Battle Cry of Freedom*, 847.

3. Hess, *In the Trenches at Petersburg*, 280.

4. Calkins, Chris M. *The Appomattox Campaign: March 29-April 9, 1865*. Lynchburg, VA: Schroeder Publications, 2018, 66–67.

5. Calkins, *The Appomattox Campaign*, 74.

6. Grant, *Annotated Memoirs*, 861.

7. *Ibid.*, 862. Hess, *In the Trenches at Petersburg*, 280. Calkins, *The Appomattox Campaign*, 75–76.

8. Calkins, *The Appomattox Campaign*, 79. Hess, *In the Trenches at Petersburg*, 280–281. Grant, *Annotated Memoirs*, 862.

9. Grant, *Annotated Memoirs*, 862.

10. McPherson, *Battle Cry of Freedom*, 847. Hess, *In the Trenches at Petersburg*, 281. Osborn Report, *Official Records*. Calkins, *The Appomattox Campaign*, 89. Anthony Taylor diary entries of April 5 and 6, 1862, 103.

11. Calkins, *The Appomattox Campaign*, 85.

12. *Ibid.*, 93. Grant, *Annotated Memoirs*, 865.

13. Taylor diary entry of April 6, 1865, 103.

14. Osborn Report, *Official Records*.

15. *Ibid.* Taylor diary entry of April 6, 1865, 103–104. Calkins, *The Appomattox Campaign*, 115.

16. Grant, *Annotated Memoirs*, 867.

17. *Ibid.* Calkins, *The Appomattox Campaign*, 114.

18. Appomattox Courthouse National Historic Park. 2018. *The Appomattox Campaign.* http://www.nps.gov/apco/appomattox-campaign.htm.

19. Osborn Report, *Official Records.* Taylor diary entry of April 6, 1865, 104. Calkins, *The Appomattox Campaign*, 116.

20. Calkins, *The Appomattox Campaign*, 115–116.

21. *Ibid.*, 123–124. Osborn Report, *Official Records.* Taylor diary entry of April 7, 1865, 104.

22. Calkins, *The Appomattox Campaign*, 131–134. Hess, *In the Trenches at Petersburg*, 281–282. Grant, *Annotated Memoirs*, 871–872. Quote from Grant to Lee on the evening of April 7, 1865, contained in *Annotated Memoirs*, 872.

23. Grant, *Annotated Memoirs*, 873.

24. Osborn Report, *Official Records.* Calkins, *The Appomattox Campaign*, 151. Taylor diary entry of April 8, 1865, 105.

25. Calkins, *The Appomattox Campaign*, 151–152.

26. *Ibid.*, 155. Osborn Report, *Official Records.*

27. Taylor diary entry of April 9, 1865, 105.

28. Clark, *History*, 263–264.

29. Osborn Report, *Official History.* Taylor diary entry of April 9, 1865, 105.

30. Calkins, *The Appomattox Campaign*, 160–161. Hess, *In the Trenches at Petersburg*, 282. Grant, *Annotated Memoirs*, 873–874.

31. Taylor diary entry of April 9, 1865, 105.

32. *Ibid.* Clark, *History*, 264. Osborn Report *Official Records.* Calkins, *The Appomattox Campaign*, 162. Homer Plimpton letter to his aunt and uncle dated April 27, 1865, contained in his journal, 381.

33. Taylor diary entry of April 9, 1865, 106.

34. Plimpton letter to his aunt and uncle dated April 27, 1865, contained in his journal, 381.

35. Clark, *History*, 264.

36. *Ibid.*, 458. Osborn Report, *Official Records.*

37. Calkins, *The Appomattox Campaign*, 162–165. Osborn Report, *Official Records.* Hess, *In the Trenches at Petersburg*, 282. Clark, *History*, 266.

38. Clark, *History*, 264.

39. Osborn Report, *Official Records.*

40. Clark, *History*, 264.

41. Plimpton letter to his aunt and uncle dated April 27, 1865, contained in his journal, 381.

42. *Ibid.*

43. "To the Bitter End." Battlefields.Org. March 23, 2015. https://www.battlefields.org/learn/articles/bitter-end.

44. *Ibid.*, 549.

EPILOGUE

1. Clark, *History*, 264–266.

2. *Ibid.*, 267–269.

3. *Ibid.*, 380, 553.

4. Ward diary entries of March 6, 1865, April 5, 1865, and letter to his wife of July 10, 1865, 221, 223, 247.

5. Clark, *History*, 486.

6. Cummins and Hohweiler, *An Enlisted Soldier's View of the Civil War*, 250.

7. Taylor diary entries of April 9–10, 1865, 107.

8. Taylor diary entries of April 10–19, 1865, 107–110. Clark, *History*, 267–268.

9. Clark, *History*, 403. Brown, *Haystacks of Limbs*, 161.

10. Engle, *Gathering to Save a Nation*, 471–472.

11. Reavis, "Life and Public Services of Richard Yates," 29–30.

12. *Ibid.*, 2.

13. Roe, Wise, *A Civil War Soldier's Diary*, 241. Clark, *History*, 521.

14. Stanley, Charles, "A Brief Biography of Valentine C. Randolph" in an appendix to Roe, Wise, *A Civil War Soldier's Diary*, 243–244.

15. Plimpton letter to his aunt and uncle dated April 27, 1865, included in his journal 382, 399.

16. Quinn, Patrick, "Homer A. Plimpton," included in Dodson, John L., *The Civil War Journals of Col. Homer A. Plimpton*, xx.

17. *Ibid.*, xx–xxi.

18. Eicher, John H., and Eicher, David J. *Civil War High Commands.* Palo Alto: Stanford University Press, 2001, 411.

19. Clark, *History*, 368–369.

20. Eicher and Eicher, *Civil War High Commands*, 411.

21. Clark, *History*, 270–272.

22. Plimpton letter of April 27, 1865, 402–403.

23. Clark, *History*, 275.

24. *Ibid.*, 277.

25. *Ibid.*, 278–279.

26. *Ibid.*, 279, 513.

27. *Ibid.*, 281.

28. *Ibid.*, 281–282. Plimpton journal entry of December 16, 1865, 412.

29. Clark, *History*, 282–283.

30. *Ibid.*, 283–284.

31. *Ibid.*, 284–285.

32. Plimpton journal entry of December 16, 1865, 415.

33. Clark, History, 401.

34. *Ibid.*, 495.

35. *Ibid.*, 428.

36. *Ibid.*, 286.

Bibliography

Articles

Bohn, Richard E. "Richard Yates: An Appraisal of His Value as the Civil War Governor of Illinois." *Journal of the Illinois State Historical Society,* Civil War Sesquicentennial Issue, 104, no. 1/2 (2011): 17–37.

Botts, Joshua. "'Brilliant and Important Victories'—Research—History of the Foreign Relations Series—Historical Documents—Office of the Historian." State.gov, July 3, 2013. https://history.state.gov/historicaldocuments/frus-history/research/brilliant-and-important-victories.

Calkins, Chris. "Petersburg: The Wearing down of Lee's Army." Battlefields.org. February 5, 2009. https://www.battlefields.org/learn/articles/petersburg-wearing-down-lees-army.

Coffey, Walter. "The Army of the Potomac: Hooker Takes Command." Civilwarmonths.com. January 26, 2018. https://civilwarmonths.com/2018/01/26/the-army-of-the-potomac-hooker-takes-command/.

Coffey, Walter. "Lincoln Visits the Virginia Peninsula." Civilwarmonths.com. July 8, 2017. https://civilwarmonths.com/2017/07/08/lincoln-visits-the-virginia-peninsula/.

Cozzens, Peter. "Shenandoah Valley Campaign of 1862." Encyclopedia Virginia, November 29, 2012. https://www.encyclopediavirginia.org/Shenandoah_Valley_Campaign_of_1862.

McFarland, Kenneth M. "James River During the Civil War." Encyclopedia Virginia, October 27, 2015. https://www.encyclopediavirginia.org/James_River_During_the_Civil_War.

"150 Years Ago Today: Christmas at the Siege of Petersburg: December 25, 1864." The Siege of Petersburg Online, February 1, 2015. http://www.beyondthecrater.com/news-and-notes/siege-of-petersburg-sesquicentennial/150-years-ago-today/150–18641225-christmas-petersburg-siege/.

Pohanka, Brian C. "Fort Wagner and the 54th Massachusetts Volunteer Infantry." Battlefields.org. February 4, 2009. https://www.battlefields.org/learn/articles/fort-wagner-and-54th-massachusetts-volunteer-infantry.

Rhea, Gordon. "The Overland Campaign of 1864." *Hallowed Ground* magazine, available at Battlefields.org. April 14, 2014. https://www.battlefields.org/learn/articles/overland-campaign-1864.

Schroeder, Patrick. "The Battles of Appomattox Station and Court House." Battlefields.org. November 5, 2009. https://www.battlefields.org/learn/articles/battles-appomattox-station-and-court-house.

Stanley, Charles. "Henry Day, 39th Illinois Infantry Company A." Illinoisgenweb.org. https://civilwar.illinoisgenweb.org/scrapbk/039-a-mh.htm.

Stanley, Charles. "In Search of Honor." *Chicago Tribune,* July 8, 1996. https://www.chicagotribune.com/news/ct-xpm-1996-07-08-9607080172-story.html.

Stanley, Charles. "When Duty Calls." *Chicago Tribune,* November 15, 1998. https://www.chicagotribune.com/news/ct-xpm-1998-11-15-9811150154-story.html.

Suderow, Bryce. "'An Ugly Looking Chance for a Charge': The Battle of Darbytown Road. October 13, 1864." February 1, 2015. https://www.beyondthecrater.com/news-and-notes/research/battles/an-ugly-looking-chance-for-a-charge-the-battle-of-darbytown-road-october-13–1864-by-bryce-suderow/.

Swansburg, John. "The Incredible Life of Lew Wallace, Civil War General and Author of Ben-Hur." Slate.com. March 26, 2013. http://www.slate.com/articles/life/history/2013/03/ben_hur_and_lew_wallace_how_the_scapegoat_of_shiloh_became_one_of_the_best.html.

Thompson, Robert. "Two Days in April: Breakthrough at Petersburg." Battlefields.org. July 25, 2011. https://www.battlefields.org/learn/articles/two-days-april-breakthrough-petersburg.

Urofsky, Melvin I. "Dred Scott Decision—Reception and Significance." In *Encyclopædia Britannica,* September 10, 2020. https://www.britannica.com/event/Dred-Scott-decision/Reception-and-significance.

Ware, Charles W. "Fort Gregg Again! A Voice from Illinois Regarding Its Capture." *National Tribune,* 3, February 19, 1891. https://chroniclingamerica.loc.gov/lccn/sn82016187/1891-02–19/ed-1/seq-3/

Wetzel, Michael. "Fort Gregg: A One-Armed Comrade's Description of Its Capture." *National Tribune*, 3 August 21, 1890. https://chroniclingamerica.loc.gov/lccn/sn82016187/1890–08–21/ed-1/seq-3/.

Books

Alexander, Edward S. *Dawn of Victory: Breakthrough at Petersburg, March 25–April 2, 1865*. El Dorado Hills, CA: Savas Beatie, 2015.

Beschloss, Michael R. *Presidents of War*. New York: Crown, 2018.

Bowery, Charles R., Ethan S. Rafuse, and Steven Stanley. *Guide to the Richmond-Petersburg Campaign*. Lawrence: University Press of Kansas, 2014.

Brands, H. W. *The Zealot and the Emancipator: John Brown, Abraham Lincoln and the Struggle for American Freedom*. 1st ed. London: Doubleday, 2020.

Brown, Bambi Rae. *Haystacks of Limbs: The Siege of Petersburg, Virginia—1864–1865: The Civil War Diary of Anthony Gaveston Taylor, 39th Illinois Regiment—Company A—Volunteer Veteran Infantry*. Parker, CO: Outskirts Press, 2017.

Calkins, Chris M. *The Appomattox Campaign: March 29–April 9, 1865*. Lynchburg, VA: Schroeder Publications, 2018.

Clark, Charles M. *The History of the Thirty-Ninth Regiment Illinois Volunteer Veteran Infantry (Yates Phalanx) in the War of the Rebellion. 1861–1865*. Chicago: Auspices of the Veteran Association of the Regiment, 1889.

Cozzens, Peter. *Shenandoah 1862: Stonewall Jackson's Valley Campaign*. Chapel Hill: University of North Carolina Press, 2013.

Dyer, Frederick H. *A Compendium of the War of the Rebellion: Compiled and Arranged from Official Records of the Federal and Confederate Armies, Reports of the Adjutant Generals of the Several States, the Army Registers, and Other Reliable Documents and Sources*. Des Moines: The Dyer Publishing Company, 1908.

Eicher, John H., and Eicher, David J. *Civil War High Commands*. Palo Alto: Stanford University Press, 2001.

Engle, Stephen Douglas. *Gathering to Save a Nation: Lincoln and the Union's War Governors*. Chapel Hill: The University of North Carolina Press, 2016.

Flotow, Mark. *In Their Letters, In Their Words: Illinois Civil War Soldiers Write Home*. Carbondale: Southern Illinois University Press, 2019.

Fox, John J. *The Confederate Alamo: Bloodbath at Petersburg's Fort Gregg on April 2, 1865*. Winchester, VA: Angle Valley Press, 2010.

Fry, Zachery A. *A Republic in the Ranks: Loyalty aand Dissent in the Army of the Potomac*. Chapel Hill: University of North Carolina Press, 2020.

Hess, Earl J. *In the Trenches at Petersburg: Field Fortifications & Confederate Defeat*. Chapel Hill: University of North Carolina Press, 2009.

Hicken, Victor. *Illinois in the Civil War*. Urbana: University of Illinois Press, 1991.

Horn, John. *The Petersburg Campaign: June 1864–April 1865*. New York: Da Capo Press, 1999.

Horn, John. *The Siege of Petersburg: The Battles for the Weldon Railroad, August 1864*. El Dorado Hills, CA: Savas Beatie, 2015.

Jackson, Holly. *American Radicals: How Nineteenth-Century Protest Shaped the Nation*. New York: Crown, 2019.

McPherson, James M. *Battle Cry of Freedom*. New York: Oxford University Press, 1988.

McPherson, James M. *For Cause and Comrades: Why Men Fought in the Civil War*. New York: Oxford University Press, 1999.

Plimpton, Homer A., and John L. Dodson. *The Civil War Journals of Col. Homer A. Plimpton: 1861–1865*. Bloomington: Trafford, 2012.

Randolph, Valentine C., David D. Roe, and Stephen R. Wise. *A Civil War Soldier's Diary: Valentine C. Randolph, 39th Illinois Regiment*. Dekalb: Northern Illinois University Press, 2006.

Reece, J.N. *Report of the Adjutant General of the State of Illinois*, Vol 3. Springfield, IL: Phillips Brothers State Printers, 1901.

Robertson, William Glenn. *Back Door to Richmond: The Bermuda Hundred Campaign, April–June 1864*. Baton Rouge: Louisiana State University Press, 1991.

Tanner, Robert G. *Stonewall in the Valley: Thomas J. "Stonewall" Jackson's Shenandoah Valley Campaign, Spring 1862*. Mechanicsburg, PA: Stackpole Books, 2002.

Wise, Stephen R. *Gate of Hell: Campaign for Charleston Harbor, 1863*. Columbia: University of South Carolina Press, 2011.

Other

"Abner P. Allen." Congressional Medal of Honor Society. https://www.cmohs.org/recipients/abner-p-allen.

"Antietam." Battlefields.org. January 12, 2009. https://www.battlefields.org/learn/articles/antietam.

Appomattox Courthouse National Historic Park. 2018. *The Appomattox Campaign*. https://www.nps.gov/apco/appomattox-campaign.htm.

"The Battle of Gaines' Mill." Nps.gov, February 26, 2015. https://www.nps.gov/rich/learn/historyculture/gainesmillbull.htm.

"The Battle of Monocacy—July 9, 1864." *American Battlefield Trust*. 16 October 2020. www.battlefields.org/learn/maps/battle-monocacy-july-9–1864.

"The Campaign to Appomattox." Nps.gov. n.d. https://www.nps.gov/parkhistory/online_books/civil_war_series/6/sec1.htm.

"Chantilly." Battlefields.org. January 14, 2009. https://www.battlefields.org/learn/civil-war/battles/chantilly.

"Chickamauga." Battlefields.org. January 14, 2009. https://www.battlefields.org/learn/articles/chickamauga.

"Civil War Army Organization." American Battlefield Trust. September 17, 2019. https://www.battlefields.org/learn/articles/civil-war-army-organization.

"Documenting Prisoners of War Held at Andersonville." Nps.gov. https://www.nps.gov/ande/learn/historyculture/documenting_union_pows.htm.

"Farewell Address." Speeches and Writings. Abraham Lincoln Online. n.d. http://www.abrahamlincolnonline.org/lincoln/speeches/farewell.htm.

"Fort Wagner." 2009. Battlefields.org. January 22, 2009. https://www.battlefields.org/learn/articles/fort-wagner.

Fox, John. *Medal of Honor—Or Not—for 39th Illinois' Corporal Henry M. Day? John Fox Books* (blog). July 30, 2011. https://www.johnfoxbooks.com/post-12-medal-of-honor-or-not-for-39th-illinois-corporal-henry-m-day/.

"Henry M. Hardenbergh." Congressional Medal of Honor Society. https://www.cmohs.org/recipients/henry-m-hardenbergh.

"House Divided Speech." Speeches and Writings. Abraham Lincoln Online. n.d. http://www.abrahamlincolnonline.org/lincoln/speeches/house.htm.

IL GenWeb Project. 39th Illinois Infantry Regiment. n.d. https://civilwar.illinoisgenweb.org/reg_html/039_reg.html.

"Jackson's Shenandoah Valley Campaign." Battlefields.org. December 13, 2016. https://www.battlefields.org/learn/civil-war/jacksons-shenandoah-valley-campaign.

"Kansas-Nebraska Act. [1854]." In *Encyclopedia Britannica*. July 31, 2019. https://www.britannica.com/topic/Kansas-Nebraska-Act.

"Kernstown." Battlefields.org. January 12, 2009. https://www.battlefields.org/learn/articles/kernstown.

"National Park Civil War Series: The Battles for Richmond, 1862." National Parks Service. U.S. Department of the Interior. https://www.nps.gov/parkhistory/online_books/civil_war_series/21/sec7.htm.

"New Market Heights." Battlefields.org. April 17, 2009. https://www.battlefields.org/learn/civil-war/battles/new-market-heights.

"Operations against the Defenses of Charleston." Battlefields.org. February 21, 2017. https://www.battlefields.org/learn/civil-war/operations-against-defenses-charleston.

"OR XL P1 #251: Report of Captain Lorey A. Baker, 39th IL, June 16, 1864." From *The War of the Rebellion: A Compilation of the Official Records of the Union and Confederate Armies, Volume XL, Part 1 (Serial Number 80), page 687*. Beyondthecrater.com. May 1, 2010. http://www.beyondthecrater.com/resources/ors/vol-xl/part-1-sn-80/or-xl-p1–251-l-a-baker-39-il-june-16/.

"OR XLII P1 #258: Report of Lieut. James Hannum, 39th IL, October 27–28, 1864." From *The War of the Rebellion: A Compilation of the Official Records of the Union and Confederate Armies*, Volume XLII, Part 1 (Serial Number 87), pages 692–693. Beyondthecrater.com. May 28, 2011. http://www.beyondthecrater.com/resources/ors/vol-xlii/part-1-sn-87/or-xlii-p1–258-j-hannum-39-il-oct-27–28/.

"OR XLII P1 #257: Report of Capt. Lewis T. Whipple, 39th IL, August 13–20, 1864." From *The War of the Rebellion: A Compilation of the Official Records of the Union and Confederate Armies*, Volume XLII, Part 1 (Serial Number 87), page 692. Beyondthecrater.com. May 27, 2011. http://www.beyondthecrater.com/resources/ors/vol- xlii/part-1-sn-87/or-xlii-p1-257-l- t-whipple-39-il-aug-13–20/.

"OR XLVI P1 #222: Report of Colonel Thomas O. Osborn, 39th IL, Commanding 1/1/XXIV/AotJ, Mar 27–Apr 9, 1865." From *The War of the Rebellion: A Compilation of the Official Records of the Union and Confederate Armies*, Volume XLVI, Part 1 (Serial Number 95), pp. 1185–1188. Beyondthecrater.com. November 12, 2012. http://www.beyondthecrater.com/resources/ors/vol-xlvi/part-1-sn-95/appomattox-campaign-reports-95/or-xlvi-p1-app-222-t-o-osborn-1–1-xxiv-aotj-mar-27-apr-9/.

"P. G. T. Beauregard." Battlefields.org. December 19, 2009. https://www.battlefields.org/learn/biographies/p-g-t-beauregard.

"Peninsula Campaign." Battlefields.org. December 13, 2016. https://www.battlefields.org/learn/civil-war/peninsula-campaign.

Reavis, L.U. *The Life and Public Services of Richard Yates, The War Governor of Illinois: A Lecture to the Illinois House of Representatives*. St. Louis: J.H. Chambers & Co., 1881.

"Richard Yates to Ward H. Lamon." Chronicling Illinois. February 1, 1862. http://www.chroniclingillinois.org/items/show/3020.

"Second Manassas." Battlefields.org. January 14, 2009. https://www.battlefields.org/learn/civil-war/battles/second-manassas.

"To the Bitter End." Battlefields.org. March 23, 2015. https://www.battlefields.org/learn/articles/bitter-end.

Index

Numbers in *bold italics* indicate entries with illustrations